THE UNDEFENDED

Simon P Walker

Book 1: *Leading Out of Who You Are:*
　　　Discovering the Secret of Undefended Leadership

Leadership involves power and influence over others—but each of us is trapped by a psychological imperative inside us to use whatever control we have for our own ends. Where does this imperative come from? The author describes four ego patterns—Shaping, Defining, Adapting and Defending—which are formed during our childhood and which are the source of our drives and fears. Our natural instinct to use our leadership to meet our own needs rather than others' is what Walker terms 'defendedness'.

Book 2: *Leading with Nothing to Lose:*
　　　Training in the Exercise of Power

This book ventures into the territory of the pragmatic leader who has to make executive decisions, manage budgets, set targets, hire and fire, resolve conflict, improve performance, organize procedures and plan strategy. Walker illustrates from history the strengths and weaknesses of eight different styles of exercising power (which he calls Foundational, Commanding, Affiliative, Serving, Pacesetting, Visionary, Consensual and Self-emptying), and explains why the ability to use not just one or two of these but all of them fluidly depends not simply on skill or training but (paradoxically) on the freedom to abandon our defences and attend to the needs of those around us.

Book 3: *Leading with Everything to Give:*
　　　Lessons from the Success and Failure of Western Capitalism

In the final volume, Walker defines the politics and economics of undefended leadership. He sets the current economic crisis within a broad narrative of social dysfunction in the West and introduces a model of social ecology that clarifies the chaos and gives perspective to envision the future. Essential, provocative and most timely reading for all leaders!

www.piquanteditions.com

"Leadership is commonly associated with dominance and power.
Simon Walker shows that there are other types of leadership capable of being more
effective."
R Meredith Belbin

THE UNDEFENDED LEADER

Leading Out of Who You Are
Leading with Nothing to Lose
Leading with Everything to Give

Simon P Walker

PiQUANT
editions

10 11 12 13 14 15   6 5 4 3 2 1

ISBN 978-1-903689-64-6

The Undefended Leader Trilogy was first published as:
Leading Out of Who You Are: Discovering the Secret of Undefended Leadership (Piquant Editions 2007, ISBN 9781903689431)
Leading with Nothing to Lose : Training in the Exercise of Power (Piquant Editions 2007, ISBN 9781903689448)
Leading with Everything to Give: Lessons from the Success and Failure of Western Capitalism (Piquant Edtiions 2009, ISBN 9781903689455)

British Library Cataloguing in Publication Data

Walker, Simon P. (Simon Patrick), 1971-
   The undefended leader.
   1. Leadership. 2. Power (Social sciences) 3. Social
   ecology.
   I. Title II. Walker, Simon P. (Simon Patrick), 1971-
   Leading out of who you are. III. Walker, Simon P. (Simon
   Patrick), 1971- Leading with nothing to lose. IV. Walker,
   Simon P. (Simon Patrick), 1971- Leading with everything to
   give.
   303.3'4-dc22

ISBN-13: 9781903689646

Book design by To a Tee (www.2at.com)

Contents

2 LEADING WITH NOTHING TO LOSE

3 LEADING WITH EVERYTHING TO GIVE

Part 3A: Deconstruction: Lessons From The Failures Of Western Capitalism

Part 3B: Reconstruction: Lessons For The Future Of Society

Acknowledgements

I am grateful to the many people who have supported me over the years as this book has taken shape. Starting with Jim, Freya, Nick and Jen and Ben and Tobyn, as well as many other dear friends. In particular, I have appreciated those many students who, during my courses, have given me valuable encouragement to take these ideas out to a wider audience.

I am grateful also to my publisher, Pieter Kwant, and my editor, Huw Spanner, who have stuck with this project from its embryonic form right through to its birth as a fully-formed trilogy.

It is with deep thankfulness that I dedicate this book to my wife, Jo, without whom it would have never been written, to my parents, and to my children, Barnaby, Jonah and Olivia, whose patience towards a distracted father has, at times, been stretched beyond the acceptable. For them, and their generation, I have written this book in the hope that I and my generation will leave the world in a better state than we found it.

Simon Walker

—1—

Leading out of Who You Are

Discovering the Secret of
Undefended Leadership

Preface to the first edition of
Leading out of Who You Are

About an hour's drive from Kingston, the capital of Jamaica, is the old Spanish port of Ocho Rios, which owes its name to the mistaken belief that eight rivers flow into the Caribbean here. The area boasts one of the island's most stunning natural features: Dunn's River Falls, whose crystal-clear waters descend six hundred feet over terraces of smooth rock to join the Caribbean on the white sands below. If you visit the falls, you will be invited to join one of the tourist groups that are taken up to the top by an official guide. As you toil slowly upwards, holding hands in a human chain, you'll be told to pause briefly at set places, where official photographers pop up and video you. You'll be instructed to sit for a few moments in a pool, to be filmed, 'beaming', before being moved on so the other 19 members of your group can go through the same routine. You'll pass by glorious cascades that tempt you to take a shower, glistening plunge pools that beg you to dive in—yet you'll leave them unexplored. You will be within arm's reach of jets of water that would massage your shoulders and neck, yet you'll stay stolidly in your chain, hands locked, and miss your chance. Through palm fronds you will glimpse magnificent views of the peaceful sea, but instead you'll focus on the grinning faces of your official cheerleaders, urging you to whoop and holler at the 'great time' you're having.

And yet no one at the falls will be doing anything different. Not one single person will be out of line, enjoying the spectacle in any other way than this. Like obedient children, you'll all be toeing the line. You'll pass by all these temptations, still linked hand-in-hand, resenting every missed opportunity, every required pose, every restriction placed on you as you climb wearily up the prescribed route until you are led, an hour or so later, out to the top of the falls. You'll arrive there feeling as if, somehow, what should have been the most exhilarating and liberating experience had been turned into an exercise in being led, against your will, where you didn't want to go.

You will probably reflect that it's a great pity that the Jamaican authorities have imposed these rules that prevent people from being free to just enjoy Dunn's falls for themselves. But at that point you may discover something quite unexpected: that there are no rules at the falls. There are no rules telling people to hold hands, or to walk in line; no rules telling people not to dive in the pools or stand under the cascades. In fact, there are no restrictions at all on how you can enjoy your visit. You can have a natural massage, you can take a jacuzzi, for as long as you like—and no one will stop you. You can do all these things; but you don't. You don't because no one else is doing them.

What happens to every visitor at Dunn's falls is what happens to everyone everywhere. People allow themselves to be constrained by imagined rules they have come to believe are real: rules that determine their lives and experiences. It is a kind of leadership that people have come to follow, a kind that invites them to toil away, in a human chain, up the side of a waterfall. It's a kind of leadership that is quite clearly unrewarding—it denies sensation, experience, pleasure. It denies the essential quality of this place, its energy and raw power—indeed, its power to heal. And yet we submit to it.

People submit to poor leadership, to leadership that is clearly wrong, to leadership that everyone can see leads us away from life and health. We submit to leadership that is full of hypocrisy and deceit, leadership that is manipulative and abusive, leadership that sells us a lie of some future utopia, leadership that lacks courage and is really concerned with securing the leader's reputation. We submit to it because we have come to believe in the imaginary rules. We convince ourselves that it must be right, that our senses deceive us: that there must be some hidden danger in the obviously better way. We accept the rule of the group and we fear being exposed as the foolish, idealistic, mistaken person who stepped out from the crowd.

Yet some of us long—and hope—for a different kind of leadership. We still believe that a leader should say what he means and mean what he says. We still believe that a leader should have integrity as well as inspiration. We still believe that a leader should work for an end greater than her own advancement. We still believe that a leader should be willing and able to make sacrifices. We still believe that a leader should be able first to serve rather than be served.

This is a book about leadership, but not the kind that leads people up waterfalls in human chains. It is about an 'undefended' leadership that invites people to break away from the group and jump into the beautiful pools we see around us. It invites us to embrace a kind of difference that is radically free and exhilarating. It offers us a horizon that is wide and blue. It encourages us to raise our gaze from the usual tacky, commercialized version of the world, compromised and exploitative, to which we have allowed ourselves to be subjected, and believe again that another, freer and more honest kind of life can be ours.

Simon Walker
Oxford, 2006

INTRODUCTION

The Beginnings of the Story

As a young adolescent, I remember being equally fascinated and appalled by the figure of Gandhi in Richard Attenborough's film of the same name. Played by Ben Kingsley, the Mahatma's frail body and defenceless demeanour, his beggar's clothing and scant belongings represented perhaps everything I despised as a young, strutting male. I could hardly imagine a figure like that winning many admiring glances from the girls at my school! And what a contrast with the heroic role models I idolized: muscular athletes, who dominated the opposition with their overwhelming physical strength and breathtaking skill. Gandhi simply didn't fit into this economy of power. In these terms, he simply had nothing to offer: he epitomized the weakness I associated with the boys who were always picked last for every team. He was, to be blunt, a physical and social embarrassment, someone who would have been a pariah if he'd been in my class.

This attitude to Gandhi was not, I came to realize, unique to me or my generation. It was typical of many of the British elite of his day, including Winston Churchill, who scoffed and fulminated at his coming to 'parley' on equal terms with the Empire's high commissioner dressed only in a loincloth.

And yet I had to admit that, despite my prejudices, Gandhi was a figure of remarkable influence, not only in his day but in world history. It was this fact that troubled my immature understanding of power and leadership, because I simply couldn't account for it. My confrontation with Gandhi was my first encounter with an extraordinary historical figure who challenged me on this issue. It was certainly not my last.

I had become a Christian at the age of 13, making my own the faith taught to me by my parents. Up to that point, I had associated Christianity with a number of things that came very low on my list of desirables: old age, buildings that were dull, cold and badly lit, ancient language and rites, out-of-date music and the strange feminine attire worn by vicars. However, the decisive moment for me was closer than I thought. It came without warning one evening in February 1985 when 80 or so pupils—a fifth of the whole school—responded to a call from a visiting preacher in chapel. And I was one of them.

Overnight, the Christian Union became the largest society in the school, and so it remained for the rest of my time there. Perhaps, in a way, that was one of its handicaps, at least in helping me to mature. The CU was influential—indeed, powerful—and so, unlike most Christian teenagers, who grow up being ridiculed and marginalized, my experience was that my religion was something with credibility. Indeed, it got you places. Most of the school prefects were Christians, deliberately chosen by the headmaster for their moral lifestyle (and maybe their compliance). Perhaps it isn't difficult to see why my faith failed to challenge the hierarchy of power I was naturally internalizing as a young adolescent male.

Ironically, Jesus himself became an increasingly awkward figure—something I would spend the next decade trying to resolve. He was a man who, at times, chose to use physical force. The depiction of him as 'gentle Jesus, meek and mild' is deeply misleading. I wouldn't have wanted to be a money-changer in the Temple on the day he overturned their stalls. I wouldn't have liked to be one of the religious leaders whose arguments were torn to shreds and their hypocrisy exposed by his wisdom and insight. He used power to quell raging storms, to multiply a few loaves and fish into enough to feed many thousands and to physically overwhelm those who came to arrest him in the garden of Gethsemane.

However, the more I looked at this historical figure, whose disciple I'd chosen to be, the more I was confronted by another truth. That Jesus had not, in accordance with the rules of the hierarchy I had come to understand, chosen to use power to achieve his greatest and most far-reaching victory. He had used weakness. His death on the cross stood as a rebuke to all attempts by the Church to establish God's kingdom through the use of power, whether physical, economic, political or military. There can be no shadow of doubt whatsoever that at the heart of God's purposes to transform the world is the way of vulnerable self-offering. Christians believe that the single most powerful act by any one person in human history was Jesus' death on the cross. Indeed, they regard it as a cosmic event, which brought into being a new order and reconfigured the entire destiny of humankind. But whether it actually was or not is irrelevant to the point I'm making here. What is beyond dispute is the fact that that crucifixion changed human history as no other human act has done.

Jesus' death has inspired literally hundreds of millions of people to follow him. There are tens of thousands of churches named after 'the holy cross'. Each year, the whole Christian world observes as its most sacred day Good Friday, the day Jesus died. The cross is held high on every Christian march and pilgrimage. It is worn by nuns as a sign of a lifelong vow. In Christian countries it is placed at the head of many graves, in the hope of a life beyond the grave to which the death of Jesus is the doorway. The sign of the cross is made countless times every day by believers who acknowledge that their God died for them on it. Jesus' journey to the cross occupies nearly a half of the Gospel accounts of his life; the entire New Testament is one long interpretation of the meaning of his death and resurrection. More books have been written and read about the day of his execution than about any other single day in history.

As I grew into adulthood, I realized that, although I had followed Jesus for nearly a decade, although I was myself in Christian leadership, my understanding of power and leadership was still basically informed not by the life and death of the man I followed but by the values of the playground, the sports field and the market. Jesus' life and death confronted me with a story of power at the centre of which lay an act of weakness and self-emptying. I had to try to grasp the reality that power is not located only in might. I had to begin to revise the terms in which I made sense of what power is and how it can be used. It wasn't that one had to eschew altogether physical strength, or verbal skill, or force of intellectual argument, in favour of frailty and ignorance. Rather, it was that these things in themselves could not be seen as the pinnacle of power. Any account of power could happily accommodate exhibitions of intellectual, political or military strength around its lower slopes, but it would have to place at its summit the exercise of vulnerability and self-emptying.

Indeed, as I looked more closely at human history I saw this pattern repeated over and over again. There were, of course, many examples of what I would conventionally have called 'powerful' men and women who had changed the course of the world. Military leaders such as Alexander and his Macedonians, Julius Caesar and his legions, Genghis Khan and his Mongol hordes, Napoleon and his *Grande Armée* have reshaped the political landscape time and again. Of course, tyrants have devastated that landscape, including in the last hundred years alone Adolf Hitler, Joseph Stalin, Mao Zedong and Pol Pot. However, in all these cases the will of the leader was imposed, by sheer force or some other kind of coercion. Dictatorship is hugely destructive and rarely lasts long. On the other hand, stable political systems, on which civilizations have been built to survive for centuries, arguably have been founded on strategies that decentralize and disseminate power.

Crude, brutal and coercive forms of power and leadership occupy the valleys and foothills of political history, but the higher you go up the mountain, the more you find forms that are democratic, consensual and educative. Power is in general located less in a single individual and more in the collective, the body of followers. The leader himself uses power for different ends: to empower, educate and enable others rather than to dominate and oppress them. Such patterns of power are associated with the more enduring and stable political systems, societies and civilizations. Certainly, without such patterns of power

European and North American civilization would never have flourished as it has or reached the heights of human freedom and culture it has attained.

Right at the summit of the mountain there are to be found the few extraordinary individuals whose occupation and application of power is of a different order altogether. These are what I call the 'undefended leaders'. These are the ones whose life and philosophy have involved deliberate acts of weakness and courageous self-sacrifice. Up here, we find the likes of Dietrich Bonhoeffer, Martin Luther King, Desmond Tutu, Mother Teresa of Calcutta, Nelson Mandela, Mikhail Gorbachev, Aung San Suu Kyi—and, of course, Mahatma Gandhi and Jesus of Nazareth. It is on these pinnacles that the highest ideals and myths of humankind have come to be staked. It is also these undefended leaders who are associated with the greatest revolutions, in which the lower forms of power are overthrown and a bright light is shone upon the truest nature of humanity.

It is in undefended leaders that we glimpse our true potential, and in undefended structures of power that people are set most truly free.

Study questions

1. Who are your leadership role models?
2. What is it about them that you admire and try to emulate?
3. How do they exercise power?
4. Write down five words that describe your own approach to leadership.
5. How would someone else know that you had these convictions from the way you lead?

⮑ On the website, www.theleadershipcommunity.org, join the online forum discussion on 'Your greatest leaders'. You will need to register as a guest member in order to join the discussion. That is a free registration.

ONE

What Makes an Undefended Leader?

What exactly makes an undefended leader? Is there something that these great ones, who occupy the peaks, have in common? To identify what it is, we need to consider the particular nature of the task of leadership. Many roles in life can be adequately fulfilled by acquiring the necessary skills. With sufficient training, you can draft architectural drawings, legal documents and financial agreements, for example. But leadership is different. Leadership is about who you are, not what you know or what skills you have. Why is this? There are two reasons: leadership is about trust and it is about power.

A leader leads people from where they currently are to another place, which at first is unknown to them and can only be imagined. To get there, they have to leave the safety and familiarity of their present situation, to embrace an unknown, and perhaps dangerous, future. The task of the leader is to make that change possible—and not only possible but actual. He achieves this by acting as a guide between the known and the unknown. The people don't know the future they are being invited to venture into, but they do know the leader. The leader represents safety and security. People follow him because they trust him. The diagram below illustrates the dynamics of power that exist in any such relationship.

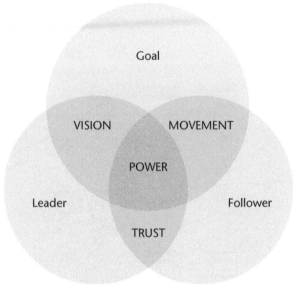

Diagram 1.1   Leader, follower and goal

In any leadership situation, there is a relationship between the leader and the goal. Without a goal, a point toward which people are being directed, it is hard to say that leadership is taking place. The leader's ability to articulate the goal is *vision*; but the relationship between the followers and the goal is *movement*. In other words, the followers have actually to move towards the goal envisioned by the leader. There must be some kind of strategy and tactics to enable this movement to take place—otherwise it will disintegrate into chaos. Finally, a healthy leader-follower dynamic is characterized by the experience of *trust* between them. This is the glue that bonds them together. This is the means by which the followers enter into the leader's own sense of confidence, vision and purpose. The followers appropriate the life the leader is living, and in this way the leader becomes a vehicle for the followers to move into the unknown. This is an appropriate exercise of *power*. If trust breaks down, the connection is broken. Then, either the followers no longer follow or the leader finds other means to ensure that they do—through coercion, manipulation or the like— and so begins to exercise power inappropriately.

When George W Bush was inaugurated as the 19th Republican president of America on 20 January 2001, he could not have known that the events that would catapult him into world history were just unfolding. Some nine months later, on 11 September, when two hijacked passenger planes were flown into the twin towers of the World Trade Center, the tectonic plates of global politics shifted. In the uproar of doubt, fear, grief and rage that followed, the world watched as America struggled to come to terms with an extraordinary and novel experience of vulnerability. Unlike the nation states of Europe and most of the rest of the world, its national security had rarely been breached. Unprecedented security measures were introduced at airports and railway stations across the country. What we were witnessing was a nation attempting to recover a sense of safety that had been shattered. In such times, people look for leadership to make them feel secure. They look for someone they can trust who will comfort them. For America at that time, Bush's simple, black-and-white rhetoric and the political ideology of his neo-conservative allies offered clarity and reassurance amidst the confusion.

Inevitably, the Bush administration has not been able to sustain the extraordinary quality and quantity of trust it at first enjoyed. Critics point to its dogged unilateralism as the cause of this decline, as well as the growing sense of scandal over illegal imprisonment and torture. Some people feel a sense of betrayal, and this feeling is all the more acute because the trust was formerly so strong. This sense of betrayal, as well as confusion, is still growing in America. For the leader, trust is everything: without it, leadership may begin to resort to unhealthy strategies to ensure that people follow. Jim Wallis, one of the foremost social activists in America today, talks of the 'moral authority' of the leader. This, he suggests, is what gives a leader her ability to lead—and this, I believe, is what all undefended leaders have acquired in abundance.[1]

Moral authority is different from the kinds of authority bestowed by election, appointment or delegation: it has to do with the kind of life one has lived. Very often it is acquired only through personal struggle and loss. Consider Nelson Mandela, Winston Churchill, Moses. What do these leaders have in common? The answer is that their most significant leadership did not begin until late in their lives, and those lives were characterized by both struggle and loss.

---

[1] Jim Wallis, *Faith Works: Lessons on Spirituality and Social Action* (SPCK, 2002), pp171ff

Mandela's story is well known. The leader of the ANC's military wing was imprisoned by the South African regime on 5 August 1962 and spent 27 years in gaol. Twenty-seven years! This is the length of time it takes for a baby to develop into a full-grown man or woman with a career well established. Twenty-seven years have elapsed since 1979, only six years after the official end to the Vietnam War. Twenty-seven years Mandela spent waiting, wondering, hoping, despairing, living without ever knowing whether he would be released or done away with, whether the cause he believed in so passionately would ever triumph, at least in his lifetime. Not knowing whether his sacrifice would make any difference at all.

Churchill's political career began at the turn of the 20th century, some 40 years before he was to take his defining role on the world stage. During those years, he experienced cycles of success and failure, marginalization, alienation and defeat. He suffered for long periods from the 'black dog' of depression, and grew used to being pilloried in the media for his military mistakes and political vacillations. It was not until the age of 65, the age at which most men in Britain retire, that he was appointed to lead his country against the wicked ideology of Nazism. He wrote: 'All my life has been a preparation for this moment.'

Moses was, according to the Jewish scriptures, the man God appointed to lead his people out of slavery in Egypt. He is regarded by both Jews and Christians as a spiritual and political giant, a man with such great faith that he led a people maybe a million strong, along with all their flocks and herds, for 40 years in the desert and gave them God's laws for healthy and holy living, the Ten Commandments. He was a man charged not only with rescuing his people virtually single-handed from the power of the Pharaoh and his armies but also with nurturing them spiritually and leading them into God's promised land. However, Moses had to wait until he was an elderly man before God gave him the authority to lead. As a young man he had tried to assert leadership by force and personal power. (Raised in the Pharaoh's palace as a member of his household, he had killed an Egyptian who was in charge of some Israelite slaves). But the Israelites had rejected him and in fear he had fled to another country, to live in exile as a shepherd for many long years. By the time God came calling, he was a crushed man. His old confidence in his own power was shattered, and he asked God many times for reassurance and assistance before he was willing to be a leader again. His early rejection and a deep realization of his weakness and inadequacy had changed him and humbled him.

Now, not all great leaders have experienced significant periods of time in the wilderness, but many have. What is it that sets a Gandhi apart from a Bush? A Mother Teresa from a Margaret Thatcher? A Gorbachev from a Vladimir Putin? It is the same factor: they earned their authority through their experience of personal sacrifice and, often, of struggle and loss. In other words, they all went through the fire of personal experience, by which their characters were tested and refined. For all to see, their personal *integrity* was put under scrutiny, their motives were examined, their commitment and dedication were exposed, their moral *courage* was revealed. In those 27 years in a South African gaol, Mandela was accruing moral authority—the right not only to make a stand against the powers of apartheid but also to command the followership of the ANC. Moral authority is connected with having been proved trustworthy, usually through trial and suffering. What made him, and others like him, remarkable leaders was their remarkable character. Their suffering refined them into more human and courageous moral agents, into people with *compassion*. In contrast, suffering makes many more ordinary leaders cruel, hard and manipulative.

Leaders, it seems, are formed, not simply appointed. This process of formation is not one that is merely passive, or merely active: it is both. Circumstances conspire to create an environment, an arena, in which character is put to the test. Here, the combatants do battle with themselves, in active, painful struggle, wrestling with their inner selves. The battle is against their inner demons—of anger, of the thirst for power that can lurk within all of us. The public, political battles are mere re-enactments of the campaign they have fought and won inside themselves. Indeed, their moral courage and conviction, their personal freedom and security, their willingness to embrace personal loss, are available to them only because they have already fought and won the war with themselves. They have nothing to win or lose on the political front that they have not already won or lost on the personal front. They are free, free of the need to dominate, to conquer and oppress, to consume, to acquire—whether it be land or power or reputation—because they are free within themselves.

Power tends to corrupt, and absolute power corrupts absolutely. The inner character of the leader is revealed and written in large letters on the pages of history because unless she has defeated the inner demons, she will never defeat those outside. Her leadership is merely an expression of who she is inside. And that is what gives such leaders their power and their authority: their freedom to be themselves, to be authentic, to choose their own paths.

It is for this reason that the journey we are going to make in this book is a vital one. We need to try to understand the mechanisms by which leaders can become free. There is an urgent need for such leaders in our world today. Think of the scale of the political and economic choices being faced by our national leaders, and of their consequences, even as you read these pages. What are they going to do about nuclear 'rogue' states such as North Korea and, potentially, Iran? Are they going to foster understanding or misunderstanding between the Islamic world and other societies? How are they going to address the root causes of the expected 3–4°C rise in global temperature over the next 50 years? To deal with the predicted two-metre rise in sea-levels over next 50 years, which could destroy millions of human lives? Are they going to allow the development of cloned and genetically screened babies? To sanction euthanasia? Will they do something to prevent the deaths of some 15,000 children a day due to infected water sources (an intervention that would cost a mere $6 billion)?

Such huge issues overshadow even the greatest of those faced by the leaders of past generations. Never before have we been so aware of the interconnectedness of the choices our leaders make. We can appreciate the impact of our social behaviour not just on our town or our county or our nation but on the entire population of the world, and not only now but for centuries to come—and not just the human population but even the other species with which we share this planet. However, notwithstanding this change in scale and complexity, the leaders of the past still set us a standard of the fundamental moral courage required by every generation of social and political leaders. The choice of Abraham Lincoln to take a stand against slavery was not without ramifications, economic and political. The choice of Martin Luther King to persist in resisting segregation non-violently was not without great cost, to him and others. The choice of Franklin D Roosevelt to throw the might of America into the war against Nazism rather than fighting exclusively against Japan was not without risk.

Virtually every significant decision that has proved to be for the good of humankind has come at a cost. It is rare that legislation that liberates slaves, or insists on a basic wage, or releases countries from debt, or creates equitable trade laws, or exposes corporate fraud, or educates the poor, or provides health care for the vulnerable, increases productivity or is otherwise cost-effective in the short term. And that is one of the great problems facing the democratic world today: change for good often costs more in the short term, but our electoral systems make it very difficult for governments to pursue long-term policies. Those who adopt policies that cost in the short term often lose power.

What we are beginning to realize is that not only do we need individual leaders to be free in themselves, we also need our systems to be liberated. Just as individuals find themselves trapped by the dynamics of power, defending their own interests, protecting themselves against various threats, so too do governments. It has always been so, but since the Second World War the structure of democracy has increasingly been influenced by the mechanisms and values not of the community but of the corporation. The dominant influence in politics now is the market, not the members of a society. Governments 'sell their ideas' to the public, who have already been assessed through focus groups to ensure that what is on offer is just what consumers want. People 'buy' policies just as they buy shampoo. In such a feedback system, where there is a rival brand offering an alternative range of goods to attract any dissatisfied customers, it's difficult for anyone in office to propose any radical or costly choices if they want to stay there.

Perhaps the greatest challenge facing the leaders of Western society is not the development of democracy in countries currently governed by other structures of power but the reformation of our own democracy, which now looks more like market economics than a political system. However, I would suggest that such goals cannot be attained unless we first establish the basis on which a person can be genuinely free. Only when individual leaders start to make different choices, embrace different aspirations and develop a different political vision can such grander questions be addressed. How such a social system as ours may be reformed is the subject of the second and third books in this trilogy. This present book considers the mechanisms of power and of 'defendedness' at the level of the individual and asks just how someone can truly become an 'undefended leader'.

Study questions 1

1. Refer to Diagram 1.1 on page 6. Describe a situation in which
   - vision was weak. What was the consequence for the followers?
   - movement was weak. What was the consequence for the followers?
   - trust was weak. What was the consequence for the followers?
2. Contrast these with a situation in which all of these factors were strong. What was the outcome in this case?
3. Complete the following table to measure a leader you admire, a leader you do not admire and yourself by these three criteria: integrity, courage and compassion.

CHARACTERISTIC	A leader you admire (1-10)	A leader you do not admire (1-10)	Yourself (1-10)
INTEGRITY			
COURAGE			
COMPASSION			

4. Reflect on the score you gave yourself. How do you think you can improve in the area you have identified as your weakest characteristic?

5. Choose two of the issues below that you are particularly concerned about:
   · the environment
   · health
   · education
   · the economy
   · national security
   · foreign policy
   · business

   What costly decisions do you believe our political leaders need to take with regard to each of those issues? How would you have to change your current lifestyle to support those decisions?

⊃ On the website, www.theleadershipcommunity.org, join in the online forum discussion 'What kind of leaders do we want?' You need to be registered as a free 'guest member' in order to join the discussion.

Part 1A

HOW LEADERS DEFEND THEMSELVES

TWO

The Hostile World of the Leader

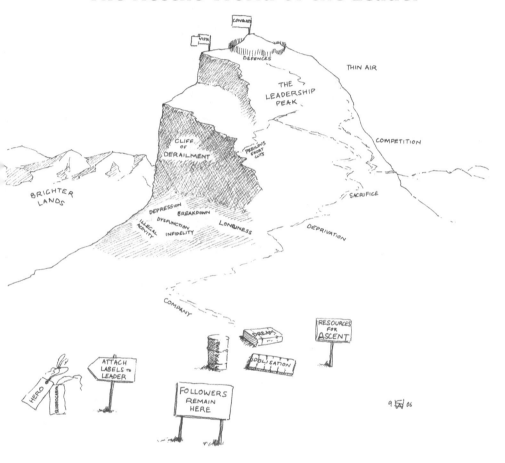

Let's begin at the beginning. We need to establish the mechanisms by which leaders become defended. In order to do so, we must examine the environment in which leadership takes place. This is a particular one, for leaders often experience three things that other people experience only to a lesser degree: idealization, idealism and unmet emotional needs.

Psychologists tell us that what lies behind 'hero worship' is the experience of idealization.[2] Every single person on this planet lives with doubt—confusion, self-doubt or even, for some, self-loathing. Yet few of us are brave enough, or have sufficient support, to deal with these flaws in our own life. So, what do we do with them? We bury them—and then we look for someone else through whom to live a surrogate life. And this person may well be our leader. Many followers need their leaders to be everything they themselves struggle to be: they need to believe in someone who doesn't doubt, who is never defeated, who doesn't fall for the same routine petty temptations that they do. As followers, we need to see someone who is 'other' than us, different and, often, more powerful. We need a superman or superwoman who is strong enough to protect us, to defend us and our way of life against the battering that all of us take. And so we idealize ordinary people who have taken up the burden of leadership and we turn them into the ideal heroes we need them to be.

By doing this, we 'deal' in a way with our deficiencies. We don't deal with them properly or honestly, within ourselves: we deal them through a kind of proxy. The leader lives out our life for us. He embodies all we would hope, but cannot manage, to be. This is at its most basic a strategy to abdicate responsibility—it lets us off the hook and allows us to carry on dallying with the compromises in our lives rather than dealing with them directly. So, a kind of transaction takes place in which we allow the leader to become the person we need him to be. At the same time, the leader, gratified by the attention and, indeed, adulation, seeks to achieve the standards we are unconsciously setting for him. When this occurs, a collusion is established in which both parties meet their needs through the other. This can result in a kind of paralysis. For the followers, it may lead to dependence; for the leader, it may lead to isolation, loneliness and intolerable strain. He cannot share any of the issues he is struggling with inside, because no one will allow him to.

The second experience common to leaders is idealism. Most leaders are to some extent idealists. They have a desire for things to be different, to be better. Thus, the leader lives all the time with a discrepancy between the world that she wants (and wants others) to inhabit and the world she (and others) actually do inhabit. Psychologists call this condition 'cognitive dissonance'—there is a discord between the reality and the ideal. Now, there is plenty of evidence to suggest that this discord produces a certain mental and emotional strain in people. This can be constructive, generating passion, drive and energy; but it can also be destructive, producing frustration, disappointment and confusion. Accordingly, one of the mind's strategies to deal with it is denial and repression.

[2] Manfred Kets de Vries, *The Leadership Mystique: A User's Manual for the Human Enterprise* (Financial Times Prentice Hall, 2001)

Most people deal with cognitive dissonance fairly effectively simply by choosing to look away from the ideal. They come to tolerate the reality by avoiding the evidence, by filtering the data they receive. They fabricate a world in which the discrepancy is less.

The leader, however, is motivated by a desire to hold on to the ideal—indeed, it is the ideal that drives her. Accordingly, she commits herself to a journey that will inevitably lead her into a dissonance between the reality and the ideal, a tension that she refuses, until she gives up leading, to deny or suppress. Unfortunately, most other people don't want to know about this tension: they are in the business of denial and they don't want to be reminded of how bad the reality is or how much better the ideal is. They prefer blissful ignorance—and the leader, in all the evangelical fervour of her vision, is a fly in the ointment. And so the leader finds herself pursuing the lonely path that all prophets and visionaries down the ages have followed—of being isolated, being a voice crying in the wilderness, travelling alone, ahead of the crowd, on the margins, in a distant land—feeling a sense of belonging but also a sense of alienation.

The third experience common to leaders is that of unmet emotional needs. Not all of those in positions of leadership are what you might call 'appropriate' leaders. The thing about appropriate leaders is that they take responsibility for people other than themselves. Not all of those who hold positions of leadership do this—and, conversely, not all those who do this are in positions of leadership. But for the purposes of this book I am defining a leader as one who takes responsibility for people other than himself. A mother in the home is a leader; a playgroup facilitator is a leader; a traffic policeman is a leader. Leadership happens when a person takes responsibility for someone other than herself. And leaders do this because, by and large, they care. They care about the welfare of the other person or people. It is not enough for them merely to live a happy, contented life: they are affected by the welfare of others around them. Many leaders respond empathetically to the emotion of the situation around them. To some extent, they 'feel' that situation themselves and experience feelings that are not originally their own. They carry other people's feelings; they are what is called 'empathically open' people. That is why psychopaths are technically the very opposite of leaders: they feel nothing and have no sense of anyone's pain or emotion or welfare but their own. One of the most worrying findings of research in recent years is the number of 'leaders' of corporate organizations who display some psychopathic tendencies. A person who feels little or nothing for another person regards them merely as a commodity or a utility for their own benefit. Other people are merely an extension of their ego, to be coerced to fulfil their agenda.

Appropriate leadership, in contrast, involves being open to the other person's agenda, and genuinely responsive to their needs. Indeed, in many cases the leader, driven by his ideals, sacrifices his own needs for the sake of others. What funds this transaction is another kind of collusion: the leader discovers that by attending to other people's needs, and neglecting his own, he receives approval and appreciation from his followers. This quickly comes to compensate for his own, unmet needs. Thus, a cycle of deprivation and collusion becomes established. The social leader does not meet his own needs directly, but instead meets them through his service to other people, who then reward him with approval. The followers are used to make up the psychological deficit within the leader.

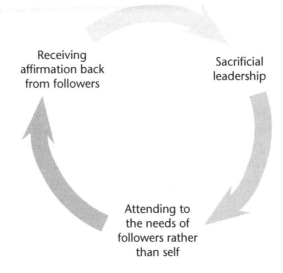

Receiving
affirmation back
from followers

Sacrificial
leadership

Attending to
the needs of
followers rather
than self

Diagram 2.1   The leadership-followership collusion cycle

The outcome of this is deeply unhealthy. The followers are, to some degree, being exploited by the leader in accordance with his own needs, rather than being led in accordance with theirs. The leadership is compromised because the motives behind it are mixed. Moreover, the leader finds it increasingly hard to manage without this emotional feedback, and so it becomes increasingly difficult for him to share his burden and accept support from others. Instead, he develops an attitude of martyred resignation. He sees himself 'pouring out' his life for the sake of others, while no one cares for him and his needs. This reinforces his sense of identity as the sacrificial one who is specially able to bear the burden of this lonely road. He agrees to travel it because it fits in with a corrupted version of the story of his identity which he continues to tell himself.

Idealization, idealism and unmet emotional needs: a triad of experiences common to those who lead. Together, they contribute to making the environment the leader inhabits an isolated and rarefied one. Leadership is rather like climbing a mountain. The motivation for the climb is the view from the top and the sense of achievement that drives you on through the hardships and privations it involves. From the summit, you will enjoy vistas unseen by others. This is what drives the leader: to find a land currently uninhabited, a better place, a bigger world—be it a happier office, a more effective and higher-performing team, a better-educated school, a more authentic church, a more potent NGO. As you climb, so the air gets a little thinner, and the flora and fauna a little less rich. The surroundings are harsher and offer less protection, and less sustenance. There are fewer travellers along the way, and long periods of isolation in which you walk alone, bearing the weight of the journey in private.

Along the way, you question whether it is really worth it. Why not be content with an easier ride back down in the valley? Were things really that bad that you had to get off your behind and set out on this great quest? Surely you could have waited for someone else to fix the problem? Alone, up on the mountain, the leader is beset with doubt. Her ability to 'self-talk' becomes a vital aid to her survival, because it is in internal conversation that she finds the motivation to continue. Some of these 'mountains' are really only foothills and can be scaled quite quickly; but others are a lifelong challenge requiring fortitude and endurance. It is not uncommon for the toil to take its toll. Many a leader of a big organization is only too conscious of the sacrifice involved in getting where they are: sacrifices they have made in working late, studying longer, putting in the extra mile; sacrifices their family has made, seeing less of Mum or Dad. The leader reckons that now she is there, up at the top, she had better make it worthwhile. She plants her flag and stakes her claim and tries to chase off any rivals. It is difficult for someone who has given up so much not to be possessive about the rewards they finally achieve.

Meredith Belbin, the author of the widely-used instrument Belbin Team Roles, has spent a lifetime investigating how human beings work together. His analysis has led him to the conclusion that for much of history leaders have come from the 'warrior' element in the human species. Belbin identifies the confluence of both genes and cultures that result in the establishment of strong cultural norms, or 'memes'. The further back in history we look, he argues, the more we see the dominance of the warrior meme in shaping the human population.

Of course, every empire has been established by military might, and this has been accompanied by a certain cultural expectation of how you behave when you are victorious. For example, the victor claims the spoils of the vanquished, taking possession of what they have fought over. He acquires goods from his victory as his rightful property. He can rightfully demand the submission of those he has defeated. In many ways, it seems we have retained at least some of these ancient 'warrior' notions in our expectations of leadership. In all too many corporations, the CEO—whether consciously or unconsciously—expects the perquisites of the victor: the vast salary, a rich tribute to the ruling monarch; cultural symbols such as a grand office, a chauffeured car, a corporate jet, which indicate social position and authority; the power to reconstruct the company, probably seeing off the old guard and establishing a new corps of acolytes and ministers. Look at it another way and we begin to see how ubiquitous this notion of the rewards of leadership really is: how many CEOs of major corporations forgo the opportunity to be rewarded in these ways?

The consequence of this is, of course, territorialism. Manfred Kets de Vries suggests that the leader spends his whole time looking for the person who is going to succeed him, so that he can kill them off before they do.[3] There seems to be plenty of evidence that the warrior attitudes of our forebears, whilst expressed today in slightly more sophisticated ways, are still prevalent in our corporations and governments. After all, testosterone—the hormone that makes males territorial and competitive—has not simply been banished by feminism and the emergence of the 'new man'. Indeed, some would argue that many women have had to adopt traditional masculine tactics to succeed in corporate cultures.

If the leader finds herself climbing a mountain, and coping with the privations that involves, she must also deal with the natural hostility of her competitors along the way. There are others just a little lower on the slopes searching hungrily for a short cut, some way to leap into the lead and depose the 'king of the hill'. When they smell blood, just watch them gathering for the kill—they won't waste a minute in seeing off a wounded rival. In the name of corporate effectiveness and share value, there is often little time for compassion in business leadership.

Of course, not all environments are as hostile and as ruthless as this. But I suspect that any of us who have set out on the ascent, be it as the mother of a family, or the governor of a school, or the chair of a multinational, will be aware of the pressures involved in the journey: idealization, idealism, unmet needs, a deprived natural environment creating a sense of loneliness, along with challenge along the way. Perhaps it is no surprise, therefore, that, according to Kets de Vries, 70 per cent of executives suffer some kind of heavy fall at some stage in their career. A recent survey of church leaders in Britain suggested that

---

[3] Ibid., p117

30 per cent had felt like leaving the ministry for a long period of time—and in fact on average 150 church leaders *do* quit every year.[4]

When I was leading a large local church in southern England, I myself suffered from a prolonged bout of depression. At 27, I had found myself in charge of an organization prematurely. However, the root cause of my depression was not circumstantial but personal: I had entered full-time Christian ministry without paying attention to the formation of my own emotional character. Many of the defences I will describe in the coming chapters I have used myself as strategies to cope. Ultimately, it was not my environment that needed addressing, it was me. I am glad to say that I sought help from my local doctor. He was an approachable and sympathetic man who was able to provide me with the appropriate medication to shore up my collapsing ego and clear some space to begin the process of rebuilding—one that would take the next four years. I can remember him looking at me as I described my symptoms on my first visit and saying, 'You would be surprised at the number of clergy I see who are in the same situation as you.'

That experience remains the spur for me to help other leaders, especially those with a social conscience, not merely to survive but to thrive in the task of leadership. It has urged me to try to gain an understanding of the psychological strategies that lead every day to the downfall of leaders. I get the chance to address a group of leaders who are about to set out on the climb—at the start of their career or their ordained ministry. I tell them first that they are all, every man and woman of them, brave people. There are many who do not have the courage to stand up and be counted, many who remain contentedly at the bottom of the mountain, who hope that someone else will fix their problems for them. Whatever they are feeling, however frightened they may be, they are brave and rare people. And then I say that I, for one, am not prepared to stand by and watch as they devote their lives to their mission to make the world a better place and end up limping, battered, bruised and maybe defeated as the reward for their courage. I don't want to reach the age of 65 and look around me only to see the wayside scattered with the broken bodies of those who got lost, or were undone, or simply fell exhausted after they had given their all. It seems to me that anyone noble enough to attempt this journey deserves better than that, and it is our responsibility to assist them.

With these thoughts in mind, let me turn to some of the bad strategies leaders will use along the way from which they will need to be rescued.

---

[4] Statistics taken from 'On the Long Haul' (Arrow Leadership Programme, CPAS), adapted from James Lawrence, *Growing Leaders: Reflections on Leadership, Life and Jesus* (BRF, 2004)

Study questions 2

1. What does it feel like to be idealized?
2. What do you do with your doubts and failings when you are idealized by your followers?
3. What were the ideals you set out with as a leader? Do you still have them?
4. Diagram 2.1 on page 18 suggests a pattern of leader-follower collusion. What are the consequences of this for both?
5. What does it feel like at the top of the mountain?
6. Think of your life as a leader like a journey:
   · What will you pack as you prepare to set out that you'll need to make it to your destination?
   · What breaks will you plan along the way?
   · Will you travel alone or will you find a trusted companion?
   · If you have already embarked on this journey, how do you think you are doing at the moment?
   · Are there any issues you need to address at the moment?
   · How will you know when you have arrived?

⊃ On the website, www.theleadershipcommunity.org, join in the online discussion 'What's your leadership journey?' You need to be registered as a free 'guest member' in order to join the discussion.

THREE

Strategies of Defence I:
Front and Back Stage

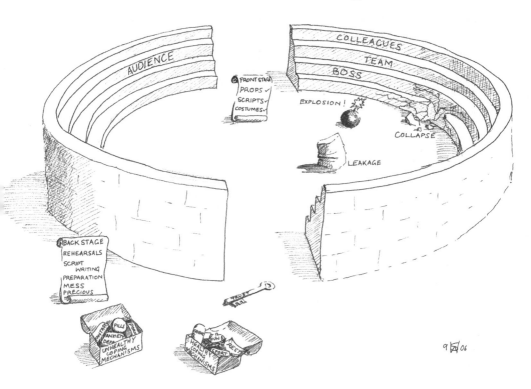

A young former executive, sitting in a chair in our garden, was telling me about his life as the managing director of a successful City consultancy. He described the tremendous stress he experienced in the role, and explained how, in the winter especially, he would often suffer from long periods of apathy, exhaustion and loss of confidence. 'How did you cope?' I asked. 'I would take myself off, snatch a moment when I could escape, and go and sit in the corner of the lobby of the neighbouring office. I could be unseen there, could curl up for a moment, have a nap, and be safe. When I went back into the office, of course, I would have to lead shareholder meetings and sales presentations. You can't stand there and look exhausted—I would have to pick myself up, smile and exude confidence again.'

I guess that everyone in positions of public leadership can identify with that experience. Even if we ourselves have not suffered so acutely, all of us will remember occasions when we have almost literally had to force ourselves out onto the stage and wring a performance out of ourselves, although every fibre of our being was crying out to find a warm, dark corner where we could simply sink out of sight.

Back in the 1960s, the psychologist Erving Goffman based a theory about human behaviour on the metaphor of a theatre. He proposed that, instead of looking inwards at where our behaviour comes from, we should look outwards, at what our behaviour is trying to achieve. Goffman suggested that over time behaviour develops as a strategy to reduce the risks and threats presented by other people. In his terms, the audience we face moment by moment may be either friendly or hostile. Our personal behaviour is a performance intended to ensure that the response is favourable. Each of us develops a routine that we perform every day, and tries to get the attention of the audience we want, who will give us the kind of reception we seek, affirming our sense of identity.

Any leader will immediately resonate with Goffman's idea, because leaders understand the 'need' for a certain amount of self-promotion. Let's imagine, for example, that we know ourselves to be highly intelligent, able to complete mental tasks quickly. We arrive in the office and are assigned a new project by our CEO. We set to work—we can accomplish the task quite easily and swiftly, perhaps more so than the colleagues who are also working on it. In order to please our CEO and secure his approval—not to mention other rewards—we want to do the task well, and we want him to notice this. Thus, we have to succeed on what Goffman calls our 'front stage'. It would be no good if we achieved the goal but kept it so quiet that no else heard about it. If we are really concerned to have our CEO's approval, we will go out of our way to make sure that he sees our success. We will become our own PR agents, publicizing our success on our front stage in subtle but unmissable ways. Thus, we learn to present on our front stage whatever will win approval.

However, suppose we are also anxious not to lose favour with our fellow board-members. We don't want to be seen as self-promoting or arrogant. Really, we want them to see us as skilled but modest, concerned about the welfare of others, not just our own. If this is the case, we will need to use our stage differently. We will still want to do the task well, but we will probably hold back from broadcasting our success. One strategy may be to achieve it but keep it 'backstage'. Then, when our CEO asks how we are all getting on with the task, other people can come out front and shout about how they have achieved it and so on. We will look pleased and applaud them, having cleared the space on our front stage for someone else to shine, not only us.

On our front stage, we ensure that we present and promote the right signs, props, evidence and script to win approval or success or make relationships.

When we do this, our back stage becomes the repository of the ideas, thoughts, relationships and experiences that could undermine our frontstage performance.

Of course, the spotlight will fall on us in due course as the CEO asks us how we have done; and then we will quietly but confidently invite him backstage to see our work. Surprised and pleased, he will be doubly impressed, not only that we have achieved the goal but also that we didn't boast about it but instead allowed others to shine. By keeping things backstage, we appear modest; but we also reduce the risk of being rejected—and if our colleagues fail, we can conveniently distance ourselves from their failure. We can make sure we don't show anyone our deepest desires, needs or achievements until that person has proved trustworthy, and until we have prepared thoroughly to ensure that they are well received. We don't want to risk them being judged and found wanting! Thus, we also learn that sometimes it can be effective to use our back stage.

We may hold back from presenting our success on our front stage and so avoid being thought of as big-headed and self-promoting.

We may hold back our real success and true performance until we trust others enough to let them see them. In that way, we protect ourselves, but also secure a deeper attachment from those we allow backstage.

So, our front stage becomes the place where we perform for our audience— often more than one audience at a time. We find ways to secure approval and praise, perhaps of many different audiences at once. Of course, there are many other strategies we will use front- and backstage. What is important to understand is that all our strategies are to do with self-presentation, or 'impression management'. Impression management is the selective revealing or concealing of our personal story in order to secure the response we need from our audience.

This behaviour is not unique to leaders—we all do it. However, as we have seen, there is a very particular and demanding audience watching the performance of the leader. Unlike that at an ordinary performance, her audience is being invited to believe in—and, indeed, often take part in—the drama that is being enacted before them. Their commitment is much greater, and their needs are much bigger. There is a heady mix of idealization and collusion and surrogacy going on, the usual implicit psychological contracts between the leader and her audience. How, then, does the leader perform in order to live up to the audience's collusive expectations? For one thing, by developing a highly refined script, one that she knows will have the desired effect. For another, by arranging certain props on the stage to reinforce the drama and persuade the audience to believe. For another, by adopting certain roles she has learned to play in order to elicit particular emotional responses from the audience. For another, by putting on different costumes to make each role more convincing. In this way, the leader develops a whole set of frontstage strategies to elicit what she needs from her audience.

But this frontstage performance cannot take place without a back stage in which a whole host of other things are going on. There are many things that the leader learns can't appear on her front stage: the audience wouldn't allow it! They need the leader to act out an idealized life, of course, so where does all the less-than-ideal stuff in her life go on? Out the back. And so the leader's back stage may become the repository for all that she cannot make visible—the doubts, the confusions, the ambiguities and the defeats. The front stage is the place for conviction and confidence, the back stage the place for struggle and uncertainty.

The leader may put on a bravura performance on the front stage, hiding away the messy stuff backstage where he hopes it will not be seen.

Nonetheless, the back stage is not only the place for the messy stuff: it is also the place where the script is written, learnt and rehearsed. Here, new ideas are generated and tried out. Here, the leader works with the material the audience could not cope with—the radical thinking, the new possibilities, the real issues. The leader protects the members of the audience from all of this, because he makes a judgement that they would find it too unsettling. Thus, he selects what he is going to put on his front stage.

The leader may hide themself away in their back stage, finding the front stage threatening. It may be hard for people to see what is really going on.

A leader who hides away his thoughts, dreams, plans, hopes and feelings backstage may suffer by being remote from his followers. He may be frustratingly detached and aloof, concealed behind a public persona that gives away little of the true story. He may himself feel trapped, obscured and misunderstood. Unless he find ways to express himself effectively on his front stage, his strongest gifts may never come to light.

Of course, the reality of the two stages is that the central experience for the leader is of living two lives: a public life frontstage and a private life backstage. The former conforms to all his followers' expectations. It represents all they need it to represent—a model of how to live by this or that set of values. It is, quite literally, a public life, a vicarious life, a surrogate life. And then there is the leader's backstage life, in which he struggles with all his own unmet needs and unresolved problems. This is where all the frustration, the disappointment, the doubt, the failure, the weariness get pushed. This is where the leader puts into effect other, private, sometimes secret, strategies to meet those needs and resolve those problems. If they are healthy strategies, they may include things such as making time for personal retreat, for physical exercise, for emotional support, for converse with friends, for sexual fulfilment with his spouse, for secure, confidential relationships in which he can be honest and real. If they are unhealthy strategies, they may include tax evasion, illicit enterprises for personal gain, infidelity, looking at pornography, lying, stealing, depression, domestic abuse and so on.

Now, what we need to grasp is that the front and the back stage are always connected. In fact, their relationship is reciprocal. What happens on the front stage drives what happens on the back stage, and vice versa. So, for example, when expectations on the front stage are very high, the back stage becomes the necessary place to live out another kind of life, free of that pressure. Reduce the pressure and the need for that backstage life will diminish; raise it, and the need will increase.

Many men masturbate, for example, not because they crave the sexual release but because they feel impotent in other areas of their life. The backstage habit is a direct response to a deficit of power on the front stage. The reverse of this is seen with many young women, whose inability to control their back stage leads to attempts to control their front stage instead. Most adolescent girls who engage in self-harm do so because they are unable to master some deeply rooted anxiety or fear within themselves— a consequence perhaps of sexual abuse, or of a breakdown in family relationships, or of a deep unhappiness about their appearance. While they cannot control whatever is causing their anxiety, they can control some element of their front stage. They can harm themselves, they can starve themselves, they can eat and then make themselves sick; they can become obsessive about some habit or practice. These disorders and neuroses all share the characteristic of displacement: dealing with something else as a substitute for the real issue. Indeed, the displacing activity often offers some kind of neurochemical compensation. So, for example, cutting yourself releases endorphins which generate a powerful sense of being alive. When someone is numb inside, such a stimulant may be the only means they have to recover feeling. In such ways, an unresolvable problem on someone's back stage will often lead to compensating strategies on the front stage.

Thus, our front and back stages work together in our complex psychological make-up to contrive ways that enable us to cope. If there is a problem or deficit on one stage, often the other can offer a compensating or displacing solution. In this way, the mind is allowed an escape route, a way to avoid dealing with the pain and attend to something else. This strategy is present in any leader.

The second thing we need to appreciate is that the more attention we consciously pay to one of our stages, the less we will be able to pay to the other. This is almost self-evident. We know very well from our own experience that if we are focusing fully on one activity, it is difficult to give much of our attention to anything else. The person who devotes themself to their frontstage performance has very little spare attention to give to their backstage life. The same is true the other way round. We see this all the time: the academic who is clearly so absorbed in his private world that he is completely unaware of his shabby appearance and poor social skills, the executive so focused on her status and performance she hardly notices the disintegration of her personal values and relationships. There are now service providers who cater for executives experiencing this kind of disintegration, who organize their laundry, their shopping, their holidays, even buy birthday presents for those they 'love', all because there's no time for a busy frontstage performer to attend to such backstage concerns.

Third, we need to realize that the two stages can never be kept completely separate—what goes on on one stage will always make itself visible in some way or another on the other. One of the ways this happens is through leakage. Very often a leader's backstage life will leak onto their front stage, and this is particularly so when the front stage requires a high degree of emotional discipline and other-person-centredness.

The leader seeks to hide a stew of feelings on their back stage and prevent it from being visible out front.

Social and spiritual leaders and those in caring professions often suffer in this way. Their own unmet emotional needs, pushed backstage, generate resentment, envy, pride, anger or even rage. The pressure of these powerful feelings builds up backstage, until they begin to leak out onto the front stage. People will detect a note of aggression in the leader's tone of voice, an unreasonable irritation when things don't go her way, a certain surliness or mean-spiritedness, or a cold detachment in the face of other people's suffering or anxiety. What has happened is that such a leader is emotionally 'full'. Like a glass that is already brimming over, her capacity for emotion is exhausted by her own unmet needs and there is no space left for anyone else's. When she is faced with another person's unresolved emotions, instead of having the capacity to deal with them, she finds that her own emotions simply overflow onto the front stage.

An alternative to a leak is an explosion. The emotional control that is required to suppress your own emotions so that you can stay focused on other people's is like the plug in the top of a volcano. As the pressure builds inside, it takes more and more effort to keep the lid on, until one day it blows and the years of resentment pour out.

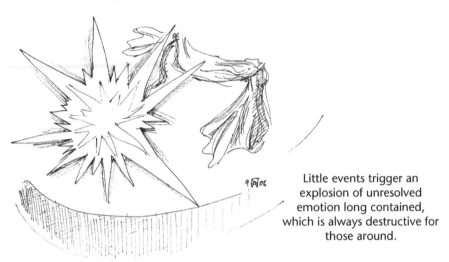

Little events trigger an explosion of unresolved emotion long contained, which is always destructive for those around.

A third option is collapse. In this case, the burden of sustaining the frontstage performance simply becomes too heavy. There is not enough strength or energy to keep it up. The exhausted leader struggles on long after he should have taken a break, driven on by the expectations of his audience (which includes, in all probability, stakeholders and shareholders demanding a higher return on their investment), until there is nothing left. His script is too tired, the props are too old. His back stage has not been able to renew them because it has been given no time or attention or resources. It is a shambles, and so one day the whole performace just falls apart. The actor has no more to give. The show can't go on.

Throughout the 1990s, one of the most highly respected preachers in Britain was a Baptist pastor I shall call 'Philip'. He led a large church in England, attended by hundreds of students and young professionals. He built a reputation for arresting and incisive Bible teaching, sharp argument and compelling rhetoric, and he was in great demand at major conferences. His line was essentially orthodox and conservative on all matters of faith and morality. Then, one day in 1998, apparently without warning, Philip left his wife and children and moved in with a male friend. Out of the blue, he severed his links with his previous existence, his previous identity, his previous role, his relationships and his beliefs. He turned his back on all that his life had meant for 50 years and embarked on an utterly new and different life, much of which contradicted what he had been hitherto. All that had mattered to him was overturned in one day. In one catastrophic revolution, he broke all the commitments he had made: of emotion, of covenant, of promise, of faith, of contract.

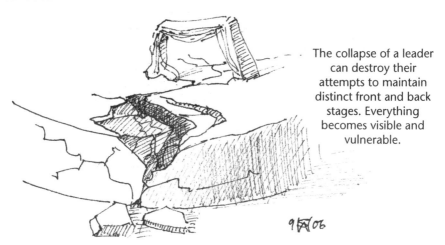

The collapse of a leader can destroy their attempts to maintain distinct front and back stages. Everything becomes visible and vulnerable.

What was it that brought him to this point, where he saw no other way forward than to destroy the life he had poured himself into for five decades? Of course I can't answer that question. But we can speculate about some of the circumstances in Philip's life that contributed to this breakdown. One of these was the frontstage performance that his audience had required him to give all those years. Obviously, he must have struggled with his sexuality for many years. Doubts about his orientation, awareness of his sexual needs, as well as confusion about Christian teaching, must have occupied his back stage for years. He must have expended enormous energy merely to keep his back stage secret, to prevent anyone even glimpsing it. And in order to do so, perhaps, he had pushed himself to perform even harder and better and more fluently on his front stage: to defend orthodoxy even more rigorously, to model the very highest ideals of the conformity his audience needed to see. He may have done so to convince not just them but also himself, to try to persuade himself that he really could hold on to this idealized life and its values. And, as he did so, day by day he must have buried his unresolved issues further and further backstage.

    Philip never succeeded in finding a way to bring these things onto his front stage. He never managed to find a few confidants he could take backstage, to share with them the mess and pain and confusion and begin to address his anxieties. Maybe no one ever offered; maybe he thought that no one would accept him if they knew; maybe he felt he would be instantly judged and would fall from grace. And so he learned to separate his back stage from his front stage and become two people. I don't know what life must have been like for him during those years—the disjuncture between who everyone perceived him to be and who he knew himself to be growing wider every day. And then one day it simply all became too much, and the show was over.

The consequences were devastating, of course—and, like many others in the audience, I am in part to blame. As a young student at the time, sitting at his feet, so to speak, I asked him to stand on that pedestal. I expected him to model the perfect life. I denied him permission to be honest about his doubts. I didn't want him to deal with them, because I didn't want to deal with my own. My life was fraught with complexity and I wanted to simplify it, and I needed him to live a life that offered me clarity, hope and vision. I kept him frontstage while his life backstage collapsed. I, and many thousands of others in Britain.

What lies behind the creation of a front and a back stage is the sense that we can't entirely trust our audience, and so we need to manage what they see of us. I can remember the relief when I finally came clean to my congregation about what was going on in my back stage. As it happened, this was precipitated by a crisis, but for which I might have remained hidden away backstage. My wife, Jo, had just lost a baby in pregnancy (having nearly lost our firstborn) and then our second son contracted meningitis at just eight weeks old. I myself was struggling to manage the reins of the large church I found myself leading. Having been brought up to keep my emotional needs to myself, I did my best to hold things together, not letting on what was really happening. Jo would despair when I sank into the sofa in a dark, morose silence, having just made myself perform as the confident church leader at the front. The darkness deepened until I descended into full-blown clinical depression for nearly two years, and had several months signed off work.

Eventually, I cried out for help and allowed people to come backstage. I reckoned I had no choice—if I didn't do it, I would end up doing something I would live to regret. Jo remembers vividly overhearing one church member saying, 'What a shame! We had such high hopes for Simon as a bishop.' When we make ourselves vulnerable, we risk rejection and judgement. Such comments were rare, however, and in the main my experience was that many other people began to confide in me their own failings, doubts and discouragements. There was an increase of honesty, acceptance and respect in our community. My admission of my weakness gave others permission to admit their own.

People only become undefended when they feel safe. For me, it was a watershed. The burden was lifted and I no longer had to play the role of a superhero. I had begun to discover the road to freedom.

Freedom comes when we start to allow people to see not only the glossy image but the mess as well.

This also means that our back stage ceases to be a place of fear, containing all the mess that we avoid, and instead becomes available for fruitful exploration.

Study questions 3

1. Use the diagram below to illustrate what you put on your front and back stage. Consider such things as your relationships, your emotions, your achievements, your needs and so on.

2. In what ways do you experience...
   · leakage between back and front stage?
   · explosion?
   · collapse?
3. How does trust influence the development of your back stage and your front stage?
   · 'People I trust I take onto my ... stage.'
   · 'People I don't trust I keep on my ... stage.'

FOUR

Strategies of Defence II: Power

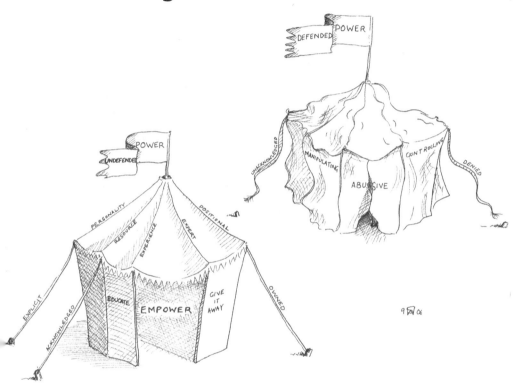

When you met him, it was like being caught off guard by a curve ball. No matter how much you prepared, you found yourself on the defensive in a matter of seconds. Tony was one of those people who somehow just seemed to know something about you or your situation that you wouldn't have expected. He had no right to know what he did, but somehow he did. Not that it was always threatening, mind you—often it would be, 'Simon, happy birthday for last week! How was London?' (How did he know I'd been to London to celebrate?) 'Simon! You're looking well—must have been the sun in Spain!' (How did he know where we'd been on holiday?) 'Simon, congratulations! You must be delighted to have won that contract!' (How on earth did he know I'd even gone for it?)

Tony made it his business to know things, and he had an uncanny ability to use what he knew at just the right time. I don't know if he intended it this way, but the effect was to unsettle you—leave you feeling a little surprised, exposed. What else did he know about you? Was nothing hidden? It meant you began the conversation, as I say, on the back foot. He had the initiative. He had set the agenda, and you were following it. By the time you had caught up with him, he was off somewhere else. Whatever you wanted to talk about, somehow you never set the terms for the encounter. Maybe it is no surprise that Tony was one of the most influential men in the region. A successful businessman, a respected industry figure—he made things happen. Tony had power, but more than one kind of power. He certainly had financial power, but he also had power that was due to his personality and his position.

In fact, as Charles Handy has suggested in his book *Understanding Organizations*, there are many kinds of power, and all of us have some power of some kind. For example, there is *personality power*. Research into the neuroscience of emotion has revealed how people are affected emotionally by others around them. The most effective leaders, by and large, are the most affective. This is because affective leaders influence the emotional state of their audience very strongly. They do this through the empathy (a cognitive ability about which we will talk at greater length later) that enables them to tune into and understand other people's emotional states. Leaders affect others because they resonate with them—an emotional chord is struck, and there is harmony. Moreover, effective leaders have developed the ability, whether through training or otherwise, to exploit social and emotional signalling to influence the emotional states of others. The body language of smiling and eye contact, listening posture, proximity, volume and tone of voice, pace and rhythm of speech, vocabulary, confidence, warmth, enthusiasm—these are the tools of personality power. On a power audit, most effective leaders score very high on their personality power. It is this that enables them to influence others to trust them, believe in them and follow them.

Second, there is *resource power*. This is to do with your ability to affect the success or failure of an operation because you have leverage with regard to the resources it needs—whether you control them yourself or have influence over others who do. The resources may be financial, technical, bureaucratic or some other kind. A person with resource power can make or break an operation simply by providing or withholding the resources required. A leader always needs to have some element of resource power, because without it the necessary means to 'make the journey' will not be available.

Third, there is *experience power*. This is the power that is acquired simply by being in a situation for a long time. Many a new initiative is stopped dead by the committee member who raises their eyebrows at the latest suggestion and quietly points out that some 20 years ago just such an idea was tried—and failed. Someone once said that experience is the comb life gives you after you have lost your hair. However, those who own the comb are usually pretty eager to use it on others with a fuller crop.

Fourth, there is *expert power*, which derives from having a greater degree of relevant expertise than your colleagues. Experts are usually brought in on any challenge or project that is technically difficult, and their knowledge and insight gives them technical power in that situation. By and large, the leader is not the greatest expert in every—or even any—situation, and so he will make use of others' expertise, and often defer to it on a consultancy basis.

Fifth, there is *positional power*. This is the power that is acquired simply by dint of being appointed to a position of authority within an organization. Since the system has legitimated this authority, there are certain executive decisions you can make. Related to positional power, as 'underneath' is related to 'from above', is *given power*. Whereas positional power is conferred by your superiors, given power is ascribed from below, by your followers. In other words, we are talking about the power gained through trust. The most powerful leaders usually have a high degree of both positional and given power. Indeed, often problems arise in leadership when there is a discrepancy between the power from below and the power from above—when the level of trust does not match the level of positional authority.

There are other kinds of power—physical power and spiritual power, for example—but what concerns us here is the fact that leaders wield power. By definition, influence is power—an ability to effect change. Whether it is a push or a pull, from above or from below, influence must involve power. What we must realize is that power is a pragmatic thing—in itself, it has no value attached to it. It is neither good nor bad to be powerful: the issue is how power is used. It is a question of praxis. The other thing we must appreciate is that power is a commodity. It is something that is possessed. You can accumulate power. You can accumulate personality power through developing social skills, resource power through hard work, experience power through longevity, expert power through education. Power is an asset that, over time, can be bought. And likewise it can be lost—taken away or given away. We give away power, for example, when we teach someone else something. The mother who teaches her child how to cook not only empowers the child but, in so doing, gives some of her own power away. Previously, there was a huge discrepancy in power between the mother and her child in this domain, but as she teaches the child, so the discrepancy grows smaller. As the child becomes more competent at cooking, so the mother loses some of her dominance. Thus, we should think of power as an asset—and recognize that, like all assets, there are many things you can do with it. Power can be spent, invested, multiplied, lost, given away, bought, sold and so on.

Most leaders have more power than others around them, and often they have a rich mixture of the six different kinds of power discussed above. The question is: What are they doing with all this power? When I speak at conferences, I often get delegates to make a simple audit of the power they actually possess in their roles. The audit considers their positional power, their experience power, their personality power, their resource power and their expert power, and also their spiritual power. Sometimes it comes as a surprise to people to discover that they probably have a lot more power than they thought. Older leaders sometimes feel that the reins are slipping from their hands, and they fail to see how much power they can exert in a planning meeting simply by dropping in the remark, 'Back in '75, we tried something very similar to that. I have to say it never really took off.' Such a comment, loaded with the weight of so much experience, can deter many a young leader from attempting something bold.

I was working with a school where the head teacher was trying to change the culture into something more collaborative. A staff meeting agreed that this new approach was a good thing, but, even with training, nothing changed. When I walked into the staffroom I sensed very quickly that the blockage was one individual: the deputy head. Clara had been on the staff longer than anyone else, and was well known and liked by the parents. Despite frequent opportunities, she had never applied to be head, preferring (as she put it) not to have all the pressure of the administration and management. Now, without ever explicitly challenging the head's plans, she was simply being very passive. The effect on the staff was slowly to drain away all their energy and confidence. I began to see that Clara had no desire to embrace change herself—she was comfortable as she was—and she was preventing it simply by remaining disengaged, by dint of her long experience and her popularity with parents. Her 'buy-in' was needed to make something happen. Otherwise, all she had to do was do nothing and nothing would change.

Sometimes, the unacknowledged power in a system can be used more positively than this. I was nurtured as a teenager in an organization in which mentoring played a major role. The mentors were usually impressive figures, whose devotion and conviction were evident to all. Unconsciously, we all aspired to impress them and be like them. Indeed, I suspect that we feared their rebuke or rejection. It was amazing how our attitudes on many issues—how we should spend our holidays, which books we should read, which university we should go to, whether or not we should get married—were determined by the unspoken opinions of these people. Officially, there was openness on all these questions, but in practice there was a clear hierarchy of values and, one after another, the choices we actually made were almost identical. In this system, power was located not so much in any obvious contract of authority as, invisibly, in the way we idealized our mentors and needed to belong and be accepted. This kind of power can derive not only from the charisma of the leaders but from the tradition of the institution as well.

I can remember how my own power was pointed out to me after I had chaired a student union meeting at university. An older and wiser postgraduate student, who used to come along to support me, took me aside and asked me whether I was aware how much power I had over the group. He explained to me that anything I said carried a lot of weight, and on reflection I could see he was right. Without realizing it, I had taken into that meeting expert, positional and personality power which had all combined to make my contribution to the discussion hard for others to oppose. No wonder decisions tended to fall my way! I also had to acknowledge the uncomfortable truth that there was something in me that enjoyed this dominance and was happy to exploit it. As a result of that insight, I often tell leaders now to 'tread lightly' when they express an opinion—they must appreciate the extra weight it will carry simply by being theirs.

Experts speak of the 'psychological contract' that exists in any organization. By this, they mean that there is something else, informal and often unacknowledged, besides the financial or structural contract that determines expectations and rewards. In a tight, familial organization, this may revolve around a single figure, an archetypal 'parent' who the 'children' feel they ought to please and emulate. In larger organizations, it can consist in the obligation you feel to 'the firm' or 'the vision'. This is often particularly the case when the 'mission' is a social, ethical or spiritual one. In one of the organizations I have worked for, we used to talk about how 'for the sake of the work' we gave up doing things we would otherwise choose to do, acknowledging that the 'mission' took precedence over our personal freedoms. 'For the sake of the work' can invoke duty and sacrifice, but it can also be used to bully legitimate objections into submission.

One of the biggest issues that have preoccupied thinkers and commentators in recent decades has been that of the ethics of power. Through the work primarily of Michel Foucault, we have become very aware of the reality and the dynamics of power in any situation. Concerns over the abuse of power have been crucial to the debates over racism and sexism, equal opportunities, gay rights and rights for disabled people, globalization, institutional religion and many other social issues of our day. In effect, we have been experiencing a sea change in the balances of power over the past four decades, and it is not finished yet.

Foucault insisted that there is always power exercised in any situation, and therefore the most dangerous kind of power is unacknowledged power. When it goes underground, when it is not recognized and owned, power becomes a liability, just as dynamite becomes a liability unless it is handled carefully and knowingly and certain safety procedures are observed. Just as it can be lethal for someone with explosive to deny—or even not be aware—that they were in possession of it, so it is with power. The most dangerous kind of person is the one with a great deal of power who denies that they have any, or who denies that power is a fundamental factor in their leadership. This is the strategy of what I call 'defended' leaders.

The undefended leader, on the other hand, does all she can to acknowledge her exercise of power, and the flow of power in her organization, and to make them both explicit and accountable.

Study questions 4

1. Rate yourself on a scale of 1–10 according to how much of these five different kinds of power you feel you exercise in your leadership:
   · Personality
   · Resource
   · Experience
   · Expert
   · Positional
2. Add up your total score, out of a possible 50. This will give you some indication of how much power you think you currently possess as a leader.
3. Is this total score more or less than you may have expected?
4. In what ways do you use your power positively in your leadership?
   · to educate and train others?
   · to help and protect the vulnerable?
   · to empower projects around you?
   · to improve the potential of the organization?
5. Are there any people in your organization who, in your opinion, possess power without realizing it? What is the impact of such people? What could you do to help them become more aware of the impact they may be having on others?

FIVE

Strategies of Defence III: Control

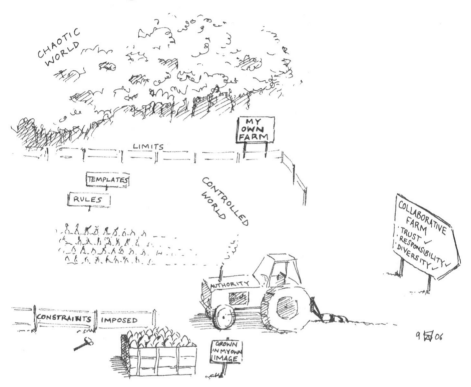

The world is an unpredictable and risky place, and it can be hostile. My task, as a human being, is to find a way to be safe in it, and one of the ways I achieve that is through control. Control offers us a sense of security—but it is perhaps wise to recognize that it is really only an illusion of security. Ultimately, nothing we have the power to do can make us truly safe. However, that does not stop me trying. For example, if I control my diary I feel secure that nothing is going to trip me up unexpectedly. If I control my money, I feel that I am protected from financial crisis and penury. If I control my followers, I feel that the project I am leading will be protected from failure. If I control what I eat, I feel that I am not merely at the mercy of overwhelming circumstances or anxieties I cannot control.

All of us use mechanisms of control, and at times these are entirely appropriate. It is appropriate to exercise control over a child when they are about to run into the road. It is appropriate for the surgeon to exercise control over an assistant who is about to slice through a major artery by mistake. It is appropriate for the authorities to exercise control over a violent criminal who would otherwise commit further crimes. Control is not in itself a bad thing. In times of crisis, when the consequences of not being in control would be disastrous, exerting control is appropriate, necessary and good.

However, wanting to be in control can become a highly destructive disorder. Obsessive-compulsive disorder, or OCD, is increasingly recognized and highlighted as an example of the way a mechanism of control can become ritualized and embedded in a very damaging way. Some people, when faced with an unresolvable concern that cannot be controlled, relieve their sense of impotence and anxiety by focusing on another, arbitrary behaviour over which they can exercise control. Unconsciously, they choose a surrogate, whether it be washing their hands, not touching people unless they're wearing gloves or whatever, and this becomes a ritual that, when engaged in, releases a certain neurochemical that soothes them. However, OCD works in much the same way as any other addiction: it offers comfort, but at a great cost. It requires loyalty and obedience. It demands attention. It occupies, and preoccupies, the mind as a craving without which you are not safe. It gives less and less reward, while insisting that more and more is sacrificed.

OCD is typically addressed, in Britain's National Health Service, through cognitive behavioural therapy, or CBT, which seeks to unlearn the neural pathways that direct the repetitive, obsessive behaviour. While only a small percentage of people suffer from acute OCD, a much higher percentage of people exhibit at least some of the behaviours that could develop into this kind of self-soothing control. One of the things I do when I feel anxious or dejected is to listen to the same track on a CD over and over again, maybe 10 or 20 times or more without stopping. I find the repetition soothing: it offers me a rhythm of predictability, it takes me into a world where I know what is coming next, where I can escape the pressure of the disorder of life around me. Listening to a track repeatedly is one of my mechanisms for sustaining an illusion of control during a period of stress. I notice how children love the repetition of characters, storylines and formats in the shows they watch, which I am sure offers them the same comfort of familiarity. For others, it will be something different. My wife will often embark on a good spring clean when she feels anxious, and she tells me that many of her friends do the same. Other people keep lists, others obsess about their health, others may insist on having everything 'just so' in their office, or on having a cigarette every evening after work (which creates its own addiction) or a glass of wine or two, or on looking at pornography.

Control offers us an illusion of escape from the chaotic world we inhabit into a constructed reality in which there is order and predictability. In general, as human beings we need to feel soothed in order to feel well, and being in control is a mechanism to achieve this. Much of our quest for control, therefore, is not actually a response to stress or crisis—mostly, we exercise control in order to make the world more familiar to us. The result of this is that we will tend to try to construct a world around us that resonates with our own personal needs. If we can achieve this, we will feel safer; we will find ourselves inhabiting a world we understand, which we can predict and interpret. It is much safer for me to inhabit my own world than to inhabit yours. I don't know you as well as I know myself; I don't trust you as much as I trust myself. So, I decide that a world shaped in my own image is my best option.

This desire to create a world in our own image in order to feel safely in control is common to all of us. However, the leader is in a unique position to achieve this desire. Being in leadership gives you the authority, the power and the resources to structure your environment. A leader has the positional power to make changes, to dictate timing and establish rhythms and determine what happens when and how. Unlike most people, who have to make the best of a world someone else has shaped, the leader can set her own rules within her particular domain. It should be no great surprise, therefore, how often you find that the personality of an organization reflects the personality of its leader.

Jeremy—not his real name—is the head teacher of an independent day school in England for 400 eight-to-thirteen-year-olds. When you visit the school, you immediately pick up a sense of focused, slightly manic energy. The children move swiftly from one activity to another; they are always on the go, always advancing towards some goal. The school is efficient, formal yet modern. The staff are motivated. Expectations are high—including standards of appearance. When you walk round with Jeremy, he is constantly spotting a pupil with a tie loose or a button undone. He will know where each of the 400 children should be at any time of day, and often will know some particular fact about them that day. He always knows more than his staff about what should be happening and when.

Jeremy has been at the school for many years as head. He would say of himself that he knows everything there is to know and that way he is in control—he will never be caught out. His roving eye is never off the ball. Like the Dark Lord in *The Lord of the Rings*, there is no corner of the school where his gaze does not penetrate. His appearance is immaculate, his manners impeccable; his eyes hold yours in a fixed stare that challenges you to find any trace of disorder. Inevitably, Jeremy finds any kind of threat to his control deeply problematic, especially if it comes in the form of an equally competent, equally experienced colleague who sees things differently.

Paul—not his real name—is the leader of a large church in England. It doesn't take you long to realize what a busy and exciting place this church is. There are dozens of children's groups, midweek activities, courses on marriage and parenting, evangelism and outreach. There are special mission weeks, children's clubs in the summer, weekends away, men's groups, women's groups, pensioner groups, homework groups. There is work in schools, work in deprived areas of the city, work the church funds in Africa, Asia, Russia and South America. The church is alive with visitors and newcomers, and overrun with children. Its services can feel like a trip to a funfair, as you are bombarded with sensations that leave you somewhat dizzy.

Here are some of the things Paul would say about himself. He finds it quite hard to be on his own. He finds it a challenge to pray privately and silently. He finds it hard to be doing nothing. He is tempted to avoid looking at the difficult stuff in his life. Other people would say of Paul that he is a fantastically confident, secure leader, always open to new opportunities, always looking forward.

Denise—not her real name—was the principal of a college in England that trained future teachers. The college had a reputation for academic excellence and prided itself on its scholarly rigour. At first glance, it was not entirely clear who was the leader of the college: the principal was often away, lecturing abroad, and responsibility was devolved to the vice-principals. When Denise was there, she was often buried in her office writing papers or books. Access to her was by appointment; informal chance meetings in corridors or at the dinner table were brief, as she struggled with small talk. Direction to the college was typically given via 'set pieces'—prepared lectures, valedictory dinners or other staged and formal events at which she could make a presentation. Decisions were made not by the principal but by the entire staff—some 18 people—who would have to come to some kind of consensus on every issue. Inevitably, decision-making was slow and often convoluted. The college was full of mature students preparing for a life in education, busily engaged in academic learning but paying rather less attention to their practical training and social skills. Often, students left the college feeling that they had made less progress emotionally or practically than academically in their time there.

Jeremy, Paul and Denise: three leaders of three different organizations. Yet in each case there is a close correspondence between their personality as leader and the personality of the organization they lead. In each case, it could fairly be said that if you wanted to know what the leader was like, you should look at the community around them. Their organization was, if you like, a projection of their personality onto the larger screen of an institution or society. The characteristics of the lives of each of these three individuals had become manifest in the character of the culture around them. That culture was like a human sculpture, fashioned by the things that drove them personally, including their needs and fears as well as their values and ideals.

For Jeremy, the culture reflected his need to be in control, to feel that he was always achieving standards and goals. It expressed his own internal struggles to live with failure and accept compromise, and his anxiety about his own competence. His demand for achievement from his pupils was a projection of the demands he made of himself. His school was his frontstage performance; and, like his own, its back stage was well hidden, in case it might spoil the immaculate polish out front.

For Paul, the culture reflected his need to be busy, always forward-looking, always on his front stage. It expressed the struggle to be still that he experienced in himself, the discomfort about 'doing nothing'. It expressed his desire for activity and growth. In Goffman's terms, it had, just like Paul, a front stage that was full of high energy and a back stage that was highly underdeveloped.

For Denise, the culture reflected her need for space and personal autonomy, and her avoidance in her own life of emotional language and the social engagement that made her feel insecure. Her demand that her students should focus on academic work was a projection of her desire to concentrate in her own life on the areas where she felt most competent. Denise vacated the front stage of the organization because that is what she did in her own personal life—she had not developed the confidence to perform comfortably out front. Set-piece presentations were the only realistic way to bring out onto the front stage of the college some of the ideas she had been beavering away over backstage.

Often, we discuss the issue of control in terms of the 'control freak': the person who has to micromanage everything, with eyes everywhere and fingers in every pie. Of course, that is one expression of control; but I am suggesting that the exertion of control is more complex and much more common than this. No leader is free from exerting control in order to create a world in which they feel safe—and, unlike others, the leader has the opportunity actually to take control. Once again, as with power, it is healthy for a leader to recognize and acknowledge their exertion of control and make it explicit. Control is one of the least acknowledged defences of the leader, and it is what often prevents them from working collaboratively with others. Collaboration always involves creating space for other people genuinely to express themselves. It is like allowing other actors on the stage to perform besides you. Attempts at genuine collaboration always fail if they merely require the other person slavishly to follow your script and your stage direction. Only when the leader is willing to follow someone else's script can collaboration truly be said to be taking place.

In October 1991, Linus Torvalds, a computer-science postgraduate student at the University of Helsinki, announced on the Internet that he had written a 'free version of a minix-lookalike for AT-386 computers' and would make it available to anyone who was interested. For the non-technical, Torvalds had created an alternative operating system to Microsoft Windows, the system that probably runs your computer. Unlike Windows, Linux (as he named his system) is what is called 'open-source' software. In other words, it is free—you don't have to buy it. Furthermore, you could, if you wanted to and had the ability, contribute to its next edition. The software has been written almost entirely by a growing group of volunteer programmers—hackers, for want of a better word—who responded to Torvalds' invitation to 'join in'. By the end of 1998, more than 264,000 lines of code had been written and more than eight million users were running Linux on a wide variety of platforms.

That year, it was estimated that Linux accounted for 17 per cent of server operating systems and it was projected to see a compound annual growth-rate of 25 per cent, two-and-a-half times greater than the rest of the market. Linux was widely regarded as being of very high quality and very reliable. In both 1997 and 1998, it won the InfoWorld award for the best operating system, and in 1997 it also won the InfoWorld award for best technical support. By 2007, it is estimated that Linux will have taken some 37 per cent of the market.[5]

But the real fascination with Linux stems from the fact that it is not the product of an organization. In its earliest years, no systems group developed the design, no management board approved the plan, the budget and the schedule, no HR department hired the programmers. Instead, volunteers from all over the world contributed code, documentation and technical support over the Internet, just because they wanted to.

Linux is a story of distributed work and collaborative leadership. Torvalds himself still exercises editorial control over the script that is contributed, and there is now a management structure in place to support the much more complex relationships between authors, editors and customers. However, the shape of the software represents the vision of a community rather than an individual. In order to achieve this, Torvalds had to take the risk of allowing others to play a leading role—literally to write the script. It involved creating the mechanisms for their contributions to be recognized and incorporated; it involved an openness to the future and an emergent approach to the market. It involved flexibility and also, dare I say it, humility on Torvalds' part. This is the case not least in terms of financial ambition: Linux makes its money from service partnerships, whereby it charges a fee for managing, maintaining and

---

[5] Jae Yun Moon and Lee Sproull, 'Essence of Distributed Work: The Case of the Linux Kernel', *First Monday*, vol 5 no 11 (November 2000)—posted at http://firstmonday.org/issues/issue5_11/moon/index.html

updating its system. Torvalds himself is no Bill Gates, paying himself only a modest $200,000 a year.

I suspect that many of us, reading this, will find ourselves admiring this achievement but also recognizing how immensely challenging we ourselves would find it to lead our organization in this way. Allowing others to be in control where appropriate may be the hallmark of the undefended leader, but that doesn't make it any the less difficult!

Leading in our own image

This is my proposition: all of us create worlds in our own image, but the difference for leaders is that they have the positional authority to do so. If I am right in this, then it is vital for leaders to appreciate that they have the mandate and the power to impose their personality on the community around them. Within the environment over which we have authority and for which we have responsibility (be it a family, a classroom, an office, a voluntary society or the boardroom of a global multinational), we impose our own personal strategy on those around us and seek to create a world that meets our own needs. The community becomes an extension of us, and our followers become performers on our stage, using our script to tell our story. There is an identification of the person of the leader with the performance of the organization they lead.

For us, therefore, there is a moral responsibility and an ethical imperative to know ourselves, not for our own benefit but for the benefit of our followers. And not only to know ourselves but to be free from our selves. It is freedom that is the critical factor: freedom to make decisions and choose courses of action that in the end may lead to personal loss rather than personal gain. I have suggested already that this moral freedom is a characteristic of all undefended leaders.

In contrast, leaders who cling to personal power and are not free always, in the end, become corrupted. Robert Mugabe, the senior executives of Enron and WorldCom—these are men who are (or were) ultimately enslaved, whose leadership of their country or company became inextricably bound up with their own personal status and ambition. Their willingness to lead their followers down the road to disaster stemmed from their slavery to their own personal needs, which they had to use their society or organization to satisfy.

If we are not free, our organization is not free. If we are still captive to our own need to achieve, to gain personal reputation and standing, wealth and influence, the organization will always be subjected to our personal strategy to accomplish this. We may wriggle and squirm to avoid this conclusion, but we can't. We may desperately want to soften it—to say that, true, some leaders become too self-interested, but a little self-interest is fine; but we must face the reality. The truth is that, until we are set free from the need to get a favourable response from our audience, everyone concerned, leaders and followers, will be trapped.

It is for this reason that civilized countries have established over the centuries checks and balances to curb the power and autonomy of their leaders. They recognize the potential for corruption in leadership and so they limit their leaders' freedom to perform their own script under their own direction. We set political and legal constraints round our leaders to prevent them from becoming dictators. The worst of the world's leaders are those who dismantle such constraints in order to give themselves more freedom. Almost invariably the temptations are too great, even for those who start out with high ideals and noble aspirations. Accountability and submission are crucial factors in leadership: no leader should be without them.

However, such constraints are not enough in themselves. They are designed to limit the damage a leader may do, but they cannot help to make a leader free within themself. We have seen in history leaders whose lives were set free from personal need and aspiration. These are the women and men who had the moral courage to take the hard road, and invite their followers to take it with them, not because it would make them rich or successful but because it was the only way to freedom. And it is to this kind of leadership and this kind of life we are called to aspire. In the end, it is about being undefended as a human being so that you can be undefended as a leader.

Our pursuit of undefended leadership must take us further into the journey to find how to live an undefended life.

Study questions 5

1. When you feel you have lost control, what strategies do you employ to regain it?
2. What strategies do you use to exert control in your leadership?
3. In what ways does the organization (or team or department or whatever) that you lead reflect your personality?
4. How does this enable you to feel in control?
5. What examples of genuinely collaborative leadership have you seen?
6. What did the leaders do to make that happen?
7. We often discover how free we are only when we lose the things we have. What things would you find it hard to lose?

· Reputation	· Role
· Status	· Power
· Income	· Autonomy
· Popularity	· Control

Part 1B

LOCATING THE ROOTS OF THE DEFENDED SELF

SIX

Our Experience of Trust

To understand the route to undefendedness, we must first understand the architecture of our ego, for ultimately it is that that we are defending. The ego is formed throughout childhood. Research suggests that there are two periods of childhood when our ego is most plastic. The first is in early childhood, when we are shaped by our parents; the second is in adolescence, when we are shaped by our peers. These periods coincide with times when our hormones make us open and impressionable, when the 'hard wiring' of our brains is more flexible and we retain experiences and memories in their architectural structure. Most important, these times coincide with periods when we are forming our attachments with our significant others.

John Bowlby's work has been seminal in developing an appreciation of the role of trust in forming our ego. Trust is, to put it simply, the degree to which you can rely upon a relationship. It is like a rope between two people: how strong the trust is determines the weight it can bear. Bowlby's basic theory is that children need to grow up attached to others by strong ropes. There is no secure attachment without trust, and it is such secure attachments that form us and give us a safe, reliable, predictable environment in which to grow.[6]

The reason that trust is so important to the formation of the ego is to do with danger. We need to appreciate just how threatening the world is, especially to a small child, surrounded by what seem like powerful giants, any one of whom can hurt them. When we are small, we are vulnerable and need protecting. Our 'ropes' protect us: they give us limits and they also mean we are attached to powerful figures who can fight on our behalf. Without these ropes, the growing child soon feels vulnerable and anxious and has to find other ways to protect themselves. The child psychologist Margot Sunderland has suggested that these ways can include being aggressive and bullying in order to appear strong. They may also include being compliant. They may involve being the class fool who does anything to win the favour of the crowd. In the absence of strong ropes, children resort to a mixture of what psychologists call 'self-holding' and 'self-promoting' in order to make themselves secure. Such patterns of behaviour, developed in early life, are robust and remarkably difficult to change.

Mark had been a community leader for many years. He had tremendous insight into his faith and strong convictions about the role of the community in society; and yet he would often be told that he lacked confidence and appeared indecisive in his leadership. Something was preventing him from expressing clearly and strongly on his front stage the values and ideas that enthused him on his back stage. He had grown up in a household with a dominating father who, while not a cruel or unkind man, could be dismissive and on occasion aggressive. As an imaginative and sensitive teenager, Mark learned to keep his thoughts private rather than take the risk of expressing them on his front stage. The threat of his ideas being belittled or ignored was too great. It was safer to keep them to himself because he couldn't trust his father's reaction.

---

[6] John Bowlby, *Attachment and Loss* (New York: Basic Books, vol 1 1969, vol 2 1973, vol 3 1980)

Despite being a grown man now in his fifties, with children of his own, Mark had retained his expectation that the 'audience' to which he had to present his ideas might be dismissive. Somehow, the experience he had had as a teenager had become applied to his relationships in general. As a result, his leadership had suffered from a lack of decisive confidence in articulating his ideas.

Mark developed a small front stage with few of the leadership skills needed to communicate his ideas.

Mark's back stage became a place of safety, where he protected himself by cultivating his thinking, and managing his emotion, so that he was fortified against criticism.

Craig had grown up as the youngest of five. His older siblings would frequently treat him as the baby, laughing at anything he said or did, carelessly putting him down, as teenagers can often do, without thought for the effect it might have. Now he was an adult, his relationship with them was much improved—indeed, they now regarded him as someone with wisdom who they would go to in a crisis. Nonetheless, Craig was left with a legacy. He would often let other people dominate conversation, and would defer to strong characters even when he had an opinion. He would fume that others would talk over him in a discussion, and yet he would never be able to find the courage to tell them they were out of order. He told me that it felt as if he was hiding just behind the curtain of his stage.

Craig became nervous and deferential in groups, because he predicted that his contribution would be laughed at.

When he came out, he expected to be greeted with jeers and laughter from an audience that would mock and belittle whatever he had to say. It simply wasn't worth the risk, so instead he had developed a deferential performance, designed to secure at least a non-hostile reaction from the crowd. Somehow, the experience Craig had had as a child had been transferred to his relationships with other people in general, even though his relationships with his siblings in particular were now much better.

Sarah went to boarding school, an environment in which weakness was instantly picked on and exploited. She learned that in order to survive she needed to give a performance of confidence and humour. She developed a quick repartee and was always at the centre of the action. As an adult, she was a master of deflection: if anything came too close for comfort, she would use her humour to bat it away, shielding any vulnerability she might have. As a leader, she was always preoccupied with what others might be thinking of her and how she could manage their impressions. Her experience of a hostile peer-group at school had been transferred to her adult peers, with the result that she expected other people to take advantage of anything she might give away of a personal nature, unless she remained in control of the encounter.

Sarah developed a large front stage, to which she devoted all her attention, to manage the impression the audience had of her and prevent them from turning against her.

Mark, Craig and Sarah are not unusual: I could relate literally hundreds of stories in which the experience of trust an individual had had as a child—both of being trusted and of finding others to be trustworthy—had determined their expectations of people in general when they had grown to adulthood. It seems as if the particular experiences of childhood become generalized and applied to everyone—even a negative experience that has since in some way been 'redeemed'. In his later work, in collaboration with another psychologist, Ingar Bretherton, Bowlby went on to propose a mechanism by which this transfer might occur. The suggestion is that in their early years children construct a working model of the way they expect that people will treat them, based on their experience of attachments.

There is a certain logic to this idea. As human beings, we have to learn how to make predictions, because we never know for sure what is going to happen even in the next 10 seconds. Certainly, when I walk into a room full of people I don't know precisely how they are going to react to me—in a sense, I am in the dark. However, my past experience of how people have treated me—and, most fundamentally, whether they have proved trustworthy or not—acts as a kind of 'psychological headlights'. I use the working model I constructed as a child predictively, to try to 'see' what is coming so I can be prepared. Mark, Craig and Sarah all developed ways to manage risk in a world in which other people could not always be trusted. When someone grows up in an environment in which those around *can* be trusted, the outcome may be very different.

Felicity grew up with parents who were consistent and reliable and who allowed her to take risks. They gave her an experience of being trusted. When she tried out her ideas in conversations, they were listened to and well received. Her audience—her parents—was essentially one that welcomed and valued all her performances. Felicity learned to trust herself on the stage, and she internalized the prediction that people would basically receive her well. She never really experienced people as threatening and so she didn't suffer from anxiety, because her working model predicted that people would probably give her a fair hearing. As an adult, she became known as a confident and secure leader who took risks and encouraged others to do so, too.

One of the factors that cause this transfer of early childhood experience into an adult working model of trust is the way the brain both forms and sorts memories. There are several regions of the brain involved in the laying down of memory, and each has a slightly different function. The memory I have of how I learned to kick a football, for example, is located in a different part of my brain from my memories of my greatest goals, which in turn are stored in a different place from the one that remembers *how* to kick a ball! The area of the brain that is associated with emotional memory in early years is very good at retaining the sensations we first experienced in any context—and the hormonal responses of fear or joy that went with them, such as a faster heart-rate, sweaty palms, dilated pupils. However, this area of the brain is very bad at discriminating which actual experience first evoked that emotional response. The actual explicit memory of that first occasion gets stored in a separate region of the brain, and the two areas do not 'talk' to each other very well. Not only that, but the memory of the occasion tends to decay quite rapidly whereas the sensations it produced linger on. The upshot of this is that we can recall—or be reminded of—powerful sensations and emotions from childhood without being able to remember what it was exactly that produced them. This means that a whole range of stimuli which may be quite different from the original can now trigger the same emotional reaction in us. To put it another way, the experience that triggers the emotional response becomes generalized from something very specific to something much more diffuse.[7]

It is in our early years in particular that we establish patterns of reaction to generalized stimuli that remind us, even inaccurately, of certain past experiences. The consequences of this way of forming memory is that early, sensory memories—for example, of fear—are retained and generalized, and resurface throughout our lives long after we have forgotten what it was that caused them. They exist as a kind of memory landscape, continuing to determine our emotional topography throughout our lives. The metaphor of a 'working model' conveys the idea that such memories, even if we are unconscious of them, may continue to inform the way we predict that people will treat us.

Explicit memories of events and experiences are laid down here but decay quite rapidly.	Analytical, explicit level of brain
Memories of sensations and emotions can flood back throughout our lives, triggered by apparently unrelated events.	Neural hinterland, where we re-experience old emotional memories
Sensory memories are stored elsewhere in the brain and are not connected to the memory of the actual event.	Emotional, sensory level of brain

Diagram 6.1   A schematic diagram illustrating the way the brain lays down explicit and emotional memories in two different, and poorly connected, areas

Over the past five years, I have worked intensively one-to-one with more than a hundred leaders. In the main, this has involved several sessions, totalling many hours, over a number of weeks or months. I have yet to come across a leader whose approach to leadership is not strongly informed by their early experiences as a child. This is not to say that it is always their parents who have shaped their behaviour. Siblings, peer groups at school, teachers and youth leaders and others can all have an influence. Nor is it to say that their genetic make-up has not had an impact—of course, it has. But invariably the root of the defendedness they exhibit as a leader, the strategy they use to make themselves safe, lies in the experience of trust they recorded as a child. Whether it is to

---

[7] Joseph LeDoux, *The Emotional Brain* (London: Phoenix, 1999)

compete, confront, negotiate or concede, the strategy they choose as an adult leader refers back to one they came to develop in their early years, in response to their experience of other people as trustworthy or otherwise. It is to these strategies we must now turn.

Study questions 6

1. What experience of being trusted did you have as a child?
2. Describe how, essentially, you expect people to react when you come out onto your front stage?

I expect that when I come onto my front stage people will...

· Is your working model basically one that trusts other people or one that does not?
· Have you had occasions when you suddenly felt powerful emotions that were apparently unrelated to anything that was happening at the time? If so, these were sensory memories that you had laid down at some stage in your past and had since generalized.

➲ On the website, www.theleadershipcommunity.org, are a number of 'visual landscaping' audio exercises. These were designed to help people to begin to become aware of and address their unconscious sensory memories, in a way that has proved powerful and useful for many. Try the exercises 'Creating your own landscape' and Exploring your landscape'. You need to be registered as a free 'guest member' in order to be able to listen to the audio exercises.

SEVEN

Our Response to Trust: The Shaping Leadership Ego—Over-Confidence and Paternalism

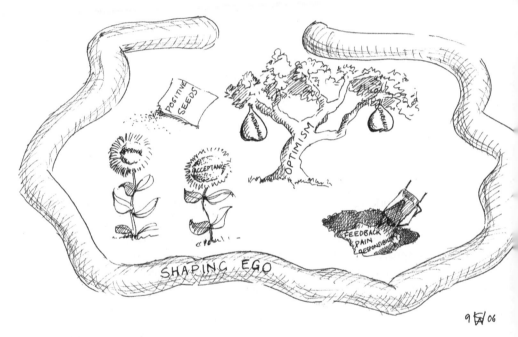

In 1991, two psychologists, Kim Bartholomew and Leonard M Horowitz, wrote a paper suggesting that there may be four different 'shapes' of ego that emerge out of different nurturing environments in infancy. The first type of ego, which they labelled *secure*, is gained by infants who have a positive view of both themselves and their caregivers. The second, which they labelled *dismissing*, is gained by those who receive over-intrusive care and as a result form a positive view of themselves but a negative one of their caregivers. The third, labelled *preoccupied*, is gained by those who fail to attract sufficient attention from their caregivers. This gives them a positive view of their caregivers but a negative view of themselves, and predisposes them to a preoccupation with trying to find secure emotional ties. The fourth type of ego, which Bartholomew and Horowitz labelled *fearful*, is gained by infants who receive unpredictable, disorientating care. This gives them a negative view of both themselves and their caregivers, predisposing them to fear being hurt.

What is interesting in these suggestions is the interplay between the infant's view of others and her view of herself. As children grow up, they try to make sense of what happens to them; and often a child will conclude that if something bad happens to them, it is because they themselves are bad and deserved it. If my parents are quarrelling, I may, as a child, conclude that it is something I have done that has made them fight—and if they split up, it is my fault: I am to blame. It is in the nature of the innate egoism of children to assume that they are the root cause of what they experience. This being the case, it is likely that a child will form a specific working model not only of other people but also of himself from the care he receives in childhood.

Let's look at this in relation to trust. Let's imagine the stories of four different individuals, each of whom choose a different way to cope with the trustworthiness or otherwise of the caregivers around them.

Imagine that a child grows up in a home in which she is trusted and supported. In Bowlby's terms, her attachments are secure. In this home, she receives approval and affection from a number of different caregivers—one or both parents, one or more close siblings, a formative teacher or whatever. I will refer to these caregivers as 'X'. The messages the child perceives from X are that she can trust both herself and, indeed, other people. Her experience is that other people are basically on her side, that they are reliable and, most important, that they are essentially safe.

Imagine this child's ego forming, rather like a landscape taking shape. At birth, the landscape is unformed and incoherent. But over time, as it is shaped by the influence of loving care around it, it begins to gain a boundary and a topography. The plants of approval and affirmation are sown; the borders of self-confidence and self-definition are marked out. Those caregivers who walk in this landscape do so with care and respect; they keep their word, they give encouragement, they are present and available.

As the child grows, she may develop the confidence and trust to allow others to come into her landscape, without fear that it will be trampled and damaged. Moreover, the boundaries and basic topography of that landscape formed in her early years will tend to prove robust and last for the rest of her life. While many other elements will be added, and some taken away, the fundamental character of her landscape, confident and strong, will probably endure. In short, her ego has a secure presence in the world.

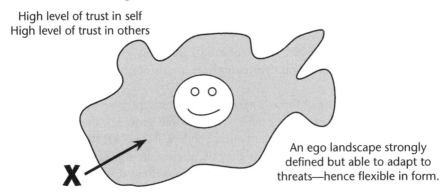

High level of trust in self
High level of trust in others

An ego landscape strongly
defined but able to adapt to
threats—hence flexible in form.

X perceived as unconditional and positive

Diagram 7.1   The pattern of the Shaping Ego

The Shaping Ego is one that perceives X to have been unconditional and positive. What develops from this is two characteristics: first, a high level of trust in themself; second, a high level of trust in others. Here is a self that tends to feel safe, that by and large hopes for and expects a positive response from other people. Many of us go through life managing a measure of anxiety—anxiety that probably stems from the unconscious expectation of some kind of threat (of failure, rejection, disapproval or the like). The Shaping Ego, in its caricature (which is what we are painting here to make the point), doesn't experience any such pervading anxiety. Life is essentially unthreatening, on two grounds: first, that you don't expect others to threaten you, and second, that even if you were threatened (by failure, rejection or disapproval, for example), it would not be catastrophic. Your sense of self is neither built upon nor destroyed by such things, and you would recover.

In Charles Dickens' novel *Bleak House*, John Jarndyce, the middle-aged master of the house in question, represents the best qualities of a Shaping Ego. Generous, trusting and forgiving, he has the care of two young wards, one of whom, Richard, seeks the settlement of a will that, he hopes, will make him immensely rich. In pursuing his claim, and against the advice of his guardian, Richard 'girds his means to the winds' and, tragically, dies penniless. Throughout, however, Jarndyce chooses not to give in to anger at the costly folly of his young ward; instead, he hopes the best for him, trusts him and supports him financially in his debts, despite Richard's resentment and distrust of his motives. At its best, the Shaping Ego is an optimistic and forgiving one, able to see and welcome the potential in others and to celebrate their successes.

Dickens also introduces to us another masterfully-drawn character, Mr Skimpole. He is a charming young fellow and a regular guest of Jarndyce who assures all he meets of his innocence. Like Jarndyce, he is not prone to judgementalism: he, too, is optimistic and forgiving of others' failings, seeing that he himself, as he tells us, 'is only a child'. However, his self-deprecation masks laziness and self-indulgence, ill discipline and lack of compassion. Skimpole has mastered the feat of never being worried or troubled by the plight of anyone, and he enjoys the goodwill and indulgence of those who overlook his selfishness on account of his charm, good humour and bonhomie. Ultimately, he is a callous character impossible to admire, whose overdeveloped view of himself is concealed behind politeness and apology. The Shaping Ego, at its worst, can be prone to self-indulgence and indifference. Sensitivity and compassion for the plight of others grow out of our own experience of anxiety, loss and sadness; and without such experience the Shaping Ego may be superficially warm but fundamentally cold, apparently concerned and yet, in reality, self-absolved of responsibility.

There is a lazy assumption widespread in the West that low self-esteem lies at the root of antisocial behaviour. Encouraged by the positive psychologies of the 1960s and '70s many people still believe that if only it were possible to give delinquent youths a more positive view of themselves, their antisocial and criminal behaviour would diminish. My wife works with emotionally and behaviourally dysfunctional children in schools and she finds that there is often a correlation between a negative, unstable and even dangerous home environment and a child's misbehaviour at school. However, it is interesting that, in a largescale review of research literature in 1996, Baumeister, Smart and Boden found that the evidence overwhelmingly contradicted the theory that low self-esteem causes violence.[8]

They observed this pattern present in people from playground bullies to abusive spouses to gang leaders to racist thugs to dictators: that the decisive cause of aggression and violence is not low self-esteem but a perceived threat to the ego. Contrary to popular belief, too much self-esteem can be a bad thing. Where it is exaggerated, unrealistic and narcissistic, it can (as other writers have suggested) have damaging effects.

The nature of the Shaping Ego explains why this is the case. This is an ego prone to self-inflation. At a moderate level, this generates a confidence (perhaps unrealistic) that solutions can be found to current problems. At a more extreme level, it can produce a will to dominate and to absolve yourself of responsibility and blame. Shapers have received unconditional feedback from the 'mirrors' around them, and the reflections have always been somewhat distorted, sometimes badly so. The feedback can be subjective and solipsistic, unrelated to any actual, external evaluations. As Shapers grow up, however, they remain

---

[8] R F Baumeister, L Smart and J M Boden, 'Relation of Threatened Egotism to Violence and Aggression: the Dark Side of High Self-Esteem', *Psychological Review*, 103, pp5–33

convinced of their own likeableness and reject any contrary feedback. In one sense, they retain the kind of childlike view of self that all of us have sometimes known—that of the infallible superhero. By and large, children do not have an accurate view of themselves.

Tony Blair is an example of this. Over the years, he has given the impression of being resistant to criticism, and of being able to convince himself of his own rightness. He seems to have an unquestioning self-regard that basically dismisses the feedback he receives from outside. He trusts himself—he also trusts others—and fails to see why people should not endlessly trust him. It is this that has given him his eternal self-assurance, so attractive at first, as well as his independence of mind on issues such as Iraq.

The Shaping Ego pattern can produce tremendous qualities, as we have seen; but at its most extreme, when morally unconstrained, it can also show itself in terrible abuses. I suspect that Ronnie and Reggie Kray, the notorious London gangsters of the 1960s, were Shapers. Brought up in a strongly matriarchal home in the East End, they were devoted to their mother and she to them. She could never see anything bad in her angels, and she never required them to be responsible or properly self-critical or to think of others. In time, the twins created an extended 'safe family', but it became clear that they would do unspeakable harm to anyone who hurt their mother in any way. Their grandiose egos created a world that made sense on their terms, according to their ethics; and neither they nor their mother ever saw beyond it. They were what psychologists would call 'sociopaths': utterly committed to their own point of view and totally indifferent to anyone else's.

The Shaping Ego and leadership

How, then, do Shapers lead? What impact does their high level of trust, in themselves and in others, have on the way they lead people and on the culture they create around themselves?

Optimism

Shapers tend to be positive about what can be achieved. Where others see threats, they see opportunities. Optimism is a tremendously powerful quality—in a crisis, it is the very oxygen you need to survive. The story of Sir Ernest Shackleton, the British Antarctic explorer, illustrates the power of undiminished optimism in the face of the severest adversity. His 1914 expedition to the Antarctic in the *Endeavour* ground to a halt in an unbreakable ice-sheet, leaving the entire party stranded hundreds of miles from Elephant Island, the nearest land. Vowing that not one life would be lost, Shackleton inspired extraordinary loyalty and comradeship in his exhausted, frostbitten men, demanding that each of them believe in his capacity to see them safe. On 30 August 1916, more than four months after he had left them to go on an 800-mile, near-suicidal voyage to reach the nearest whaling station, Shackleton returned to rescue every single one.

Paternalism

Shapers tend to want to rescue people. This may be what is needed in Antarctic exploration, but for the long-term development of healthy adult followers it is, perhaps, less desirable. Outside of moments of crisis, it is often necessary for a leader to stay with his followers in their pain rather than simply sort out their problems for them. Dependence is a close cousin of paternalism.

Self-defined reality

Shapers tend to define their own reality. This gives them their ability to survive in tough situations that would overwhelm others: they simply do not experience those situations in the same way. Of all people, as leaders they need least approval or encouragement from others around them, and this can make them free in their choices—witness Blair's independence of mind on Iraq. Shapers do things their own way and believe that others should simply join them. This gives them the capacity for both the greatest service to and the greatest abuse of others. Often, they will work for a greater good when few others will; but they can also take their followers down a road that leads to nothing but their own personal vision.

It also gives them their tendency to unrealism. 'Power tends to corrupts, and absolute power corrupts absolutely.' Lying behind Lord Acton's observation is the Shaper, whose moral compass never points to quite the same north as everyone else's. Most of us align our behaviour to the norms of our wider society; but if my sensitivity to those norms is weak, because I define my own world, then normal social restraints will constrain my behaviour less. A warped morality (or even amorality) may result—and when that encounters political or military opportunity the results can be catastrophic. Dictators from Hitler to Mao have lacked the socializing norms that commonly restrain people.

Frontstage Shapers

The impression a frontstage Shaper gives is of self-assurance, even swagger. The audience watches with a mixture of admiration and awe as the leader rises to the challenges that lie ahead with supreme confidence. His regime smells of power, and in the face of his dominance the pretenders find other corners in which to exert their subordinate influence. There is often something pheromonal about frontstage Shapers when they get into leadership, something basic, biological and territorial. The options they offer are: compete or go elsewhere. The classic gun-slinging persona of Clint Eastwood, lounging through town, draws on the almost visceral appeal of the dominant frontstage Shaper. (Of course, the role can be played by women as well as men. The other most influential person in town could well be the madam of the local brothel, exercising a different but maybe equally exciting mix of power and seduction.) We are drawn to Eastwood's character: we want to be rescued by this mysterious and potent hero.

It's interesting to note how the world of the frontstage Shaper is either very safe or very unsafe. It is very safe if you are 'on his side'—protection is yours. However, for those on the back stage, in the shadows, life is very unsafe. The reality is that, while the Shaper exhibits a high level of trust in both himself and others on his front stage, backstage the opposite is true. There, his world is characterized by defensiveness and suspicion. It seems that, for a Shaper, once someone falls out of favour and is no longer seen as safe, they become a source of fear. Although the Shaper experiences most of the world as very safe, he experiences a part of it as very threatening.

Backstage Shapers

Nowhere is this more evident than in Mafia culture. The concept of 'cosa nostra' is classic backstage Shaping culture imprinted on family tradition, psychology and social consciousness. *Cosa nostra*—literally 'our thing'—expresses loyalty and commitment to your own community. To be inside 'the family' is to be safe, utterly safe. You will be protected, provided for, nurtured—a dependant of the 'family' which defines your reality. Within the 'family', morality is entirely self-referential: any action is justified to protect its interests and there is no need to take note of the rules of the world outside. Perhaps in organizations such as Enron and Arthur Andersen similar cultures evolved over time.

Cosa nostra is backstage Shaping culture where the only thing that matters is that you belong. In this culture, the world is divided between those who are trusted and those who are not. Those on the outside—in this case, on the front stage—are the dangerous ones. Mafia culture revolves around managing a world of suspicion and fear. It works because it creates a terrifying world for those on the front stage, outside the 'family'—they must either face being permanently under threat or find some way of 'buying into' the values (and favour) of those backstage. Membership of the 'family' promises safety; but for those members who jeopardize the 'family', by disloyalty or indiscretion, no punishment is too severe.

Many organizations, institutions and communities exhibit the influence of a Shaping Ego at the top. These are not necessarily hostile places; indeed, they are probably warm, comfortable places for which their members feel a great deal of affection. The insider's experience is of security, and probably also of privilege leading to loyalty. Often, the members of such a community are devoted, willing to make sacrifices and put up with privations for the sake of the family or firm. For many of us, this is very appealing. We crave the sense of belonging, as well as the perks. Businesses that cultivate talk of 'family' encourage just such an emotional attachment. And, of course, organizations such as the Freemasons have traded on such human needs for centuries.

Much about this culture is good and healing. But as leaders we must never forget that the seeds of paternalism and dependence are also sown in this kind of culture, and here, too, lie the roots of cold rejection. Whether they grow into full flower depends on the sensitivity of the leader, as well as the supporting scaffolds she places around her.

Study questions 7

1. What childhood influences form a Shaping Ego?
2. What characteristics does a Shaping Ego display in terms of
   - behaviours?
   - attitudes to others?
   - attitudes to themself?
3. What leadership characteristics tend to be seen in a Shaper?
4. How is the Shaping Ego expressed on
   - the front stage?
   - the back stage?
5. Who have you experienced as a Shaping leader? What was their impact on their followers
   - positively?
   - negatively?

EIGHT

Our Response to Trust: The Defining Leadership Ego—Drivenness and Ambition

What marks out the person with the Shaping Ego is their general feeling of security. The other three egos have one, opposite characteristic in common: to them, the world can never be unconditionally safe—and for the Defining Ego it is predominantly a critical and judgemental place.

Imagine a child growing up in a home where expectations about behaviour are very clear. For example, her parents may encourage good behaviour through some system of rewards and sanctions—a 'star chart' perhaps, or a pocket-money scheme. They may try to model good behaviour to their child, seeing it as their role to exemplify the kind of life she should aspire to. They may shower praise on her when she does well at school and take an enthusiastic interest in any good news she brings home. They may teach her to make sound and sensible judgements thoughout her life. In such ways, a moral curriculum is pursued, in which certain values are taught by them and 'caught' by her. In Bowlby's terms, the attachments are strong, but conditional.

Imagine the child's ego forming in such an environment. Little by little, she may interpret the 'sense-making' system of her parents and learn how to flourish within it. She may understand that, as long as she stays within the boundaries, she will generally receive plenty of approval and affirmation. She may find that it pays to do things that are within the canon of worthy and good behaviours, because that is how to get attention. She may also discover, to her cost, the sense of dismay when she falls short. No doubt many such children are spared full-on condemnation, but those that are sensitive may still pick up the unspoken disappointment.

What happens in the landscape of the ego is that the child starts to 'seed' the plants that will win favour. It may be a matter of achievement at school, or the development of a talent, or displays of such qualities as kindness or drive. The landscape is soon well defined by a string of successes, which have been received with delight and praise. Achievement in itself is reduced to a Pavlovian stimulus, providing the cue for X—her caregivers—to give approval. The child learns to provide the cue in order to get the approval. Increasingly, she also learns to avoid activities that might lead to disapproval. Thus, her landscape begins to tell a tale of both successes achieved and failures averted. Indeed, as she develops her own self-concept, the potential critic ceases to be her parents, or her teacher or youth-group leader, and becomes her herself. She is increasingly self-critical, evaluating what she does by her own, internal standards.

The child learns that it is always best to win. Losing is something to avoid because when she loses, the approval is (or she expects it to be) withdrawn. She learns that it is up to her whether she gains approval: she has the power in herself to get it—or not. She learns to trust herself, but not trust others. Other people, she predicts, will always look at her conditionally, will always score her and rank her. Approval will be withdrawn if she does not demonstrate competence in every field. She learns to weed out of her life anything she isn't good at. Life becomes highly selective, a matter of avoiding situations in which she might fail. She comes to think of herself as competent, but always under pressure. She is only as good as her last win.

What emerges from this is a high level of trust in herself but little trust in others. Her trust of self is high because, by and large, her life has been a catalogue of achievement of the targets she has set. There is a positive story to tell here that probably involves individual discipline and sacrifice. While other children have been larking around, rebelling or just drifting through their teenage years, the Defining Ego has been training herself to live up to the required standard. Her trust in others is low, however, because the fear lurks that, if for some reason she was unable to maintain the standard she has set, criticism and condemnation would follow. Her expectation is that others will judge her on the basis of her performance, not of who she is.

Somehow, all her cumulative achievement means nothing to her: it is as if she keeps on winning trophies but each new one is an illusion, because each one merely gives her the message that she has met the standard this time. She is trapped by the sense that she can always fail next time and must therefore drive herself on, avoiding failure, avoiding letting herself down. Whereas once she achieved in order to secure the approval of X, now it has become an internal imperative simply to sustain her sense of self, regardless of who is watching. She is driven by insatiable inner standards that can never really be attained. Each day, she is set another target and feels she has to hit it. She is defined by what she achieves, and afraid of what she can't.

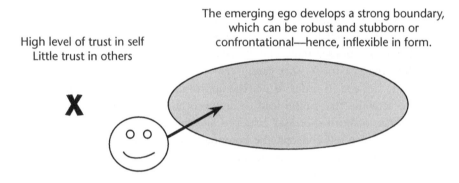

High level of trust in self
Little trust in others

The emerging ego develops a strong boundary, which can be robust and stubborn or confrontational—hence, inflexible in form.

X perceived as conditional

Diagram 8.1   The pattern of the Defining Ego

It doesn't take a highly judgemental home for a child to develop such an ego. Merely the good intentions of a caring and educative environment can be enough. Of course, most parents want to be encouraging, praising the positive, and it is often only a short step to become parents who give out subtle signals of disappointment when the standard is not met. There are many educational and nurturing institutions that are set up to give the same kinds of feedback: do well and you get rewarded, fail and there are consequences. Schools promote achievement with all kinds of status and status symbols, creating a hierarchy of those who are successful and those who are not. 'Doing well' is a way to secure power, prestige and reputation.

Some children are particularly sensitive to the praise of adults and fear letting them down. Indeed, sometimes the most loving and affirming homes can foster an over-conscientious desire on the part of children to live up to their parents' expectations and dreams. Nasser Hussein was captain of the England cricket team between 1999 and 2003. As a child, he had been intense and, as his talent began to emerge, he was aware that his father took pride in him as a promising sportsman. Those early years of strong parental approval of a gift he worked hard to cultivate established an ego whose standards Hussein had to measure up to throughout his professional career. He described how, as captain of England, he would dread the prospect of batting, the very thing he excelled at. The night before he was due to bat, he would sleep fitfully, waking up to rehearse strokes in his mind. He could hardly bear to go to sleep again, for fear of hastening the time when he would have to walk out to the crease. Instead, he would count the minutes, allowing himself to fend off the fear of his forthcoming ordeal for as long as possible.

For Hussein, what had started as a delightful gift that he enjoyed became a terrible threat that robbed him of joy and filled him with fear at the prospect of failure. However good his last innings had been, however many centuries he had scored to date, each time he went to the crease it was to have his worth as a batsman—indeed, his whole life—scrutinized and possibly trashed. Failure would mean not merely a bad innings to get over but the dismissal of his gift, perhaps even of his identity. Faced with such a prospect, it is no wonder that he found the anxiety so exhausting. In the end, Hussein resigned the captaincy and a burden visibly lifted from his shoulders. The following year, he retired altogether from first-class cricket, only three days after scoring a match-winning century against New Zealand.

The Defining Ego can be understood as a house of cards. In terms of achievement and accomplishment, the standards set and the discipline and sacrifice required to meet them, it is impressive indeed. You may marvel at what has been attempted and attained: others would have given up, or would never have aimed so high. The Defining Ego flatters itself by its commitment to live up to its own self-expectations. However, like a house of cards, the edifice is precarious. If the next card falls, it will send the whole thing crashing to the ground. The reason for this is easy to appreciate: others cannot be trusted to give unconditional acceptance, and you expect them to be judgemental. You have prevented their criticism by perpetual success, but if once you fail, your whole life will be evaluated and found wanting. The one thing the Definer has 'bought' with his avoidance of failure is avoidance of rejection. To experience failure is, in his mind, to face rejection, and that is the one thing he is most afraid of. However, like a high jumper who has to set the bar higher and higher, the Definer is condemned to fail in the end. One day, the bar will simply be too high. And when it is, the prospect that faces him will be the rejection he fears, or even self-annihilation.

The Defining Ego and leadership

How, then, do Definers lead? What impact do this high level of trust in themselves and little trust in others have on the way they lead people and on the culture they create around themselves?

Performance, not success

Definers will create around them a culture driven by the pursuit of better performance. This may be in terms of quality, productivity, sales, costs or efficiency, depending on their field of operation. However, improving performance is not the same as achieving success. Success, as something to be enjoyed and celebrated, is not experienced. What is achieved is the avoidance of failure. Current victories are soon left behind, 'good but not as good as they could be'. If 9 out of 10 is attained, the focus will be on why it wasn't 10. If 19 positive things are said in the feedback, the focus will be on the one negative. The joy of success is chilled by the spectre of failure, preventing celebration and inner peace, creating an incessant demand for more or better that can never be satisfied.

In the television series *The Apprentice*, Alan Sugar (or, in the American original, Donald Trump) puts a group of 14 potential employees through a series of business challenges in what amounts to a 12-week job interview. One by one, they are weeded out in a culture that epitomizes the leadership of the Defining Ego. Only one thing matters: performance. Nothing is ever as good as it could be, and even the best performances are criticized rather than celebrated. The entire project is fuelled by fear—you can almost smell the adrenalin. Such is the corporate world today, very often, where success consists in seeing your rival go under, and you are only as good as your last deal.

Control and lack of delegation

In an environment of fear, control is everything. To lose control is to risk error and therefore failure. The Defining Ego inevitably and relentlessly moves away from diversity and spontaneity towards conformity and homogeneity. Systems become increasingly sophisticated and complex in an effort to reduce the threat of disorder. Delegation becomes little more than instrumental execution of the operational orders. Freedom to trust yourself and think for yourself is sacrificed on the altar of control.

The England rugby union team won the World Cup in 2003 on a Defining regime. The fact of the matter was that they were better prepared, had spent more money, had left less to chance and followed a tighter game plan than any other team. Their head coach, Clive Woodward, was ruthless in dumping established members of the team if they lost form. His favourite comment after a game, whether they had won or lost, was 'We move on, we move on.'

However, while the strategy served the team well for a time, it hit the rocks soon after, when many of the same players returned to New Zealand with the same head coach to play for the British and Irish Lions. By then, the All Blacks had learned Woodward's game plan and adapted. None of the Lions thought for themselves or trusted their own judgement on the field. They looked like automata playing out a pre-programmed set of moves, without the flexibility or the confidence in their own and each other's ability to adapt to a fluid game. Paralysed by fear of 'getting it wrong', the legacy of the Defining Ego culture is a lack of freedom to take risks. The Lions lost the series 0-3 and conceded more points than ever before in the process.

Avoiding risk

Taking risks involves freedom to fail. Once failure has been identified as the arch-enemy, the possibility of taking risks diminishes. A few years back, I did some work for a large multinational pharmaceutical company. It coincided with an ambiguous set of results from its clinical trials for a new 'wonder' drug for lung cancer. The value of the company's shares plummeted as investors reacted to the news. What was interesting was what happened to the culture of this company. Previously known for its willingness to innovate in staff welfare as well as drug development, it changed its emphasis to systems controls. It tightened up the way supplies and services were ordered and managed, abandoned drug-development programmes which didn't have an almost cast-iron guarantee of success and concentrated on exploiting the markets for existing, already proven drugs.

The current shareholder-capital system of our publicly quoted companies is, in essence, a Defining culture. All that matters is performance: you are only as good as your last deal (or, in this case, drug). To thrive in such an environment as a leader, you would need yourself to be totally performance-focused, for the system doesn't tolerate failure.

Frontstage Definers

Definers are often the highest achievers, able to marshal considerable personal resources of discipline, focus and self-belief. Many of the world's most extraordinary achievements—in mathematics, art, engineering, medicine, science, exploration and war—would have been possible only through the drive of often a single Defining Ego. However, in order to sustain their sense of self, Definers invest huge amounts of energy in working hard, and very often they become driven or full of anxiety, never able to relax. This may lead them in one of two directions. The first is to avoid going onto their back stage. They spend their energy achieving on their front stage, amassing the trophies and the acolytes they need around them to reassure themselves of their potency; but they rarely spend any time backstage, because to do that would require taking their eye off their frontstage performance. They may come to deplore self-reflection, which they see as negative. Sadly, they may neglect their personal and emotional lives, allowing personal relationships to decay. They are sometimes willing to sacrifice all manner of values backstage in order to sustain what is going on out front.

Then, of course, the day may come when they crash. They lose their job, or their spouse announces that they have had enough of years of neglect, or their grown-up son or daughter says they don't want to know them—and who are they anyway? Then, amidst the pain, they realize what it has cost them to maintain that frontstage performance, and truth may come bearing down on them like a tidal wave. Tragically, things are too far gone for some Definers for them to recover. Relationships may be lost irrevocably. For some it may be too late to develop any kind of personal and emotional language even to begin to address all the hurts and deficits there are. They may now simply be ill equipped to make that kind of journey. All that is left to them is to try and hold onto the fragments. Some remain broken, others turn sadly back to their careers and become even more driven and ruthless than before, denying those around them the freedom to do what they have denied themselves. As leaders, they tend to become territorial, defending their status from everyone they perceive as a threat. Every situation is seen as a win-lose situation. Losing becomes even more fearful, failure is not tolerated, poor performance is eliminated.

They may begin to develop a culture of 'deliver or be delivered from the company'. Often, the success of the firm becomes *their* success, and they resist any attempts to be dislodged from their position. In the end, they may go into retirement, probably with a sense of fear in their guts, having lost most of their relationships, consigned to a one-dimensional life, picking over the bones of the good things they have allowed to rot around them. Big cars and golfing holidays are scant consolation for their restless loneliness. Moreover, they tend to age gracelessly, raging against their diminishing faculties, never having learned how to trust others and receive as they have to let go of their beloved control and autonomy and power. They have the indignity of having to allow others to serve them and clean them. They discover their mortality but they face their demise ill prepared, finding that all the scripts and performances they have delivered were on the wrong stage. On the back stage, which is all that really matters now, they have little on which to draw.

Such a bleak prognosis need not be the case, however. For those who are willing to humble themselves, seek forgiveness from those they have hurt and try to learn again what it means to be human, redemption and even restoration are possible. Hope still remains.

Backstage Definers

The second direction the Defining Ego can go in in leadership is away from their front stage towards their back stage. They begin to find that the safest way to sustain the high standards they expect of themselves is to hide them away backstage, behind the curtain. There are several advantages in doing this. First, it means that if they fail, they fail privately. Public failure is what they really fear, but if they keep their standards secret—nursing them late into the night, in their hearts where no one else can see—only they will know whether they have succeeded or failed. This way, if they do fall short they can usually find a way of 'rescripting' it. 'It wasn't a failure, it was a learning opportunity. The pass mark was unachievable. The examiners were wrong. I could have done better if I'd really put everything into it, but I chose to hold back. My best is still to come!'

They become experts at avoiding defeat and sustaining their sense that they really have lived up to their own standards by embracing little fantasies and self-delusions. Meanwhile, they eliminate from their lives all the things they can't succeed in. They avoid any risk and start using aphorisms such as 'If a job's worth doing, it's worth doing well!' They become 'all or nothing' people, committing themselves only to those things in which they can win. They exhibit a strange mixture of passion and commitment on some occasions and passive detachment, apathy or depression on others, when they see no point in trying at all.

These backstage Definers have learned that no one likes a bighead, so they keep their achievements to themselves. They are known as modest, self-deprecating and understated, qualities that are all the more appealing because of their obvious gifts and skills. They choose to present a compliant face to the world. However, locked in their private world of secret goals and visions, they risk falling into fantasy and solipsism. Many feel frustrated on a daily basis that they aren't able to turn their dreams into reality. Many feel endlessly disappointed that they cannot be publicly who they privately think themselves to be. Many live in a lonely world in which they just accept that no one will ever know who they really are.

Some develop an anxiety syndrome to do with control, or Obsessive-Compulsive Disorder as an external mechanism to establish control of things that in themselves they cannot resolve. Others develop a depression, a mental cage into which they retreat and lock themselves away. In there it may be dark, it may be grey, but at least it can be still. When you're depressed, you can let yourself off the hook—nothing can be expected of you. Depression is a mechanism many Definers adopt unconsciously as the only way to loosen the chains of self-imposed expectations that bind them every day. And in that depression they may nurse a fatalistic belief that the world will never be any different and they are consigned to live in their private world, alone. There is no point to anything.

As leaders, backstage Definers often fluctuate between being passionate and being apathetic, being committed and being world-weary and cynical, being involved and being withdrawn. Deep down, they long for the freedom that 'being found and accepted for who they are' would bring. Tragically, some never find such honesty and safety. However, others do make the difficult journey out of that lonely place. It is wonderful how the intimate support of a faithful, loving relationship can foster confidence in a defended soul and encourage them to climb into light and freedom.

Of course, the pictures I have painted here are extreme, caricatures designed to draw attention to the most dramatic of behaviours. Many readers will relate in small ways to milder versions of these attitudes at times in their life. It is helpful for all of us to be aware of our own pathologies, however moderate they may seem to be.

Study questions 8

1. What childhood influences form a Defining Ego?
2. What characteristics does a Defining Ego display in terms of
   · behaviours?
   · attitudes to others?
   · attitudes to themself?
3. What leadership characteristics tend to be seen in a Defining leader?
4. How is the Defining Ego expressed on
   · the front stage?
   · the back stage?
5. Who have you experienced as a Defining leader? What was their impact on their followers
   · positively?
   · negatively?

NINE

Our Response to Trust: The Adapting Leadership Ego—Anxiety and Over-Responsibility

The one thing the Shaping Ego and the Defining Ego have in common is a high level of trust in themselves. For different reasons, both back themselves and expect to succeed. The third ego doesn't share this presumption. The Adapter has little trust in themselves, but a high level of trust in others.

Imagine a child growing up in an environment in which he sees his relationship with his caregivers, X, as fragile—or, in Bowlby's terms, insecure. In other words, his perception is that the rope may easily break. There may be several reasons for this, and it is worth looking at each in turn.

In one home, X is remote or even absent. Dad is preoccupied with work and has little time or attention to give to the child; Mum is detached and withdrawn as a result of things she is struggling with in her own life. Maybe they are busy with the emotional needs of his many other siblings and so there is little adult attention to go round. In such circumstances, the child must develop a coping mechanism. One such may be to try to secure a parent's attention in some way. He may develop a funny routine—he's discovered that when he does such-and-such, other people watch and laugh. Or he may make himself useful, finding ways to help out around the home. He cultivates his 'performance' because it clearly 'works'—it attracts and holds the audience's attention for a few minutes, which is what he needs. In fact, he sees other people much as an uncertain stage-performer may see their audience. People may lose interest at any time, there are many other shows they could go and watch. What the performer has to do is to master techniques that secure their continuing interest and attention. What both performer and child are trying to achieve is to prevent the fragile relationship breaking so that they are rejected. They sense that unless they continue to secure it, this is what may happen.

In another home, a child experiences the significant adults around them as emotionally 'full'. People become like this when they are unable to deal with all the emotions inside them. This could be the case if a parent is sad or depressed, perhaps having suffered a loss or bereavement. The child may sense that she can't 'risk' expressing any of her own feelings or needs because that would 'break' the adult, who is not robust enough to contain it. This could also be the case if a parent is full of unresolved anger. The child experiences them as volatile and so can't take the risk of doing anything to 'set the explosion off'. Psychologists recognize that in order for a person to express their own emotional needs, they need to feel that they will be heard and 'held'—in other words, that there is a space for their own needs to be contained. Many of us will recognize this ourselves. Think for a moment of the person you would go to talk to if you were anxious or depressed. There are probably lots of people who instantly come to mind who, despite being good friends or even family, you *wouldn't* want to go to. The person you would choose is the one who will listen without judging or condemning you, who will accept you and 'hold' your emotions without making you argue them away or bottle them up again. What we want and need is a container into which to pour out our own emotional mess and for it to be held by someone else. We need the relationship to be 'big and strong enough' to cope with that.

There is another situation that, ironically, creates a sense of fragility, and that is when conflict and confrontation are not appropriately modelled in the home. Many leaders I deal with talk about how loving and peaceful their childhood home was. Press them a little further and you discover that theirs was a home in which no one ever got angry, conflict was not done, issues were buried. They never saw Mum or Dad lose their temper, shout or yell. Everything was quiet and, apparently, happy. The consequence of this apparent idyll is that the child never discovers whether his relationship with X is strong enough to survive a conflict. It is as if he were growing up not knowing whether the ropes around him are strong or weak. He is terrified that they will break, because he has no experience of ropes coping with a good 'tug of war', or being repaired when they become frayed. The child internalizes the idea that, because the ropes have never been tested, they may be fragile; and he predicts that it would be devastating if they broke, because he has never experienced this happening. And he will do anything to avoid it happening. The irony of an apparently secure home in which arguments never have to be resolved because they never take place is that it can produce not a secure child but one who grows up to be insecure.

In all three of these situations, an ego can form that has little trust in itself but a high level of trust in others. The child does all he can to prevent the relationship breaking.

Little trust in self
High level of trust in others

The emerging ego develops only
a weak boundary, which remains
open but is extremely flexible
and accommodating.

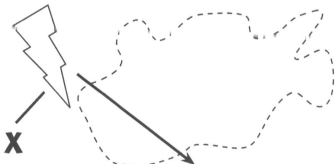

The relation with X perceived as fragile

Diagram 9.1   The pattern of the Adapting Ego

Frontstage Adapters

This pattern can work itself out in one of two ways. First, on the front stage, the child develops an attention-seeking performance and maintains this strategy into her adult life. In any group, there is usually someone who needs to have the attention on them all or most of the time. Often, they are the first to speak in a discussion. Often, they find a question to ask the group leader, and have their hand up first in a lecture. They seem to need to have other people's eyes upon them. The reality is that they 'know who they are' when they have other people's attention—and they don't when that attention turns elsewhere. The borders of their ego 'landscape' are wide open and they invite people to come in and approve of what they find inside. Because of this, they tend to seek out exciting situations where there is plenty of warmth and optimism about. They need to feel part of something that gives them worth and purpose.

Many of the characters played by Woody Allen suffer from this kind of extreme neurosis about their social relationships. Insecure about their looks, worried about the impression they are making, they try to be helpful but often end up being a nuisance instead. Perhaps the character played by Ben Stiller in the recent film *Meet the Fockers* sends up such an ego best. Stiller plays the son-in-law attempting to ingratiate himself in the ruthlessly Defining culture of his fiancée's family. He is up against Robert de Niro's father-in-law, a former CIA agent who is the epitome of distrust of others. Every attempt Stiller makes to be useful and pleasant of course only adds to the disaster, culminating in him burning down the whole wedding reception. Such social neurosis is easy to send up, but a lower level of it is prevalent in much of the population—which is, of course, why we laugh at it: we can see enough of ourselves to feel the pain!

Then, there is often the Adapter person who is the team 'glue'. This is the person who goes around ensuring that everyone is doing OK. They sense when people are being excluded or overlooked and will go and make sure they are all right. They detect disagreement and will find ways to placate people and play down differences in order to smooth over any conflict in the group. They secure the affection of others around them by being caring, supportive and positive, drawing attention to others rather than themselves. The thing they fear is being left out of the group, so they stop the group leaving people out.

Finally, there are the problem solvers in the group, the ones who cannot be without something to contribute. They are the ones who are always coming up with a better way to do things—indeed, even if it works fine just as it is they seem to manufacture a problem so they can fix it. If they can make a drama out of a crisis, they will. Indeed, the real problem for them is when there is no problem, because having something to fix is what assures them of their worth and secures the relationships they feel are fragile. It is no surprise that often these people end up in the caring professions, working in contexts where everyone is in need and they can be reassured every day that their need, and the relationships with those around them, will not be taken away.

At its best, this kind of behaviour can create warmth and care for those around. Many voluntary organizations are staffed by Adapters sacrificially giving their time, skill and energy to make a difference. However, the darker side of this character is what I sometimes refer to as 'emotional incontinence': an inability to control appropriately the effluence of your emotion, and a need to seek reassurance all the time from those around you. 'High-maintenance people' is another term we sometimes use to describe such people. In effect, they co-opt others around them into 'maintaining' them by containing their emotion for them. Like leaky sieves, their feelings and responses simply pour out of them. The answer, of course, is for the sieve to become a pan and develop the capacity and responsibility to contain emotion itself. For the frontstage Adapter, this feels very risky, because emotion is the principal currency with which they purchase attention and affection. To contain it would be to reduce their buying power.

Backstage Adapters

The second way the Adapting Ego can work itself out is on the back stage. If frontstage Adapting can sometimes end up as emotional incontinence, backstage adapting can be thought of as emotional containment. This occurs when someone habitually bottles up their feelings rather than taking the risk of expressing them. The trigger for them will have been the sense that it is just too dangerous to express your own feelings. Millions of people habitually 'self-hold' (the psychological term to describe the mechanism by which a person retains their own emotions within themselves rather than allowing them to be dealt with by others). When a person does this, they manage to preserve a fragile relationship from breaking by not putting any undue stress on it. Rather than expressing their own needs, or articulating their anger, or asking for help, they bottle it up. They internalize blame and guilt and idealize others around them, absolving others of responsibility for their actions—even, at times, the cruellest and grossest actions.

Over time, of course, this produces a deficit of affection and self-love: crushed self-esteem. Years of suppressing your own needs and serving other people's leaves a legacy of anxiety, guilt, resentment or self-loathing as well as exhaustion. At its most extreme, this is the kind of ego that will allow itself to be used and abused.

Ironically, and tragically, the self-destruction involved in an abusive relationship can become the very thing such a person believes they must experience.

This kind of person tends, as they grow into adulthood, to become compliant and adaptive, finding ways of fitting in and repressing their own needs. They will often allow others to win rather than them; and, in order to protect their perception of someone else, will appropriate blame that is not properly theirs. Their opinion of themselves becomes too low as they continually put themselves in situations where they allow others to win by letting themselves lose. They seek to serve others and say 'yes' to them. They find saying 'no' to people very difficult, because unconsciously they fear that, if they do, the relationship may well break down. They become people with an overdeveloped sense of duty, conscientiousness and commitment.

In Steven Spielberg's war film *Saving Private Ryan*, the Rangers captain played by Tom Hanks is sent with his platoon to rescue Private James Ryan from the front line. All of Ryan's brothers have been killed in combat and American military policy demanded that the last remaining son should be brought home. In the event, the rescue costs the lives of many men and the scene of battle ends poignantly with Hanks's captain gasping his dying words to the young private: 'Earn it! Earn it!'

Ryan gets out alive, and we see him finally as an old man, visiting a cemetery in France some 50 years later with his family to pay his respects at the graves of the men who died to bring him home. 'Tell me I have been a good man,' he begs his wife, in tears. 'Tell me I have been a good man!' The rest of his life had been almost a penance for the price that was paid to save him. He bore on his shoulders the weight of the captain's exhortation, the duty that had to be fulfilled, the perpetual guilt that his life should have been saved while others were lost. Such is the moral and emotional burden of the Adapter.

Such is the emotional appeal made by some Christian teaching in the church. In this case, it is not a platoon of soldiers sent to save a life but Jesus, the man Christians believe to be the Son of God. In accomplishing his rescue mission, Jesus willingly laid down his life—indeed, Christians believe that this act of self-sacrifice is central to how we can obtain forgiveness and be reconciled with God. In response to such sacrifice, the writers in the New Testament encourage followers of Jesus to 'live a life worthy of the Lord'. There is, of course, a right and healthy sense of thankfulness and love to someone who has given his life to save yours. However, unless you are careful, being a Christian can become a daily penance, an observance of a duty of gratitude, burdened by a perpetual feeling of guilt for what was done for you. When the death of Jesus is understood in this way, the gospel of life becomes just another kind of slavery.

The Adapting Ego and leadership

How, then, do Adapters lead?

Following, not leading

For the Adapter, leadership is a daily battle. Once again, things can go one of two ways. On the one hand, the leader may seek to do his adapting on the front stage of the organization—usually, with regard to the relationships around him. For him, leadership involves popularity, approval and attention. Consequently, Adapters lead by 'licking their fingers and sticking them into the wind,' as Jim Wallis says of politicians.[9]

In fact, they follow rather than lead. They find ways of ingratiating themselves, of staying in, of keeping people on board. This may mean that they get into patterns of playing off one group against another or of telling half-truths rather than the whole, uncomfortable truth. They rarely confront bullies properly or resolve conflict by dealing with the issues. Usually, they look for a way to paper over the cracks rather than finding the courage to try to repair the widening fissure. Of course they work very hard—too hard—giving every hour of the day to justify their existence and demonstrate their worth.

Denial, not freedom

On the other hand, the Adapter in leadership may go backstage. When this happens, he keeps his insecure, adaptive self well hidden. Instead, he presents a persona that is excessively confident and in control, which is designed to mask his insecurities and deny his need for love and affection. So determined are they that no one will ever find out quite how insecure they feel behind the curtain that they put on a bravura performance, saying all the right things, talking the talk. Driven by their sense of obligation, they push themselves harder and harder, getting exhausted, wrung out, while the organization takes more and more. In the end, they find they are trapped: they cannot give any less at work, but how can they ever own up to what is going on behind the mask? How can they be honest? How can they be real? Will anyone ever know the real them? They long to be known, and accepted for who they are; and yet they can't take the risk of letting anyone see—in case they see what they're really like and walk away.

Meanwhile, the duty they offer increasingly has strings attached. They serve (unconsciously) in order to get some return. They hope for thanks and approval and if they don't get them they feel resentful. They deny themselves to serve others, but envy those who are preferred over them. Their own unmet emotional deficit starts to leak out. It may come out in angry outbursts and

---

[9] Wallis, *Faith Works*, p173

irrational decisions. It may come out in anxiety and panic. It may express itself in physical ways, in stress-related illnesses, irritable bowel syndrome or high blood pressure. The pressure the Adapter puts themself under will find a way to escape, whether managed or unmanaged. The long-term legacy will probably be ill health of one form or another, resulting in loss of productivity or performance—the very thing they despise in themselves.

Giving, not receiving

Adapters are almost certainly the hardest workers in an organization, working longer hours and going the extra mile. Giving to others is the thing that gives them their sense of identity. In the Bible, there is a story of two sisters, Mary and Martha, who Jesus visited one day as their friend. Martha busied herself preparing a meal for their guest, while Mary sat at Jesus' feet listening to him. In the end, Martha's frustration boiled over. 'Lord, don't you care that my sister has left me to do the work by myself? Tell her to help me!' Expecting his support and some criticism of Mary's laziness, she was taken aback when Jesus replied, 'Martha, Martha, you are upset and worried about many things, but only one thing is needed. Mary has chosen what is better and it will not be taken away from her.'[10]

To her surprise, Martha was invited to discover that giving is not always better than receiving. Indeed, for the Adapting Ego receiving is far more of a challenge. It involves placing yourself in someone's debt and accepting with humility the service of another. It takes away your control and invites you to allow someone else to love you and have power over you.

In an organization, the ability to receive as a leader is a mark of trust and health. Leaders must first allow themselves to be led. Otherwise, they will end up leading people in order to satisfy their own unmet needs.

---

[10] Luke 10.38-42

Study questions 9

1. What childhood influences form an Adapting Ego?
2. What characteristics does an Adapting Ego display in terms of
   - behaviours?
   - attitudes to others?
   - attitudes to themself?
3. What leadership characteristics tend to be seen in an Adapting leader?
4. How is the Adapting Ego expressed on
   - the front stage?
   - the back stage?
5. Who have you experienced as an Adapting leader? What was their impact on their followers
   - positively?
   - negatively?

TEN

Our Response to Trust: The Defending Leadership Ego—Suspicion and Over-Sensitivity

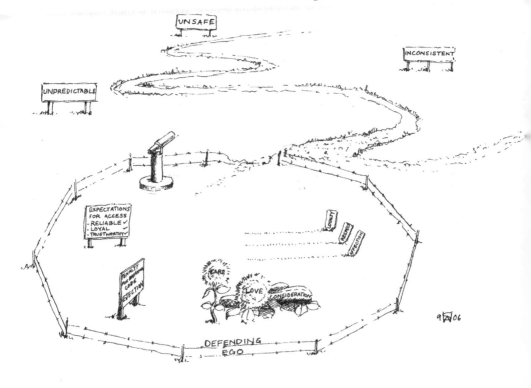

The fourth and last of the egos we need to explore is the one that has little trust either of self or of others: the Defending Ego.

Imagine a child who grows up in a relationship with X that she perceives as being unreliable (and it is important to note that we are talking about perception, which may or may not reflect reality). In Bowlby's terms, we would call this 'disorganized'. Let me tell you about Max. Max is five and lives with his nan, Paula, along with his brother, who is eight, and his sister, who is 11. The reason they live with Paula is that both their parents are drug addicts. Max was born into a dangerous and dysfunctional home and Paula's generous and sacrificial care has been nothing short of a rescue. However, life for her is tough—very tough: she is in her sixties and has already brought up a family of her own as a single mother. She manages mainly on benefits, and yet will always spend lavishly on the children for birthdays and Christmas, running herself into debt.

Max's experience of home is of inconsistency. Sometimes, he is showered with love—spoiled, even. At other times, he is left in the unreliable care of his father, when his nan is just too exhausted to cope. If his father is not around, it may be his mother, who pops up out of the blue when she is not off her head. Or Max may be looked after by his uncle and his current girlfriend, who will (on past form) probably be around for a year or so. Max's experience of caregivers is unpredictable and chaotic. Sometimes it is secure, at other times it is precarious; sometimes he feels safe, at other times, he doesn't. He knows what to expect on some mornings, but on others he may not get breakfast or make it to school on time. It's hard for Max to grow up with any sense of stability, order and predictability about his attachments.

Max's situation may seem quite extreme, but there are many who experience far worse. It is not just the obviously dysfunctional families, however, that give their children unreliable care. A father who is volatile, aggressive or just bad-tempered and difficult to predict is an unreliable caregiver. So is a mother who suffers from some form of manic depression, or simply mood swings, who is intimate and affectionate one day but remote and closed in on herself the next. A family that uproots from one culture and moves to another, perhaps one with a different language, breaking up friendships and rocking the child's sense of place and routine; or a family in which Mum and Dad have split up and one of them is now an unpredictable presence, sometimes present, sometimes not—they, too, may give unreliable care. A child who is misunderstood at school from an early age and labelled as a troublemaker and untrustworthy, and therefore is treated with suspicion by people who should be on his side—he, too, experiences unreliable care.

In fact, disorganized and unreliable attachments are becoming ever more prevalent in our society as the family as an institution fractures, as peoples are displaced and migrate for work, as the proportion of parents on antidepressants or anxiety-related drugs increases. In Britain, it is estimated that the number of marriages that will end in divorce will soon reach nearly 50 per cent, and that one in every two people experiences a broken family, as a child or an adult. That is not to say that all who experience such things develop Defending strategies; but it is to say that for many children the world is unreliable and hard to predict—and adults are difficult to trust.

Faced with such a world, the child has to develop a strategy to cope, and one such strategy is a low trust of other people. Let me illustrate it this way. Imagine I am playing in an American football team and you are on my side. I'm a running back and you're an offensive linesman. Your job is to stop people 'hitting' me by blocking opponents and creating a pathway for me to run through. If you don't do that, I'm going to get whacked. Imagine now that I discover that sometimes you're reliable and on your game, but at other times you are simply not. Maybe you get distracted sometimes, or simply don't fancy taking the hits yourself. If that is the case, I can't rely on you to create holes for me to run through; I can't rely on you to protect me. I can't rely on you to be on my side. Now what do I do? Well, one thing I can do is to avoid running down the channel you should be protecting. Even though sometimes you put up a great block, it's not worth me taking the risk, so I simply opt out of trusting you. Another thing I can do is to become an expert at spotting whether you seem to be 'in the game'. If I can learn how to pick up your signals, when you are losing interest, or are distracted, or are not up for it, if I can tell whether you're about to let me down, then I can choose whether to run down your channel or not. It gives me some control and it gives me a measure of safety, in what would otherwise be a dangerous situation.

Now, a child is much the same. She will learn not to trust someone who is inconsistent and unreliable—it's just not worth the risk of getting let down or hurt, especially if it is their job to protect her. Remember that children are small people and face a big world: if their 'blocker' isn't on their side, they may well get hit by some heavy traffic coming the other way. They will come to distrust others around them, to be suspicious and cautious of placing themselves in another's care. Moreover, if they *do* trust someone and that person then lets them down, they will withdraw, no question. That will be it. For the child, the only way to make that dangerous situation safe is to pull back, to avoid the same thing happening again.

At the same time, this child may develop the skill to 'read' people to see if they're going to be on her side. She becomes good at interpreting expressions, tones of voice, body language. She knows when to get out of the way, to avoid the hit before it comes. She develops a number of defensive strategies to avoid being hurt or let down: she will probably be oversensitive when she is criticized, she may interpret people as being against her when they are not, she may personalize issues and blame people she feels are being disloyal. She will be good at seeing who is on her side and will cultivate those relationships to make her secure. She will value loyalty and be loyal herself—to those she does trust—as a means of securing the same commitment in return.

Pauline was someone who had been let down throughout her life—by her mum and her dad, her convent school and her tutors. When I met her, I quickly came to see that there were two kinds of people in Pauline's world: those who were safe and those who were not. The safe people were those who had never let her down. These, like her husband and other priests she had known, she adored and relied on—she would have done anything for them. She trusted every word they said and hung on them, sometimes with a misguided loyalty, I felt. The unsafe people were those who had let her down. On this list were her arch-enemies of old, but also recent friends who had not quite lived up to expectations.

Knowing Pauline was like joining a private members' club. At first, she was suspicious of you. You felt as if you were under inspection as she checked you out at a distance and evaluated you to see if you could be trusted. Then, when she felt sure enough that you were reliable, she began to let you in; and this gave you access to all kinds of benefits—she was generous and kind and affirming, your greatest supporter and ally. In this way, you came to enjoy membership of an intimate, special and (you were conscious) somewhat exclusive club.

At the same time, you were aware that you yourself could be blackballed at any time: if you let her down, if you didn't keep your word, if you went behind her back, if you dared to criticize her or were not entirely supportive of her opinions, you were out. The doors would be shut, the trust gone. I felt as if I was permanently on probation. I was proud that, unlike others, I was not on Pauline's blacklist; and I was anxious not to earn a place on it by being unreliable.

The Defending strategy is all about dividing the world up into the safe and the unsafe. People are seen as falling into one or other category—there is nothing in between. The world to a Defender is a dangerous place, from which you have to protect yourself. To do that, you have to become cautious, suspicious and fiercely loyal to those you have admitted into your personal life. I have known many Defenders. Steve was a football coach who regarded me as his greatest ally through the season when I was 'on his side', but after I questioned a decision I was blackballed, shouted at, given the 'I don't know how you can do this to me' treatment. Clare was a teacher in a small school who regarded me as a threat the moment I arrived. When it became clear that I would not be drawn into her 'gossip circle', then I was out, verbally bullied and subjected to malicious rumours.

I suspect that many entrepreneurs are Defenders. Their ego prepares them well for the ruthless cut-and-thrust of business. They are habitually distrustful of others and can sniff out the slightest whiff of danger in a deal. They are shrewd and cunning. On the other hand, they often find ways to create strong loyalty around them—but woe betide anyone who falls out of that circle of trust!

Behind the Defending strategy lies a sense of powerlessness. It involves not only little trust in others, but also little trust of self. Children who experience unreliable care will often conclude that the reason X doesn't remain on their side is because of a problem in themselves—it is *their* fault, they are to blame. Thus, they internalize the message that they, too, cannot be trusted. Sadly, Defenders find it hard to trust both others and themselves to be able to secure a long-term relationship.

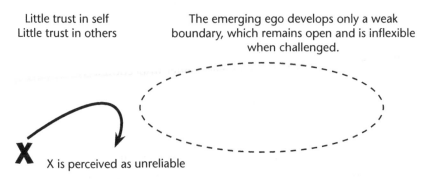

Little trust in self
Little trust in others

The emerging ego develops only a weak boundary, which remains open and is inflexible when challenged.

X X is perceived as unreliable

Diagram 10.1   The pattern of the Defending Ego

The Defending Ego and leadership

For the Defender, life is about stopping people from hurting them. They long for secure, loyal, intimate relationships, but sometimes prevent themselves finding them by ending a relationship the moment there is any doubt or hint of rejection. They often frustrate their own longings and sometimes seem willing to sacrifice both themselves and others in a cycle of destruction and loss. How, then, does this ego work out in leadership?

Respect and suspicion

Defenders offer people one of two things: respect or suspicion. As leaders, they will tend to gather round themselves people to whom they are deeply loyal—perhaps being willing to accept a judgement or a piece of advice apparently on the basis of who gives it, rather than on its actual merits. They will tend to signal that they value loyalty, perhaps in both explicit and implicit ways. 'It's great to have you on board, Tom. You see, we're a close family here...' (Whoa! You thought you were joining a team, not a family!). 'Jane, we have very few rules in our department. What matters here is trust, simple, plain trust. We back each other up, see?' (It sounds great, but what's the subtext? If you show any dissent, or air an unpopular opinion, what may happen?) 'Mary, let me tell you how much I value you. You see, in the past we've suffered from people who've let us down. I know you're not going to be like them, so I want to let you into the plans we're making for where this ship is going...' (Great! You feel so privileged. But you also feel that I've somehow clipped your wings. It's much harder for you to show any dissent now that I've pulled you into this place of trust. And you didn't seem to have any choice in the matter, either. What happens if you don't want to be in here?)

Unpredictability

It should be no surprise that the Defending leader, who himself experienced unreliable care, tends to offer unreliable care to others. At times, you will be his greatest friend, a real insider, with all the benefits, and the warm feelings, that entails. And then, inexplicably, you will be pushed to the outside, for some perceived disloyalty, some minor betrayal, maybe insufficient enthusiasm for a pet project. Working for a Defending leader feels unsafe because you are on a knife-edge—and there's little you can do to change this, because being an insider is not, in a Defender's world, a matter of performance (which you can control) but a matter of threat (which you can't).

Corporate policemen

Corporations sometimes attract Defenders who act as corporate policemen to sniff out dissent—people for whom the organization is an extension of their identity. Disloyalty to the organization is disloyalty to them: it jeopardizes their whole world and they will not tolerate it. This, of course, can create a culture of mistrust. Their influence, though in the short term good for conformity and submission, is bad in the long term for humanity and health. For Defenders, the perennial issue of whether they can trust others rarely sets people free, because their freedom is contingent on their loyalty to their leader, not on truth or goodness. Of course, those on the outside may also be tarred inappropriately as enemies and so genuine, open collaboration becomes difficult. Partnership involves trust and real freedom, and for Defenders this is usually a challenge.

Leaders who are Defenders desperately need to be liberated from their sense of vulnerability. At their best, they can create strong communities that revolve around loyalty. At their worst, they can be suspicious and mean, willing to sabotage a project in order to protect themselves.

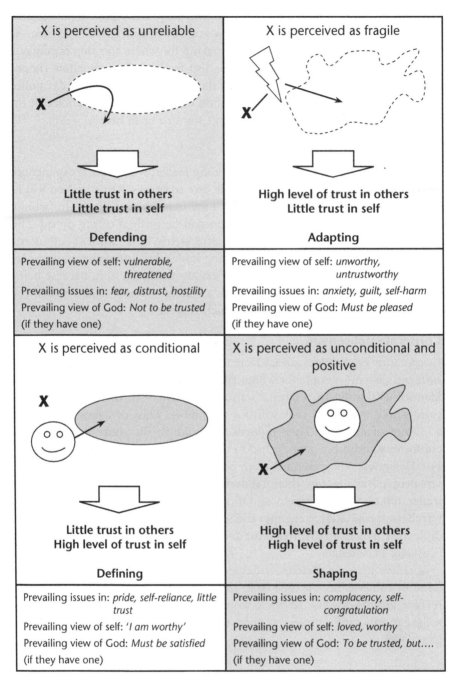

X is perceived as unreliable	X is perceived as fragile
Little trust in others **Little trust in self** **Defending**	**High level of trust in others** **Little trust in self** **Adapting**
Prevailing view of self: *vulnerable, threatened* Prevailing issues in: *fear, distrust, hostility* Prevailing view of God: *Not to be trusted* (if they have one)	Prevailing view of self: *unworthy, untrustworthy* Prevailing issues in: *anxiety, guilt, self-harm* Prevailing view of God: *Must be pleased* (if they have one)
X is perceived as conditional	X is perceived as unconditional and positive
Little trust in others **High level of trust in self** **Defining**	**High level of trust in others** **High level of trust in self** **Shaping**
Prevailing issues in: *pride, self-reliance, little trust* Prevailing view of self: *'I am worthy'* Prevailing view of God: *Must be satisfied* (if they have one)	Prevailing issues in: *complacency, self-congratulation* Prevailing view of self: *loved, worthy* Prevailing view of God: *To be trusted, but....* (if they have one)

Diagram 10.2   Summary of Ego formation

Where does this in-depth discussion about the formation of egos leave us? We should recognize that no single pattern will define us. This is because the strategy we have developed on our back stage will be the obverse of the one we pursue on our front stage. If, for example, we show a high degree of trust in both ourselves and others on our back stage—the Shaping pattern—we will tend to show the opposite on our front stage: little trust in either ourselves or others, the Defending pattern. This seems a strange, contradictory conclusion to come to. How could this ever be true?

First, we must remember what this separation of two stages does for us. We develop a front and a back stage in order to manage our fear, to protect and promote ourselves in the world. Our performance on the stage is designed to secure a certain response from the audience. It should come as no surprise, therefore, that what we do on one stage is different from what we do on the other: our intention in developing these two stages is that this should be the case. It lies at the heart of our strategy, to reveal one thing but conceal another. The Adapter may choose to hide his vulnerable self away on his back stage and promote instead a self that is anything but: that is driven and focused and apparently confident—the Defining pattern. Or the Definer may choose to hide her need to avoid failure away on her back stage and show instead a more Adaptable, accommodating frontstage persona to divert the audience from seeing how much it all really matters. In fact, the four patterns work as two pairs: Adapting/Defining is one, and Shaping/Defending is the other.

Second, many of us know ourselves to be contradictory. Ask yourself this question: Am I entirely consistent? Your answer will be 'No,' because every one of us is inconsistent. We all say and do things that don't fit with our stated beliefs or our idea of ourselves. You may say you're a placid and laid-back person, and yet there are times when you lose your temper and fly off the handle. You may say you're a driven person, but there are situations in which you are lazy, self-indulgent and unfocused. You may say you're loyal in your friendships, but there are relationships you have allowed to break. None of us is consistent; none of us live up to our words. How refreshing, therefore, to find a reason for this! Contradiction—or, at least, paradox—lies at the heart of our strategy. We intentionally develop a side of ourselves, a persona perhaps, that is more concealed. It is real, nonetheless, a dimension of who we are, a theme in our story, an act in our drama. What a relief to find a way of making sense of its existence!

I often deal with leaders who suffer anxiety or guilt because a part of their lives doesn't match the rest. There are men with high sexual ethics who bewail the fact that they continue to give in to Internet pornography. There are confident women who crumble when they have to give a presentation to a meeting, their heart racing and their blood pressure rising. There are clergy who spend hours listening to the problems of church members and then come home and yell at their children and their spouse, who they love the most. There are executives who can confidently command boardrooms and oversee multi-million-dollar deals, but lack the authority and consistency to lead their families and win their respect. There are high-flying businesswomen who are bold and assured in all their professional relationships and comfortable in social gatherings and have flocks of friends and admirers, but who cannot, but cannot, let anyone into their inner fear and loneliness.

Contradiction is at the core of us, and to some extent will always be part of us. This shouldn't surprise us or worry us, and it is unhealthier to deny it than to acknowledge it. It has been observed of Churchill and Hitler that whereas the former was prone to excessive drinking, cigar-smoking and depression, the latter was a model of self-discipline and created a Reich that was intolerant of prostitution, gambling and all forms of unhealthy self-indulgence. And yet the unacknowledged contradiction within that one single life accounted for the murder of six million Jews. Beware the leader who has no knowledge of their own failings and who demands excessive purity! Behind the curtain may lurk devils too dark to show themselves. Devils tend to shrink when they are unmasked, and lose their power when they are named. I am not consistent, and you are not consistent, and it is better that we admit it.

So, where have we got to? We set out to find the root cause of our defendedness and we have located it right under our noses. It is our very selves that we are defending. At its most basic, we are not defending our jobs or our reputations or even our relationships: we are defending our egos. We are battling for our personal survival. Everything else represents the particular currency with which we have come to promote and protect ourselves in the world. As we have seen, there are four basic strategies of defence. In the Shaping strategy, the security of childhood ties remains intact and immunizes the individual from future feedback. In the Defining strategy, the continuing achievement of high standards defines the individual. In the Adapting strategy, the attraction of praise, approval and attention compensate for a lack of self-worth. In the Defending strategy, suspicion and loyalty are the keys to safety in a hostile world.

Underlying each strategy is an experience of trust—the degree to which we trust ourselves and the degree to which we trust other people. And the root of our strategy goes down to our experience of being trusted and of trusting others while we were growing up. The question is: Can we change? Can we ever be different from what and who we are now? Can we escape the patterns that have become embedded so deeply over the years and truly learn to live differently? Can we be liberated from the recurring attitudes and anxieties that have plagued us all our lives?

The answer to that question must be a resounding yes! I do believe we can be set free; I do believe we can be changed. If I didn't, I would have hesitated to write this book, for fear of raising expectations only to dash them. However, I do not believe that the answer lies within our own ability to change. Categorically, I believe it is not possible for an individual to will themself to change. I do not subscribe to the psychology that suggests that we have all the potential we need inside ourselves. The solution does not lie within. It can't lie within us, because the problem did not originate and does not lie within us. The root of our problem does not consist in some flaw in our character which we may be able to fix—no, it lies, and has always lain, in the formation of our relationships with others. What has been distorted, and continues to be so, is our experience of ourselves in relationship: the space we create between ourselves and others, the kinds of attachments we continue to form, the patterns of trust, or distrust, we establish. The problem lies not within us, but between us and others. And therefore the solution must also lie, not within us, but between us and others.

The solution must lie, in fact, in locating relationships with the world, with others and perhaps, uniquely, with Another, in which we are both trusted and able to trust. What we need are sources of love, affirmation and affection that can make us safe, can secure us against negative experiences in our own fragile histories: sources that are big enough, secure enough and unconditional enough to make us safe regardless of the threats that surround us.

Study questions 10

1. What childhood influences form a Defending Ego?
2. What characteristics does a Defending Ego display in terms of
   · behaviours?
   · attitudes to others?
   · attitudes to themself?
3. What leadership characteristics tend to be seen in a Defender?
4. How is the Defending Ego expressed on
   · the front stage?
   · the back stage?
5. Who have you experienced as a Defending leader? What was their impact on their followers
   · positively?
   · negatively?

Part 1C

THE SECRET OF THE UNDEFENDED LEADER

ELEVEN

The Freedom to Fail: Locating the Source of Approval

Imagine you are performing Shakespeare for the first time on Broadway. This is your big night, something you seem to have prepared for and looked forward to all your life. Out there are waiting hundreds of expectant theatregoers, all knowledgeable and informed about what they like and don't like. Out there, too, is a hostile gang of theatre critics, ready to write their acerbic assessments of your performance, reviews that may determine the success or failure of your show, if not your career. Adrenalin is pulsing round your veins. The threat of potential failure and judgement makes your hair stand on end, your pupils dilate and your stomach twist into knots.

Now imagine that you hear a whisper from a stage hand: 'So-and-so'—a famous actor—'is backstage and wants to meet you!' You scarcely believe it, until you hear a knock at your dressing-room door and sure enough, there is the great man himself! He introduces himself and explains that he was in town and wanted to see you perform. He's heard such things about you and, from what he has seen on screen, senses that you have a great gift. He tells you that, whatever happens tonight, whatever tomorrow's papers say, he will be clapping you all the way.

Wouldn't the way you act this night be totally transformed by that one, single encounter, those few hurried words? The encouragement you had been given, the affirmation and unconditional support would change your experience from one of fear and anxiety to one of excitement, and perhaps even calm. What would be different, of course, is that the sense of threat had gone. The threat of the audience and the critics would be replaced by the safety of approval and an evaluation you respected more than any other. Indeed, even if your performance got the thumbs down from the critics, the sight of that one smiling, clapping figure in the stalls, the person who mattered most, would banish the fear of that criticism. It wouldn't necessarily improve your performance, but it would set you free.

Freedom comes from knowing that you are approved of. Freedom to perform comes from the knowledge that there is someone rooting for you in the audience, whose opinion you value more than anyone else's and who is smiling and cheering just for you. In such a relationship you become free from the need to succeed. Indeed, you can perform with nothing to lose, because you are secure that your identity, your future, your wellbeing, does not depend on the quality of your performance.

In the 2000 Olympics in Sydney, Jonathan Edwards had the weight of destiny resting on his shoulders. Some five years earlier he had broken the world record three times in his event, the triple jump, and since then he had been far and away the best triple jumper the world had ever seen. His record distance of 18.29 metres had never been challenged—no one had even come close. Season after season, he dominated the event. And yet, somehow, at the 1996 Games in Atlanta he had contrived to lose. 2000 was to be his year. He also acknowledged that this was going to be his last Olympics—his last opportunity to establish himself in his rightful place before he retired. Conventional sporting wisdom would have it that Edwards should have prepared mentally by eliminating the possibility of failure from his mind. He should have played over in his head, again and again, the image of himself jumping the perfect jump and winning the gold.

But that was not how he prepared. Instead, he contemplated defeat and stared it right between the eyes. Instead of blocking out failure, he chose to embrace it: he chose to embrace the idea of loss and reflect on what it would actually mean for him never to win the Olympic title. And when he considered that future, he discovered that it was not the threat he had feared it to be. He realized that he could survive such an outcome: he would still know who he was and, indeed, being a man of faith, his identity and worth in God's eyes would still be intact. In short, he found that his sense of who he was did not depend on how he performed as an athlete. In the event, Edwards ran down the runway free of fear, won convincingly and was rewarded with the medal he deserved.

Freedom to lead depends on us finding a source of unconditional approval that is not jeopardized by our performance. Leadership, like acting on Broadway or jumping in an Olympic final, is a threatening activity, one in which we may be observed and evaluated by a host of critics. As long as we fear the reaction of this audience, we can't be free in our leadership. Freedom comes when we are concerned only about the opinion of the one in the audience who truly matters.

As long as we fear for our job, as long as we fear for our salary, as long as we fear for our reputation, as long as we fear for our popularity, as long as we fear for our credibility, as long as we fear for our wealth, as long as we fear for our control, we cannot be truly free in our leadership. We will defend ourselves against the loss of the asset we value most. Only the person who is secure against the loss of all these things can be truly undefended, truly free. The secret of effective leadership is the freedom to live an undefended life.

Conventional wisdom insists that, in leadership, success come from dismissing the very idea of failure. The leader is the one who, through diligent training, preparation and foresight, can face any eventuality. The British Army supplies its officer cadets as they begin their training at the Royal Military Academy at Sandhurst with a little red book entitled *Serve to Lead*. Compiled in the 1950s, the book has a consistent message: that the leader is the one who is not threatened by failure because he has at his disposal tremendous resources. In short, he has mustered his defences, material, physical, mental and spiritual. The Army prizes defended leaders and trains men to become defended leaders. Arguably, this is the kind of mentality you need for combat. I often take former army officers through my course on undefended leadership, and I recall one describing the process as a kind of 'reprogramming'. Instead of controlling and suppressing his fear through competence, preparation and control, I was inviting him to trust that his ultimate security is assured, by a relationship that cannot be destroyed, even by bullets or bombs.

The idea of undefended leadership is that we are secured not by our skills and resources but by our attachment to another—one who is big enough not to be overwhelmed by our failures and weaknesses. Imagine that you walk into a room and find it full of all the people you have ever known. They are all there—all there because this is a party for you. As you enter, they turn and smile and welcome you, and you find yourself walking through a throng of friends. Music is playing and the air is full of chatter and laughter. Stories are being shared and connections made. There is apparently plenty of time to talk with everyone you want to and you converse with friends and relations, heroes and neighbours. Some you haven't seen for many years, and some you left on bad terms the last time you met; and there are conversations that need to be finished, or even begun. You realize that this room sums up your life, your presence in the world, for it contains all the people you have touched and affected in some way or another. Inside, you experience a wonderful, warm glow as you feel known and cared for and understood.

Slowly, one by one, the guests start to leave, and the room begins to empty. The music quietens down and you are left with your family. The host of memories and stories you share is like treasure—treasure that you gave them to cherish and look after: your deepest, most significant, most vulnerable being. The cracks where it has been dropped in the past remind you of the fragility and the pain you felt in earlier, unhappier times. But today, it seems, is not to be such a time. Today, you are held carefully and with respect, and you feel secure.

Finally, they, too, begin to go, one by one, and you are left, standing alone.

'Hello there,' says a voice. You turn and there, leaning against the wall, is a young man, smiling. 'You haven't seen me before, but I've seen you. Or, should I say, I've been watching you, since—oooh, well, since before you even existed, actually. I knew you when you were no bigger than a plum, growing inside your mother's womb. You see, I was there. I was there with you.

'I was there in the room when you were born, when you took your first gasp of air. I was there in those early months—I know what happened to you, I saw inside you, the things you couldn't see. I saw your fear when you were left alone and your joy when your mum returned. It was like an explosion of warmth inside you, swamping your little body. I was there when your first tooth came—and when the first tooth fell out. I saw you take your first step, and when you screamed with pain that day when you fell on your nose. I watched your hair grow. I watched it being washed and cut. I was there at the school gates when you went in, aching and scared inside where no one else could see. I knew your first house. I was there at your birthday when you were given that toy you had asked for and asked for.

'I was there, too, when you thought no one else was looking, no one could see. Yeah, I saw it all. I was there when you thought no one knew or cared or understood, in the night when you were alone, crying inside. I felt it with you. I have felt everything with you. And, now, I know what you do—each morning, when you wake, how you feel about the day, and about yourself. I know what it means for you to face another day. I have been there at your greatest victories and your greatest defeats. I have watched your life take shape. I've watched as you've hidden those parts of you away; I know the scars, and that surge of anxiety when that person comes near. I know what you long for in the deepest part of your being. I know what you believe you can achieve, and I know the frustration you feel at not being able to do it. Each night, I hold one by one your regrets for all the mistakes you have made, and I hold the shards of your shattered hopes so that they don't fall to the ground.'

He pauses and then says your name, and he says it as if he knows it very well—as if he has been saying it for years. 'I came here because you need to know one thing: that to me you are the most special and precious person in the world. And you need to know that whatever happens to you now, in the rest of your life, nothing will change that and you will never be alone.'

Freedom to lead an undefended life, freedom to lead others as an undefended leader, involves finding a relationship like that. A relationship in which we are safe, secured by an unconditional regard and affection, an unbroken attachment, that holds us despite the threats we face. As someone has said, it is another kind of defendedness, in which we are defended by Another rather than by our own strategies. It should be clear by now that even the best of relationships and attachments leave a legacy—a deficit. Even the most secure Shaper will be in danger of abusing others, and will one day face the fragility of losing her relationship with X. Human relationships are simply not big enough. They are not strong enough to survive death, or true enough to give us a proper sense of perspective, a proper sense of ourselves.

What I need is for an X to come and pour into me the love and acceptance I have craved. I need an X to say to me: 'I know what you're like and I still accept you.' I need an X who will always be in the audience rooting for me. I need an X who, even when I blow it, will come backstage, talk through the things that went wrong and tell me how to get up on my feet again. I need an X whose commitment to me is so tough, so strong that it can survive the worst I can do. I need an X in whose presence I feel utterly secure—when I'm with them, I don't need to worry about what others think of me or how I appear or whether I'm successful or not. I need an X whose view of me is true and fair and unbiased. I need an X who will lay out a pathway to the ideals and values that should direct me, but even when I fail to achieve them will not condemn me or cast me off. I need an X who is bigger than me, and bigger than all my worries—and that includes my boss, my relationships, my ambitions, my needs, my financial anxieties. I need an X who knows and understands my hopes and dreams; who will hold them and nurture them with me, and for me, and not drop them and let them break. I need an X who can work with the broken Simon as well as the whole and healthy and confident Simon.

Of course, the X I am talking about can't be human—at least, not merely human. This X has to be divine—but they also have to be personal. An X that is merely a force or a way of being or an organizing principle in the world is no good to me: I can't be loved and accepted and approved of by a cosmic energy. I need an X who is *for* me, not in a sloppy, sentimental, cuddly-grandfather way, but leading me on to greater things, better things, higher things. I need an X who is big enough to know and hold me in my suffering, but also hold the world in its suffering. An X who merely avoids looking at or dealing with injustice is no good to me, or to anyone. I need an X who takes evil and injustice, abuse and pain seriously, an X who sets boundaries, but safe, secure ones.

If I can find such a relationship, it will begin to make courageous, self-sacrificial leadership possible. Choices that previously were unavailable to me because they would jeopardize my success or reputation, will now become available because I won't need to safeguard my success or reputation.

Of course, the impact of such a relationship will vary according to which of the four ego patterns a leader manifests. Its impact on a leader with a Shaping Ego pattern will be different from that on a leader with an Adapting, Defining or Defending Ego pattern. The security and intimacy of such an attachment will penetrate to the very heart of our defendedness.

The Shaping Ego

Key transforming truth: The world is neither as safe nor as unsafe as you think.

Shapers believe that the world can be truly safe—on their terms. However, this is something of a fantasy, and the reality a Shaper needs to discover is that the world is neither as safe nor as unsafe as they feel it to be. The Shaper needs to grow up into a more mature understanding of life in which problems may remain unresolved and mysteries unsolved, and in which relationships may break down irrevocably. Instead of seeking a harmonious world, from which, under their governance, every disorder is eliminated, the Shaper must learn to tolerate difficulty, division and diversity.

Likewise, the Shaper may at times feel bitterly betrayed by people close to them who they trusted. The Shaper must learn to move beyond recrimination, to learn from the breakdown and to choose to trust others once more, but with greater discernment.

Key action: Stop trying to rescue people.

Shapers tend to act instinctively as rescuers, to try to save people from experiencing pain. In so doing, they prevent people taking responsibility themselves. They can also become burnt out in the process. Shapers need to restrain their impulse to fix, and instead must learn to be with others in the mess they're in and help them to shoulder their responsibility rather than trying to take it away. At the same time, they must allow others to give to *them*, to see their own need. As they do this, Shapers will become more sensitive to the complexity of the pain around them and will eschew simplistic, superficial or premature solutions in favour of the goals of maturity and wisdom.

Key attitude: Allow feedback to touch you.

Shapers find it all too easy to allow feedback to bounce off them. They may listen, but they often don't hear. As they are led into freedom, a Shaper begins to give a more open account of themselves, to tell a story of failure as well as success, problems as well as results. They choose to take responsibility for a sense of self that is not all sorted and secure but is being defined each day by their choices. Feedback from close colleagues and friends is an important source of material that they are eager to incorporate into their unfolding story.

The Shaper can make this journey into freedom only with the support of that secure relationship in which their need to defend themself is slowly dismantled.

The Defining Ego

Key transforming truth: You are not as successful as you think you are—but you cannot be as unsuccessful as you fear.

Definers live with a carefully nurtured sense of self, defined by exceeding personal standards and targets. Within that range, they can be extremely confident—in fact, over-confident. However, beneath that confidence lurks a fear of failure, and Definers need to be freed from this. They need to be released from the fear that their identity and worth will be devastated if they fall short of these standards. They need to be liberated from the sense that other people's affection for them is conditional on their good behaviour.

Instead of seeking to maintain their performance, Definers must discover the freedom to fail, to learn that they can fail and survive. They need to acknowledge their failures rather than burying them in denial as they are tempted to do. (Audit the things about yourself you're tempted to deny if you don't believe me!) They need to articulate their failures as part of the story they tell themselves and others. They need to live happily with both success and failure. As they do so, they will discover that they never were quite as good as they thought they were—but it doesn't matter as much as they thought it did anyway.

Key action: Stop wanting to win at all costs.

Definers find it hard to let others win. They are instinctively competitive, whether it be to do the shopping in the fastest time, to be the youngest person to reach that level in the firm or to be the only one to hit their targets that quarter. This can make it difficult for them to take pleasure in other people's success, or to seek win-win outcomes. Others around them may feel dominated and overwhelmed by their superiority, rather than empowered and enabled. Definers must consciously restrain their impulse to win while others lose, and should try out the experience of allowing others to win for a change. Most of all, they should look for win-win outcomes. Collaborative success through partnership should be the hallmark of their leadership: if they aim for this, they will not go far wrong.

Definers should also watch out for the activities they simply 'opt out of' because they secretly fear they can't win at them. Having a go at things at which they are less than the best is an excellent way to grow in freedom.

Key attitude: Enjoy the moment and stay in it.

Many Definers live entirely in the future: What is the outcome going to be? Where is the next challenge? How can I beat the competition in the next quarter? Once I've got this promotion, then I'll be able to invest time in my family… As a result, they often fail to appreciate the moment, the here and now. Definers who want to walk into freedom need consciously to resist the urge always to be moving on and living for tomorrow. Instead, they need to cultivate an awareness of what is happening now. This involves developing the ability to listen to their body, to notice how people are feeling in the office today, to enjoy their successes and celebrate them—as well as stay in touch with their feelings of fragility and inadequacy. As they do so, their experience of life will be much richer, and others will find their leadership more liberating.

The only route to freedom for the Definer is the daily appropriation of a source of affection and approval that is unconditional.

The Adapting Ego

Key transforming truth: Relationships are not as fragile as you believe.

Adapters live with the fear that relationships around them may fracture. As a result, they pursue strategies that are designed to shore up those relationships, which may involve attention-seeking, self-containment or acquiescence and accommodation. The long-term outcome can be exhaustion, anxiety, self-neglect or even self-harm. Adapters need to be set free from this fear of fragile attachments and the low self-esteem and self-trust that it produces. Instead of living to preserve something they fear may be taken away, they need to learn to trust themselves as people who are worth knowing.

As they grow in self-trust and self-respect, so they will be less afraid of what others may think of them. They will begin to believe that when they offer people their friendship they are actually offering them a valuable gift. They will begin to be able to say no to the demands of others and respect their own boundaries and limits.

Key action: Say no.

Adapters find it incredibly hard to say no. They fear rejection if they do so, they fear that the relationship will break if they don't always make themselves available. As a result, they are often exhausted themselves as they are used and abused by others: the firm, the family and the like. For Adapters, there is no more important choice than simply to choose to say no. This is a matter of respecting yourself and recognizing your limits. It is not self-indulgent, it isn't something you should feel guilty about. Often by saying no you help the other person to take appropriate responsibility: they benefit as a result, and (more important) so do you.

Adapters should recognize that their instinct is to take too much responsibility for problems around them, often blaming themselves for things that go wrong. Their route to freedom is to take less responsibility and ensure that others take more.

Key attitude: Trust yourself.

Behind this difficulty in saying no lies a lack of self-trust. Adapters often live with scripts that say such things as 'I don't merit their friendship,' 'If they really knew what I was like…' and 'I don't deserve this gift.' Their source of freedom lies in listening to the voice that says: 'You are of value because I love you.' These words are hard for them to hear and receive, but heard and received they must be. If you are an Adapter, write them beautifully on a sign to put on your desk, or make them your screensaver. And whenever someone offers you a compliment, don't just shrug it off and forget about it: treasure it as a genuine and precious gift! Write it down, put it in a beautiful box along with all the other gifts of approval and affirmation you have been given. It's time to start prizing the praise.

The Defending Ego

Key transforming truth: You are safer than you realize.

Defenders live in the expectation of an imminent breakdown in relationships. They are on the alert for it, anticipating it—and often actually making it happen by pushing other people into a corner. If you have been let down many times in the past by people you trusted, needed, relied on, it's easy to fear that the same thing is about to happen to you again—and that fear can drive Defenders to lash out before it's too late.

As they grow in confidence in the one relationship that will not let them down, Defenders will begin to be free from this fear. It is a question of where they turn their attention: towards the relationships that may let them down or towards the one in which they're secure.

Key action: Stay in the relationship.

The route to freedom is no quick fix, but instead is a settled, determined choice to restrain the impulse to cut and run when people appear to be disloyal or hostile. This takes courage—courage to confront your fear and not give in to it, to choose to take the risk of believing in others and yourself and offering your best. It involves accepting criticism without simmering with rage (or boiling over). It involves not withdrawing but continuing to offer yourself to be known.

Key attitude: Trust others.

As Defenders learn to trust themselves more, their highest priority should then be to trust others. Defenders fear that this is a great risk that leaves them exposed and vulnerable, but over time, as they discover that other relationships can be relied on, they will find that they are more able to take the risk of not withdrawing. If you are a Defender, make it a discipline to give trust away as much as you can. Choose to overlook the times when you have been let down and instead think the best of other people. As you discover what it is like to be trusted, in a trustworthy relationship, so all kinds of other trusting relationships will grow up around you. You will flourish and become welcoming, hospitable and generous, a 'safe place' not only for yourself but also for the many people who will be blessed through you.

Study questions 11

1. Which of the four Ego patterns do you most relate to?
   - Shaping
   - Defining
   - Adapting
   - Defending
2. In what ways does that pattern affect and determine your relationships
   - in your leadership?
   - with your family and loved ones?
   - with friends?
3. How much do you want to find a relationship that can secure you at the deepest level?

⮑ On the website, www.theleadershipcommunity.org, listen to the audio file with the 'visual landscaping' exercise 'Encountering God in your landscape'. This will help you to become more aware of being known by a spiritual source of approval. You need to be registered as a free 'guest member' in order to listen to the audio file.

TWELVE

The Freedom to Give: Cultivating Undefended Leadership

Robert K Greenleaf was born in Terre Haute, Indiana and spent most of his organizational life in the fields of management, research, development and education. Just before his retirement, he embarked on a whole new career and became a noted author. In 1970, he published 'The Servant as Leader', the first in a series of essays he wrote on the concept of the servant-leader.

Greenleaf argued: 'The servant-leader is servant first. ... It begins with the natural feeling that one wants to serve, to serve first. Then conscious choice brings one to aspire to lead. He or she is sharply different from the person who is leader first, perhaps because of the need to assuage an unusual power drive or

---

[11] At http://www.greenleaf.org

to acquire material possessions. For such it will be a later choice to serve—after leadership is established.'[11]

As this quote indicates, the heart of the concept of servant leadership is that service precedes leadership. For anyone concerned about the moral condition of the world—and, indeed, the need for human beings to serve one another rather than exploit each other— Greenleaf's message is captivating. It cuts directly across the attitudes that prevail in so much of life and leadership in contemporary society. It insists on the moral priority of the other; it demands that leadership is not self-serving but other-person-centred.

The concept of servant leadership has been seized on eagerly by faith groups who find in it support for the vocation to service offered by the religious life. Many Christian authors have baptized Greenleaf's ideas, arguing that Jesus was the servant leader par excellence. Popular hymns have been written about Jesus the Servant King. A theology of leadership as service has readily emerged. This has, in part, been responsible for the strong emphasis in the last two decades that qualities of pastoral leadership are the most important attributes to look for in candidates for the ministry.

Greenleaf's message also resonates with the suspicions of postmodern and feminist critics that all acts of power are intrinsically oppressive: they disempower and restrict the liberty of others. In the light of this philosophical critique, leadership has been seen by many people as legitimate only in its posture as service—as something that is done from behind, from underneath, in the background. Essentially, leadership must meet the needs of others rather than dominating them and imposing the leader's own needs. As Greenleaf put it:

'As we near the end of the twentieth century, we are beginning to see that traditional autocratic and hierarchical modes of leadership are slowly yielding to a newer model—one that attempts to simultaneously enhance the personal growth of workers and improve the quality and caring of our many institutions through a combination of teamwork and community, personal involvement in decision making, and ethical and caring behaviour.'[12]

Greenleaf is not alone, nor even the first, to assert the primacy of service in leadership. As I have already mentioned, the British Army has been training its officers for more than half a century to 'serve to lead'. The notion of the leader who serves is quite deeply rooted in a military culture that prizes self-discipline, self-denial and the repression of emotion. There can be no doubt that the only legitimate goal of leadership is service. However, I wonder whether Greenleaf's

[12] Robert K Greenleaf, taken from the introduction to Larry C Spears (ed), *Reflections on Leadership: How Robert K. Greenleaf's Theory of Servant-Leadership Influenced Today's Top Management Thinkers* (John Wiley & Sons, 1995)

very worthy and significant insights need to be developed a little further when we consider the context of social leadership.

I have had several years' experience of working with social leaders (including voluntary leaders)—some of whom, interestingly, have come out of the armed forces. In most cases, people give their time, skills and energy not in hope of reward or to advance their careers but out of a desire to do good. They exemplify, if you like, the kind of leaders for whom Greenleaf appeals. Furthermore, I have no doubt that many of them also applied the same mentality to their paid employment. However, in the course of working with a great number of such people and, indeed, being responsible for both their welfare and the welfare of those they led, I have encountered four problems.

The first is that some of these people are unable to give up their roles as volunteers when it is time for them to do so. What I have found is that, though they are willing and able, in service to others, to take these worthwhile roles, they find it much harder to let them go again. So often there are tensions when someone is asked to step down, when their leader suggests that a change is required. Then it becomes clear that, while they are ostensibly serving in this role for the benefit of others, they are also receiving something in return which they are unwilling to give up. If some such transaction was not taking place, they would be free to let go of the role when the community no longer needed them to do it. But they are not. The role makes up for some kind of psychological deficit they have within themselves. Perhaps it gives them an identity, perhaps it makes them feel valuable. Whatever it is, they are not free.

The second is that many people require affirmation or approval for everything they do. Of course, expressing appreciation is one of those things that all of us ought to do—there is rarely a person whose day is not brightened by a warm 'Thank you' or a grateful gesture. Cultures of positivity and praise are extremely important and I am not decrying them. However, it is important that we learn to lead others regardless of whether we are appreciated, regardless of whether we are thanked. When Winston Churchill lost the general election in 1945, many people, including his daughter, felt that it showed appalling ingratitude. Churchill himself took it hard. However, when he was asked once whether he resented it he replied that he did not, because he felt that the British people had suffered a lot during the war. Churchill experienced the sadness of being rejected but he did not blame those who did it and nor was he crushed by it. Many other people do and are, however. When they are not thanked for what they have given (freely), they are quick to complain. It seems that the appreciation they receive has become for them more than something they are simply free to enjoy. It has become a vital need, without which they can't thrive—without which they are reluctant to give more. In fact, it becomes clear that they are not serving freely but in order to receive thanks. Their service is not a gift but work to earn a wage of praise.

Third, there is the problem of those who cannot be served. Perhaps this is an aspect of those people I have already mentioned who can't give up their roles, but in this case they find it very difficult to receive from others. Many people in caring professions spend their lives giving to others but find it hard to be on the receiving end. It seems to be a place where they are uncomfortable. They are not, then, entirely free.

Finally, there are people who resent what they have given. Many volunteers and people in caring professions give for little return, but when someone feels bitter when they think of all they have given, something has gone wrong. Their service was not given as a gift but as a duty.

Many people in social leadership roles—for example, in health care, social work or community work—serve for reasons other than merely financial reward or preferment. It seems to me that Greenleaf's message is addressed to another kind of leader, the leader who habitually exploits others for his own personal gain. To this kind of person, Greenleaf offers a vital redress. However, in doing so I suggest that he opens the door to an alternative error: that the leader must somehow find within themself the love and grace to serve others. A significant percentage of people in social leadership, motivated by his vision of servant leadership, may fail to find these resources within themselves and instead run dry. So, they resort to constructing other kinds of collusion that secure them other, emotional rewards for their work. The danger in this is that not only will they end up exhausted and bitter but their followers will end up hurt.

I entirely approve of the high calling of leaders who serve rather than dominate and seek prestige. However, I am not convinced that Greenleaf is right to give serving priority over receiving. The British clinical psychologist Beau Stevenson describes a cycle of nurture and deprivation that can be found especially in those involved in the caring professions. He suggests that a high proportion of people in these professions have experienced homes where there is some kind of want. In such homes, a sense prevails that if anything is given away, it leaves a deficit. If, for example, a visitor came to the door unannounced, they would be duly invited in, but it would create anxiety about whether there was enough food to go round. The guest would be regarded as an inconvenience who would eat into the household's carefully rationed supplies. Their presence would 'take' from the family and leave a deficit. In contrast, in a culture of generosity the unexpected guest is welcome and the meal is gladly shared. It is not a duty or a cost. The guest is regarded as a blessing that brings something to the family that they are pleased to receive.

In the culture of deprivation, the transaction is one of taking and denying; in the culture of generosity, it is one of giving and receiving. In the first, the guest's presence leaves a gap; in the second, it represents a gift. Those who experience cultures of deprivation, Stephenson argues, grow up feeling a sense of obligation to make up for the deficit. The child feels the need always to give something to her parents in return for what they have given her. She grows up feeling guilty for the hard work they have to do, very grateful for every meal they provide, very overtly concerned when one of them is tired or ill. She learns that when something is given to her, she has to give something back. A transaction becomes established in which receiving always involves giving back. In time, as an adult, she comes to repeat this pattern. Serving others becomes the mechanism for earning appreciation. Stevenson suggests that such people are drawn to caring occupations in which they offer service to others. In return, they seek the appreciation of those they serve. I have encountered many people who conform to this pattern. In our terms, they fall within the category of either Definer or Adapter. They live with a sense that they and other people have to meet obligations. When these people enter leadership, it is usually social leadership and their motives are apparently philanthropic. However, in reality they do expect a return for their work—it's just not financial.

In contrast, those who grow up in a culture of generosity develop with a greater freedom. Their childhood experience is of resources abundant enough to supply their needs without leaving a deficit. There is enough love for them to be able to take it without feeling they have to pay for it in some way. Of course, there is no reason why someone used to plenty should want to give what they have away. They do not necessarily become generous just because they have experienced bounty. They, too, need to hear Greenleaf's message of service. However, it is clear to me that, as leaders, we can never give unless we have first received. Receiving should always come before giving. If that order is reversed, the gift becomes corrupted in some way. It tends to be given no longer freely but with strings attached.

Undoubtedly, the freest and most generous leaders I have come across are those from generous backgrounds. However, it does not need to be the nature of our home environment that determines our freedom and generosity as adult leaders: we must find and cultivate a generous source of approval elsewhere. As a Christian, I find that ultimately in God, who invites me as my divine Father back into a loving, intimate relationship. There are lots of striking observations in the Bible, but one of the most significant and extraordinary is the one Jesus is recorded as making in Mark's Gospel: 'The Son of Man did not come to be served, but to serve, and to give his life as a ransom for many.'[13]

---

[13] Mark 10.45

The Son of Man—a reference to himself as God's anointed—comes as leader, not to be served but to serve. What the rest of the New Testament makes clear is that it is in the character of God himself to serve. Arguably the most unprecedented idea in the Bible, one with which I think we all have to wrestle, is this: that, unlike the Deity we are used to imagining, the God revealed in this book does not primarily demand to be served by us but instead seeks to serve. The God of the Bible is set on serving us, our needs, rather than on us serving him.

Now, of course, this God is no benign old man doling out heavenly favours to his spoilt children. Nor is it that humankind is so wonderful that in some strange reversal human beings themselves become divine. Rather, it is the compassion and unconditional generosity of God that compels him to reach out to those in need, even though they do not deserve it. This idea, of course, turns religion on its head. Religion is the social phenomenon in which human beings offer service to various divinities. According to Jesus and the writers of the New Testament, this activity of religion has nothing to do with God at all. God is not someone who is served, but someone who serves. If it is true that there is a personal God, who offers me love, affection, intimacy, acceptance, approval, simply because it is his nature and character to do so, then it is possible for me to receive from this source and so be free from needing others to give me these things.

This is like discovering a spring of fresh water that can begin to well up within you. Instead of having to make the effort every day to fetch water from various wells around about, a spring is available inside you which can pour out a stream of life-giving water. Indeed, this water can not only quench your thirst but can also flow out of you and be available to other people. Instead of leading out of our emptiness, there is the possibility that we can lead out of fullness. Instead of a deficit within us, that we make up through our success or power or influence, there is a fullness that meets all our needs, which we can offer to others as a gift. If this is the case, then it is possible that our leadership can change from being something that always in some way takes from others—as may happen to the servant leader—to being something that gives to others freely, in undefended generosity.

I love the story of undefended generosity told in the film *Babette's Feast*. In this tale, a female traveller arrives in a small, remote Lutheran community in Denmark. Her origins are mysterious and the closed community is naturally suspicious. It struggles to welcome this glamorous and flamboyant woman into its restrained and rigorous life. One day, Babette receives an unexpected letter, in which she finds a considerable sum of inherited money, and she decides that she is going to spend it on a great feast for all the villagers. She is, we learn, in fact a chef from Paris, trained in the finest cuisine. Over the next few weeks, strange parcels begin to arrive, containing all manner of exotic goods. The villagers are intrigued but also confirmed in their suspicions that Babette is a thoroughly dubious, worldly creature who does not know the discipline of spirit and body that their religion has taught them.

Finally, the day for the feast arrives and Babette invites all the villagers to come to her home. As they step in though the door, they are greeted by a world transformed. Instead of the grey ordinariness they have always known, there are colour and scent, and a stunning banquet of the most exquisite food laid out for them. There are even bottles of 'illicit' wine! Babette offers her hospitality to the villagers, who enjoy an evening they will never forget. She spends her entire inheritance on it, in a gesture of grace, generosity and freedom. Indeed, she spends herself, and in so doing she transforms her friends. During the meal, old rivalries and resentments, fostered for years between neighbours, are brought out and forgiven. Their eyes are opened and their own meanness and shrunkenness of heart, after years of self-denial, is transformed into generosity through the grace they receive.

My personal experience is that at the centre of the universe there is a God whose characteristic act is to give, to give freely, to give from limitless resources: who gives not in order to meet some need in himself but to establish relationship. So liberal is his creation that people who do not see a Creator behind it will still talk of 'the abundance of Nature', and may refer to the beauty, fertility and even love of the universe, which 'calls us into synchronicity' with the world around us. In such a world, we experience life 'coming to us as a gift'.

My two-year-old daughter likes to stand in front of me with a bag of crisps (or whatever she happens to be eating) and feed them to me, one after another. She puts her hand into the bag, takes out a crisp and offers it to me, watching expectantly as I take it, smile, say thankyou and eat it. Then she does the same again. Smiling, enquiring, enjoying giving to me. Doesn't she worry that the bag will run out and she'll have none for herself? Isn't she anxious about going hungry that night? Not at all! She hasn't given it a moment's thought! It never occurs to her that she may not be given all her stomach needs to be satisfied. Because she lives in a home blessed with plentiful supplies of food, she has never known what it is to be without; and so she trusts, and receives, and gives.

However, there is a choice to be made. Do we choose to experience life as a possession that may be taken away from us, or as a gift generously bestowed on us? For the leader who sees her life as a possession, leadership is a matter of acquiring more. It means protecting her assets and watching out for threats. It means maximizing her investments and exploiting opportunities. It means being tied to a plan, because you can't be still, listen to the moment and move where you need to. It means working with others only when self-interest dictates. It means a life ruled, ultimately, by a creeping, gnawing fear of what she might lose and a hunger for what she could gain. There is, of course, great motivation to be found from such a choice—fear motivates, as we have seen in the Defining and Adapting patterns, and it creates great drive. But the consequences may not be the freedom and peace that we seek, and that others we lead also seek.

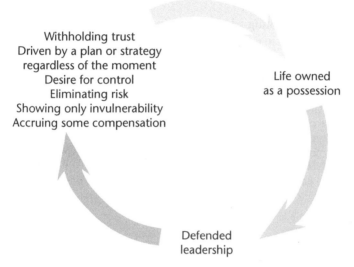

Withholding trust
Driven by a plan or strategy
regardless of the moment
Desire for control
Eliminating risk
Showing only invulnerability
Accruing some compensation

Life owned
as a possession

Defended
leadership

Diagram 12.1   A summary of defended leadership

In contrast, choosing to receive life as a gift leads to a very different set of consequences for the leader. Leadership becomes a matter of energetically joining in a movement of life and love around us that is already in full flow. A matter of finding ways to encourage and cultivate the gifts of others. A matter of choosing to trust others and take the risk of setting them free to succeed and fail. This leadership resists becoming merely executive management and instead remains attentive to the critical decisions of the moment, able to adapt and choose the right thing to do. It is not possessive about achievements. It is playful and compassionate and generous with praise.

When I ask groups of leaders to list the two things that would change if they started to act as an undefended leader, the things they suggest are very simple, even obvious. These are some of the things that come up time and again:

· Experience less duty and obligation around key tasks
· Celebrate more!
· Ask for help, work in teams and become dependent on others as often as possible
· Go to bed earlier
· Play more sport
· Get excited about stuff

- Be chaotic and messy
- Revel in each new discovery made
- Enjoy freedom of emotional expression
- Enjoy the moment
- Rest!
- Be intrigued by people
- Go for every exciting adventure you can
- Go into every day not knowing what to expect

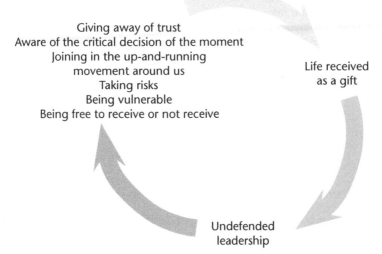

Giving away of trust
Aware of the critical decision of the moment
Joining in the up-and-running
movement around us
Taking risks
Being vulnerable
Being free to receive or not receive

Life received
as a gift

Undefended
leadership

Diagram 12.2   A summary of undefended leadership

We could extend that list endlessly, and you will already be adding your own suggestions. The funny thing about this list, whenever my groups compile it, is how liberated and excited it makes people feel just to think that some of these things could actually become a reality in their lives. It is almost as if they dare not believe it is true. But it is true! A veil has been cast over our eyes to make us believe that the world is one of duty, fear and self-protection. We must choose to tear away this veil and see a different world. We must choose to inhabit a world that is basically generous and make a commitment to trust ourselves to it. As we do so, the kind of leaders we are will change inevitably—change without any great effort or strain, without us learning new techniques or going on more training courses. The question is: How much do we want it?

We shouldn't confuse liberty with licence, however. In saying that change will happen to our leadership without effort or strain, I mean that, once we deliberately choose, and go on choosing, to live in the world 'as a gift', changes in our leadership will inevitably flow from that freedom. However, we should be under no illusion: attaining that way of being in the world requires intention, will and discipline. Discipline in leadership is often taken to involve a subjugation of your own instincts and feelings for the sake of a greater goal. There is something subtly different about the discipline an undefended leader requires: it is needed to prevent the defences reforming. Our defended way of being in the world is deeply embedded in us, like a habit or even an addiction. Ask a junkie what self-discipline is involved in coming off the substance they have depended on for years! They will tell you that the hardest thing is to say no to the continual, relentless urge to assuage your cravings by resorting to the drug again.

The greatest thing our defendedness gave us was a sense of security and control, and so the moments when we feel insecure and out of control will be when we are most tempted to resort to those strategies once again. Those are the times when we will reach for a shot of attention to give us that boost when our confidence is low. Those are the times when, with a shaking hand, we will pour ourselves a tumbler of success laced with the CEO's praise and a pay rise. Those are the times when we will inhale deeply the smoke of corporate denial and chicanery to enjoy the high of complicity and the rush of power.

Living as an undefended leader is a matter of cultivating an undefended life, deliberately and with discipline and focus, over years, not months. The specific choices we need to make will always relate to the particular pattern of defendedness we have embedded in our egos.

In order to sustain an undefended life, *Shapers* need to choose

- to set extra time aside when appraising their staff so that they can genuinely listen to them and create space for their personal and emotional stuff to be heard rather than being suppressed for the sake of the corporate goal;
- to be honest about an issue they are struggling with in the boardroom, risking vulnerability but inviting empathy and creating an opportunity for a humanizing encounter to take place;
- to be committed to a relationship that has lost its sparkle, because they have made vows and promises to do so.

Definers need to choose

- to make changes to their frenetic routine, planning in times to retreat and receive a renewal of their sense of identity and approval;
- to let go of a possession that has become an idol that enslaves them: a car they love, a treasured role, a carefully nurtured ambition...;
- not to read the business press so obsessively, or to get the latest downloads of the market on their mobiles every hour, but instead to

trust that if they spend the time they gain reflecting and waiting, it will prove a better guide to their decisions;

· to let go of some habit they have relied on, something that is not bad in itself but has become a crutch, perhaps an exercise routine they observe religiously, or a diet.

Adapters need to choose

· to switch off their mobiles and be unavailable at times they have set aside to play, or pray, or be with their family;

· to resist the urge to plough into their e-mails at the start of the day without first stilling themselves and handing over all their fears and hopes to their source of safety;

· to hand over to someone else a role they have become possessive about: perhaps a department, or a ministry in a faith community, or the chair of a council;

· to ask for help when they need it, rather than taking on all the responsibility themselves.

Defenders need to choose

· to put themselves in unfamiliar and even frightening situations at work that they would naturally avoid, in order to experience the freedom of being undefended by their normal skills and scripts;

· to notice their emotions as they arise, taking responsibility for their fear or anger rather than allowing them to dominate them and dictate their reactions;

· not to try to manipulate their situation in order to preserve their status or reputation;

· to risk confrontation by being honest about their feelings without blowing up in an aggressive, out-of-control way.

Living out an undefended life as a leader by and large involves living in a place that feels provisional and perhaps uncomfortable. Beware the times when we feel competent in everything we do! I find myself impressed with the philanthropy of Bill Gates and Warren Buffett not so much because of the vast scale of the wealth they have both given away ($28 billion and $37 billion respectively) but because of what it represents: a willingness to embrace their humanity again—with a measure of vulnerability along with it. Beware our sense of mastery of our universe. Be sure that, if we ever experience this, or make it our goal, we are selling our souls to a false god. We will find ourselves serving only a reflection in a mirror, an idol with clay feet, who cannot make us truly safe or fulfilled. We will have been seduced by the illusion that life can be free of pain and difficulty, only to discover that we cannot, in the end, preserve ourselves from these.

Finally, I need to make it clear that I am not talking here about living a balanced life. You might read this chapter superficially and conclude that I am appealing for leaders to balance their lives. The call to avoid extremes of activity or passivity is a worthwhile one, but not one I am making here. On the contrary, I am calling for leaders to live extreme lives: lives that exhibit radical and risky characteristics shared by only a few. The choices you make to start to live an undefended life, to lead as an undefended leader, are made not for the sake of balance or wellbeing; they are made for a greater good. And that greater good is to set people free. The undefended leader doesn't live by a manual for wellbeing, nor does she aspire to a healthy balance as an end in itself; she aspires only to bring freedom wherever there is enslavement. At times, this results in the freedom to choose not to work, to choose not to be driven, to choose not to burn out. At other times, it issues in the freedom to exhaust yourself for the cause, to take huge risks, to set everything up to succeed or fail. What governs these choices is not self-preservation, or some notion of a stress-free and integrated life. Rather, it is born out of the conviction that only the radically undefended life is a free life; that only choices made to embrace the generosity of the world around us issue in abundant life.

This perspective also gives us a new angle on the often asked question: What is the difference between the task of leadership and that of management? Frequently, the answer is given that the leader is the one with vision and the manager is the one with hands to implement it. Sometimes it is said that the manager is the person who climbs up the ladder, efficiently and within budget, while the leader is the one who notices that 'the ladder is leaning against the wrong wall.' Other images are common. The leader has a 'helicopter perspective' and can see the overview. Or he is the one who climbs to the top of the mountain and from there he can see the workers working on every side, whereas they can see only the slope on which they themselves are toiling away.

Such metaphors are helpful enough, and encourage leaders to look for the bigger picture rather than a mere detail. What I think they are all reaching for is the sense that leadership is, at its purest, concerned with truth. In its highest calling, it is not concerned with pragmatic solutions, with getting the job done: it is a matter of seeing something more truly than others around you.

Many things darken and cloud the eyes of those who seek this kind of 'sight'. In the first place, as I have said, our own unmet needs distort our vision, determining the way we see things. Our own self-interest (as opposed to the interests and needs of others) muddies the waters we swim in. In the murk, people start to panic and thrash around, flailing after passing shadows, only stirring up more mud in the process. Stillness is what is needed if the mud is to settle and the waters to begin to clear. And this is the posture of the leader. While others are still urgently straining away, towards some unclear goal, the leader is the one who stops—and perhaps makes other people stop around her. And when she has stopped, she waits. And as she waits, she listens, and feels, and looks. And as she does so, shapes begin to emerge and the scene begins to become a little clearer.

Leadership has little to do with making lots of decisions, with getting a great deal done. It is about getting the right things done. As leaders, the crucial quality we need is the courage to stop. The courage to wait and be still. While everyone around us is clamouring for a decision, the leader waits until she is confident and clear.

Study questions 12

1. Why does this chapter suggest that the concept of the servant-leader may be problematic?
2. What kind of culture did you experience growing up?
   · a culture of deprivation?
   · a culture of generosity?
3. What kind of culture do you tend to create around you?
4. How would your life be changed for the better if you experienced the world as essentially generous?
5. What three changes would you make to your life to begin to live out an undefended life?
   a)
   b)
   c)

⮑ On the website, www.theleadershipcommunity.org, listen to the audio file with the 'visual landscaping' exercise 'Responding to needs around you'. This will help you to become more aware of how to experience the world as a generous place and how to receive from a source of generous approval. You need to be registered as a free 'guest member' in order to listen to the audio file.

THIRTEEN

Leading as a Child

The bullying had got worse and something had to be done. The problem was that the bully had the power and influence to make life hell for anyone who crossed him, and most people just accepted it and tried to avoid becoming a target. But one victim decided that, after all the racial and sexual abuse, the derision and humiliation, he wouldn't stand for it. He could have gone up the chain and lodged a formal complaint. He could have set disciplinary procedures in motion. He could have got revenge in more subversive and spiteful ways. But instead he chose another course of action.

He gathered the team together and found out how many others had had the same experience as him. Stories began to come out that had been kept quiet out of shame and fear of further victimization. As the full scale of the problem emerged, the collective anger grew, and a resolve that this had to be stopped. Everyone looked for a lead from the person who had called the meeting. 'We're going to confront this guy together,' he said, 'and show him this has got to stop.' So, they set a time and everyone agreed to be ready to tell their story.

The bully was invited to a meeting about something important that he should know about. When he walked in, he was shocked to find that it was about him. The door was shut and he was made to listen as person and person told the group what he had done to them. Then the appointed leader stood up. He told the bully that he had a choice. He could carry on as before, in which case he would find that everyone, every day, was against him. His requests would be ignored, his projects allowed to fail; he would eat alone and he would be excluded from every future assignment the group took on. Or he could apologize to each and every person he had hurt and write a statement saying how he planned to change. In that case, the group would agree not only to accept it but to help him to live up to it. The man's face crumpled as he recognized both the shame of his actions and the grace of the chance that was being given to him to come back into the group—but on new terms. He knew which option he wanted to take.

This story of leadership illustrates the power of the community collectively to deal with its own problems. Without resorting to expensive legal proceedings and the structures of bureaucracy, the problem was addressed and sorted out locally and directly. Instead of acting out of fear, the group chose to trust one another and, indeed, to trust the bully. Instead of seeking to defend themselves or to retaliate, they chose courageously to make themselves vulnerable. Different forces were brought into play, forces of social belonging, shame and guilt, forgiveness and acceptance, help and mutual support. These forces proved powerful enough to resolve the situation more quickly and less expensively than any formal proceedings could have done, and without the organizational damage.

Think how many millions of dollars in lawsuits would be saved if disputes in the workplace were solved like this. Think how many conflicts between warring communities would be resolved in weeks if a similar process was followed. Think what potential there would be to reduce violence and fear in the neighbourhood if communities would take that kind of collective responsibility. All it took was the mobilization of the forces of social belonging, shame and guilt, forgiveness and acceptance, help and mutual support. And a leader who was willing not to give in to feelings of hate, not to seek revenge, but instead to act courageously and make himself undefended. It took a leader who decided that trust was more powerful than fear. And he was right.

However, the thing that is most striking about this story is that the person who took the lead was not a business manager, a corporate executive or a community leader: he was an eight-year-old child. The whole thing took place in a classroom at a primary school.

I expect that that comes as a surprise. To some, it may even come as a shock. You might find yourself resisting its implications. 'Well, of course', you may say, 'the child didn't have much idea about what was really going on—it just happened to work out for him.' But isn't that just the point? A child is unaware of all the theory about why things do or don't work. He comes at things without years of experience and baggage, and sometimes that is just what enables you to see the situation as it really is rather than as you might have expected it to be. Our problem is our difficulty in seeing the world as it is and not through the distorting lenses and filters of our experience, knowledge and prejudice.

Or you may say: 'Well, it's easy for a child of eight—he hasn't yet had to cope with the knocks of life. He won't be so trusting of others after he's been let down a few times.' Once again, isn't that exactly the point? As adult leaders, we bring into every situation the baggage of our past. Indeed, we have spent much of this book exploring the architecture of that past and the legacy of (dis)trust it has left us. Of course, we can't undo the past, but we can become aware of it, and this allows us to reverse the strategies we have used to cope with that which enslaved us. It isn't difficult to appreciate the freedom the child had to face this situation. The question is not whether this is desirable—of course it is! The question is whether it is attainable for us, hard-bitten, cynical and defended grown-ups.

Or you may say: 'It was an unthreatening scenario—nothing like as nasty as things get in adult life! As leaders, we have to deal with people who threaten our very jobs, our salaries, our careers. We have to handle multimillion-dollar deals that will affect the lives of hundreds of employees. It's all very well being undefended when the stakes are so low; it's quite another matter when the stakes are so high!' And yet to argue like this is to miss the point. For a child, that bully was the embodiment of threat and fear. A child isn't aware of or concerned about global warming or the state of the market. They are concerned about whether they get assaulted in the loos or on the way home from school. What more direct threat do you want than that? In fact, the reality is that we, as adult leaders in the West, very rarely face a situation that is physically menacing. The threat of material harm, such as losing a job, is probably the biggest danger most of us would face in a decision we had to take. And you can recover from losing a job—we are fortunate enough to live in a society in which we would receive benefits. We probably have some assets, some savings. We probably have sufficient skills to get ourselves another job. In reality, the threat is not fundamentally threatening. Yet we make it so because we habitually avoid pain. In fact, the West has become a society bent on eliminating pain and struggle from our lives. When we are threatened in the slightest degree—by a loss of earnings, by not being able to go on holiday, by missing out on a promotion—we become anxious and depressed, fearful and defended. The point is that children are usually far less guarded about their own safety than grown-ups. Think of your average teenager bombing down a ski slope, past the cautious and rather genteel descent of the 'sensible' adults!

Or you may say: 'A child's an idealist. You can't be idealistic in life as a leader. Speak to any politician! Leadership is about pragmatism. There are no neat, black-and-white solutions—life is too complex and interconnected. Choices always involve shades of grey, compromise, give-and-take. Leadership in the real world is about being able to make those compromises and still come up with some kind of way forward.' Sure, the life we live is complicated and compromised—because we make it so. What guided that child was some basic values and principles of action which cut through the complications. It would have been far more complicated to file a complaint with the school authorities.

By acting locally and directly, the child actually simplified the task of leadership. Imagine if he had gone up the chain. What would have happened? First of all, a lengthy process of gathering data would have taken place. Teachers would have asked questions and conducted interviews, filled out forms and written reports. Meetings would have been called with the appropriate agencies. The bully's background would have had to be taken into account. Maybe social services would have been brought in. Maybe they would have concluded that the source of the problem was a dysfunctional home, a violent father who beat his mother, neglect and lack of love. Yes, the bully would have been more understood by adults if this process had taken place; but the solution would have been no better. Probably a behaviour therapist would have been sent in to 'work with the child' and support the teacher, an intervention that would have been costly and lengthy. In any case, it would only have been successful if the other children had been included in the process so that the procedures could be supported within the classroom—otherwise, the bully would only have ended up feeling more excluded and ostracized. In truth, the 'adult leadership' solution would have been more complicated, more time-consuming and more expensive—and would still in the end have had to rely on the same social and emotional mechanisms to solve the problem.

All this prompts the question: Is there any way in which a child offers us a model of what undefended leadership might look like?

Maintaining a light and playful touch

First and most important, a child does not think of themself fundamentally as a leader. A child thinks of themself as a child—a child who, in this situation, is doing a particular activity. A child's principal frame of reference is not learning, or leadership, or performance: it is play. Children engage with the world essentially through play. I can vividly remember making it to the national finals of the school hockey championships. My team had beaten all comers that season and we were going to play in a major stadium. Our nerves were jangling as we sat in the changing room before the match—the biggest sporting occasion of our lives to date, and possibly ever. Our coach looked at us and said: 'Now, there's one thing I want you to promise me to do when you get out there on the pitch today: enjoy it! Enjoy the next 80 minutes! This is a one-off experience, and the most important thing is not to miss it.'

Winston Churchill spent five years summoning the energy and self-belief to lead the British nation from 1940 to 1945 in resistance to the mighty forces of Germany and later Japan. Renowned for his inexhaustible energy and focus, Churchill almost burned out other, far younger ministers and aides, despite being in his late sixties. Not only was he battling Hitler but on the home front he had to contend with his deputy prime minister, Clement Attlee, the leader of the Labour Party. After a particularly grey and difficult few days, late one evening, when the news from Europe was especially disheartening and Attlee was being a thorn in his side, the lowering Churchill was seen to turn to his wife, Clemmie, and growl, 'Enough of Hittlee and Atler—let's go and watch a film, shall we?' Amidst the pressure of the greatest military conflict in history, he didn't lose touch with his childlike side. Known as a man who took his own destiny very seriously, he still managed to retain a sense of humour in the darkest hour.

Think about your challenges at work right now. Now think about how many of them have come to daunt or oppress or even overwhelm you. Now think about how some of them have taken on a sense of absolute reality—they have started to define your horizons. Now think about how that would change if you were to reposition those same challenges as if you were a child joining in with work that was actually his dad's responsibility. When a father invites his child to come and help him in the garden, he gives her a trowel and the child makes some scrapes and perhaps digs a few small holes for some seedlings. However, the reality is that the father doesn't need the child to get the gardening done— in fact, the job probably takes far longer with her 'help' than if he'd done it on his own! He invites her to join him not because he can't do it without her but because he doesn't want to. He delights to share this activity with his child out of the joy of 'working together with' her—for the sake of their relationship, their love, their fun, her learning.

Humankind has achieved astonishing things in its history, and we have seen astonishing men and women accomplish great tasks of leadership. But none of them are absolute; none of them surpass the great mysteries and deep beauties of the universe. Remember that your greatest achievement as a leader will not solve the world's problems. It will not bring about heaven on earth or save the planet. Make your contribution with a smile, thankful for the opportunity and delighted to see other people make theirs.

Retaining the capacity to wonder

It is said that in the course of a long evening of government business, Abraham Lincoln would lead his colleagues outside and there in the night sky he would point out a small smudge of light. 'That, gentlemen,' he would say, 'is the nebula Andromeda. It is the nearest galaxy in the universe to our own Milky Way. It is three million light years away. It is composed of more than a hundred billion stars, most of which are bigger than our own sun. It is one of more than a thousand million galaxies in the universe. Now that I think we feel small enough, we can go back inside.'

Wonder begins with awareness and could be said to be the basis of all leadership. Awareness is our ability to perceive ourselves and others and the world as we are. Self-awareness is the first of the competencies that constitute emotional intelligence. Awareness of the Other is the foundation of what some people have called 'spiritual intelligence'. But the valuing of awareness is much older than these new ideas. In the fourth century, the Desert Fathers, the pioneers of Christian monasticism, understood that awareness of the distorted nature of the self lies at the beginning of the journey out of that self towards *theoria* (contemplation). Ignatius Loyola's 'Spiritual Exercises', written in 1548, are based on developing an awareness of yourself within the accounts of biblical events. John Calvin, the 16th-century Swiss Reformer, asserts in his *Institutes of the Christian Religion* that Man never attains a true self-knowledge until he has previously contemplated the face of God. The purpose of meditation in Buddhism is to achieve a greater awareness of your desires and drives. Through awareness of your attachments, you are able to detach and so be 'free' from the illusion of this material reality. In Islam, the rhythm of daily prayer returns the individual to a God-consciousness amidst the activities of the day.

Children often exhibit a remarkable, naive awareness of themselves and their world. They tell you when their body hurts or feels hot or cold, they're conscious of fear, excitement, shock and loss in a more immediate way than we grown-ups. The journey into adult life often involves suppressing and dismissing feelings, which in turn lowers our body-awareness. Awareness of self is in dialogue with awareness of others and our world. As we become more aware of our participation in the ecology of life around us, we become aware of our appropriate scale, humanity and interdependence. Our mistake as leaders is often to think we are bigger than we really are. We come to believe, because we inhabit the small worlds of offices and institutions, that we are masters of our worlds. Of course, we are not—when a natural disaster strikes, we soon realize how weak and powerless we really are.

How our use of time, our priorities and our decisions as leaders would change if we retained a sense of wonder from moment to moment—about breath and molecules and photosynthesis and scents and birth and death. During the American Civil Rights movement in the mid 1960s, the aggressive Black Power movement arose in response to the apparent impotence of the black population and the violence and intimidation it was suffering. On 16 June 1967, Martin Luther King distanced himself from Stokely Carmichael, his friend and a former colleague in the Southern Christian Leadership Conference (SCLC). He refused to accept that, as Malcolm X proposed and Carmichael increasingly was advocating, the way to resolve political, economic and social injustice was through violence. At the heart of King's philosophy was his belief in the shared humanity and equal worth of black and white and his conviction that the solution was to find a way of mutual respect. Without a sense of the dignity of creation, King's ideology would have been susceptible to become a clarion call for domination. Wonder, rooted in an awed awareness of the world in which our lives are a gift we have received, does not lead only to poetic idealism: it also produces hard-headed politics, social strategy and some of the most courageous leadership of the 20th century.

Not that a leadership of wonder always issues in success! In 1982, Joe Montana, the stellar quarterback for the San Francisco 49ers since being drafted in 1979, went out on the pitch in his first Super Bowl. Inexplicably, in the midst of one 49ers drive, he stopped and just stood still. When the time limit for the play expired, he was fined a 10-yard penalty. After the game he was asked why he didn't get the play off—something a schoolboy quarterback would know to do—Montana replied that he decided he was not going to miss this great event, and in the midst of the game he was going to stop for a moment and just take it all in. Sometimes, life is just too wonderful to miss!

Strengthening the bonds of trust

Children trust. Implicitly. It's what makes them so vulnerable. I put my children in the car and we head off on a journey, and they simply trust that they will be safe, that there will be a meal provided, that they will have a bed to sleep in at the end of the day and probably some sweets along the way. As we grow, we learn to trust less. There are good reasons for this, but if we lose the ability to trust we lose the basis of all human relating. Robert Galford and Anne Seibold Drapeau's book *The Trusted Leader*[14] argues the case for the role of trust in organizations. They illustrate their point with numerous examples of companies whose performance falls when there is a systemic lack of trust in the firm. Trust involves risk—there is no legal safeguard. Trust involves making yourself vulnerable, putting yourself in someone else's hands; trust involves letting down the barrier of self-protection and allowing someone else to help us. Trust involves securing the relational bond between two people not by contract but by mere promise. Of course, in a culture where 'promise' means so little, trust is hard to come by.

Trust does things, though. Remember what it feels like to be trusted: trusted with a task, a treasure, a secret, trusted to keep a promise. When you are trusted by someone else you feel important: valued, respected, needed. Children who are habitually trusted by their parents develop a healthy trust of themselves and others, a positive self-regard. Children who are not trusted feel vulnerable and lack self-respect and self-belief. Remember what it feels like to be trusted. It feels good, doesn't it? As leaders, we can give that experience to another person this very week, this very day, this very hour.

Not only does trust make people grow, it also heals social ills and reduces the burdens on any civil society. In 1947, following independence, the subcontinent of India faced a massive and violent internal struggle. The majority Hindu and minority Muslim populations proved unwilling to coexist and, despite Gandhi's pleas that the land should not be divided, it was indeed partitioned and the states of India and Pakistan were formed on 14 August 1947. However, no one had envisaged the chaos that was to follow as literally millions of Hindus and Sikhs living in Pakistan began a mass migration across the new border into India, passing en route the millions of Muslims migrating the other way. Conflict erupted, and the ensuing bloodbath was catastrophic. In charge of the partition and the transition to statehood was Lord Mountbatten, the British Governor General of India, who positioned his troops at various flashpoints, and Delhi and Calcutta in particular. However, there was another force at work restraining the violence: Mahatma Gandhi. Central to his campaign was the rebuilding of trust between the divided communities. In the heart of the fighting, Gandhi would walk, barefoot, from one village to the next. When he arrived at a village, he would find the Hindu and Muslim leaders and would invite them to live together under the same roof, guaranteeing the peace between their respective communities. If one Hindu was killed, he charged the Muslim leader to fast

---

[14] Galford, Robert and Drapeau, Anne Seibold, *The Trusted Leader* (The Free Press: Simon and Schuster, 2002)

until the murderer was brought to justice; and vice versa. Gandhi's weapon was not the gun but the embrace. He compelled people to trust one another again and resist the suspicion that leads to fear, that leads to prejudice, that leads to hostility, that leads to bloodshed.

Mountbatten's forces were literally overrun by the scale of the violence. He dubbed Gandhi his 'one-man boundary force' and heard to remark: 'On the western front I have 100,000 crack troops and unstoppable bloodshed. On my east, I have one old man and no bloodshed.' Gandhi's one-man peace corps was to prove more powerful than the might of the Army in restraining violence, in town after town, by building trust and strengthening the bonds of humanity.

Learning to take responsibility

It's a basic lesson of the kindergarten that we ought to take responsibility for the consequences of our actions. Robert Fulghum begins his delightful little bestseller *All I Really Need to Know I Learned in Kindergarten* with a credo. He writes, 'These are the things I learned [at kindergarten]:

> *'...Clean up your own mess.*
> *'Say you're sorry when you hurt somebody.*
> *'Put things back where you found them...'*

Then he extrapolates: 'Think what a better world it would be if ... all governments had as a basic policy to always put things back where they found them and to clean up their own mess.'[15]

It's so simple, isn't it? It makes sense in the playground, but out in the big, wide world what seemed black-and-white dissolves into murky shades of grey. To lead in a childlike way may, to some, imply a lack of responsibility, or duty or obligation. Far from it! Children tend to have a straightforward morality and instinctive senses of right and wrong, duty and loyalty. It is as we grow up that these may get confused. Many leaders devise complex schemes to avoid taking responsibility—to avoid paying corporation tax, avoid the expense of disposing of the company's waste, turn a blind eye to the impact of their supply-chain control on their suppliers, ignore the effects of their products on the consumers who buy them, ignore the impact of their energy consumption on the planet.

The thing about taking responsibility as a leader is that it often breeds responsibility in those around you. Eleanor was not an obvious leader. As owner of the local newsagent, her life had been a simple one. She had never

---

[15] Fulghum, Robert, *All I Really Needed to Know I Learned in Kindergarten* (Ballentine, New York, this ed. 2003)

stood for the local council or played any kind of civic role. All she did was run her shop. One day, however, she decided she was going to take responsibility, for something very small but very important nonetheless: the litter outside her shop. She lived in a little town in north-west England called Middlewich, a town that was neglected by the local authorities and had consequently lost its self-respect. Walking down the small, narrow high street on a Sunday morning was like wading through a garbage tip—filthy and foul and stinking with the refuse of the night before. And it was not much better by Monday!

Eleanor began by taping a black binbag to the wall (the council provided no bins) with a misspelt handwritten sign requesting that shoppers throw their litter in the bag rather than drop it. Then she went next door and gave the neighbouring shop a bag and asked them to put it out. Next, she wrote to the council and asked whether Middlewich could have some proper, smart, new bins. Next, she began to talk to her customers about the litter problem, and pretty soon she had a band of locals equally fed-up and eager to make a difference. On Saturday mornings, you would see her Middlewich Clean Team out in brightly coloured rainbow tops clearing up the rubbish in the parks. Next, she got the council to put up hanging baskets in the summer and dared to enter the town in the Best-Kept Town in Cheshire competition. To everyone's surprise, Middlewich won—and not just the county title but the accolade of the North-West 'most improved town'. The miraculous change held good, and within two years Eleanor was meeting the Deputy Prime Minister and being asked to act as a consultant to other towns struggling to deal with poor social behaviour.

Eleanor did nothing more than decide to take responsibility. Others began to follow her lead and soon the entire culture had begun to change. It's all too easy to turn a blind eye as a leader and simply not see what is not convenient. Many of the big issues are not screaming out at you, slashing your market share: they are simply going on in the background. We pass them by and hope that someone else will take responsibility for them. There are probably places on your territory right now where that is happening. It's what happened at Enron. And WorldCom. And Abu Ghraib.

Not all children are the same...

	Shapers	Definers	Adapters	Defenders
Rather like....	*an eight-year-old who is 'comfortable in their own skin'*	*an intense and dutiful 21-year-old heir*	*an over-anxious 11-year-old who is eager to please*	*a wary 16-year-old*
Maintaining a light and playful touch	Often have no problem with this as they are generally not overwrought by their jobs.	Are often terribly earnest, intense and driven in their role. May lose sight of play altogether.	May feel guilty about play, assuming that all worthwhile work is in some sense costly and hard.	May be sceptical of such 'innocent' motives and unwilling to let themselves go.
Retaining the capacity for wonder	Are drawn to the unusual and the novel without necessarily dwelling too deeply on it.	Think that wonder doesn't get the job done, and probably put it off as a 'luxury' for a later date.	Probably suppress their sense of wonder in case it is disparaged.	May be very sensitive to awe as it feels 'big' and 'authentic'.
Strengthening the bonds of trust	Have no problem trusting others. In fact, they are probably too trusting and need to be more discerning.	Never give unqualified trust but believe that trust is earned through performance and success.	Find it very hard to ask anyone else to take things on, and as a result may prevent others from learning to trust themselves.	Are desperate to do so, but may demand such loyalty from other people that they can only disappoint.
Learning to take responsibility	Shoulder considerable weights, but may abdicate responsibility for harder and more uncomfortable tasks.	Want exclusive responsibility most of the time, but occasionally refuse to accept any responsibility at all.	Usually take inappropriate responsibility on themselves when they should be ensuring that others take it.	May not expect to be given responsibility and may at first fail—but, when trusted, prove to be highly responsible.

The challenges of leading as a child are specific to each of the four ego patterns. Each has a different set of issues, born out of their own particular 'childlike posture'. The table above outlines some of the specific responses Shapers, Definers, Adapters and Defenders will tend to make to the call to lead 'as a child'.

The invitation to lead as a child involves a specific response that will leave behind the comfortable and familiar way in which we inhabit the world. Undefended leadership turns on its head the world's conception of power and embraces the notion that we must become as little children in order to lead others. Being childlike is an essential component of leadership—I believe, because we are fundamentally, by our very nature, always children of God. If we fail to acknowledge this, our childlike needs become suppressed and channelled into unhealthy childish fantasies, destructive, unnamed and irresponsible. Mature childlikeness is a quality of playfulness, awareness and wonder, trust and taking responsibility that overturns society's conventional priorities. It replaces fear with confidence and offers others a courageous generosity.

Study questions 13

1. How would you have dealt with that bullying problem?
2. This chapter suggests that childlike leadership can be more efficient. Why, and how?
3. Do you agree?
4. Can you think of a similar situation you have encountered in your own role as a leader?
5. What are the chief characteristics of childlike leadership?
6. How do you react to Eleanor's story?
7. What does it make you want to go and do?
8. This chapter suggests that if we don't lead in a childlike way, it may result in childishness. How might this be manifested?

➲ On the website, www.theleadershipcommunity.org, join in the online discussion on 'Leading like a child'. You need to be registered as a free 'guest member' in order to join the discussion.

9. How does this chapter challenge you to change
   · as a person?
   · as a leader?

FOURTEEN

The Formation of Moral Authority

We began this book by observing the lives of some of the world's most undefended leaders. The characteristic common to them all was what I called 'moral authority'—that quality in their lives, values and ideals that in itself gave them authority among their peers. What we also noticed was that another thing these leaders often shared was a history of struggle. If we are to know what it is to truly lead, we need to look more closely at the nature of struggle and how leaders respond to it.

Nature should alert us to the intrinsic good of struggle. If you see a butterfly struggling to escape from its chrysalis, you may be tempted to lend it a helping hand. Most of us don't like to see creatures struggle and it would seem a kind thing to do. However, you would be condemning it to an early death. The struggle the butterfly has to fight its way out is vital for strengthening its wing muscles. Nature builds in struggle as an essential part of the formation and development of healthy life.

It is, perhaps, a uniquely modern ideal that we should eliminate struggle through constant improvements in our socio-economic conditions. We have become increasingly defended against pain and loss, through technological advances and growing economic power. It hasn't been so for most of human history—and, indeed, it still isn't so for most of the global community to this day. It is the preserve of the global elite to contemplate a life from which struggle may be banished. But perhaps, like the emerging butterfly, we risk being fatally weakened if we embrace such a vision of ease. Could our defendedness against hardship render us more fragile as a result? Could there be a strength to those who, through choice, live lives undefended against distress? Could there be qualities of endurance, fortitude, courage, determination and patience that are formed only through such experiences? Again, as parents we often encourage our children not to give up, whether learning an instrument or practising their basketball skills. We seem to know that the effort they put in, however boring or hard, is worthwhile. And yet at the same time we take it as our prerogative as adults to avoid such 'labour' and 'pain' as far as possible.

Struggle takes many forms, and one man's effort is another man's ease. It may be physical: the father who labours to earn enough so his family can eat that night, or the mother who walks five miles with a child on her back to fetch water from a clean well, or the disabled person for whom simply cooking an ordinary meal is a huge task, or the child who walks eight miles to school every day because there isn't one in her village. I remember watching an elderly woman, crippled with rheumatoid arthritis, hobbling, inch by inch over five minutes, to make it up to the rail in church to take holy communion. It struck me that every action of my day, which I do without a second thought, would be for her a struggle, a battle of will against pain.

Struggle may be physical. It may also be emotional: the mother who has lost her daughter in a car accident, for whom each day begins and ends with the sickening emptiness and loneliness of that loss, or the sufferer from depression who fights to keep his head above the grey tide of pointlessness that threatens to overwhelm him, or the victim of rape trying desperately to control her rising panic when she finds herself alone in a room with a strange man, or the couple who have watched each of their tiny babies, born prematurely, die within a few hours from some unknown condition.

Struggle may be physical, it may be emotional. It may also be intellectual: the writer who defies a tide of critical opinion to find the courage and self-belief to express what he feels called to say, or the child, battling against a school system that has labelled him 'low-performing' in his first year, or the scientist, searching for a solution to the medical condition to which he has devoted the whole of his working life, or the chief executive endeavouring to lead his company through a major transition when the welfare of hundreds of employees depends on his choices, or the leader of a community whose beliefs are ridiculed and marginalized by the society in which they live.

Struggle may be physical, it may be emotional, it may be intellectual. And it may also be spiritual. Perhaps the great struggles all end up being spiritual in the sense that they pose us ultimate questions. Victor Frankl was a Jew incarcerated in the Nazi concentration camp at Auschwitz. As he looked around him, he saw his fellow inmates succumbing to the appalling conditions. What he noticed was often those who received news of the death of a loved one died soon after. It was as if they lost the will to live, lost the reason to endure the pain. Frankl resolved not to lose his sense of meaning and purpose himself. Everything else could be taken from him, but the Nazis could not take that. In the face of his suffering, his own personal meaning became the one thing that was secure.

Having survived the war, Frankl went on to develop a psychological tradition that places at its centre the need of each human being to find their own meaning. His ideas have been rather trivialized in the post-war boom as 'meaning' has become synonymous with little more than personal fulfilment; but for Frankl it was always far more than that. Meaning was not 'the icing on the cake' which you added once you had accumulated all the possessions you needed to be comfortable. Meaning was the irreducible core of our human being, which could never be taken away. For Frankl, meaning was found through the struggle for life, through the deprivation of virtually all other human needs.

His story alerts us to the essential role of suffering in the formation of leaders. Suffering in itself is not the 'good': we are not called to be masochists, seeking out painful situations as if there were some nobility in them. No, it is a stimulus that causes us to struggle, and in this struggle it is possible for certain qualities to be fashioned. However, it is also possible that the pain will prove overwhelming and, rather than forming our humanity, will have the effect of dehumanizing us. What makes the difference, it seems, is the choices the struggler makes: their response to their pain. It is this that determines whether the knife will shape or cripple, whether the fire will consume or refine.

When we are made to struggle, we are assailed by all kinds of emotions, emotions that can, at worst, harden into negative and destructive attitudes. The emotion of fear makes us instinctively defend ourselves, for example. What matters is how we then process our experience of it. Do we allow it to become anxiety, which may in turn express itself in depression or self-harm or other anxiety disorders as we try to 'hold' our feelings? Or do we allow the fear to turn into anger? Anger may turn into rage, and rage into hate; and hate may harden into suspicion, hostility and aggression and erupt into actual violence. Violence may in turn bring retribution, and thus you find yourself in a cycle of destruction chosen from the outset by your reaction to pain and struggle. It is all too easy for an experience of suffering to lead to a cycle of defendedness, territoriality and aggression.

Struggle offers us choices: it sets before us diverging paths, as it were, and obliges us to choose between them. This is its nature. Much of life allows us to drift along indecisively, not committing ourselves to one thing or another. Pain and struggle allow no such ambivalence. We are forced to choose, and often the path we take becomes one that determines our destiny. What choices, then, do those who we recognize as leaders with moral authority make when they are faced with pain in their own lives?

Purpose and purposelessness

The first choice is between purpose and purposelessness. When we are in pain, we ask the question: Why? Why us? Why now? In the face of such questions, the need to find a purpose to the experience, a meaning that makes it significant, is acute and pressing. Churchill's political career up to the age of 65 was chequered with failure. He had suffered for most of his life from depression, an experience so familiar he named it his 'black dog', like an old hound always lurking in the background. On his appointment as Prime Minister in 1940, he remarked that his whole life had been a preparation for this moment. He had been born with a sense of destiny, an expectation that one day he would be called to some great act. This sense of purpose drove him on through his depressions and mistakes. It made sense of his failures and prevented him from sinking into self-pity.

Two 20th-century poets, one American and one Welsh, express the contrasting choices that lie before us when we encounter pain. T S Eliot in 1942 wrote that

> *The one discharge from sin and error...*
> *Lies in the choice of pyre or pyre—*
> *To be redeemed from fire by fire.*[16]

For Eliot, the necessary, unavoidable route by which we are purged of self-attachment and fear was a painful one; to be defended against it would have been comfortable but ultimately self-defeating. By contrast, Dylan Thomas wrote possibly his best-known lines about the prospect of old age and death:

---

[16] T S Eliot, 'Little Gidding' from *The Four Quartets,* in *Collected Poems 1909–1962* (this edn Faber and Faber, 1963). Reprinted by permission of Faber and Faber Ltd, London and Harcourt, Inc., Florida

Do not go gentle into that good night,
Old age should burn and rave at close of day;
Rage, rage against the dying of the light.[17]

In the face of purposeless loss (in this case, the loss of youth and faculties), suffering and ultimately annihilation, rage and fury become valid options, which Thomas would encourage us to embrace. The stark difference between the two responses lies in the meaning of the suffering. For Eliot, it had significance in the formation of his ultimate identity. For Thomas, it was meaningless and in itself confirmed only the futility of human life. I want to suggest that the formation of the leader is to be found in Eliot's choice as opposed to Thomas's. This is not to be insensitive, I hope, to the trauma of pain or to insist that we stoically battle on with a stiff upper lip. Grief often accompanies pain and loss and we must support those who journey with that dark companion. However, slowly, over time, that journey may become more purposeful again. The person who chooses courageously to hold on to a belief in the purpose of their life and the value of their experience of pain will emerge refined, able to carry others through their own suffering. People find purpose through pain in different ways: a mother may find purpose in the loss of a child to illness by starting a campaign in their memory for better awareness of the condition and better funding for research. An athlete may find purpose in the loss of a limb in a car accident in the appreciation of mobility that it gives her and the way it inspires her to campaign for greater resources for disabled children to enjoy sport.

The journey through pain that the Shaper must make is, of course, different from the one that lies ahead of the Definer, or the Adapter, or the Defender. For the Shaper, pain may be something of which they have relatively little knowledge, and that which they have experienced they have buried. Their hunger for safety can lead them to deny their pain and seek relationships in which they will be insulated from it. For the Definer, the pain of failure, or of a broken relationship, can be the catalyst for monumental life-change. Often, they will perceive such moments as 'conversions' that turned their lives around. These can fill their lives with purpose and meaning, as they become evangelists for the new reality they have discovered. For Adapters, pain is the very stuff of life: they have learnt to live with it, to accommodate it. For them, the threat is to be defeated by it, whereas freedom involves believing in the greater purposes that can be achieved through it. Defenders are often motivated by pain, and their experiences of injustice, marginalization and exclusion can drive them to try to build a different and (one hopes) better world.

---

[17] Dylan Thomas, 'Do Not Go Gentle'. By Dylan Thomas, from THE POEMS OF DYLAN THOMAS, copyright ©1952 by Dylan Thomas. Reprinted by permission of New Directions Publishing Corp. and David Higham Associates

Love and anger

There are those who manage to make meaning out of their own pain and, in so doing, overcome the potential futility of their struggle and the rage and resentment that could have festered in their loss. However, this kind of passion can be fuelled as much by unresolved pain as by genuine freedom, and it is this that alerts us to the second choice that has to be made at the crossroads of pain: that between love and anger. The emotion of anger is powerful and it is not in itself wrong. However, for an activity to be inspired and driven by anger, let alone a mission, is dangerous. Ultimately, anger overturns and tears down. Anything energized by it will in the end prove destructive.

Emma had been damaged at birth through faulty medical procedures. The neurological consequences meant that she was significantly disabled, both physically and mentally. Her father struggled with anger at the negligence that had caused this, though he chose not to sue the hospital. His way of coping with his sadness was to see purpose in Emma's life as it was. He believed she was someone who would teach others about disability, acceptance, tolerance and humanity. This became a purpose in which he invested enormous and ever-growing energy. As he came up against systems that marginalized her and ignored her, as a child, a pupil or a member of the community, he fought them and refused to give in. Those around him, however, detected increasing rage in his zeal. Conversations with him continually turned back to the subject of injustice. His concern became blinkered as he saw everything in terms of the cause. Increasingly, he fell out with those who were trying to help, regarding them as lacking the necessary fight for the crusade he believed in so passionately. He reduced his friends to confused outsiders and become confrontational. In a way, he increasingly manifested the patterns of behaviour of the Defending Ego: seeing others as threats and seeking to protect the vulnerable from them. In the end, he seemed to have been robbed of his ability to trust.

Emma's father was tanked up as a social leader with a purpose; but his fuel was not love but anger, an unresolved resentment that leaked out and damaged others around him. There are many in social leadership like him. Sometimes, those who themselves have experienced life as unjust, those who have an embedded Defending pattern, become the most vociferous campaigners for social justice. However, their actions are fuelled not by love but by anger, and so they are not free. The pain we suffer forces us to struggle to find the resources to cope, and sometimes anger can seem to offer us a wellspring of motivation that could get us through it. The deeper struggle, however, is to find a source of power and energy drawn not from anger but from love.

Love seems so absent when we are suffering. Surely love would protect us from pain? Surely love would not allow us to struggle so? Once again, Eliot offers us his conclusion about the ultimate source of pain. He writes:

> *Who then devised the torment? Love.*
> *Love is the unfamiliar Name*
> *Behind the hands that wove*
> *The intolerable shirt of flame...*[18]

Can it be that Love allows us to suffer, to struggle? What kind of love is that? We may catch a glimpse of such love in the choice some parents make for their child, suffering from cancer, to undergo painful surgery and nauseating chemotherapy. In the face of illness for which the only cure is painful, love chooses that path. Could it be that, if as a human being each one of us is sickly, infected with the wrong kind of self-protection, the only cure available to us is one that involves pain and suffering? Could it be that, if we have taken refuge in a place we think is safe that is actually full of danger, it is through pain that Love calls us to escape? Not that we seek pain, of course; but when it finds us, we may choose to see it as a tool to be used in our formation.

In the place of struggle, where can we find the face of Love? We may find it in the tender hand of a loving partner who nurses us. We may find it in the patient ear of a friend who listens to us hour after hour. We may find it in the warm embrace of a child who presses their love into us. We may find it in the gentle breeze and warm sun on an afternoon's walk. We may find it in the letters and e-mails and flowers we receive from those concerned for our wellbeing. We may find it in the prayers of a faith community that upholds us in our hours of darkness. We may find it in mystery: simply in a deep knowledge that One loves us and we are not alone.

The unconditional regard, approval and affection that we all need to make us safe is most deeply needed when we are in pain—but often hardest to find. Accessing Love is not a one-off experience, not something that 'just happens to us' when we're not looking. We need to continue deliberately and in a disciplined way to put ourselves in the place of Love so that we can continue to draw on its strength.

For Shapers, experiencing and receiving this love for ourselves may not be difficult, but we have to take care that complacency and ill-discipline don't creep in. At the same time, we need to recognize that love is always received as a gift, to be generously given away. If instead we see it as a possession and hoard it, it quickly turns sour and rancid.

---

[18] T S Eliot, 'Little Gidding'

For Definers, receiving love is an alien experience: we are more at home doing something to earn it or justify it. We may find it helpful to look out for how often we clench a hand into a fist, or grip a bag or a briefcase like a vice—when we find ourselves doing so, it's time to smile and relax that grip that reveals our determination not to be robbed of what is ours. Instead, we should open our hands and allow them to receive, and then give away, the things that briefly come into our stewardship.

For Adapters, receiving love involves believing we are worthy of it. The trick is to make sure that we capture every single act of love, gesture of blessing and word of grace and affirmation. We could try keeping a little book in which we note down all these little instances and experiences—it is a great discipline, as long as we make sure that it's an expensive book, beautifully bound, not a scrappy, dog-eared old notebook!

For Defenders, the key is perhaps to let go of our anger. Anger can become bottled up inside us, a dangerous source of passion and drive. It needs to be released, like the pressure in a volcano that will produce a violent eruption if it finds no other escape. Then, we must take the risk of entrusting ourselves to others again. Even though it feels immensely risky, it is a risk worth taking so that our wounds can be gently healed.

Many leaders have found it essential to practise a spiritual discipline of prayer on a regular basis to sustain this. Gandhi was well known for adhering to his routine of praying and reading scripture in the early morning and resting in the afternoon, even if it meant that meetings with political leaders had to be delayed! Such a rigorous regime and rhythm, I suspect, gave him the steel to survive the enormous pressure—including hostility—he often faced. Today, a growing number of business leaders are planning-in regular retreats on which they can refresh their inner being. As one of the Bible's maxims puts it: 'Above all else, guard your heart, for it is the wellspring of life' (Proverbs 4.23).

Knowing who we are and knowing what we do

The choice between purpose and purposelessness, the choice between Love and anger. The third choice that struggle forces us to make is that between knowing who we are and knowing what we do. Leaders are often busy people; many are instinctive activists, bursting to take on any new challenge that presents itself. In such a life, it is all too easy for someone to know themselves only through the things they do, the roles they play. Indeed, their activism may be a strategy to distract them from the emptiness behind the amazing things they're achieving. Struggle changes all that. Often, it takes from us our ability to be busy, to be in control through our own managerial skill, our expertise and the systems we have put in place. When we're in pain, we're often incapacitated, taken out of the action and unable to influence it. From this position of enforced passivity and powerlessness, we have to confront a stark question: Who are we? The Definer will ask: Who am I, without the props of my job around me? The Adapter will ask: Who am I, without the feedback from my acolytes and underlings? Or without the affirmation of being essential to every board meeting, vital to the corporation, indispensable to everyone around? All four egos will ask: Who am I, when I am alone, when the mobile is silent and the in-box is empty and the world goes on without me? Who am I then?

In a place of struggle, we must find an answer that is not related to our activities or roles. We are challenged to find an identity that is not threatened by the loss of such things, that is deep enough and robust enough to survive when the props of our old lives are removed. The question becomes simply: Do I know who I am? At this point, when everything else has been taken away from us, this question is not an academic one—it is urgently practical. The solution is not to speculate philosophically on the nature of identity. Rather, it is to look for the enduring qualities and characteristics that have survived, and can survive even a devastating loss.

One of the most striking things about the Jewish religion is the centrality of memory and storytelling. The Jewish scriptures tell the story of the nation, from the call of the patriarch Abraham, back in Genesis 12, to the return of the people from exile in Babylon in the seventh century BC. The faith of the Jews involves retelling this story as well as enacting rituals that remind them of central events within it. Chief among these are the rescue and exodus of the people from Egypt, an event remembered in the festival of the Passover. The Jews find a sense of corporate identity in the story that is told of how God accompanied them through their history. In the face even of devastating loss—even of their homeland during their exile—they retained this sense by retelling the story of God being with them.

In a place of struggle, we are forced to choose: whether we see our pain as a pointless agony against which to rail or, as the Jews did, as a period of growth, possibly even of transformation, in which a deeper and bigger Presence accompanies us. Oppressed by loss—of our role, or our job, or our health, or a loved one—we are forced to come to know ourselves, not as people defined by such things but as people who choose not to be overcome. We might say we are invited to see ourselves as those who, like the Jewish people, have walked an accompanied journey, one on which we were not alone. And we are invited to regard this journey, like them, not as one that has no purpose but as one that has brought us to the meaningful place in which we now confidently stand. Once again, it is the presence of and our relationship with Another through our journey that enable us to endure. The man or woman who can look back on their life and see it as a series of accompanied events and transitions in which they 'found themselves' is the man or woman who can not only survive struggle but can face any threat without fear.

Many Shapers and Definers have coped with life's harsh challenges through denial, blocking out the pain and the memory of pain and pressing on. For them, there can be no freedom: they can't go back to their story for a knowledge of who they are because they have spent a lifetime erasing it from their remembrance. They have chosen the path of defendedness, and, faced with a new threat, they can survive only by continuing denial.

Many Definers have coped with failure in their past through domination. Seeking to prevent a recurrence of such experiences, they have amassed skills and competencies so that they are 'in control' of their circumstances, able to cope. They, too, have chosen the path of defendedness. Faced with a new threat, they can only hope they have the power to overcome it.

Many Adapters have coped with the pain in their past through fear and anxiety, allowing themselves to be pushed back into a corner, ruled—indeed, continually assaulted—by their memories of what was done to them. They, too, have chosen the path of defendedness. Faced with a new threat, they can survive only by cowering and hoping not to be overwhelmed.

Many Defenders have coped with their past struggles through anger, not allowing the wounds ever to be healed or forgotten, but instead letting them fester and infect everything they do. And they, too, have chosen the path of defendedness. Faced with a new threat, they can survive only by lashing out.

Denial, domination, defeat and anger over our past cannot help us to grow through suffering and struggle in the present. The only route to growth lies through owning our past and taking responsibility for it. More than that, it lies through finding meaning in it and recognizing that it has not been a solitary journey but one on which we have been accompanied, known, loved and understood. It is then we can begin to find meaning and healing in the story we have told, and the freedom to face the future. It is then that as leaders we find the freedom to 'lead out of who we are'.

We could say that the leader who has not reached this point is a leader who doesn't know whether they are anything more than their success. Indeed, if we are to become leaders who are able to embrace the prospect of our own personal demise for the sake of the choices we believe are right, then answering the question of our ultimate worth, beyond the roles we play, becomes not optional but imperative. Our great leaders all had the courage to offer their followers not an easy ride to ensure their own popularity, but struggle and hardship to achieve the greater goal. On 13 May 1940, in his first speech as Prime Minister, Winston Churchill said: 'I have nothing to offer but blood, toil, tears and sweat.' Not a great manifesto—but the embattled British responded to what they perceived as his total commitment. They may not have liked the message, but in the coming years a depth of admiration, affection and even, perhaps, dependence was forged between Churchill and the nation he led that has rarely been surpassed in a political leader. Undefended leaders are perhaps not often the most popular at the outset, but they are usually the most needed by the end.

None more so than Mahatma Gandhi. 'Rivers of blood may have to flow before we gain our freedom, but it must be our blood!' said the frail, birdlike man to his people. Yet people followed him because of his authenticity and trustworthiness. All the positional power of Lord Mountbatten, as well as the military power of his troops, could not shape the fate of India as that one man could. This kind of leadership does not offer easy promises or wide, open roads; rather, it recognizes and embraces a future of obstacles and opposition. Such leadership requires the leader to be in a place of personal security, where their own success, comfort, reputation and popularity do not impinge upon their purpose and direction, where they are genuinely free to 'lose' their personal status to achieve the greater goal of leading others to freedom. They are free because, ultimately, their identity does not depend upon their success; and they are followed because everyone else recognizes this to be the case. Their moral authority, forged in the flames, is clear for all to see.

Study questions 14

1. Do you agree with the assertion of this chapter that struggle is 'a good thing'?
2. In what ways have you personally grown through struggle?
3. Do you ever regret avoiding struggle that might have been beneficial?
4. What are the three choices that struggle sets before us?
5. Which poet, T S Eliot or Dylan Thomas, inspires you more in this regard? Why?
6. How can you begin to draw from a well of love rather than anger?
7. What changes to your routine or regime may you need to make to ensure that this happens?
8. Are there parts of your life where you live in denial, in defeat or in anger?

⮑ On the website, www.theleadershipcommunity.org, listen to the audio file with the 'visual landscaping' exercise 'Remembering the journey of your formation'. This important exercise will help you to become more aware of your own accompanied journey and to understand it as meaningful and known. You need to be registered as a free 'guest member' in order to listen to the audio file.

FIFTEEN

Setting Undefended Goals

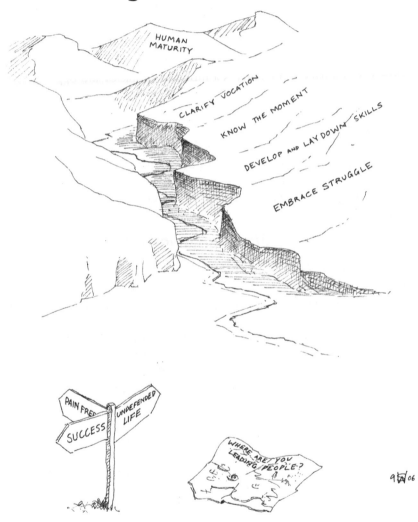

Virtually every book on leadership you read emphasizes the importance of setting goals and having clear, achievable objectives. The value of being clear, purposeful and deliberate in your choices is without doubt; the value in helping others to become clear, purposeful and deliberate in their choices is also without doubt. However, what is less clear is what those choices should be in favour of. The mere fact that someone can identify clear targets does not make them a good leader. There was no doubt that Adolf Eichmann was a highly efficient goal-setter: he determined to execute the 'final solution of the Jewish question' (the extermination of the Jews in Europe) hammered out at the now infamous Wannsee Conference outside Berlin on 20 January 1942. History tells of the horrible efficiency with which he and the Nazi machine he mobilized put it into effect. Setting goals and achieving targets are of no value in themselves unless the goal we have in mind is the right one.

What, then, is the right goal of leadership? Of course, there is, in an obvious sense, a different goal in every situation: to get the children safely across the road, to prepare the product for launch, to take the country through a war or the company through a 'downsizing', to captain the team to win a tournament and so on. However, beneath these specific goals, is there a deeper goal to leadership? Is there a greater task that unifies the act of leading?

One answer to that might be that the goal of leadership is success. The leader always leads her followers towards success, whether that is making it across the road or winning the tournament or the war. Many people define the goal of leadership as success: they point out that the alternative is to be happy with failure. No leader wants to lead people to that. Consider how much leadership you experience is aimed towards the goal of succeeding. What is the goal in business? Better sales, stronger forecasts, shorter turnaround. How about in education? Better Sats results, better degree results. How about in life in general? A better salary, a nicer house, a smarter car, more exotic holidays, a better healthcare policy, a better pension. Life, as a whole, is oriented around success, and leadership at almost all levels takes this as the unquestioned target. To succeed is good; to fail is bad. Good leaders aim for success. Good leaders achieve a better rate of success than bad leaders.

But I am not so sure. For a start, success in itself is not always a good thing. It may come at a price—an unreasonable price, be it financial or moral or personal. I can get my children to succeed in their homework. I can do it for them, or help them to search for answers on the Internet. I can get them extra tuition. I could probably ensure that they get good grades in all their coursework throughout school if I chose. That would be success of a kind—academic success. Maybe they would get to go to a fine university if so. That, too, would be success in one sense. But in another sense my strategy might have been very unsuccessful. It would probably have failed to enable them to grow up: to learn themselves, take responsibility, have integrity and deal with failure.

I can lead my family towards a better lifestyle—move to a smarter area, drive them around in a bigger car, take them on nicer holidays—but at the end of the day I could find myself cursed by children who never saw me because I was working such long hours. I can push my children to find 'suitable' spouses of such a standard (in other words, good enough in my eyes) that they will never be happy in their relationships. I can leave a wife who is unable to explore and develop her own gifts because I need her to be around to maintain the domestic ecology. Leadership in life, if measured in terms purely of 'success' (if these are understood as they usually are), does not necessarily equate with good leadership at all. Conversely, undeniable examples of good leadership often fail by the criterion of 'success', at least in the short term. The situation in India got worse, not better, following independence. Mother Teresa never persuaded the world to change its trade policies, never secured significant sums of aid to transform Calcutta. Aung San Suu Kyi remains under house arrest in Myanmar, where the brutal military dictatorship has only tightened its grip on power. And there have been occasions when quite exceptional leaders have lost their lives—surely the ultimate sign of personal defeat—as martyrs for their cause.

This should alert us to the fact that the general goal of success in leadership that we may set ourselves is mistaken. I want to suggest that the only proper goal of leadership is this: to enable people to take responsibility. My belief is that leadership is concerned with the task of helping people to move towards fully mature, responsible personhood. 'A responsible person'—a term that slips off the tongue, almost a cliché. Yet so much of our lives often involves the rejection of responsibility. Some of us live in deceit, concealing things about ourselves and our habits. Some of us live in blame, charging other people with things for which we should be taking responsibility. Some of us live in hypocrisy, expecting other people to live up to standards we would never dream of attempting. Some of us live in denial, choosing to forget about things we have done or had done to us for ill. Taking appropriate responsibility is more difficult than it seems—we have spent much of this book examining the mechanisms in all of us that often cause us to take either too much or too little. My suggestion is that enabling people to take responsibility is the primary task of leadership. It is not part of the task. It is not something we hope will occur as a spin-off. It is the explicit target at which we aim. Everything else is secondary.

My suggestion is that the goal towards which we lead our followers is in fact a human goal: it is for both the leader and the followers to be changed. This, after all, is the only thing that both the leader and the followers have in their power to change. It's not in our power to create success. It's not in our power to make other people do things. It's not in our power to dictate the course of world events (though we may believe it is). We cannot predict, let alone dictate, whether the stock market will go up or down, whether our team will win the league or not. But what we can take responsibility for is ourselves, and those we are responsible for leading. That is our sphere of influence. It is (to put it in spiritual terms) God's job to raise up rulers, and to bring them down again. What folly to think we have the power of success and failure! What conceit to think it is our gift to decide who lives and who dies! We do not have the power of life and death—those keys belong to Another.

Our task, as human beings, as human leaders, is far more humble and close to home. It is to grow up. It is to learn, through the experiences we are given, who we are—what it means to be courageous, what it is to serve, what it is to be loved and to love, what it is to be real, what it is to be fully human. True leadership is leadership of ourselves and others into this kind of life: embracing our full humanity, discovering what it is to be fully human, to participate fully in the world. Once we understand this, we begin to understand that leadership is not restricted to the narrow range of activities it is often supposed to be. It is not simply 'motivation'; it is not simply 'inspiring others to great efforts', nor is it simply courage. Leadership is not simply executive decision-making or being clear about strategy and how to achieve your goals. Leadership is the activity—any activity—that leads other people more deeply into this full humanity: which enables them to take hold of, and take responsibility for, the life that they, as a unique, particular person within the created human race, have been given to live.

Leadership, therefore, is a task that occurs at every level of life and in every kind of sphere—at the swimming pool, in the nursery, around the dinner table, in the car, on the phone, in the classroom, in front of the television, in the garden. Leadership is a way of offering life to the world, in order to draw life out of the world. As such, it is a spiritual activity.

What, then, are the goals we should set for ourselves if we are to develop into significant leaders? There are, of course, skills we need to develop: skills such as communicating, listening, thinking, planning, enabling, negotiating, persuading and so on. Leaders should set themselves goals to develop such skills, and we will be addressing how to do this in the second book of this trilogy. However, there are some more fundamental goals for which we must aim, which take priority over the developing of any skills.

Enabling people to embrace struggle

We may need to put a health warning on leadership for the benefit of those who seek to avoid pain, or want others to avoid it: Leadership is not for you! Leadership is fatally undermined by two flaws in the leader. The first is when she cannot allow either her work or those she leads to fail. Most of the time, the people we lead don't want to take responsibility for their actions—they would rather we did it. As long as the leader comes along after them, mops up their mistakes, patches the whole project back together, prevents the show coming off the rails, their followers will allow them to do so. The show may go on, but the followers themselves are not being led. They're being protected and pampered.

Sometimes a leader can behave like a footballer trying to win the game single-handed, who runs everything himself instead of passing the ball to someone else. Even if such a leader succeeds, she will not have helped the team to improve. What she usually does succeed in doing is running herself ragged, getting frustrated and probably angry at everyone else. I see team after team whose leader in effect carries the 'children'. They are quite happy to be carried, and they never have to stand on their own two feet. Most people (including us) only take responsibility when things start actually to go wrong. Then, the pain motivates us to do something about it. If the leader can't stay with the pain and face failure herself, how will the followers ever manage to? All the undefended leader has to focus on is making the pass—getting the ball into the right zone. If the other player doesn't get to it, this is an issue the whole team has to deal with, not just the leader. Being undefended in this way is immensely liberating: rather than feeling under pressure to succeed all the time, the undefended leader is free to take risks, to delegate, try new challenges and, above all, be honest. Moreover, when things go wrong, she can avoid blaming others (when it's their responsibility) or herself (when it's not). Get the ball into the right zone—that's all she has to do.

The second fatal flaw in a leader is offering premature solutions. All too often, I see business leaders, frantic to get improvements in their company's performance, come up with new idea after new idea, and none of them last. Why is that? Because they are premature solutions. A solution will only work when its time has come. And that time is when people are crying out for it, desperate for something to change. The role of the leader is often, in fact, to make the situation worse so that it can get better. He needs to be the one who can allow things to go wrong and let people struggle and fail—for only then will people start to take responsibility for the situation and the choices they make. A leader who is a Mr Fixit is no leader at all. The basic role of the leader is to 'push the problem back to the followers'—push it back under their noses, so they can't try to deny it and bury it. It is to make sure that the truth of the situation remains visible, rather than hiding it away. Then people start to experience being trusted; they start to learn and begin to trust themselves. In this regard, undefended leading is rather like being a skilled teacher: you could tell your students all the answers, but you don't. You hold back, allowing them to work them out for themselves. Your role is to help them apply themselves to the problem, trust themselves and find the resources to solve it.

Enabling people to both develop and 'lay down' their skills

The concept of the leader as someone who makes it possible for the gifts of others to emerge is well established. She doesn't seek to be the most competent person on her staff; she doesn't seek, or need, to be the expert. Instead, she seeks to gather around herself capable, skilled people who she can then develop further. She releases the gifts in others, through her trust, her support, her encouragement and inspiration. The cliché that a leader should 'do herself out of a job' is true.

However, what is less widely understood is the role of the leader in enabling people to 'lay down' their skills. This is, perhaps, much harder than developing and releasing the skills of others. The possession of a skill is not in itself necessarily a gift to the community or organization. We have seen how our skills are, in fact, assets we use to acquire the approval, power and control we need to make ourselves secure in the world. As long as they are used in this way, they can't set other people free. That is not to say that your skills cannot be used to train and help others—of course they can. That's what you might call 'low-level leadership', in which skills are imparted. What I mean, however, is that for higher levels of leadership, in which the leader's task is less practical and more emotional, social and spiritual, the leader's own freedom from the need to use her skills to acquire anything is paramount. The power we possess and the skills we have cultivated are of no use in higher-level leadership until they have been laid down, let go. The leader is called to relinquish control over what binds her, and what she binds to herself, in order to be truly free. Only then can she set others free. She herself is called to let go of what she owns. This is the journey a leader must make, to the quiet, still, sanctified place of self-offering where she is available to be used. All the mystical writers acknowledge this journey. The great leaders such as Jesus, Gandhi and King speak of their knowledge and acceptance of this place: the place where they have let go and laid down their own power to make change happen.

The goal of the leader, therefore, must be not only to develop skills in others but to enable others to be willing to lay down their skills. Often this involves the leader inviting people periodically to step down from their leadership roles in order to renew their experience of freedom. I myself believe that all leaders should lay down their roles every five years or so. A period in which we are shorn of our power is good for us and reveals whether we are truly free. This is more than a sabbatical. It should be undertaken on an understanding that that role and that power may not necessarily be taken up again. They should be genuinely let go and handed over. This also ensures that a leader experiences once more what it is like to be led, and to receive before she gives.

Many good leaders cannot get to this place: it is too painful, it asks too much of them. Their skills remain their own personal possessions. As such, they remain skills—they cannot become 'gifts'. A gift is something we give away to others, for their benefit, not our own. This means—tragically—that they will always exercise their leadership with a desire to preserve themselves. Of course, this is a place where all of us, not only leaders, need to go to be set free. But this is a book about leadership, and it's worth pointing out that most leaders have more to give up than most other people. They are probably leaders by virtue of their skills: their power and training and personality. They lead because people accept their influence. For them, then, it is harder to let go. They have more to lose. However, what they will discover when they do let go is that what they have let go is given back to them once more.

Self-emptying leads to transformation; it leads to empowerment. In my own experience, I have found that many of the skills I have possessed that I have also let go have been given back to me, but with a power they did not have before. My intellectual skills were given back to me, but not in the field I thought best—medicine, for which I was highly unsuited—but in theology, in which I have found the greatest and deepest challenge I could have imagined. My skills as an athlete were given back to me. The very year I let them go, after three years of underperforming on the track, I set new college records, beyond all my expectations. And I am finding now that the professional work I gave up as lost, and handed over, has been given back to me—except that it is new, different and (I sense) better. Giving things up is always painful, but once the battle is over, there is a great sense of freedom, of lightness.

Enabling people to identify and embrace their vocations

It is the central proposition of this book that life observes a fundamental principle. When someone is willing and able to give away what they possess, they find that it is given back to them transformed into something greater. This is the argument I have been developing, from different angles, from the first page. The leaders who leave the finest legacies in history are those who participate in this transaction. Leaders who fail to do so will always be limited in their power and their ability to create lasting freedom through their influence. I believe it is through this act of consecration that a leader becomes aware of what may properly be called his 'vocation'. Vocation, from the Latin *voco*, means simply a calling. It doesn't refer only to a religious calling. Rather, a sense of vocation is available to each of us. Vocation is that clarity of identity and purpose, power and freedom, that you gain when you are truly available. Vocation occurs when the gifts and opportunities you were willing to 'lay on the altar' are given back to you, now shining bright, transformed by some other Power and Presence.

If I am right in this, then the task of leading is no longer primarily a complex business of theories and ideas and training schemes (though all of these things could undoubtedly enhance your work). Instead, it is fundamentally this: the single focus of the consecrated man or woman who has laid aside their personal interest and made their whole being, their skills and their resources, available to be used for the good of others. At this point, I believe, they find themself playing in harmony with the universe, taking part in a drama much bigger than themselves. This means that potent leadership—undefended leadership—can be offered by the simplest person to the most qualified. Intelligence, wealth, status become irrelevant. The only relevant factor is the degree of consecration, of availability.

Thus, a leader enables others to identify and embrace their own vocations. This is not career guidance. This is more than identifying some passion or drive or skill that might suit a particular job or role. This is helping someone else to come to understand what their unique and specific calling in the world may involve. Of course, vocation emerges slowly and continues to deepen over time, and it needs testing from many different sources. No single leader should presume to tell another person what their vocation is with absolute certainty. But this question should be in the back of every higher-level leader's mind: What sense of vocation do I find emerging in the person in front of me? I often look out for people with exceptional listening skills—the ability to sit quietly without interrupting or interpreting, to notice little things and to reserve judgement. These, rather than the confidence of power, are the things I would look for in a potential leader.

Enabling people to 'know the moment'

There is a distinction in classical Greek between two kinds of time. *Chronos* means 'time' as in minutes, hours or years, but *kairos* means a significant time—a season, a moment, an occasion. It is not unreasonable to say that Western civilization have been built largely on an appreciation of *chronos* but with very little appreciation of *kairos*. As a Westerner, I am brought up to worry about how long things take, whether things are late or not, how much time I have wasted. Western industry is based on the principle of efficiency: achieving the maximum output in the least amount of time. We often appoint and 'incentivize' men and women as our 'leaders' on the basis of their skill and with a mandate to 'make the system more efficient'. In fact, this virtually defines the role of the CEO in any corporation—to reduce costs and increase productivity. And for this they are handsomely remunerated.

Our system rewards those who have skills in managing *chronos* better than others. However, as leaders our goal is to develop in our followers a growing confidence in their *kairos*. Higher-level leadership involves helping people to understand the times in which they live. In part, this is a matter of appreciating the historical, social, political and spiritual context we find ourselves in. It is about helping people to learn how to see under the surface, to read between the lines, to discern the larger patterns and bigger forces at work. It is about helping people to notice things that would otherwise pass them by, to teach them to be good 'seers' whose eyes are always open. It is about helping people to discriminate between truth and lies and to pursue the truth with all their heart. It is about fostering the poet, the artist and the prophet in our followers: those who see beyond the veil that is drawn over our eyes. Leaders need to allow such diverse skills to flourish—which is why any healthy society encourages and funds the arts and allows freedom of speech. We should be cautious of leadership that sacrifices depth on the altar of efficiency.

Our society greatly undervalues those who have the ability to recognize *kairos*, yet we do so at our peril. We live in a day when mere increases in productivity are not going to solve the world's problems. Whatever our governments may tell us, the answer to global warming does not lie in more efficient technology. At current rates, it would require two Earths to allow the present population of the world the levels of consumption Britain now enjoys, and five Earths to allow them all American levels of consumption! There simply is not enough planet to solve our problems through increasing our efficiency and reducing our waste. The only answer is going to be cutting our consumption.

I find myself looking for leaders who already choose to live according to such principles. Whether or not they can afford more, I am impressed by the person who has chosen to limit their spending to moderate levels and invest their income in the greater things they believe in. It tells me that they are free from the need to acquire more. In an age when all of us have to become more acutely aware of how we are consuming the Earth's resources, this is the kind of person I want leading me.

This, then, is our *kairos*, the time we find ourselves in. Of course, the *chronos* system is resisting this conclusion for all it is worth, insisting that the world is not going to change, that time (*chronos*) will march on as it always has, insisting that rumours of crisis (*kairos*) are exaggerated. Indeed, we do need to beware those leaders whose claim to status rests on their predictions of apocalypse. But recognizing the significance of the time we live in does not mean we must become apocalyptic. Often, this is just another way of abdicating responsibility. Rather, we must recognize that today (as on all days) we are called to have moral courage, to pursue an undefended life, to resist the forces in and around us that lead people into defended places. That moral choice begins in simple ways with our lifestyle and ends, simply, in our own enjoyment of undefended freedom. The happy coincidence is that as we ourselves enjoy this undefended life, so others, too, begin to be led into freedom.

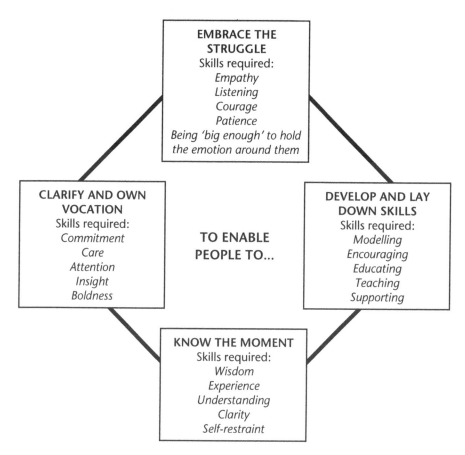

EMBRACE THE STRUGGLE
Skills required:
Empathy
Listening
Courage
Patience
Being 'big enough' to hold the emotion around them

CLARIFY AND OWN VOCATION
Skills required:
Commitment
Care
Attention
Insight
Boldness

TO ENABLE PEOPLE TO...

DEVELOP AND LAY DOWN SKILLS
Skills required:
Modelling
Encouraging
Educating
Teaching
Supporting

KNOW THE MOMENT
Skills required:
Wisdom
Experience
Understanding
Clarity
Self-restraint

Diagram 15.1   The goals of the undefended leader

Study questions 15

1. What, in your opinion, are the strengths and weaknesses of a *chronos* leader and a *kairos* leader?
   · *chronos*
   · *kairos*

➲ On the website, www.theleadershipcommunity.org, join in the online discussion '*Chronos* or *kairos*?' You need to be registered as a guest member in order to join the discussion.

2. What is the most lasting thought this book will leave you with?
3. Imagine being able to stand and watch your own funeral. What would you want those who give tributes to say about you, as a person and as a leader?
4. What are the greatest obstacles standing in the way of you being the person or leader you'd like to hear described?
5. What support do you need now to help you?
   - a peer mentoring group?
   - training on leadership strategies?
   - reflection on and development of your own character?
   - a community of fellow leaders facing similar challenges to you?

➲ We may be able to help you with some of these. The website www.theleadershipcommunity.org has many useful links to further training and resources. There may be fees payable for these further resources.

—2—

Leading with Nothing to Lose

Training in the Exercise of Power

Preface to the first edition of
Leading with Nothing to Lose

Leading with Nothing to Lose, the second book in the trilogy The Undefended Leader, continues where *Leading out of Who You Are* left off. If you have not read that first book, perhaps it will help if I give you a very brief résumé of its central ideas. Here it is, in two paragraphs.

Leadership involves power and influence over others, and it is incumbent upon a leader to use that power and influence benignly. However, each of us is trapped by a psychological imperative which was shaped during our childhood and which is at the root of our very ego, our sense of self. It is the source of our drives and fears. I identified four particular ego patterns (called Shaping, Defining, Adapting and Defending) and showed how they determine the personal needs we will be prone to try to meet in our lives as leaders. The greater the pressure to meet those needs, the more 'defended' we become.

One of the principal strategies we develop to defend our selves is to divide our leadership performance between a 'front stage' and a 'back stage'. This allows us to either reveal or conceal certain aspects of our selves, to manage audiences we see as potentially threatening. We can become less defended only if our perception of that audience changes: from being intimidating, critical or dismissive to being unconditionally and reliably affirming. This cannot be simply a matter of believing something we know is untrue; we need genuinely to find a new audience that has that characteristic. The best human audiences (secure relationships, loving marriages, deep friendships and so forth) can go some way towards fulfilling that need, but ultimately we have to find a spiritual source of approval if we are to be set free. The undefended life is available only to those who can locate such a source and learn to pay attention to it. This is the calling of the undefended leader.

However, the journey to undefended leadership does not stop there. Locating the source of freedom is only the beginning of the path, not the end, which has to lead, in practice, to a new approach to the tasks of leadership. And so we come to the second part of the trilogy, which you are holding in your hands. *Leading with Nothing to Lose* travels on into the territory of the leader who has to make hard-nosed executive decisions every day: managing budgets, setting targets, hiring and firing personnel, negotiating conflict, improving performance, organising procedures, planning strategy, getting his hands dirty in the bump and grind of routine leadership.

If *Leading out of Who You Are* dealt with the fundamentals of the person of the leader, *Leading with Nothing to Lose* deals with the fundamentals of their power. The practicalities of leadership are just as important as the ethics and ideals. These things are, rightly and necessarily, bedfellows and the aim of this book is to get them back under the quilt together: an undefended leader with undefended tools of leadership who is inspired by an undefended vision.

Simon Walker

ONE

The Power of Weakness: the Overlooked Source

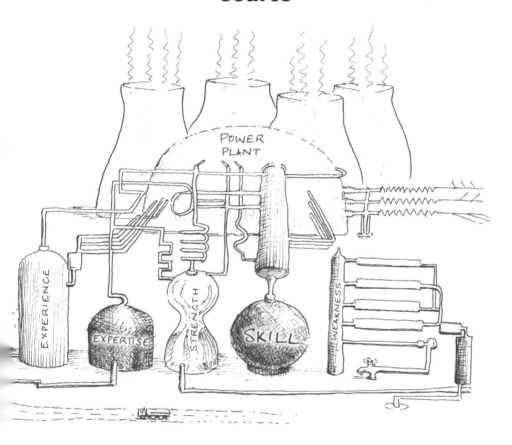

Most of us have, at some stage in our lives, discovered that being weak does not always mean being powerless. We probably stumbled on this realization unexpectedly, for our instinct and culture alike tend to tell us that the reverse is true—that to be weak means to be ineffectual and at the mercy of others. Imagine, for example, someone advertising a seminar on 'How being weak can make you strong'. You won't find this class being taught in Basic Military

Theory, or on an MBA course in business management. You will find plenty of sessions on how to be more effective, how to be more productive, how to be more potent in your leadership. You'll find dozens of courses offering you ways to build up your portfolio of skills or develop a more influential social network. You'll find courses on time management and 'personal impact skills'; but you'll struggle to find a single class that suggests that learning to be weak may actually be a part of being strong—and not just *quite* strong but the strongest a person can be.

And yet, nonetheless, I would bet you have had experiences in your life that might suggest that sometimes, in certain situations, the weakest person can actually be the most powerful. Maybe it was as a small child, when you discovered that even though you were the smallest member of your family, the one with the least education and the emptiest piggy bank, you could get your own way—just by screaming. Or maybe it was when you were sick and were let off school, and your whole day was transformed as the dread of the spelling test lifted and for 12 hours the world revolved around you. Your mum took the day off work and you were waited on, soothed and allowed to lounge in bed—simply because you croaked and whispered and shivered.

Maybe, if you are a woman, it was when you discovered that men will stop and spend hours helping you if you stand by your car staring anxiously into the engine and looking flustered and helpless. Or maybe it was when you realized that sometimes it is better to lose a battle than to win it but lose the war. Or that sometimes it's better to waive your rights and so demonstrate your moral superiority, or to give away something precious and so win a friend for life.

Perhaps in a history class you learned about the Norman conquest of England in 1066. Remember how the Saxon king Harold met the invading army of William at Hastings in the famous battle that was to be recorded on the Bayeux Tapestry? Harold's troops occupied the higher ground and had the upper hand when they saw the Normans falling back in apparent defeat. The Saxons charged down the hill after them, only to find themselves enveloped in an ambush. The Norman retreat had been a ruse, a pretence of weakness intended to lure the Saxons into a trap. And it worked.

Perhaps in the gym, practising judo, you mastered the 'sacrifice throw' of *tio toshi*, rolling back onto the ground and using your opponent's forward momentum to propel him over your head. The sight of his adversary falling to the ground, apparently overwhelmed, tempts him into a final surge, an overbalance—and the very opposite of the outcome he was expecting. In fact, judo throws almost all exploit the 'advantage' of your opponent, their weight and power, and use it against them.

Perhaps you watched the celebrated 'Rumble in the Jungle' between Muhammad Ali and George Foreman on 30 October 1974. Ali, the underdog who had lost his heavyweight title, faced the much younger, larger and stronger Foreman, a brutal puncher who literally bludgeoned his opponents into submission. Ali carried off a magnificent victory against all the odds by allowing Foreman to batter him for most of the fight as he leant back on the ropes, absorbing unimaginable punishment. When Foreman's strength was eventually spent, Ali launched his own brilliant counter-attack in the eighth round and knocked his demoralized opponent out on his feet.

Or perhaps you observed the final years and months of the life of the previous pope, John Paul II. As the world looked on, this frail, bent and feeble old man made his way towards his own death. And yet, in those closing weeks, larger crowds than ever gathered outside the Vatican to catch a glimpse of him on the balcony, and people spoke of the inspiration he gave them, the power they sensed in him, though he had never been weaker or less able to speak. It seemed that, when almost all human strength had left him, he had found strength from another source that transcended human limitations.

These are not isolated examples. In fact, when you think about it, weakness is often more powerful than strength. Of course, you could object that sometimes the power of weakness seems to lie in manipulation and cunning, subversive actions that are not altogether honourable or even honest in intent—and that may indeed be the case. Weakness, just as much as strength, can be used for ignoble purposes. But there is nothing inherently bad about the force of weakness. Like strength, it is a question of what it is used to achieve.

Weakness can be so potent it can pierce the most hardened of hearts, so forceful it can break through any resolve, so appealing it can win more allies, funds and support than all the marketing campaigns in the world. More than that, it can achieve different kinds of things that strength can never achieve, as we will discover in this book. It isn't just that it can be strong, it's that it can exert a particular kind of strength, a particular type of power, that simply is not available from any other source. There are things that can only be accomplished through the exercise of weakness.

It is somewhat strange, therefore, that weakness is so little talked of in books about leadership. Those that have sold in their millions, that line the shelves of every executive's office in the developed world, do so because they talk about strength, and about power. They explain how to become more effective, how to run the show faster and sleeker and for greater profit. They give away secrets of how to win and they promise success to those who obey their rules.

However, they allow very little space for any consideration of the power of weakness. Why is this? Surely, if weakness is a kind of power—and we all know it is, because all of us have used it at some time in our lives to great effect—then it ought to feature in discussions about leadership. The answer, of course, is that weakness is threatening. I remember a course I led for some senior leaders.

One of them, who ran a large, thriving organization, looked at me in disbelief when I suggested that they should allow weakness to be expressed on his staff team. 'That would be a disaster!' he objected. 'We wouldn't get any work done. Every board meeting would be reduced to a therapy session. I'd have people in floods of tears all the time. How would that be productive?'

That reaction is typical of many leaders. If I talk about the value of weakness, they feel: 'What does that say about all the macho stuff I pump up my troops with at the beginning of each quarter? If I start talking about weakness, I'm going to have an office full of weeping and wailing, of workers sharing all their failings and limitations. If I start talking about weakness, *I* may have to start showing some—and then I'll have a mutiny: I'll have people taking advantage, using my weakness against me. Before I know it, I'll lose control— I'll be upstaged, I'll be out. No, weakness is far too messy, too dangerous, too complicated and threatening to let out of the box. Better to keep it nailed up and pretend it doesn't exist. Sure, we can't get rid of it completely, but we can make damn sure we keep the lid on it as tightly as possible!'

Many leaders—though not all—are terrified of weakness. They see it only as something negative, both in themselves and in their followers. And what frightens them most deeply is what they might lose. They see their leadership as a medieval lord might have regarded his castle: as their own realm, in which they can do as they choose. Through strength, skill, hard work (and maybe birthright), a feudal lord won power and would build a stronghold to subdue those who would take it from him. His castle protected everything that was valuable to him: his wife, his children, his money, his lands, his serfs, his reputation. In a similar way, most leaders today regard themselves as defending their territory and the privileges that come with it. Their banner flies from their high towers and they will see off all intruders and assailants. Indeed, they suspect that most people around them, though they may call themselves allies, colleagues and friends, are secretly rivals or rebels in waiting. Everyone who has not actually worked their way inside their castle walls to feed from their table is out there plotting how to overthrow them. That's why many leaders surround themselves with people less talented than themselves and many choose sycophants as followers. It's why many maintain such control over their organizations, in case a threat should emerge beneath them that they were not aware of. Most leaders—though not all—are heavily defended and insist to themselves that only the best defended can survive.

We tried out the title for this trilogy on a number of leaders in business and politics. We'd ask: 'Imagine you saw a book on the shelf in Borders or Barnes & Noble entitled *The Undefended Leader*. Would you take it down?' Almost without exception they said they would, out of curiosity. Then, we asked them what they thought the book would be about. 'Well,' one would reply, 'I would think it was about a leader who had landed themself in a bit of trouble—you know, lacked back-up and support.' Or another would say, 'My guess is it would be a leader who didn't clearly know where he was going.' Or another: 'I'm not sure quite what the book would be saying, but I do know I wouldn't want to be that leader. He's vulnerable!'

For many men and some women, the idea of weakness is unthinkable: it's the very contradiction of all they believe in. They assume that being undefended is a negative thing, that it spells trouble. They assume that all leaders are trying to be as defended as possible. They expect books on leadership to explain how to become better defended, more competent, fitter, faster, stronger. Yet, at its most basic, leadership is concerned simply with the application of power to exert influence, to achieve things. Leaders need every tool they can lay their hands on to do the best job possible—and if weakness is one of the tools in the kit, they need to know about it. And not only know about it, but understand what it does and how and when to use it.

One of the tasks of this book is to take the risk of hauling up that box from wherever you have buried it, prising open the lid and taking a good look inside. And what we will find in there is a whole new way of thinking about power. What we are going to discover is that not only is weakness a source of power but there are seven other distinct kinds of power, which work in different ways and are appropriate and available for different situations.

Imagine if I told you there was a new source of energy that had the potential to revolutionize our lives and solve the global energy crisis. You might say, 'Great! Where can I get some?' Imagine if you were not just a consumer of energy but a supplier. In fact, imagine if you were the CEO of one of the biggest energy suppliers in the country. How would you react when I told you of this new source of energy? You'd say, 'Well, Mr Walker, that's very interesting, but I'd like to know a little more. Where's the evidence that this new energy source is more efficient? Has it ever been used before? How do we know it's safe? How expensive is it to harness? How much of it is there and why haven't the geologists or physicists told us about it before? I want to know a bit more about this new source of energy before I take this any further.'

And that would be fair enough. These are appropriate questions for someone to ask who is charged with the responsibility of supplying energy to millions of people. Their choices will affect thousands of businesses and hundreds of thousands of homes. They need to be properly informed. Just the practicalities will usually be enough for the consumer, who is probably most concerned about whether the new source of energy will cut their bills a little; but for the expert who has to manage this power professionally, only a rigorous understanding will do.

Now, the same is true of those of us who are called to be leaders in wider social situations. Like that CEO in the energy industry, we have at our disposal large sources of power to influence the lives of other people—in some cases, of many other people, even millions. It might be acceptable if we were merely consumers of power to say, 'Weakness? Great! That's a new one I must try some time.' But for those of us in leadership the only responsible choice is first to try to understand it a little better. What exactly is weakness? And, for that matter, what is strength? What do they do to people around them? Do they always work the same way? How do they relate to other forms of power? Can they be controlled? Are they dangerous? What are the safeguards we need to have in place? How do we access them appropriately?

If we want to be effective leaders, we will find it worthwhile to get an understanding not only of weakness but also of power: its source, its structure and its very nature. The aim of this book is to try to do just that. There are hundreds of books on leadership available, and many of them refer to the use of power; but there are rather fewer that actually dissect what power is. This book attempts to analyse its structure. In the next few chapters we will look at the key elements of power, the particular forces involved in any transaction. Then, having established the basic elements, we will go on to look at how they combine to form *patterns* of power. Rather than seeing these in terms of architecture (which might be appropriate if we were talking about physical forces applied to physical structures), we will use the image of an ecology of power, because the forces in play are social and the structure being built is not physical but social and emotional.

Once we have understood how the ecology of power is put together from its basic elements, it then becomes possible for the leader to learn how to combine these forces strategically. Throughout this book, you will find stories, illustrations and applications to explain how and when to use a particular strategy and what it can achieve. There are eight different strategies, and they have been represented powerfully by eight significant historical leaders: Abraham Lincoln, Franklin D Roosevelt, Ronald Reagan, Jimmy Carter, Winston Churchill, Martin Luther King, Nelson Mandela and Jesus of Nazareth.

The book ends by considering how leaders can progress from using perhaps one or two of these strategies to the freedom and mobility to use them all. We will explore the idea that, while to some extent this freedom can be achieved by practice, more fundamentally it is connected with the freedom to 'lead with nothing to lose'. And I shall suggest that the one essential characteristic of all the most mobile, flexible and ultimately effective leaders is that they have been undefended.

Part 2A

THE ECOLOGY OF POWER

TWO

A Choice of Forces: Front Stage or Back Stage?

It was Alexander Pope who said, 'The proper study of Mankind is Man.' We might adapt that dictum and suggest that the 'proper study' of the leader is the follower. If as leaders we are to research anything, the most worthwhile thing to investigate is the nature of the people we seek to influence. Until we understand that, we will not understand what we are doing at all.

Another way to look at this is to consider that power is the application of force in a human system. A leader exercises power in order to achieve an effect. Just as on a bicycle the power of our legs is applied as a physical force through the pedals to the wheels, so a leader applies social and emotional force through various mechanisms to the system of the human community in which they operate. That force has an effect, just as the force applied by pedalling a bike does. Just as the bike is set in motion, so the human system is set in motion by the force applied by the leader. Like a professional cyclist, the leader must therefore train herself to be able to exert the maximum force, and to do it in the right way and at the right time. There is no point applying full power all the time—indeed, it could be fatal if you were going round a sharp bend. Power without control can be lethal. The cyclist has an instinctive appreciation of the physics of the system and therefore knows how to apply power to the mechanisms of their bike appropriately and successfully.

What is the human system within which the leader applies force? Unlike the bike, it is held together not by physical bolts and nuts but by emotional and contractual ties, whether they be formal or informal. Those ties may be familial: a family is a human system in which a group of individuals are interconnected and bound together, by their genetic and cultural heritage, the emotional and legal bonds between them and their recognition as a group by the wider community. An event that affects one member of the family ultimately affects them all. Those ties may be contractual: a company is a human system in which, through formal, legal bonds, individuals make a commitment to expend a proportion of their time, energy and skills in a shared enterprise for the good of the system. Those ties may be ideological: a faith group is a human system in which, through informal but shared spiritual and historical perspectives, a group of individuals see themselves as bound together, with a common cause. Such bonds, though not legal, can often be as strong as (if not stronger than) those enshrined in law and contract, because they draw on deeper resources such as willpower, hope, trust and love. Finally, those ties may be aspirational: a sports team is a human system in which, through a common aspiration not just to play the same sport but to win the competition, a group of individuals participate in shared activities and disciplines.

Each of these human systems is different, but the kinds of forces that can be applied to each are the same. The leader must choose which force they will apply, and when. They have to decide

- whether to use front- or back-stage force
- whether to use strong or weak force
- whether to use expanding or consolidating force.

I will explain these terms as we look at each of these choices in turn in this and the next two chapters.

Front stage or back stage?

In 1960, Dwight Eisenhower's term as the 34th president of America came to an end, and the candidates who emerged to succeed him were his vice-president, Richard Nixon, and John F Kennedy. It was to be the first campaign in which television played a significant role, as in September and October of that year Nixon and Kennedy engaged in the first televized presidential debates. Nixon sweated under the lights and looked tense and ill-at-ease, but his opponent, groomed for power, influence and attention as a member of a political dynasty, was composed, confident and fluent. Unlike Nixon, the image-conscious and visually astute Kennedy came across as cool and collected. Those who heard the debates on the radio generally thought either that Nixon had won them or that the two men were equally matched; but those who watched them on television tended to find Kennedy the winner.

This outcome illustrates well the distinction between the use of force on the front stage and on the back. Kennedy was a classic exponent of the front stage. He was instinctively aware of his audience and their perception of him, and knew what was needed to manage their impression of him. Years of small talk at cocktail parties had prepared him for the easy, relaxing chat that appealed to the new visual medium, a medium that presents its viewers with the surface. The camera invites us to focus on what appears within its frame, encouraging us to think that what we can see is all there is to reality. Like visual theatre, TV offers us a captivating front stage, in which we are convinced by the characters, the action and the props we see before us. The medium is best suited to entertainment rather than education—documentaries tend to focus on visual information and padding and are sparsely annotated with dialogue, which must be pared down and simple. Television is a prime example of the front stage, and Kennedy was one of the first politicians to exploit it.

In contrast, Nixon remained wedded to older forms of communication and debate involving rhetoric, analysis and argument. Such methods, developed over many centuries, derive from cultures in which communication was largely verbal and the visual, if it was used at all, was mere illustration to add a little life. Like a traditional preacher, Nixon sought to compel his audience through force of argument. Unlike his opponent, he paid little attention to his appearance and refused to wear make-up. Instead, he concentrated on what one might call the 'backstage' elements of any communication: sound preparation, thorough reasoning. Like a well-organized producer, he had an effective backstage machine, well-planned, well-financed and well-rehearsed, which he believed would prove his substance to the audience and win their votes. The radio audience, who engaged mostly with the argument, were mostly convinced. However, for the TV audience, captivated by the front stage, it was like being taken on a tour of the backstage area of a theatre—important, no doubt, but not what most people would pay to see. They knew that this stuff was necessary, but they didn't want to have to understand it all. They took the gamble that behind the polished set of Kennedy's front stage, the back stage was in good order. Whether they were right or not is another question—and one whose answer history never allowed us to find out, of course.

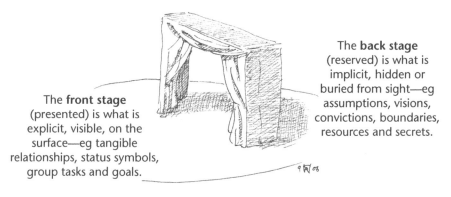

The **front stage** (presented) is what is explicit, visible, on the surface—eg tangible relationships, status symbols, group tasks and goals.

The **back stage** (reserved) is what is implicit, hidden or buried from sight—eg assumptions, visions, convictions, boundaries, resources and secrets.

Diagram 2.1: Front- and backstage forces

Every leader must be aware that they can apply force on either the front or the back stage. These two approaches are very different, and so are their effects. The back stage involves activities such as negotiation, research, intelligence; the front stage, on the other hand, involves the public agreement after the negotiation, the product delivered at the end of the research, the campaign that is fought after the intelligence has come in. A good leader is in command of the overall theatre of his organization, community or society, and for this to function well he must be able to perform effectively on both the front stage and the back. Frontstage leadership addresses the visible and tangible aspects of a situation and its explicit concerns; backstage leadership addresses the foundations of a situation and its hidden assumptions and implicit concerns.

Very often, frontstage leadership is a social activity, involving the management of relationships. Very often, it involves conversation. Often, it is an 'output activity'—it focuses on the outputs of the task, not the inputs. Very often, it is concerned with the results of decisions, and determines the process that lies ahead. Here are some examples of this kind of leadership:

- A coach at the football club setting out the team's targets in the league that season
- A consultant surgeon in the operating theatre deciding who his team will be and organizing the operation
- A mother at the lunch table establishing a consensus amongst her children about whether to go to the park or the library that afternoon
- A salesman persuading a customer to buy the latest laptop
- A teacher encouraging and inspiring a group of students to come up with better ideas in a science project for Speech Day
- A executive making a decision to dismiss a member of staff for gross misconduct
- A conductor leading his orchestra through Beethoven's Fifth Symphony

On the other hand, backstage leadership is often less directive than frontstage leadership. Often, it's quiet, unnoticed and in the background. Often, it involves providing a kind of support, whether moral or emotional or practical. Often, it relates to preparation or inspiration for a future event. It provides the basis for a successful delivery on the front stage. It's usually concerned with inputs into a situation, such as teaching, agreeing, planning or saving, rather than outputs. Here are some examples of backstage leadership:

- A family reaching agreement on what behaviour is or is not acceptable in the home
- A husband doing the washing up after the dinner party while the others have coffee
- A wife sorting out the finances of a holiday in advance
- A coach teaching the basketball team the basics of dribbling so they can practise on their own
- A woman accompanying a friend to an important meeting to provide moral support

- A head teacher preparing an inspirational speech for the first staff meeting of term...

- ...or planning the curriculum for the new school year over the summer

Arguably, backstage leadership is more self-effacing than frontstage leadership. The frontstage leader accepts the challenge and responsibility of 'performing on stage'. She will be the one in the spotlight if things go wrong; she will be the visible face of success or failure. There is no hiding on the front stage. In contrast, backstage leadership takes responsibility but in a way that does not control the outputs on the front stage. A backstage leader such as a film producer may ensure that all the finance for the production has been secured and all the rehearsals organized, but it is the director who will ultimately oversee the performances of the actors on the front stage. The director gets the glory, while the producer may be the unsung hero.

In every situation there is always a back and a front stage, and leadership is necessary on both. Leaders who lead only on the front stage will be in danger of running out of resources, supplies and inputs backstage. After a while, their followers will feel tired, hungry or stressed because nothing is being put into the back stage—of the project, the followers or the leader. This kind of internal collapse is very common in the lives of highly frontstage leaders, such as the driven executive who works all the hours he can and is concerned only with his salary and bonus or with rising sales. There comes a time when his personal back stage says, 'Enough!' This may be expressed in the form of a breakdown, physical, mental or emotional; or he may begin to develop unhealthy behaviours backstage that have a destructive life of their own. Leaders who lead only on their front stages burn themselves out, while their followers wither from lack of nourishment, or feel oppressed, or are simply unable to keep up. It was said of Churchill that his generals could scarcely keep up with the pace he set himself relentlessly on his front stage. This kind of leadership can be sustainable in the short term, however, and it may be necessary for a while during a crisis.

Less common is the backstage leader who is unwilling or unable to come onto his front stage. He is less common for one main reason: someone like this will tend not to succeed as a leader. Leadership is necessarily a social enterprise, involving public skills and performance. A leader who finds himself shying away from such encounters and is unable to present himself will struggle in the long run to persuade others to trust and follow him. Any situation in which the leader has retreated backstage for the long term is one in which there will be confusion over authority and a struggle for power, simply because the leader does not occupy the front stage. It is significant how powerful world leaders will do all they can to retain their frontstage presence, even in a personal crisis. Boris Yeltsin managed to make brief public appearances long after his faculties began to fail, Pope John Paul II asked to be propped up in a chair on the balcony of St Peter's Basilica, despite the acute pain and weakness of his last days, because he knew what his visible presence meant to the church. In 2006, Fidel Castro made sure that Cuban TV broadcast footage of him chatting with Hugo Chavez from his hospital bed. Osama bin Laden, too, though long in hiding backstage, has shown that he knows very well the impact of a well-timed appearance on video on al-Jazeera.

Leadership always involves a degree of frontstage 'theatre'. To some extent it is an act put on to convince an audience. Successful leaders are aware of this and set their stage accordingly. They understand the role of context and timing; they appreciate the 'dramatic climax', the appearance of the leader in the hour of triumph. Remember how George W Bush delivered his speech declaring that 'major combat operations in Iraq have ended' wearing pilot's overalls on the flight deck of the aircraft carrier *Abraham Lincoln* (which was steaming in a circle 30 miles off the coast of California at the time). The stage had been set and, when the moment arrived, the leader came on to crown the victory with his presence.

Such 'appearances' on the front stage are all the more significant when a leader has become important as a symbol to her followers. Symbolism is a vital aspect of leadership that every emerging leader needs to appreciate. When someone accepts the role of leader to take a group of people through a difficult challenge, she will always become symbolic in her followers' minds. She comes to represent 'that which will make us safe', a presence that will protect them against an otherwise insuperable enemy. This is an emotional transaction concerned with trust in the face of danger, and when it occurs, people cease to appreciate their leader and relate to her primarily as a person and instead engage with her as a 'sign'.

Symbolization is a powerful mechanism that can work for good or ill, but happens whether or not we choose to acknowledge and welcome it. It is, however, far more dangerous not to acknowledge it, because then a leader cannot choose how to manage it. I suspect that John Paul II understood his status as a symbol and knew that his appearance on the balcony of St Peter's would bring reassurance to anxious souls. He used his presence to soothe. At the same time, he also sought to make his followers aware both of his impending death and of their own attitude to losing him.

This language of 'theatre' and 'performance' will make some leaders a little uneasy. They will feel that it suggests something that is false and lacks the authenticity they believe is essential to leadership. After all, in the first part of this trilogy, *Leading out of Who You Are*, I argued for the moral integrity and authority of the leader at some length. Am I now contradicting myself and advocating that a leader must learn to put on a performance even if it doesn't really represent them as a person? The answer is no. I am not saying for a minute that you should adopt a persona that contradicts your own values. What I am saying is that, at times, a leader chooses to put himself on the front stage in order to deliver a message that underlines the fundamental principles of his leadership, regardless of how he happens to feel at the time. I am saying that being a leader involves a public responsibility: it is not simply a private or personal act. When you accept a role in leadership, you accept a public life in which your behaviour is identified with the institution you represent.

The leader always comes onto the front stage 'in costume'. The costume they wear represents the organization they belong to: it is not their own personal clothing but that of a public body, which they represent to the wider public. In so doing, they accept that they must act on the front stage in accordance with the values, standards and scripts of that body. They are not at liberty to go 'off-script', to fail to come on stage that night or to appear in their own clothes.

The private morality of leaders must be taken seriously by the public bodies they represent. A leader who in his private life breaches trust by evading tax, for example, does not have the right to insist that the employees of his organization shouldn't fiddle the books. A leader who drives to work in a supercharged four-litre sports car doesn't have the right to argue that others in her company must take the bus or cycle to work so that the company can claim it's committed to saving the planet through its corporate transport policy. A leader who flies everywhere when he could 'videoconference' has no right to argue for cuts elsewhere in business travel so that the firm can meet its CO_2 emissions targets. The leader who demands a six-figure bonus for herself has no right to instigate a round of salary freezes or cuts to meet a budget deficit.

If a public body does not have a public line on an issue, I take it that this is an area in which its leaders are free to make their own choices in their personal lives. If there is no obligatory script frontstage, they are at liberty to write their own script backstage. However, if anything is prescribed out front, what the leaders do backstage needs to be congruent with it.

THREE

A Choice of Forces: Strong or Weak?

Arguably, no single figure in the last hundred years represents so clearly the stark choice between strong and weak force as Mahatma Gandhi, the central figure in the story of India's independence. The British had ruled the vast subcontinent since 1858 and were reluctant to give up the jewel of their empire, despite agitation from the early 1900s and actual insurrection from 1919. Gandhi's campaign was unprecedented in that he called for non-violent resistance (sometimes referred to as 'passive resistance' or 'civil disobedience'). Instead of riots, or even warfare, the principles of non-violence committed the rebels not to defend themselves in the face of aggression.

The British response was a classic illustration of the systemic use of strong force. The authorities suppressed peaceful protests brutally with staves, rifle butts and bullets, most notoriously at Amritsar in 1919, when 379 Indians were shot dead and some 1,200 wounded. They maintained control through law enforcement, arrest and imprisonment, and managed the country by bureaucracy, fostering fear rather than trust. Strong force is that which imposes shape and direction in any situation in order to effect an outcome decided by whoever is applying that force.

In contrast, the protesters used a kind of weak force to exert influence. The bonds that bound them to each other were those of belief, not of contract. The determination to resist British rule was based on kinship rather than compulsion. Their chief weapons were respect and courage rather than the baton and the gun. Gandhi and others exercised their leadership through setting an example that inspired trust rather than through legal or military control. Thus the strong force of British rule was ultimately overturned by the weak force of the resistance. There has been no clearer or more challenging demonstration of weak force in action in the political arena, and within a decade it had inspired the Civil Rights movement led by Martin Luther King in America. However, while non-violence is perhaps the most extreme example of the application of weak force, there are many other, less demanding and more domestic examples.

Strong force sets the agenda. It irrupts into a situation and reconfigures the social, emotional or contractual landscape to suit its own requirements. Strong force is morally neutral—it can be used for good or ill, it can set people free or it can enslave and destroy them. It enforces its will, and is often unilateral and decisive. It generates confrontation and competition. It creates winners and losers.

Other examples of the use of strong force might be:

- Pulling a child out of the road when they run out in front of a car
- Attracting an audience when telling a story at a party
- Dominating a discussion in a meeting
- Exercising authority to make a final decision after a debate
- Choosing whether to hire or fire an employee
- Determining the values and standards of behaviour that are acceptable in your home
- 'Casting a vision' that is so compelling that it energizes people
- Selling a product to a customer through your powers of persuasion

In contrast, weak force comes into a situation and respects what it finds there. Often, it forgoes its own, individual success in order to enable the whole group to succeed. Often, it downplays its expertise in order to allow others to shine. It uses its knowledge and strength to empower others and give them confidence. It works by fostering respect, belief and good will. It finds solutions that all parties believe they have a share in. It is responsive, and seeks win-win outcomes. Here are some examples of the use of weak force:

- Submitting to the 'due process' in a democracy that gives each adult one vote
- Reaching a consensus around the meal table about which film the family is going to watch
- Encouraging a pupil to find his own answers by asking him the right questions
- Listening to a patient to enable her to feel 'held', heard and respected
- Building trust and a sense of belonging in a team through open and respectful listening
- Responding to an emergency call, even in the middle of your dinner
- Hitting easy shots on the tennis court so your young daughter can win the point and feel good
- Instigating a corporate listening exercise as chair of the board in order to collect, hear and respond to the views of the workforce

We are familiar with situations that exploit the advantages of both strong and weak force. For example, the 'good cop, bad cop' routine used by interrogators and teachers alike works on this principle. The 'good cop' applies weak force, winning your trust, showing friendship and understanding, making you feel you have an ally you can trust, while the 'bad cop' exerts strong force through threats and sanctions. Your fear of the bad cop makes the appeal of the good cop all the more compelling.

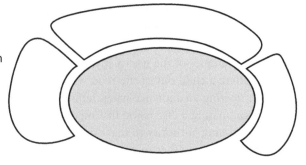

Strong force is that which imposes shape, direction or constraint—eg strong personalities, positional power, formal authority and 'vision casting'.

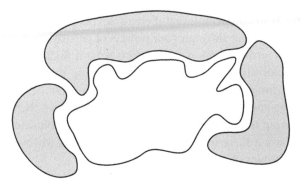

Weak force is that which resources people through affiliation, respect or trust—eg responding to need, creating consensus, fostering trust, offering an invitation and making a sacrifice.

Diagram 3.1: Strong and weak forces in a situation

When I introduce these ideas in seminars, I find that some people feel uncomfortable with the juxtaposition of the words 'weak' and 'force'. They argue that this is surely a contradiction in terms—to be weak is to have little force. Our society has come to associate force, like power, with being strong and dominant, and to associate weakness with being submissive and having no influence. However, we may question this assumption that weakness cannot be forceful and influential.

One way of considering strong and weak force is to think of them in terms of ties or bonds. Strong force creates unilateral ties that give your followers little choice—they are simply overwhelmed by force of argument or personality, the weight of the law or the size of the enemy's army. The relationship between leader and follower is one of imperative: the follower has no choice but to consent and follow. When you yield to strong force you may be doing so against your will, and often it is because it is the least bad of all possible options. Strong force creates ties that may sometimes (though not always) fail to excite the deeper emotions people feel for each other, such as respect, trust, love, affection and compassion. In contrast, weak force relies on all these emotions to create an attachment—the only ties that weak force involves are the free will, desire, hope and belief of the follower. The leader, through her use of weak force, elicits trust from the follower, which is freely given to her in informed consent. In this way, both leader and follower are explicitly, consciously committed to the same outcome.

Weak force often takes longer to exercise than strong force, which is one of the reasons why it is not always suitable in an emergency. You need to move fast when the threats are imminent—the time for reflection comes later, when the crisis has passed. Strong force appears to be dominant and it achieves its ends; but in fact it often happens that resolutions achieved through strong force alone, without the use of weak force as well, do not last.

Consider the political realm. A dictator exercises strong force, using torture and terror to create fear and submission. There is no weak force binding the people to the regime. On the other hand, all kinds of 'weak' ties are forming amongst the oppressed populace. Midnight meetings by candlelight bind people together and a sense of solidarity and mutual commitment emerges as former enemies become united against the tyrant. Bridges are built, hopes are kindled, plans are laid, songs of emancipation are sung. As a result, when finally the people have a chance to muster their own strong force, its power is explosive and the tyrant is overwhelmed. However, often what ensues is a sad consequence of the redistribution of power. The very allies who had been bound together in the shared task of overthrowing a strong ruler now find themselves having to share power. They find that now they can and must exercise legitimate strong force, can and must establish a political system in which different groups are represented, can and must organize the infrastructure of the state, can and must define a common national and political identity. Often, this new way of exercising force is very difficult, as we are seeing at present in Iraq. The 'weak' ties that held the oppressed together under the tyrant have loosened and now have to be made tighter in other ways.

Strong force is indeed seductive, but regimes that are unable to establish proper mechanisms for the flow of weak force remain precarious. The establishing of democracy is the only proven mechanism we have to exercise weak force politically. It enshrines the rights, and also curbs the influence, of each single individual: one person, (only) one vote. It is the political and structural means by which we distribute force equally and create 'weak' ties. Of course, it's imperfect. It does not necessarily create unity or harmony. It offers victory often to the largest minority and can overlook the views of the sizeable majority (unless the system employs proportional representation, which is beset with its own problems of paralysis). It doesn't necessarily create trust or affection, though it does help to prevent domination.

Importantly, strong and weak force can be exercised on both the front and the back stage. Strong force on the front stage is an exercise of might.

America classically employs strong force in its foreign policy: it prefers to work alone rather than through the 'weak' agency of the United Nations. It believes (often with good reason) that the UN is ineffectual in providing protection for the global community, especially in the face of crises (couldn't we have predicted that a 'weak' organization such as the UN was going to prove ill-equipped to take quick, decisive action in response to an emergency such as the genocide in Rwanda?). America sees itself as getting things done, and in a culture where results matter it has the evidence to prove the impact it makes on the global stage. The UN is a 'weak', frontstage organization which needs to go through protracted democratic processes that can appear paralysed in the face of provocation.

Interestingly, however, America also uses force on its back stage, behind the political scenes. And there it tends to use not strong but *weak* force. Since the end of the Second World War, it has supported regimes that were opposed to other regimes it regarded as a threat, sometimes by secretly supplying arms, for example, sometimes by giving them intelligence. It supported the *mujahedin* in Afghanistan against the Soviets in the 1980s, and throughout that decade armed the Iraqis to fight the Iranians. It prefers to operate in the international back stage with secret deals and favours, rather than fight all its battles on its front stage with 'strong' military force. In fact, some people might argue that it is because of America's covert backstage pacts in one generation that it is left to deal with frontstage conflicts in the next!

FOUR

A Choice of Forces: Expanding or Consolidating?

In the late summer of 1990, Saddam Hussein ordered a massive build-up of troops on the border with Iraq's southerly neighbour Kuwait. He claimed that it had illegally been drilling for oil diagonally and encroaching beyond its own borders. Perhaps his real reason for wanting to annexe Kuwait, however, was that it would give him access to valuable ports in the Gulf, as well as the possibility of seizing the larger oilfields of Saudi Arabia next door. The invasion of Kuwait precipitated what has come to be known in Britain as the First Gulf War and in America as the First Persian Gulf War. In early 1991, President George H W Bush, having assembled a huge alliance of 28 countries and massed their forces on the Saudi border, ordered the start of Operation Desert Storm. Thus began the campaign that broke the Iraqi army's hold on Kuwait and drove it back to Baghdad.

One of the great controversies at the time was whether the Allies should have prosecuted the war to its logical conclusion and removed Saddam from power altogether. In the light of future events, which ended in the Second Gulf War, many have said that they should. But President Bush would later argue that the cost in lives would have been too great. In 1992, his then Secretary of Defense, Dick Cheney, made the same point: 'I don't think you could have done all of that without significant additional US casualties, and while everybody was tremendously impressed with the low cost of the conflict, for the 146 Americans who were killed in action and for their families it wasn't a cheap war. And the question in my mind is: how many additional American casualties is Saddam worth? And the answer is: not very damned many.'[1]

The choices made by all sides in this sequence of events reflect the choices we make between applying what I call 'Expanding' and 'Consolidating' force. In the first instance, Saddam's invasion of Kuwait was a blatant act of expansionism—pushing beyond the current limits of his territory to occupy ground that did not belong to him. The action of America and its allies in

---

[1] Charles Pope, 'Cheney Changed His View on Iraq', *Seattle Post-Intelligencer*, 29 September 2004

response was equally expansionist: the execution of a war on foreign soil implicitly extended their reach.

However, the purpose of their response was, in fact, consolidation. Chiefly, it was feared by America, Japan and other powers that if Saddam not only annexed the oilfields of Kuwait but also managed to seize the Saudi fields nearby, he would control a large proportion of the world's oil supplies—a situation they deemed too dangerous to risk. That first invasion of Iraq, therefore, was motivated by a desire to prevent the destabilization of the global oil market, and with it the global economy. It was an exercise of consolidating force to restore the status quo ante, which had favoured the allies.

Eventually, Bush faced another choice between expansion and consolidation: should he go on extending the operation and remove Saddam from power altogether, or should he settle for the less costly and less risky outcome of merely liberating Kuwait? Perhaps the likely cost of the expansionist option outweighed the potential gains, as Cheney maintained. You always have to weigh the possible benefits of expansion against the possible costs, and in this case, they were deemed to be simply not worth it. Such is the terrain of a leader's daily choices.

One of a leader's principal tasks is to make such choices. For a CEO, it may be between diversifying her company's products or services and improving what it has been making or doing hitherto. For a government, it may be between welcoming immigrants in the hope that they will contribute to the common wealth and turning them away to protect the privileges enjoyed by the existing population. For a church leader, it may be between changing the way the congregation worships and preserving traditions that have endured for centuries. For a quarterback in a game of American football, it may be between going for the high-risk throw to the wide receiver that might gain fifty yards and settling for the security of the running back, who might just sneak a few extra yards.

Every change involves a degree of risk, and leadership is supremely about choices in the face of risk and the hope of reward. The quarterback may choose to use the running back for the first two downs, knowing there is always third down to come; but he may choose to go for the higher-risk strategy—risking an interception—when on that third down there is less to lose, with eight yards still needed. Conventionally, this is conceived as a balance of risk and reward. Models exist to help decision-makers predict whether the risks involved in a particular deal will be outweighed by the rewards if it works out. Western capitalism has been based on the assumption that growth (just another word for financial expansion) is a good thing if it can be achieved at a low enough cost. Growth in sales figures, growth in corporate profits, growth in a country's gross domestic product—these are all things to which we instinctively aspire in the West. We hear endless news reports celebrating our burgeoning national wealth—or despairing when the figures fall. Growth, expansion, taking more ground, selling more goods, this is what the capitalist machine does. It taps into that basic human drive to possess, control and dominate. Western capitalists—business leaders, politicians, educationalists and the like—have never understood the fundamental idea of communism: that the goal is to share our goods rather than to acquire more of them. The capitalist ideology assumes that it's always better to have a larger pie, even if you get a smallish slice of it, than a smaller pie that is shared out more equally.

Western civilization has been built, since its beginnings in ancient Greece and Rome, on the assumption of the benefits of expansion. The Greeks taught us to aspire to expand our knowledge and our intellectual range, the Romans to aspire to extend our territory and improve our technology. Likewise, the Renaissance taught us to aspire to a richer and more diverse culture, the Enlightenment to aspire to greater freedom and autonomy, the Industrial Revolution to aspire to greater efficiency and productivity. Today, the communications revolution is teaching us to aspire to omniscience and omnipresence. Aspiration lies at the heart of the Western enterprise, an enterprise that has been the engine of the world for the past five hundred years. Aspiration to own more, control more, understand more boils down to the simple, unequivocal belief that expansion is a good. It's better to have more rather than less.

We find ourselves now at a time in history when such assumptions are no longer axiomatic. We no longer accept unlimited expansion as necessarily morally valid, or even materially possible. In the 20th century, people began to question the moral right of imperialists to lay claim to lands not their own, and in due course imperial rule across the world was dismantled and power was given back to the nations and cultures from which it had been taken. We became aware that our expansionist drives were not morally neutral, because they almost always involved taking something from other people. Expansion involves moving into a space you don't currently occupy and claiming it for your own. In the West, we simply assumed our right to do so—the land grab was legitimate. However, territory is rarely unoccupied and just available. Western expansionism has involved a fair amount of theft, and by that I mean more than just complicity in the robbery of the slave trade.

Nor is that theft merely from other peoples whose lands or resources we have taken as our own. We are also stealing from our own children and grandchildren. We are now aware that the legacy of our expansionism is an ecological burden that not we but future generations will have to bear. Whether it is the side-effects of our energy-profligate lifestyles, which are changing the climate of the planet, or the exhaustion of its mineral resources to build and power our transport systems, or the depletion of its soil and water as we farm the earth intensively to feed our growing population, or the extinction of its other species as we invade their habitats. These are footprints we are leaving not primarily on our earth but on the earth of our descendants. It will be they who look back with horror and anger at the way we squandered and destroyed the wealth we should rightly have bequeathed to them.

In short, having been built on the assumption that expansion is good, industrial society now finds itself reaching the limits of the space into which it can expand. In fact, 'space' is now the big issue facing the population of this planet: not as in fanciful notions of colonising Mars, but space here on Earth—how we occupy space. A hundred years ago, there were enough lands uncharted, species undiscovered, sources of mineral wealth untapped to sustain continued exploitation. Now, the end is in sight, and we are only too aware of the finiteness of the system we live in. The Earth and its people are not simply inexhaustible. Resources can run out. And some of those that do can never be replenished.

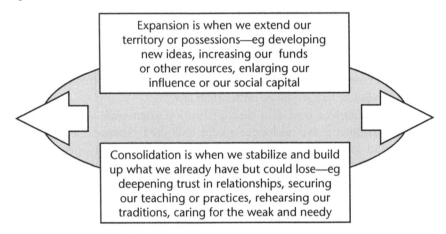

Diagram 4.1: Expanding and consolidating forces

And so a new ethic is beginning to emerge. Previously, business books on leadership extolled the benefits of growth unequivocally, with no thought for the consequences. Those that told you how to double your profit, squeeze your supply chain and exploit the next emerging market opportunity sold by the million. Now, however, those reckless days are coming to an end, and instead a more responsible and (dare I say?) mature counsel is beginning to be heard. The environmental impact of our supply chains and our packaging, the conditions of our labour force, the contribution we are making back to the community are now live issues in the business world, issues that are becoming more urgent by the day. There is a realization that relentless expansion has imposed a cost not only far away in developing countries but here in our own country: it has weakened the bonds and disrupted the rhythms of society, put pressure on families and homes and created a growing underclass. We have shredded the social fabric and now find ourselves engaged in ever more urgent repairs. While our expansionism is not yet dead, we are increasingly appreciating the value of consolidation and the necessity of it.

Expansion and consolidation are not merely alternative business strategies for making the next buck. Those days, we should all hope, are gone. The need for human beings to have goals to aspire to remains as strong as ever; but now those goals need to be reconsidered. As we consume the earth's material resources, the horizons we need to broaden are the non-material ones—horizons of intellectual growth, cultural enrichment, social diversity and spiritual depth. We have grown fat on a rich material diet in the West, but in many other respects we are starved. What we require today is not a business culture in which growth is penalized and executives are risk-averse, but one that sees itself as serving these other human needs—whose meeting in fact consolidates our welfare, protects our health and secures our long-term future on this planet.

Expansionism is always about pushing existing boundaries. It may be reactive or proactive; it may create new circumstances or respond to a demand. It improves performance and delivers more output. Expansionism takes risks by changing things; it doesn't settle for what it already has, it's restless and always wants more efficiency. Examples of expansionist leadership include:
- Driving business to achieve growth and increased sales
- Diversifying into new areas of business
- Caring for more patients by reducing the time you give to each
- Writing a book full of original ideas
- Extending your network of relationships to increase your social capital
- Getting a better performance from your team by offering them performance-related rewards
- Motivating your team to come up with new and better solutions by taking them away on a retreat

Examples of leadership that consolidates include:
- Deepening the shared convictions, values and beliefs in a group or organization
- Giving up a difficult and risky project to avert the possibility of failure
- Insisting on due process, financial, managerial or whatever, in any organization
- Stopping on the journey to look after those who are tired or hungry or whose feet are sore
- Resisting the pressure to reduce the time per patient because that would compromise patient care
- Establishing a consensus in a group discussion before continuing

FIVE

Combining Forces

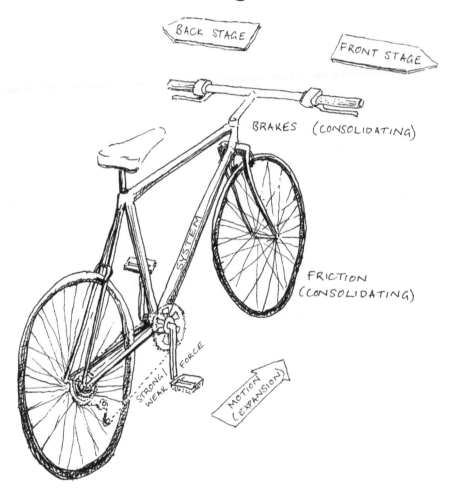

There are, then, three different pairs of forces that can be applied in any situation:

- · Frontstage/backstage force
- · Strong/weak force
- · Expanding/consolidating force

Of course, these forces are not applied in isolation: they are applied in combination, and work in concert with each other. Again, it's rather like the way a cyclist has to apply force to the pedals, the handlebars and the brakes. Turning the handlebars enables her to steer it in the direction she wants to go, and in a similar way a leader has to choose whether to steer towards the front stage or the back stage. Then the cyclist must decide how much force to apply to the pedals. She could pedal as hard as she can all the time, but then she might fall off going round a sharp bend and in any event she would exhaust herself. So, what is needed is the *judicious* use of force. In the same way, a leader cannot apply strong force to his organization all the time without the risk that it will either become exhausted or will lose its balance on more difficult terrain that must be navigated with gentler weak force.

Finally, the cyclist knows when to accelerate and when to use the brake. Both her feet on the pedals and her grip on the brake levers apply force, but their effects are opposite. One speeds the machine up, the other slows it down. Slowing down requires force just as much as speeding up—which is worth noting, as some people equate consolidation with laziness and lack of application. Of course, the bike could be allowed to freewheel and after a time friction will slow it down and bring it to a halt. But the wise leader, too, knows when to accelerate and when to brake.

The cyclist must learn to do all three of these things at the same time and must understand how each relates to the others. Pedalling faster while turning sharply changes the bike's orientation and position rapidly and is a difficult move to master. On the other hand, freewheeling and braking at the same time brings the bike to a gentle standstill, but only if the handlebars are kept upright; to turn sharply would result in a dramatic, possibly catastrophic, loss of balance. The cyclist must use the three forces—pedalling, steering and braking—in concert with each other if she is successfully to navigate the road she is travelling on.

If we think about the three different pairs of forces—frontstage/backstage, strong/weak and expanding/consolidating—we find that there are eight different ways they can be applied in concert. First, there are the four ways that force can be applied through and to the front stage (or what I will call the 'presented' stage, which I abbreviate to P):

Front stage (presented) +	Strong/weak	Expanding/consolidating	Legend
	Strong +	*Consolidating*	*(PSC)*
	Strong +	*Expanding*	*(PSX)*
	Weak +	*Consolidating*	*(PWC)*
	Weak +	*Expanding*	*(PWX)*

Then there are the four ways that force can be applied through and to the back (or 'reserved') stage (which I abbreviate as R):

Back stage (reserved) +	Strong/weak	Expanding/consolidating	Legend
	Strong +	*Consolidating*	*(RSC)*
	Strong +	*Expanding*	*(RSX)*
	Weak +	*Consolidating*	*(RWC)*
	Weak +	*Expanding*	*(RWX)*

These eight combinations represent eight different patterns of power, each with its own character. We can consider their unique properties by building up the descriptions. The chart below presents the kind of characteristics that would be present if (for example) strong and consolidating (SC) forces were combined, and then goes on to show how these would be affected if a leader exerted them on the front stage (P) or the back stage (R). The chart then looks at the combinations strong/expanding (SX), weak/consolidating (WC) and weak/expanding (WX).

Strong/weak with Expanding/consolidating	Frontstage/backstage
SC The combination of strong force and the drive to consolidate means the leadership is concerned with territorial control. Effectiveness, reliability and consistency are the key outcomes. Risk, diversity and ambiguity are reduced in favour of clarity and control.	PSC When this combination is applied on the front stage, it creates a *commanding*, authoritative style. Force is used directively to assert control. Disagreement may lead to confrontation, as the leader perceives it as a territorial threat. Followers are required to conform.
	RSC When this combination is applied on the back stage, it creates a *foundational*, enabling style. Force is used to establish solid values, method and practice. The leader establishes clear boundaries, processes and expectations that enable followers to feel secure without being micromanaged.

Strong/weak with Expanding/consolidating	Frontstage/backstage
SX The combination of strong force and the drive to expand means the leadership is concerned with creating the confidence, motivation and means to achieve more. Change, belief, hope and challenge are the key outcomes. Inconsistencies are no longer tolerated and the status quo and accepted norms are rejected in favour of opportunity and growth.	**PSX** When this combination is applied on the front stage, it creates a *pacesetting*, performance-focused style. Force is used directively to generate greater output. Failure to improve performance and attain targets will tend not to be tolerated. Followers are required to show a desire and commitment to excel.
	RSX When this combination is applied on the back stage, it creates a *visionary*, inspirational style. Force is used to capture the imagination, hope and belief of the followers, possibly through vision, passion or personality. The leader challenges their limited horizons, presenting a bigger world into which she can lead them.
WC The combination of weak force and the drive to consolidate means the leadership is concerned with creating space for others to act and ensuring that others take responsibility. Openness and the abilities to listen, accept consensus and tolerate diversity are key outcomes. The associated risks of a lack of centralized control are accepted.	**PWC** When this combination is applied on the front stage, it creates a *consensual*, democratic style. Processes are adopted that allow the collective voice to emerge without being controlled, dominated or manipulated. This social cohesion is the goal of the leadership, which fosters a sense of unity and gives the followers collective responsibility for choice.
	RWC When this combination is applied on the back stage, it creates a *self-emptying*, passive style. The leader allows others to take prominence and follow through their own initiatives, whatever the outcomes. By relinquishing active influence, the leader allows other leaders to emerge and accepts the risks associated with this lack of authority and control.
WX The combination of weak force and the drive to expand means the leadership is concerned with being responsive, reactive and alert to opportunity. Flexibility, fluidity and dynamism are the key outcomes. The leader finds ways to capitalize on the situation that emerges by responding to and adding to its growing momentum.	**PWX** When this combination is applied on the front stage, it creates an *affiliative,* coaching style. The leader fosters a dynamic atmosphere of adventure and mutual belief—'the whole is greater than the sum of the parts.' Central to strategy is that gifts and skills are affirmed and responsibility is delegated—leader and followers alike feel part of a single community with a single goal.
	RWX When this combination is applied on the back stage, it creates a responsive, *serving* style. The leader maintains a low-key presence in the background, working with individuals or small groups to encourage or persuade or solve problems. Like a second in a boxing ring, the leader seeks only to prepare his team for the contest.

We can present this information in the form of a chart that I call the Leadership Strategy model.

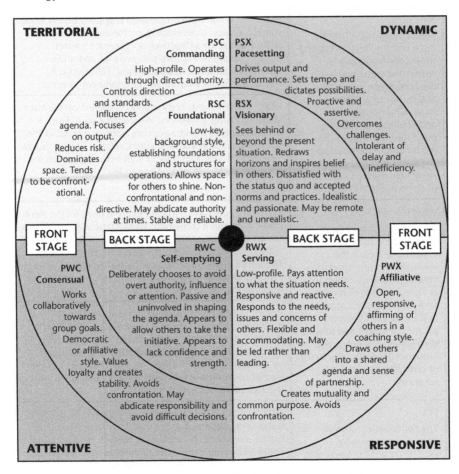

Diagram 5.1: The Leadership Strategy model

These eight different strategies represent the full repertoire of skills that are involved in effective leadership. However, before you can learn to use them all in concert, you need to understand exactly what they do and how and when to use them.

Throughout history, there have been leaders who exemplified one of these strategies in particular. Of course, they all employed other strategies at other times—they were not limited to just the one—but it was perhaps their use of one particular strategy at a particular juncture in history that really marked them out as leaders. I have picked out the following:

RSC: Abraham Lincoln and the Foundational strategy
PSC: Franklin D Roosevelt and the Commanding strategy
PWX: Ronald Reagan and the Affiliative strategy
RWX: Jimmy Carter and the Serving strategy
PSX: Winston Churchill and the Pacesetting strategy
RSX: Martin Luther King and the Visionary strategy
PWC: Nelson Mandela and the Consensual strategy
RWC: Jesus of Nazareth and the Self-emptying strategy
We shall look at each of these in turn in the next few chapters.

Part 2B

THE EIGHT STRATEGIES OF POWER IN AN ORGANIZATION

SIX

Abraham Lincoln and the Foundational Strategy (RSC)

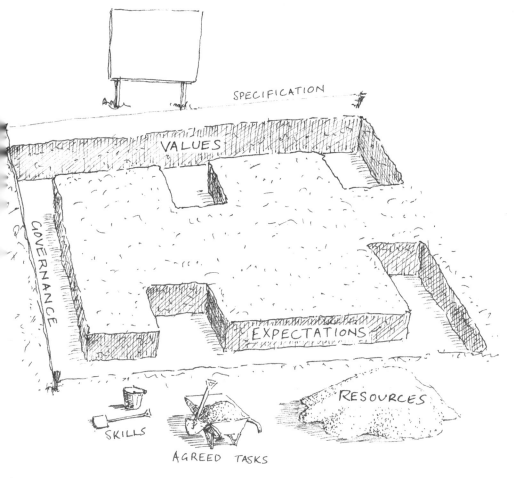

The American Civil War, which began in 1861, was largely predicated on one divisive issue, which threatened the very foundations of the Union. On the one hand, the Northern Yankees regarded slavery as morally repugnant and demanded its abolition; on the other, the Confederates defended the right of the Southern states to make their own choices. At the heart of the bloody struggle that ensued was the tall, angular figure of Abraham Lincoln, the Republican who had been elected president in November 1860. His appeal for the electorate had had much to do with the perceived chaos and corruption in the previous, Democrat administration, which the Republican press portrayed as having sunk the nation into 'a gulf of corruption and misrule'. The times demanded 'moral independence in politics and a new Luther'.[2] In the eyes of many, Lincoln met that need.

He was presented as a man who upheld the doctrines of the Bible as the foundation for all human good. Although he was not in any way a preacher or an evangelist for his faith, Lincoln's stature, style and rhetoric reinforced the quiet but powerful impact of his perspective on life and his fundamental values. What is noteworthy is that, like the German Reformer Martin Luther three centuries before him, who went back to the roots of Christianity, Lincoln constantly appealed to the roots or foundations of the Constitution as the basis of his leadership and his political agenda. For him, the Union was fundamental. 'I hold that in contemplation of universal law and of the Constitution the Union of these States is perpetual,' he argued in his first inaugural address. It was that Union that he believed must exist to bear the weight of all other social and cultural enterprise. Thus he could argue that the Union itself was more essential to him even than the abolition of slavery. In response to an editorial in the *New York Tribune*, he wrote on 22 August 1862: 'I would save the Union. I would save it the shortest way under the Constitution. The sooner the national authority can be restored; the nearer the Union will be "the Union as it was". If there be those who would not save the Union, unless they could at the same time save slavery, I do not agree with them. If there be those who would not save the Union unless they could at the same time destroy slavery, I do not agree with them. My paramount object in this struggle is to save the Union, and is not either to save or to destroy slavery.'

Lincoln understood that no freedom could stand securely except on strong social and political foundations. He believed it would be dangerous (to risk being anachronistic) to play the game without a clear set of agreed rules and a referee to enforce them—such a situation would quickly deteriorate into anarchy. His instinct was for an orderly society in which freedom was made possible by the assumptions shared by all.

His political posture and legacy demonstrate the use and advantages of the RSC strategy in a political arena. The strategy works by applying strong force to the backstage ('reserved') in order to consolidate the situation. For Lincoln,

---

[2] *Cincinnati Gazette*, 26 March 1858; *New York Tribune*, 16 May and 25 June 1860

the Constitution was foundational: the nation would be built on it. Undermine it, and the Union it created, and the entire edifice would become unstable. This foundation didn't dominate the front stage of American life, but without it the American way of life was impossible. Without the clarity of its control and the legal boundaries it set, the freedom that characterized the front stage would have been in jeopardy. Lincoln illustrates the role of the RSC strategy in leadership and the benefits it brings. It is the most basic and most important ingredient in any leadership initiative—without it, the initiative is bound to fail. When a leader employs this strategy, his followers understand what is expected of them in terms of values, standards and practice. This sets the boundaries of acceptable behaviour and the terms of all discussion. Leadership is concerned with creating a stable foundation by establishing underlying values and clear procedures, securing adequate resources, skills and competences and defining good practice.

What the Foundational strategy can achieve

Imagine being in a play for which no rehearsals have been scheduled. The actors turn up when they like and learn their lines if they can find the time. There is no clear guidance from the director, and the lighting team are unpredictable. The wardrobe is badly resourced, and no one can agree on what kind of set is wanted. To act in such a situation would be extremely stressful. In fact, the production would be a shambles. All of these things, the backstage concerns of a theatre, need to be decided, resourced and organized. Otherwise, the frontstage performance becomes chaotic.

When a leader employs the RSC Foundational strategy, she is laying out the backstage area of her theatre of operations: setting in place the agreements, boundaries, rules and expectations. What this does is to make the space 'safe' for the people occupying it. A good example of this at a domestic level is a family routine. Children who grow up in homes where mealtimes and bedtimes are set live in a world that they can predict. Where there are clear guidelines on behaviour, and they know the consequences of misbehaviour, they are able to predict what will happen to them if they choose to do X or Y. This makes children feel safe: they know their boundaries. In contrast, children who lack such social boundaries tend to betray signs of anxiety. They may seek attention or try to take control of a situation in order to make it safer. The 'backstage' foundations provide the stability for children to enjoy freedom on the front stage.

This is rather like the function of rules in sport. It isn't the rules of basketball that the fans turn up to watch—they turn up to watch the game; but in order for there to be a game to watch, the players have to consent to certain behaviours, according to a common code of practice with agreed rewards and penalties. The rules of the game are what gives their interaction on the court both shape and meaning. Everyone agrees to abide by them, and if anyone opts out, it is the game itself that censures them.

Action and reaction

According to Newton's Third Law of Motion, in the physical world every action has an equal and opposite reaction. Social systems are too complex and confused, and involve too many unknown variables, for anyone to try to propose a similar general law governing social actions and reactions. Nonetheless, allowing an inevitable degree of latitude, it is possible to find some reasonably predictable patterns emerging in any social system when social forces are applied. The idea of an *ecology* of power suggests that, if a force is applied to one part of a system, insofar as that system is closed there will be a reaction in another part of it.

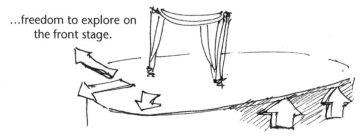

...freedom to explore on the front stage.

Strong foundational power backstage underpins...

We have been thinking about the RSC Foundational strategy, which applies a strong force to the back stage to consolidate the situation. What is opposite to the back stage is, of course, the front stage, and this is where you would expect a reaction. Moreover, you would expect it to be opposite in character and direction to the action that provokes it. Accordingly, you would predict that on the front stage the reaction would be weak rather than strong and expanding rather than consolidating. In other words, if an RSC strategy is pursued on the back stage, you would look for a PWX reaction to introduce a weak and expansive force on the front stage.

Consider what tends to happen when an RSC strategy is applied to a social system. For example, if you watch a brilliant soccer team such as Brazil you will notice how they are able to adapt their play depending on the nature of the opposition. They can keep it tight or go wide, play defensively or go all-out in attack. This flexibility is the fruit of hundreds of hours of work on their back stage, the training ground, where skills are honed, communication is developed, moves are learned. Their ability to adapt has not come by chance: it is the product of practice.

Or consider the family that has clear, established boundaries and expectations of behaviour. Because those RSC foundations are in place, the children are free to explore and discover, play and have fun on the front stage, knowing the limits they must remain within. They know that as long as they tidy their bedrooms before bedtime they are free to make as much mess as they want. As long as they are kind to one another, they can play as they like. They know they will be given such-and-such an amount of pocket money on a Friday, and they can then spend it, within reason, on whatever they choose.

The same is true of any organization. If you want your staff to feel trusted and empowered and free from micromanagement, work as hard as you can to establish the goals of the project and your expectations with regard to behaviour and to arrange all the resources that are needed—and then let the staff work with them (and, indeed, improve on them) as best they can. In 2004, the BMW management told the assembly-line workers in its Oxford factory they would like to know of any ways the workers thought the production process could be improved. Over the next few months, more than 500 suggestions were forthcoming, which even extended to enhancing the design of the Mini, the car the factory manufactured. Many of these ideas were acted on and as a result BMW reckoned it saved millions. The company trusted its workers. The management explained what they were trying to do, and the workers understood their goals, their principles and their needs. They were asked to improve on the manufacturing process within those constraints, and they did.

Lincoln's insistence on the Constitution was a crucial turning-point in American political history. It established the Constitution as the basis of American society, and shaped a policy towards slavery that was to bear fruit in emancipation and eventually, after the advent of the Civil Rights movement a hundred years or so later, desegregation. Moreover, it proved that the 'backstage' foundations were strong and broad enough to sustain the changes modern life entailed. Ultimately, it made possible the freedom and security America has enjoyed for more than a century, and its continuing expansion.

Most leadership situations go wrong because the foundations were not properly laid. By the time things break down, it is often too late to do much about it. Like underpinning a house once it has been built, strengthening the foundations of an ill-thought-out project is very difficult once it is under way. This is the current position in Iraq. The lack of any considered strategy to rebuild that society, let alone any consensus on how it should be structured, has plunged the country into chaos and civil war. No one can be safe because that society has no agreed boundaries to hold it together. It matches Emile Durkheim's definition of anomie (literally, lawlessness): the absence in a society of any shared values or morals or other agreements, which rapidly descends into anarchy.

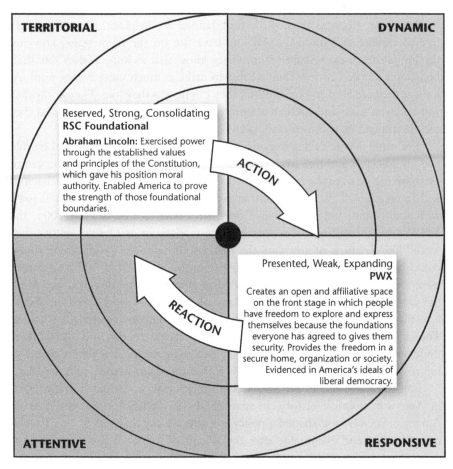

TERRITORIAL

DYNAMIC

Reserved, Strong, Consolidating
RSC Foundational

Abraham Lincoln: Exercised power through the established values and principles of the Constitution, which gave his position moral authority. Enabled America to prove the strength of those foundational boundaries.

ACTION

Presented, Weak, Expanding
PWX

Creates an open and affiliative space on the front stage in which people have freedom to explore and express themselves because the foundations everyone has agreed to gives them security. Provides the freedom in a secure home, organization or society. Evidenced in America's ideals of liberal democracy.

REACTION

ATTENTIVE

RESPONSIVE

Diagram 6.1: Foundational (RSC) action and PWX reaction

How does a leader implement an RSC strategy?

There are four key elements to implementing this strategy effectively:

1. Establish a culture of ownership and membership at the outset

The essence of RSC is that everyone agrees what they are there to do and how they are going to go about it. The development of shared rules, customs and traditions is critical for any group, organization or society. Not only do they organize life, they create a sense of belonging and membership. The retired British general Sir John Hackett insists that an army relies on such common cultural assumptions: 'Many of the military forms—the worship of regimental totems, eccentricities of dress and customs, the cultivation of the separate identity of the group—these have been developed to the creation and maintenance of that coherence on which the effective performance of a group under pressure depends.'[3]

- Establish what is expected from any activity or project. Why is each person taking part? What does he or she expect to achieve by when? What will they be making available for the project in terms of time, resources, skills and so on?
- Establish the parameters you expect of people. How many meetings will be involved? When will they take place? What is expected from each? How will people communicate and who do they need to keep informed of their progress?
- Establish the shared practices and behaviours that *you* as leader will commit yourself to—for example, always discussing things with the team before making any decision on spending over a specified amount, attending all meetings, always listening when someone else is talking, being kind...
- Make it clear that membership of the team entails both privileges and responsibilities. If anyone chooses to join the team, they are choosing to commit themselves to behave as agreed.
- Offer people the chance to opt out of the agreement at the start if they choose not to commit themselves.

2. Delegate responsibilities clearly

Build up a culture of trust in which people are trained and then trusted to deliver on their responsibilities.

I had been trying to build up Andrew's confidence. He lacked belief in himself as a person and would deny that he had anything to offer. Whenever I reminded him of his talents, he would simply shake his head and explain them away. One day, I became fed up. I was tired and I was losing patience with Andrew's fragile ego, so I changed tack.

'Andrew,' I said, 'I need some help. Badly, in fact. I need you to take this group of visitors around the centre. I should be doing it, but I desperately need to get some work finished. Could you do it for me?' Andrew's eyes widened. 'You want me to take visitors around the centre?'

'Yes, I do. And I think you'd do it fine. I need your help on this one. I can't cope without you.'

---

[3] *Serve to Lead*, British Army officers' manual, p23

At this, his demeanour changed. 'Well, OK, I'll give it a go—if you think I'm up to it.'

Andrew took those visitors round, and he has been taking visitors round ever since. He does it brilliantly—and more besides.

What I learned from that experience was that motivation is not just a matter of encouragement and affirmation: it's about delegation and control. What Andrew responded to was being trusted—trusted by me, the head guy, to do something. He rose to the challenge because I believed in him. He also responded to my need. He had always seen me as strong and capable, and scripted himself as weak and needy. I was the one who had always helped him out; but that only had the effect of disabling him, making him believe that he needed people to help *him* all the time. What he required was a little shove into the swimming pool to discover that he could swim after all.

· Delegate clearly if you want individuals to 'represent' the team in certain situations (for example, on certain committees). Ensure that each one is sufficiently informed and able to speak for the team on those occasions.

· Assign responsibilities to specific individuals. There are various reasons why you might give particular people particular jobs—because they need the practice or because you want to boost their self-esteem or to encourage them to work in partnership with others.

· Provide sufficient resources so that everyone can fulfil the roles they have been given.

3. Enable the group to take responsibility for the behaviour of individuals

I had been asked to lead a sales team whose performance had been tailing off in recent months. Its members were relieved when I arrived—they expected me to come up with some new ideas to boost their figures. I was keen to make a success of it, as it was my first job in the organization. However, as I listened to the team it became clear that they were looking for me to carry them out of the mess. I realized that if I tried to do so, and even if I succeeded, I would be making a rod for my own back: the team would simply rely on me in future to sort out their problems. So, instead of starting new initiatives, I simply let things go on as they were for a few months. I instituted fortnightly review meetings and when my colleagues looked at me to fix their problems, I told them that it was their team and their results and if they wanted to improve them, we'd have to do it together. For a while, things got worse, not better, because nothing actually changed; but I stuck to my message and pushed the problem back to them.

After a few months, they came to me and said, 'Look, we're desperate! We've got to change!' 'Good!' I said. 'Well, let's have a look at what might change.' Then we sat down together and agreed where we had been letting each other down on our responsibilities. We reviewed our strategy and together we came up with a new one. And it succeeded. The key to its success was the fact that the team owned it. They had come up with it, not me. They wanted it—things had got so bad, they had no choice. They got the praise when it worked. The solution involved staying in the mess for a little longer than was comfortable—but in the end it was worth it.

- When an individual fails to meet the agreed standards, push the problem back to the group. Resist the temptation to see it as your personal problem—it isn't, it's a problem for the group. Enable them to choose how to take responsibility for the issue.
- Allow the group to come up with solutions to such problems, rather than feeling you have to solve them yourself.
- Be content to allow messy, inefficient situations to continue until the group solves its own problems. Your task is to continue to confront them with the consequences of their choices. If they opt to leave a situation unresolved, make it clear what the consequences will be (for example, loss of revenue, the breakdown of relationships, even the failure of the project). If they choose to do nothing, they choose to allow these consequences to occur.
- A solution they come up with is always better than one you find for them.

4. Enable people to take individual responsibility for the consequences of their actions

Whenever anyone loses their temper, has a tantrum, sulks or moans, their behaviour is not without consequences—it has an effect on others. Leadership involves getting others to take responsibility for their actions. You might do this by saying something like:

- 'When you did X, it made everyone in the team feel Y.'
- 'The consequence of your outburst was that we weren't able to achieve Z in the meeting.'
- 'Is there anything you need to do to put things right?'

The 'putting right' might take one of many forms: writing an apology, seeing and speaking to someone who has been hurt, making up for lost time in their own hours, fixing whatever has been broken. Usually, accepting the consequences involves facing those who have been affected—and, often, asking them what they would like to say about it.

Some examples of RSC leadership in action

- A teacher establishing an agreed set of appropriate values and behaviours for the class
- A corporate health-and-safety policy governing good practice
- A job description that sets out what is expected of the post-holder
- A list, pinned to the fridge, of family rules such as 'Be kind,' 'Take responsibility' and 'Always listen'
- A regular team-meeting that gives rhythm to the week and provides a formal mechanism for feedback
- A set of values and behaviours underpinning a 'citizens' charter'
- A shared set of values and beliefs that bind a religious community together
- A shared story that informs and helps to define the boundaries of a tradition, community or country

When to use an RSC strategy

This strategy is most effective if it's used right from the outset of any endeavour. You wouldn't build a house without laying solid foundations first, and in the same way a leader should not start building her project, team or organization (or anything else) until she has established its foundations. This is especially important when a task is very complex and people may have different expectations.

- When you are setting up a new department
- When there is confusion and uncertainty in the group
- When the team have become disunited or are underperforming
- When you are working with a high-powered team that would react badly to being micromanaged
- When you are moving from the vision or initiation stage of a new enterprise to a period of more settled, efficient productivity
- As a basic, background strategy that you run all the time in 'maintenance mode'

SEVEN

Franklin D Roosevelt and the Commanding Strategy (PSC)

When Franklin Delano Roosevelt was elected president in 1933, he took the helm of a country crippled by the Great Depression. A quarter of the workforce was unemployed. Industrial production had dropped by more than half since 1929. Farming was on its knees, as prices fell by 60 per cent. In a country with limited government-funded social services outside the cities, two million people were homeless. The banking system had collapsed completely. Into this crisis stepped a man who would shape the economics of the next two decades and, arguably, start an engine that has not stopped to this day.

Roosevelt's response to a dire situation was to intervene: to take responsibility and take action. He began his term with an attack on the greed of the private sector, which he saw as a critical element in the recession. In an early address, he delivered this verdict: 'Primarily this is because rulers of the exchange of mankind's goods have failed through their own stubbornness and their own incompetence, have admitted their failure, and have abdicated. ... The money changers have fled from their high seats in the temple of our civilization. We may now restore that temple to the ancient truths. The measure of the restoration lies in the extent to which we apply social values more noble than mere monetary profit.'

His action took the form of the two 'New Deals' between 1934 and 1937. These involved government initiatives to employ young men and enforce codes of practice on industry that reduced competition and encouraged opportunity and reward for the whole workforce. They promoted recovery by 'pump-priming'—injecting $3.3 billion of federal money into the economy and creating the largest government-owned industrial enterprise in American history, the Tennessee Valley Authority (TVA), which built dams and power stations, controlled flooding and modernized agriculture and living conditions in the poverty-stricken Tennessee Valley. Roosevelt also cut costs, slashing the regular federal budget. He cut by 40 per cent the benefits received by veterans, and removed half a million veterans and war widows from the pension rolls. Protests erupted, led by the Veterans of Foreign Wars, but Roosevelt held his ground. He succeeded in cutting federal salaries and reducing spending on research and education, the Army and the Navy.

The situation was so bad that only an imposition from above of a draconian regime could arrest the decline. As it happened, the industrial engine that Roosevelt had started was about to begin firing on all cylinders when the Second World War broke out. The German advance through Poland, Belgium and France was unstoppable, and the Wehrmacht was soon poised for an invasion of Britain. Only 26 miles of water stood between Hitler and total domination of Europe. Britain desperately needed supplies, both military and civil, and Winston Churchill had long been urging Roosevelt to join the war against the Nazis. Roosevelt was to resist until the attack on Pearl Harbor in December 1941, but already a series of addresses to the nation (his 'fireside chats') had prepared the way for 'lend-lease', whereby America's industrial machine was directed to the production of weapons, munitions and other supplies for loan or lease to its European allies. 'We Americans are vitally concerned in your defence of freedom. We are putting forth our energies, our resources, and our organizing powers to give you the strength to regain and maintain a free world. We shall send you, in ever-increasing numbers, ships, planes, tanks, guns. That is our purpose and our pledge.'[4] When Germany invaded the Soviet Union in June 1941, Roosevelt extended lend-lease to the Soviets.

Roosevelt was shrewd in his response to the situation, for he knew that not only would lend-lease generate employment immediately, it would pay dividends in the future, ensuring that America's economy was best placed to prosper after the war. As he put it: 'What we send abroad we shall be repaid, repaid within a reasonable time following the close of hostilities, repaid in similar materials, or at our option in other goods of many kinds which they can produce and which we need.'[5] The military build-up duly generated nationwide prosperity and the number of Americans out of work fell below a million.

Roosevelt's instinctive leadership strategy was a frontstage one: from the outset, he took on the opposition—in this case, business. He demonstrates the role of the PSC strategy, and the benefits it brings. This strategy involves taking control of the situation around you through direct authority. In terms of power, it is the application of force in order to reduce risk and limit diversity and impose order on a chaotic or problematic situation. The leader metaphorically 'fills the space', both with his personality and with the initiatives he sets up. It is the impact a headmaster may have on schoolchildren who are called into his office, or a policeman may have when he arrives on a scene of unrest: both of them have the positional authority and power to impose order and take control. They have the means—including even physical means—to confront and subdue opposition. They act with authority vested in them by an institution or state and convey by the way they stand, the way they walk, the way they talk, that they expect to be obeyed. In their presence, you are immediately aware that the position of authority on the front stage is now filled and that it can only be taken from them by confrontation or subversion.

In 1933, a year of desperate economic crisis, what America needed was just such a figure of authority. Roosevelt took that role, and put in place a centralized system of reforms to drive the economy back towards growth. He was not afraid to intervene from above, to dictate a way forward. The fact that the nation accepted his leadership was much to do with the dire circumstances it found itself in. Much the same could be said of Margaret Thatcher when she hit her stride in the Eighties as Conservative Prime Minister. Britain was in the grip of strikes that were paralysing enterprise and strangling the economy. Thatcher approached her office with the same attitude and mentality as Roosevelt, willing

---

[4] From 'An Arsenal for Democracy', the first of the *Fireside Chats*
[5] Ibid.

to take the opposition on. In both cases, it was an act of confrontation—like a new teacher putting his foot down with an unruly class of children, imposing order and demanding compliance with his rules.

This is one of the key benefits of the Commanding strategy: where disorder is rife, and even fear, it brings order and control. When people feel unsafe, when they have no sense of any boundaries, they need Commanding leadership. PSC is concerned with ensuring that followers know that the leadership 'space' is inhabited and that there are very clear expectations regarding standards of behaviour and practice which will be defended against any challenge. Discussion is always seen in territorial terms and is therefore often confrontational. The leader uses his influence to establish territorial control through forceful authority and clear channels of command. Effectiveness, reliability, consistency and efficiency in delivery are key outcomes. Risk, diversity and ambiguity are reduced in favour of clarity and control.

Such powerful, direct, commanding leadership is often understood in the armed forces to be almost the *only* kind of leadership there is. Every cadet in the British Army receives a copy of a slim, red hardback entitled *Serve to Lead*. In it, the collected wisdom of the Army's great leaders of the past is offered to aspiring young officers. Bernard Montgomery was perhaps the most effective and celebrated military commander in the Second World War, and his campaigns, against Erwin Rommel in the desert of North Africa and later in northern France, were hugely significant in the defeat of the Nazis. This is what he wrote: 'A leader has to learn to dominate events which surround him; he must never let these events get the better of him; he must always be on top of his job and be prepared to accept responsibility.'[6] He suggests that the only appropriate posture for the military leader is domination, the subduing of all around him. For him, a leader who is overtaken by events, who is caught unawares, who loses control, is dangerously negligent. This kind of domination requires of a leader a certain mentality: they must be able to show 'calmness in crisis and decision in action'. Their self-control is such that when crises occur they themselves are composed, measured and focused, and in the heat of battle, with the smell of cordite in their nostrils and the frenzy of combat all around them, they remain clear-thinking and decisive.

Of course, the context for such leadership is primarily one of fear. 'All men are afraid at one time or another,' stated Montgomery. The emotion of fear is not found only on the battlefield, but it is certainly at its strongest in that arena. Safety is the most basic human need—more basic than food or company or love. If you feel that you are threatened, your first act, before anything else, is to try to make yourself safe. You don't sit down for a meal or worry

---

[6] *Serve to Lead*, p21

about being lonely or unpopular when you are in danger. These other needs matter, but not at that moment. And it is for this reason that the emotional response to danger—that of fear—is the most dramatic and compelling of all emotional responses. When the 'fear centres' of the brain, in the region called the 'amygdala', are stimulated, a cascade of hormonal reactions are triggered. Adrenaline and cortisol flood the blood system, flowing round the body and priming it for instant action. The pupils dilate, the pulse quickens, the hands sweat as the body prepares for fight or flight. Self-preservation is the one goal to which all its systems are directed at this moment.

All of us have experienced such physical reactions, no doubt. They may not have occurred in response to a life-threatening situation—it may have been simply during a heated argument, or on a dark night walking home alone, or before a sports match. However, any situation in which control seems to have been lost can feel threatening and can provoke the same kinds of response. The depression of the 1930s was just such a time, when the feeling of fear—for livelihoods, for homes, for futures, for children—was heightened and at times came close to panic. In such situations, what we need is for that fear to be contained. Fear can either be destructive, leading to panic or paralysis, or it can be channelled to produce extraordinary strength and speed of thought and a willingness to sacrifice your less fundamental needs in the greater cause of survival. The effect of adrenaline on the body is to prepare us for action, for our 'fear conditioning system' has evolved to maximize our chance of survival. There can be no better situation for the leader using the PSC strategy to release the very finest performances from those around her.

What the Commanding strategy can achieve

Fear must be channelled, and the key to channelling fear productively is containment. When a small child is frightened, he feels that the world may overwhelm him and he needs to know that there is someone who can stay with him who is bigger than the crisis, big enough not to be overwhelmed. Such a person will act like a container for his fear, preventing it from escaping into unmanaged panic. The calm, strong authority of an adult, the assurance that they know what is going on, that while they, too, may be afraid, they are not panicking—these are the signals that reassure the child that he is not about to be overwhelmed, and contain his fear.

Much the same is required of a leader in a crisis. Her task is to contain and manage people's fear, by being 'big enough' to stay in the situation and show that she herself is not overwhelmed by it. This is the leadership that Montgomery and others call for on the battlefield; but there are all kinds of other situations where this kind of leadership is essential. The brain surgeon needs to exude this kind of authority in the theatre. It would be no good if he started a discussion about the methodology of surgery just as his assistant was about to slice through a major artery! Moreover, it would be disastrous if he allowed poor-quality colleagues to work with him in order to give them a chance to experiment if it meant a threat to the patient. It would be catastrophic if he allowed his team to be lax about hygiene because he didn't want to be dictatorial but wanted to make room for freedom and diversity. Likewise, if you are walking down the road and you see a small child run out in front of a car, you impose PSC leadership on the situation—you grab him and drag him back to safety. This is not the time to start a discussion with him about road safety, or to allow him to take responsibility for his actions!

There are times in life when immediate control is needed, in order to manage and contain fear and danger. There are times when commanding, PSC leadership that 'fills the space' and dominates all around is the only appropriate strategy and not to use it would be a dereliction of duty. However, there are also less immediately critical situations in which the dynamics of PSC leadership are needed. For example, imagine you go for a job interview. You're nervous and keen to impress. But the interview process is shambolic: you weren't told what you should have prepared, no one on the panel introduces themself and it isn't clear who is in charge or how the decision is going to be made. You spend the whole time feeling anxious and uncertain, as the lack of explicit PSC authority leaves you insecure and at a loss. None of your fear is contained: instead, it swills around inside you, making you more and more apprehensive and unsure. You underperform because you try to take some control yourself, and as a result come across as a dominating person.

Now cast your mind back to your first day at school. Your mum takes you in, you find your new classroom and she hands you over to your teacher, who greets you by name (she's obviously learned it) and shows you to your desk (she's obviously prepared it and labelled it). Once everyone has arrived, she stands in front of the class and explains how school works and what's going to happen next. She always waits until there is quiet before she speaks, and then she speaks clearly and calmly. Your first day at school, which is traumatic enough as it is, is made manageable by the strong, clear, calm authority of the teacher. Your anxiety is contained by her reassuring presence. You sense that she is in control and you are safe with her; you feel that, though the situation is frightening, it's not overwhelming. You can cope because you are held together by someone else's authority.

Life is full of little situations like that, where people feel insecure and anxious: at the start of a project, when you are introducing a change in strategy, welcoming new team members, managing uncertainty. In all those situations, the anxiety of the followers needs to be contained by the authority of the leader.

When this strategy is not used in such situations, anxiety rises and what results is a power bid: people sense that there is a leadership vacuum and, to get a grip on the situation, someone or some group will start to exert control. The likelihood is that this will be improper and illegitimate, but in part it happens because there has previously been a failure to contain emotions appropriately. Fear is a powerful emotion, and there are those who will exploit it and those who will run from it. The leader's role is to manage it.

For the past two decades, the credibility of commanding leadership like this has taken a bit of a battering. Accusations of being authoritarian, directive, bullying and even abusive have made people wary of this kind of strategy. The advent of feminism and the growing number of women in leadership have made a previously male-dominated environment more sensitive about some of the more extreme expressions of masculinity. Many men in leadership feel somewhat confused about how to exercise authority without being seen as domineering. At the same time, the language of servant leadership, coined by Robert K Greenleaf in 1970, has encouraged leaders to see themselves in a submissive posture, preferring collaborative and consensual approaches to directive ones.

Many, indeed, would say that the revolution has not gone far enough. They point to continuing examples of bullying, discrimination and executive abuse of authority to show that power is still being used inappropriately. Some thinkers go as far as to dismiss leadership altogether, labelling it 'male patriarchy'. They often make the broad generalization that women do not use power in this way and are basically more collaborative and less dominating. They argue that leadership should eschew power, and that power itself lies at the root of the problems organizations encounter.

Whether or not women are indeed more collaborative and less dominating is beside the point (though I happen to think that, on the whole, they are). What matters to me as a leader, rather than as a male or female leader, is being able to use the right kind of power at the right time on the right occasion. It is absurd to suggest that power itself is the root of the problem. The root of the problem is not power but the *misuse* of power—its incorrect application. This debate has had the unfortunate effect of distracting us from the proper question, which is: How should you *use* power? It has also tended to deny permission altogether for the use of directive force. What I want to help you to understand is that in certain circumstances the use of PSC power is appropriate and, indeed, vital. In fact, not to use in such circumstances would be an abdication of responsibility.

The basic rule for when to use the Commanding strategy is this: when the consequence of *not* intervening would be dangerous if not catastrophic, then is the time to use it. So, for the brain surgeon not to use a PSC strategy in surgery could be fatal, and would be a dereliction of duty. To allow the toddler to run into the path of a car for fear of intervening in a directive way would be absurd and appallingly perverse. This is why such PSC leadership is appropriate in much of military life, where you are dealing often with life-or-death situations. It is also why military institutions schooled in this kind of power from the beginning struggle to adjust to more civilian peacekeeping roles that require the exercise of other kinds of power.

The reaction to the action

One of the reasons for the bad press for the PSC strategy is that often it has been the only strategy a leader, organization or society has exercised. One thinks, for example, of totalitarian regimes, Fascist, Communist or theocratic. In each such case, PSC power is virtually the only kind of power in the system. Or of a feudal system, in which the landowner dominates the peasant farmers. Or of a domineering parent, who crushes his children's freedom to grow up. Or of a bullying executive, who refuses to listen to feedback and defies all challenges to her authority. The result is always the same: the only 'space' available to the followers under such domination is on the other side of the ecology of power, in the Serving posture of RWX. There is no room to compete on the front stage, so the followers retreat to the back. There is no way to exert strong power, unless they stage a coup; so instead the followers are compelled either to be submissive or to find ways of evading the authority and being subversive.

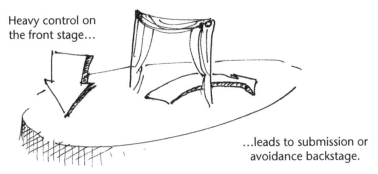

Heavy control on the front stage...

...leads to submission or avoidance backstage.

When they are continually dominated by PSC Commanding power, followers are forced to yield to its demands. The front stage is filled with a strong presence that insists on submission. In reality, it insists that followers must be servants. The RWX Serving posture is the opposite to the PSC posture, and in the ecology of power is the natural response to such domineering authority. Over the long term, the effects are always negative. On the one hand, domination can breed a kind of broken servility, as it did amongst African Americans; a diminished, dehumanized spirit, a lack of self-respect, dignity and regard bred in by decades if not centuries of serving another man's needs. Such use of power is never justified. Those of us who believe that to be human is to be created in the image of God are glad of the courage of those fellow Christians who, armed with the same conviction, fought against the slave trade in the 18th and 19th centuries.

It isn't only in political leadership that such a use of PSC power is unhealthy. The story of Enron illustrates the corrosive effect it can have when it is part of the culture of a corporation. Enron was committed to dominating the market, a strategy that ultimately led its leadership into a dangerous spiral in which, each quarter, it had to undertake more and more devious financial deceptions in order to create the illusion of billions of dollars in profits when the company was actually losing money. This drove up its share price to record levels—at which point, its executives began illegally trading millions of dollars' worth of Enron stock. These insiders knew about the offshore accounts that were hiding the company's losses, but other investors did not. It was a gross example of the abuse of power. Enron executives treated the company's shareholders and its other employees as pawns they could use to their own ends, much as a dictator controls and manipulates a populace without any regard for its welfare. Enron's European operations filed for bankruptcy on 30 November 2001, and Enron itself sought Chapter 11 protection in America two days later. At the time it was the biggest bankruptcy in American history, and it cost 4,000 people their jobs.

Not only does PSC power over the long term often result in a crippling servility, but in the end it can also provoke revolt. Marx was right in his diagnosis that the dominance of the bourgeoisie was unbalanced and would one day precipitate revolution. However, he was wrong in believing that this would inevitably lead to a more stable, egalitarian system. History testifies otherwise. Those who have been dominated and oppressed rarely seek to establish a more equitable system once they come to power. Instead, their experiences under the yoke seem often to foster in them a desire to impose the yoke on others. It seems as if the memories of subjugation and suffering are not so easily erased from the consciousness of the newly empowered. It is the same reason why people who were abused as children often (though not always) go on to abuse as adults; why power-sharing in Northern Ireland has proved so difficult and so unstable since the paramilitaries laid aside their weapons; why Robert Mugabe's regime in Zimbabwe has become increasingly violent and oppressive towards white landowners; and why the more supremacist end of the Black Power movement in America was such an appealing alternative to the civil rights movement in the 1960s.

In most cases, it takes monumental leadership, convinced of the need for generosity and forgiveness, as well as (usually) considerable assistance to establish proper structures of governance, to help people who have been subjugated to make the transition to a more equitable and empowered life without resorting to violence.

The PSC Commanding strategy has, throughout history, been the primary form of power that has ruled countries, organizations and families. The realization in the past 50-odd years that it has often been oppressive is something we should rejoice at. However, it would be a mistake to reject it altogether. It remains a vital application of power that must be available to us if we are to exercise authority properly and develop societies and organizations that are free from fear.

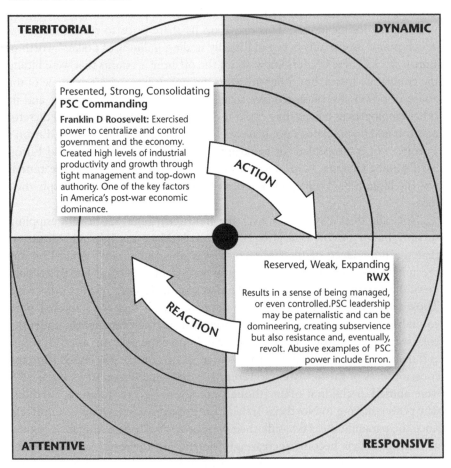

TERRITORIAL   **DYNAMIC**

Presented, Strong, Consolidating
PSC Commanding

Franklin D Roosevelt: Exercised power to centralize and control government and the economy. Created high levels of industrial productivity and growth through tight management and top-down authority. One of the key factors in America's post-war economic dominance.

ACTION

Reserved, Weak, Expanding
RWX

Results in a sense of being managed, or even controlled. PSC leadership may be paternalistic and can be domineering, creating subservience but also resistance and, eventually, revolt. Abusive examples of PSC power include Enron.

REACTION

ATTENTIVE   **RESPONSIVE**

Diagram 7.1: Commanding (PSC) action and RWX reaction

How does a leader implement a PSC strategy?

There are four key elements to implementing this strategy effectively:

1. Establish your presence

- Be at team meetings first so that when others come in you are ready to greet them, rather than looking for something, preparing your notes etc. This is a powerful way of 'shaping the space'. It sets you apart as the secure leader and sets the tone for every session.
- Stand up, straight and tall, make eye contact, smile and look secure and confident.

One of Roosevelt's characteristics was a certain paternalism. His criticism of business was like a father's rebuke to sons who should have known better and were now being called back into line. The forceful 'fireside chats' whereby he coaxed Americans into supporting their country's involvement in the Second World War likewise brought to mind a father teaching his children what was the right decision to make. Arguably, Americans wanted a father figure at the time to rescue them from the mess they were in, as well as to protect them from other, abusive authorities.

2. Command undivided attention and concentration by exuding confident authority, but without undermining other people's dignity and self-esteem

- When introducing any idea at a meeting, dominate the space by ensuring that all eyes are focused on you. Don't begin until they are. You can develop different tactics to achieve this, which may include standing in silence looking straight ahead, reminding the team of the agreement they made always to listen.
- Thank people for their attention in advance, because you expect to receive it!

3. Take unilateral control of a situation when you need to create stability

- When confronted with a volatile or escalating situation, it is your responsibility to take control and re-establish security.
- Deal with the situation through direct presence rather than by e-mail or phone.
- Be more than usually visible during this time, to reassure the rest of the team
- 'Think ahead and don't waste time' (*Serve to Lead*, p26)

4. Engender trust through 'warm' authority when dealing with conflicts

- When possible, get the two sides together in the same room and negotiate between them. Greet each individual with a handshake and a warm smile when they come into the room (you are there first, of course—it's your space they are coming into!). Remember that people will be coming through the door 'emotionally charged'. By receiving them with warmth but also with a sense of formality and professionalism, you are setting the right tone. Hold eye contact, sit up with your shoulders back and talk slowly, clearly and calmly.

- Being authoritative need not make you detached, hard and 'closed'. Warm authority is about having the confidence to be empathetic without losing your objectivity. This means you can say things such as 'I can hear that you're very frustrated,' 'I understand why you're upset' and 'I can relate to your anxiety.'

- Listen carefully to what each person says and ask them if you can repeat it back to them to ensure that you have understood their meaning. This will ensure that they feel heard and that you understand what they are saying and are not misinterpreting it.

- Enable everyone concerned to take responsibility for their behaviour and its consequences. This involves ensuring that they answer two questions:

  What am I responsible for in this situation?

  What do I need to do about it now to put it right? (This could include an apology, a change of behaviour, restitution...)

Some examples of PSC leadership in action

- An executive demanding a 10-per-cent reduction in costs from his board of directors in the next quarter
- A teacher correcting mistakes of spelling and grammar in a student's work
- A parent disciplining a child with a strong 'No!' and immediate repercussions if he transgresses
- A law court passing judgement on a criminal and sentencing him to a term in jail
- A parent strapping a toddler into a buggy
- An officer carrying out a battle plan as directly and effectively as possible

- A consultant surgeon organizing and managing his team in order to perform a safe, effective operation

When to use a PSC strategy

- Always when starting a meeting or a new project, to create reassurance and confidence before moving on to the RSC Foundational strategy to set out the boundaries, expectations etc
- When people are anxious or uneasy
- When there is conflict and you are determining the context in which to bring the two sides together
- When the consequences of not intervening immediately and decisively could be catastrophic (for example, to prevent an accident or a fight)
- When dealing with bullying or with dangerous or immoral behaviour
- When required to attain strategic goals as efficiently as possible

EIGHT

Ronald Reagan and the Affiliative Strategy (PWX)

Ronald Reagan was the 40th president of America. Elected at the age of 69 in 1981, he was the oldest person to hold that office. 'The Great Communicator', as he was called by some, was celebrated for his ability to express ideas and feelings in an almost personal manner, even when delivering state addresses. These were skills he developed in his early career as a movie actor, when he was sometimes compared to the gun-slinging John Wayne. He moved from acting to radio hosting and live television; the rhetoric of politics followed later. As President, Reagan showed that he clearly understood the importance of style in communication and knew that he needed to make an emotional connection with his audience—two lessons he had learned in Hollywood. He hired skilled speechwriters who could capture his folksy charm and he varied his rhetoric according to who he was addressing. He used strong, even ideological, language to condemn the Soviet Union and Communism, but could also invoke a lofty and idealistic vision of America as a defender of liberty.

Arguably, it was Reagan's humour—and especially his one-liners—that most disarmed his opponents and endeared him to the public. During the 1984 campaign, discussion of his advanced years led him to quip in his second debate with Walter Mondale, 'I will not make age an issue of this campaign. I am not going to exploit, for political purposes, my opponent's youth and inexperience.' His opponents and supporters alike noted his 'sunny optimism'. A frequent complaint by his critics was that his personal charm allowed him to say almost anything and still win, a quality that earned him the nickname 'the Teflon President'.

Reagan's positive outlook, his broad, movie-star shoulders and his slightly heroic and romanticized image appealed to a public who wanted to feel better about themselves. The Eighties began with America watching with growing unease the lengthening shadow of Soviet threat: its enemies appeared to be winning the arms race and at the time it wasn't at all clear who would win the Cold War. Nonetheless, Reagan was the first world leader to suggest, in 1983, that Communism was nothing but another bizarre chapter in human history and it would soon come to an end. To hasten this outcome, he built up spending on defence once again, aiming to bankrupt the Soviets if they tried to keep pace. He trusted in the power of capitalism to outperform the Communist machine, and after the anxious smile of Jimmy Carter his confidence was attractive to many Americans, as it reassured them that their country was strong and its prospects good. Perhaps he appealed to something buried in the national psyche—the belief in the potential for growth, the brighter day yet to dawn, the upward curve of the future. Without putting it explicitly into words, his emotional posture epitomized the American Dream, an almost unconscious sense that a better life was available to all.

At an emotional level, Reagan classically exploited the PWX Affiliative strategy. This focuses on the front stage but, in contrast to the PSC Commanding strategy, primarily exerts weak force, appealing to people's need, hope and trust rather than compelling them through obligation or force of will. Also, instead of seeking to consolidate his situation, this kind of leader is expansive, tuning in to its energy and hopes for the future and amplifying them. Being Affiliative is about winning hearts and minds, about finding that emotional resonance with your audience that has them captivated.

This is a subtle business. The finest exponents of this strategy are adept at reading what their audience wants to hear and how it wants to hear it. They are attuned to the transaction going on between them, the principal actor on the stage, and their audience, whose attention they know they must win. Like any actor, they understand that their performance is sustained by the audience, and if the theatre were to empty, the show would come to an end. Leadership involves finding the right style—and the right lines—to keep a possibly fickle audience enthralled. Reagan's performance was one a somewhat tense and fragile nation wanted to see. They wanted to believe in a strong, dominant, warm and kindly figure who was leading them towards a more benign world order. The style Reagan used on the political stage resembled the one he had used in the movies. Many commentators would say that Tony Blair has a similar ability as a leader. He tunes in to the public mood (with the help of focus groups and other market research, of course) and then adopts a position that resonates with 'where people are at'.

In economic terms, Reagan wanted to foster the growth of the free market by reducing the size and scope of government and encouraging enterprise. In 1954, he had regarded Roosevelt's 'New Deal' as 'approaching fascism'. As his former speech-writer Peggy Noonan suggests, 'Reagan had a libertarian conviction, that power is best and most justly wielded from the individual to the community to the state and then the Federal Government—and not from the Federal Government on down. He thought, as Jefferson said, that that government governs best that governs least. He wanted to shrink the bloated monster; he wanted to cut very seriously the amount of money the monster took from the citizenry each year in taxes.' Reagan was sceptical about the ability of the federal government to deal with problems, particularly economic ones. His solution was to reduce its role in planning and control by cutting taxation and regulation in order to allow the allegedly self-correcting mechanism of the free market to operate. On the day of his first inauguration, he said: 'Government is not the solution to our problem; government is the problem.'

Of course, such a message appeals. It sounds good to the hard-working store-owner who is motivated to expand his business if he knows that half his profits will not be taken by the government. This is classic PWX politics—creating freedom on the front stage rather than restricting it, encouraging growth and spending rather than prudence and saving. Many people give credit to Reagan for restoring optimism to a nation that in 1980 was in deep malaise and for advocating a freer rein for the private sector rather than greater government control. Perhaps his hostility to Communism was rooted in his suspicion of any system imposed from the top down rather than arising out of human freedom, ambition and desire.

What the Affiliative strategy can achieve

PWX leadership always looks for ways to motivate rather than restrict people. It is no coincidence that Reagan had previously been a motivational speaker: he understood what people needed to bring out the best in them. The past two decades, since his presidency in the Eighties, have seen the 'motivational industry' swell to colossal size. Organizations pay huge sums for coaches who promise to improve the performance of a team. The psychology of the Eighties was grounded in the feel-good factor of growth, the optimism that arises from the realistic hope that you may acquire more than you currently own. It tapped into raw aspiration. One of the differences between that heady climate of free-market growth in the Eighties and the mood today is the growing awareness that the boom cannot be sustained. Not only have stock crashes come and gone, not only have we lived through 1989's Black Monday and the 'dot-com' boom and bust of the following decade, not only are we more sensitive to the inevitable, predictable cycles of growth and decline in any market, we are also aware now that the entire global system is reaching its limits. The current talk of sustainability and renewability is in marked contrast to that of expansion and acquisition in the late Eighties.

A lot of thinking on leadership over the past two decades has emphasized the role of leader as motivator and visionary, the one who has big, exciting ideas and is able to inspire her staff to work harder to achieve their dreams. Those firms in which the rewards the employees receive are in line with the success of the business are held up as models of excellence. As we have become more suspicious of the directive approaches of the Commanding strategy, so we have favoured this more Affiliative, coaching style, in which the leader comes alongside us. Her language is of 'us' and 'we' as opposed to 'you' and 'I'; her tone is not demanding, not hectoring, but understanding, appealing and encouraging. Her message is 'I know where you are at present and I sense that together we can get to a better place in the future.' We see her as one of us, but also as someone who busily goes around keeping our spirits up, believing always in the brighter day to come.

There is no doubt that, in the sweep of history, such optimistic affirmation made a welcome change from the somewhat dour, puritanical style of much of the first half of the 20th century. Replacing duty with freedom and grim obligation with the energy of hope released Western society from some of its more repressive behaviours. It cultivated personal expression, individual liberty and human rights, while opposing the centralizing influences of government and other institutions. It encouraged us to look forward rather than back and fostered a generation of 'boomers' who have exploited (and, arguably, squandered) the opportunities of post-war society in their pursuit of individual happiness. The psychologies of our day endlessly repeat their mantras of 'releasing your potential', 'achieving personal fulfilment', 'unblocking your obstacles to growth' and 'moving from good to great'.

There are, however, three pitfalls into which such a message can lead us unless we are careful. The first is that assurances of a rosy and expansive future may simply be false. Relentless optimism does not itself make our prospects better. Nor does the urge to bury bad stories in the press and put a positive spin on events help us to grow up and take responsibility. Second, the leader can end up being more pal than boss. If you are just 'one of the boys' and can't stand apart, you quickly lose authority, respect and control. Third, the PWX message of fulfilment may ultimately be little more than straightforward, old-fashioned selfishness. The term 'selfish' itself sounds rather quaint to our ears, being reminiscent of the narrow-minded post-war restrictiveness of our parents' and grandparents' generations, and by replacing the idea of selfishness with 'self-fulfilment' we have whitewashed the negative connotations of self-orientated activity.

Appropriate and healthy Affiliative leadership is a subtly but significantly different matter from merely appealing to 'personal growth'. For a start, it is communitarian rather than individualistic. The PWX leader appeals to 'us', not 'me'. The picture she paints is of the group setting out on the journey together, where the happiness, freedom and fulfilment of each one depend on the happiness, freedom and fulfilment of all. Moreover, if the group is to attain its goal, each individual has to maintain certain disciplines and make certain sacrifices for the sake of the group. Imagine that you're one of a party of mountaineers climbing Everest. You're obviously excited by the thought of achieving that goal and you want to do it. You've trained and got yourself in shape for the climb, as have your nine fellow climbers. If any of you is going to make it to the summit, you all need to consent to some basic rules before you start out. You agree not to wander off on your own, to carry your share of the common kit, to leave the final decision about your route to your leader. You accept that you must limit how much you eat so that there is enough for all, that you will share your gear if someone else loses theirs, that you will not abandon a colleague on the mountain. These are the sort of compacts mountaineers tend to make. They constitute a code of ethics, a set of shared values, that are crucial to any climb. Without them, everyone knows, mountains can be extremely dangerous: people can get injured, lost or frozen to death.

Such agreements are like ropes that hold the team together on the difficult ascent. When they are broken, tragedies happen. One of the horrors of the ascent to Everest is that the route to the summit takes you past the frozen bodies of those who have died in the attempt. Often, the reason they perished was that they were passed by other mountaineers who, with the summit in sight and at the limits of their own endurance, chose not to stop to help them but pressed on to their personal goal. The upper slopes of Everest are a chilling witness to that tendency in us that, in extreme circumstances, will put our own interests above the wellbeing of others, even if it means leaving them to die.

Could the same be said for some of the ruthless self-interest of businesses, governments and other organizations over the past two decades in particular? In the race for the summit and the rewards it offers, have we become horribly selfish, willing to close our eyes to the consequences for others around us? Have we, like those climbers, contravened the unwritten codes of behaviour that are so important if mountaineering is not to descend into moral chaos? The reality is that unrestrained growth—in the market, in a church, in our personal liberties—is dangerously unstable and risks catastrophe. Like mountaineers, we need an ethical framework, a shared set of values, if we are to make the ascent without sacrificing our humanity.

Reaction to the action

To see how this need is manifested in the ecology of power, we must look at what is diametrically opposite to the Affiliative strategy. If we look at our model, we see that opposite to PWX is R (reserved, or backstage), S (strong) and C (consolidating)—in other words, that what is required to balance the Affiliative strategy is the Foundational strategy. This RSC strategy needs to be in operation on the back stage if the frontstage PWX strategy is to be applied safely and responsibly. The RSC strategy is the one exemplified by Abraham Lincoln, in his appeals to the foundations of the Union as the moral and social basis for government. We saw that it is the agreed rules and boundaries, assumptions and expectations that sustain any social edifice, be it a family, school, church, business, state or nation.

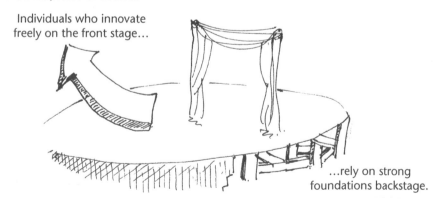

Individuals who innovate freely on the front stage...

...rely on strong foundations backstage.

If we are to enjoy the freedom of Affiliative leadership, it must stand on RSC foundations. It is interesting to note what Ronald Reagan had on his back stage. He was a committed Christian, whose morality was informed by the ethics and values he found in the Bible. He was not afraid to speak out on such issues as prayer in schools and abortion, though his aides warned him it hurt him in the polls. Abortion is wrong, he said, because it both kills and coarsens. There was a toughness to Reagan that many who knew him experienced as a kind of detachment: a willingness to set aside other people's feelings, as well as his own, for the sake of the cause he believed in. He always thought that it was his social and political message, rather than his manner, that had made a lasting impact. In his farewell address, he said: 'I never thought it was my style or the words I used that made a difference: it was the content. I wasn't a great communicator, but I communicated great things...' Underneath this lay a sense

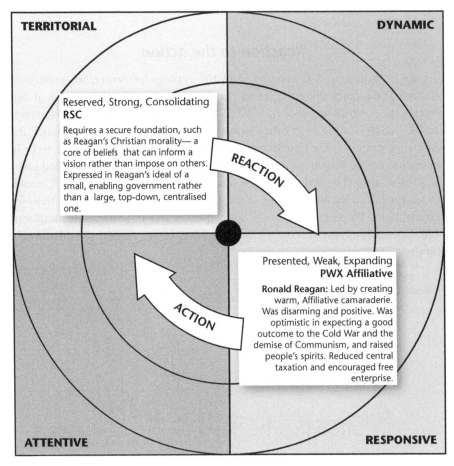

TERRITORIAL   DYNAMIC

Reserved, Strong, Consolidating
RSC
Requires a secure foundation, such
as Reagan's Christian morality— a
core of beliefs that can inform a
vision rather than impose on others.
Expressed in Reagan's ideal of a
small, enabling government rather
than a large, top-down, centralised
one.

REACTION

ACTION

Presented, Weak, Expanding
PWX Affiliative
Ronald Reagan: Led by creating
warm, Affiliative camaraderie.
Was disarming and positive. Was
optimistic in expecting a good
outcome to the Cold War and the
demise of Communism, and raised
people's spirits. Reduced central
taxation and encouraged free
enterprise.

ATTENTIVE   RESPONSIVE

Diagram 8.1: Affiliative (PWX) action and RSC reaction

of an obligation to serve others that fed a desire to see people free. Reagan once said: 'The lessons of leadership were ... hard work, a knowledge of the facts, a willingness to listen and be understanding, a strong sense of duty and direction, and a determination to do your best on behalf of the people you serve.'

Without such a moral underpinning, PWX leadership descends into mere rampant aspirationalism, the kind of chaotic, ill-disciplined and unattractive indulgence you see in some families in which the children have not been given any boundaries to their self-expression and gratification. PWX leadership can function in a healthy way only if social and moral foundations have first been laid that define the shape of the edifice to be built on top of them. Perhaps it was this familial feeling of security that led one member of staff at the White House, parodying a 1950s TV show, to call out whenever Reagan came back, 'Daddy's home!' 'Daddy's home. A wise and brave and responsible man is running things. And that's a good way to feel,' Peggy Noonan recalled of Reagan in *Time* on 13 April 1998.

How does a leader implement a PWX strategy?

There are four key elements to implementing this strategy effectively:

1. Encourage the sharing of ideas for tackling issues that concern the whole team

- Invite suggestions for solving team-management issues. Asking others to help to find a solution requires them to try to understand the problem, to see it from other people's perspectives and to acknowledge the consequences of not solving it, and inevitably will remind them of their shared responsibility for causing it!
- Create your own, unique team 'contract' or 'agreement' which has been generated by all (for example, 'As a team, we agree always to take responsibility for our behaviour, always to listen in meetings...'). Once it is written up, get each member of the team to sign the sheet, including yourself, and display it for all to see. This is a wonderful way to make individuals accountable for their behaviour: it enables you to remind the team of the agreed rules and gives you criteria for what constitutes unacceptable behaviour.

2. Engender a sense of responsibility for learning

- Create a 'buddy' system in which everyone pairs with a colleague to help to solve each other's problems.

- Encourage people to try to solve their own problems on their own before asking for help. You might introduce the mantra 'brain, buddy, boss' as a way to remind them.
- Encourage independence and responsibility by allocating office jobs— someone to buy the croissants, someone to buy the flowers, someone to update the 'challenge' charts, someone to check whether projects are at 'red', 'amber' or 'green'.

3. Foster a culture of affirmation in the team

- Set an example in giving praise. People will notice and will start to use the same vocabulary.
- Set up a 'Gotcha! pot', into which a bit of pasta (say) is put every time someone is 'caught' doing something good, kind or helpful. When the pot is full, the whole team gets a reward—something the team itself can agree on. Set aside a small budget for these rewards, which need not be expensive. The key thing is that anyone can award a Gotcha! when they spot someone else doing something great, and in this way you foster a culture in which everyone is rewarded for noticing and affirming good practice.
- Set aside time in team meetings for opportunities to hear about and see each other's work.

4. Invite members of the team to create shared rituals and routines

- Have a birthday book.
- Bring croissants into the office every Thursday morning at 9am.
- Bring bags of sweets (one particular type?) to team meetings. Everyone loves sweets, even when they are on a diet!

Some examples of PWX leadership in action

- A mentor encouraging a protégée to work her way through problems facing her
- A man expressing his support and admiration for his wife as she begins a new career
- A team coach finding positive things to say about each individual's performance
- A line manager thanking someone for his contribution to the team and citing three specific ways in which his input is valued
- A teacher inviting the class to clap a child who normally struggles with good behaviour when she achieves a modest goal
- A sports team putting their arms round each other in a 'huddle' before a match

When to use a PWX strategy

- As the underlying approach in leadership, it ensures that the best is encouraged and released in people
- To create a culture of affirmation and praise when the mood has been critical or downbeat
- To foster an enabling leadership in which people are trusted to take responsibility
- To engender teamwork and mutual responsibility, breaking down barriers between groups or individuals
- With individuals whose confidence is low
- When a team has previously experienced a dominating, authoritarian, PSC leader and people therefore lack confidence in themselves
- Where a large element of team output is demanded, requiring individuals to work together

NINE

Jimmy Carter and the Serving Strategy (RWX)

The political landscape on which Ronald Reagan strode with such confidence in 1981 had been a more uncertain place in 1976, when Jimmy Carter defeated the incumbent Gerald Ford in the presidential election. The Democrat candidate had been a dark horse and historians say that one of the principal reasons he won was the pardon Ford had granted to Richard Nixon after the Watergate scandal. It was often alleged (though never proved) that Ford and Nixon had made a pact that if the former succeeded to the presidency once Nixon had resigned, he would pardon his old boss. It was against this backdrop of moral uncertainty that Carter arrived in the White House: an earnest, well-meaning and deeply committed Christian man.

One of his first acts in office was to order the unilateral removal of all nuclear weapons from South Korea. He also announced his intention to remove all American troops from that country. In his first month as president, he cut the defence budget by $6 billion. His early instinct was to scale down America's military operations worldwide. The Vietnam War had ended the year before he took office, and Carter seemed uncomfortable with the high-profile, dominating approach of his predecessors. One of his most controversial achievements was the final negotiation of the Panama Canal Treaties, which were signed in September 1977. These in effect transferred control of the (American-built) canal to the state of Panama, and they were bitterly opposed by both the Republican Party and a section of the American public. The move was regarded as a major mistake, which reduced America's ability both to control the flow of goods through the canal and to extract revenue from it; yet it expressed Carter's moral instinct that power, control and ownership should be given, as far as possible, to local peoples rather than being retained in the hands of a centralized empire. His domestic policies similarly showed a commitment to decentralize services. He brought in strong environmental legislation, deregulated the trucking, airline, rail, finance, communications and oil industries and bolstered the social-security system. At the same time, reflecting his bias towards people who had been marginalized and overlooked, he appointed record numbers of women and people from ethnic minorities to significant positions in the government.

Carter's early posture in both domestic and foreign policy represented a marked shift from previous administrations. Small in stature and a man of strong religious convictions, he lacked the personal charisma and flair to dominate the public stage and seemed more at home in the roles of pastor and preacher than as president of the most powerful country on earth. His emphasis on the rights of others was not what Americans had come to expect from their leaders. That is not to say that previous administrations had been casual about human rights, but that such concerns had probably been seen as secondary to American growth and dominance. For Carter, they came first. Other things—economic success, military power, global political control—he believed would follow if America got its priorities right.

One incident is more revealing than any other about the workings of his mind. In 1979, the energy market collapsed, sending oil prices spiralling. Carter was due to deliver his fifth major speech on energy; but he felt that the American people were no longer listening and so instead he went to Camp David and for 10 days met with governors, mayors, religious leaders, scientists, economists and ordinary citizens. Sitting on the floor, he took notes on their comments, and especially wanted to hear criticism. His pollster told him that the people simply faced a crisis of confidence after the assassination of John F Kennedy, the Vietnam War and Watergate. Carter went on national television and said: 'I want to talk to you right now about a fundamental threat to American democracy. ... The threat is nearly invisible in ordinary ways. It is a crisis of confidence. It is a crisis that strikes at the very heart and soul and spirit of our national will. We can see this crisis in the growing doubt about the meaning of our own lives and in the loss of a unity of purpose for our nation.'

Carter's instinct was to listen rather than to command. He felt the need both to understand and to share in the problems of the people he led. Following the recommendations of the Department of Energy he had created, he wore sweaters, installed solar panels on the roof of the White House, installed a wood stove in his living quarters and ordered the General Services Administration to turn off the hot water supply in some government buildings. Across the country, thermostats were installed in both government and commercial buildings to stop people turning up the heating in the winter and the air conditioning in the summer.

There is something powerful and challenging about Carter's integrity in these choices. He felt deeply uncomfortable about calling on others to make sacrifices that he and his staff were not ready to make. The congruence of his words and actions was remarkable in a world in which so many politicians are busy constructing an image. He was willing to be openly vulnerable and ask for help: to reveal to the world his weakness rather than bluster and pretend to be strong. It is difficult to dismiss his conduct as anything other than authentic.

Authenticity is something that is mentioned a great deal in leadership thinking today. However, the reality is often rather less challenging and disconcerting than it should be. The leader who allows herself to identify personally with suffering is a rare creature. Of course, politicians put in brief appearances in slums and ghettoes, but how many actually make sacrifices themselves that match those of the general population? As the people of Paris starved in 1789, Marie Antoinette was accused (wrongly, as it happens) of uttering the infamous words 'Let them eat cake!' George W Bush was severely criticized for his 'fly over' New Orleans after the devastation of Hurricane Katrina, rather than getting his feet (let alone his hands) dirty. We are quick to charge our leaders with hypocrisy, with saying one thing and doing another—and yet we are taken aback when we encounter a leader who is committed enough to get personally involved, in a costly, self-sacrificial way, in the cause they are working for.

In recent years, such a figure has been the Burmese democrat Aung San Suu Kyi. Held under house arrest in Rangoon for many years, she was given the opportunity by the military junta to travel to London, where her British husband (whom she had not seen for over three years) was dying of cancer. However, she suspected that once she had left the country she would not be allowed to return, and so she gave up the last chance to see her husband and chose instead to remain in Burma, in captivity alongside her people. On a smaller scale, in 2006, John Sentamu, the Archbishop of York (the second most important see in the Church of England), felt compelled to identify himself with the plight of the victims of war in the Middle East. Instead of waging a political campaign, however, he had his head shaved and spent a week living in the cathedral in a tent, praying and fasting. The sight of a purple-robed archbishop on his knees under canvas was both disturbing and compelling and there are several stories of people finding faith or hope after meeting him.

What the Serving strategy can achieve

This is the RWX Serving strategy. It involves the leader paying attention to the back stage of each situation rather than the front. Instead of concentrating on appearances and public perceptions and the management of political or corporate image, he chooses to attend to what is going on round the back, behind the scenes rather than in the limelight. Thus, Carter sensed that behind the scenes the American people were no longer listening, they were gripped by some unease, some angst, and he needed to listen to this and understand it before he acted. And on this back stage the leader *keeps his emotional and strategic boundaries open* (using weak rather than strong force). Instead of having a set policy or approach that he is going to follow no matter what, he seeks to respond to the needs of each situation even as they emerge. He chooses to allow himself to submit to the agenda of those around him and follow that—rather like a good sister in charge of a hospital ward, who knows the needs of her patients and is always busy moving from one situation to another.

One of the most potent counters to the emphasis on the competence, strength and dominance of leaders over the past two decades has been Robert K Greenleaf's book *Servant Leadership*. His original essay 'The Servant as Leader' set out what he saw as the antithesis between 'the servant-led leader' and 'the leader-led servant'. 'The servant-leader is servant first. ... He or she is sharply different from the person who is leader first, perhaps because of the need to assuage an unusual power drive or to acquire material possessions. For such it will be a later choice to serve—after leadership is established.' For Greenleaf, there is a clear moral difference between leading others from a desire to dominate and leading them from a desire to serve. This perspective has rightly found a powerful voice in a leadership industry that all too often cultivates (whether overtly or covertly) the power of the leader to dominate.

Many have seen echoes of religion in the paradigm of the servant-leader. For many in the Christian church, the phrase is deeply evocative of the language

Jesus used about himself and about the call to leadership. One day, two of his disciples were squabbling about which of them was the more important. When Jesus heard them, he said: 'If anyone wants to be first, he must be the very last, and the servant of all' (Mark 9.35). He went on to say that this priority was crucial to his own identity, for 'the Son of Man did not come to be served, but to serve, and to give his life as a ransom for many' (Mark 10.45). Jesus epitomized this in the way he spent time with the rejects of his day, the homeless, the sick, the dysfunctional, the overlooked. He hung out with those who were weak and poor—indeed, it was usually the rich and the powerful who opposed him, in part because they were shamed by his generosity. Jesus saw beauty in those whom others thought ugly, and potential in those whom others had written off. His paradoxical 'last shall be first' teachings were nowhere more explicit than in what has come to be known as the Beatitudes: the list of blessings he promises for those who seek the kingdom of God. 'Blessed are the poor in spirit, for theirs is the kingdom of heaven. Blessed are those who mourn, for they will be comforted. Blessed are the meek, for they will inherit the earth...' (Matthew 5.3-5).

Two years later, when Jesus got down on his knees to wash the calloused feet of his disciples, an act that only a servant would be expected to do, it was so unsettling that one of them, Simon Peter, at first refused to let him to do it. He couldn't reconcile the lordship of Jesus with such a menial task. His own paradigm of power and leadership resisted the idea that his Lord should do anything so humiliating. Jesus' life of service was problematic also for the leaders of his day, as it has been for others since. The Jews were waiting for a Messiah who would overthrow the imperial rule of Rome. Muslims believe that Jesus was rescued from the cross before he died, as it is impossible that a great prophet could die in such a way. The servanthood of Jesus, which is at the centre of the Christian faith, is deeply disconcerting.

In recent decades, figures such as Mahatma Gandhi, Mother Teresa and Archbishop Desmond Tutu have likewise been deeply unsettling in the way they have poured out their lives sacrificially for the good of others, pricking our consciences and compelling us to reconsider our attitude to others. However, as *leaders* they are all too easily dismissed as mavericks and eccentrics. Of course, it is true that there is a difference between a politician and a prophet, a statesman and a servant—these callings are not the same. But does that have to mean that a politician cannot be a prophet as well, and a statesman can't be a servant? It all depends on how that service is practised.

Arguably, the failure of someone like Carter to succeed as a political leader was due not to his attitude of service (which only gave him authenticity) but to his inability to act decisively and with appropriate strength when required. Two days after his speech about America's 'malaise', and in the face of the energy crisis, Carter asked for the resignations of his entire Cabinet. In his eyes, this was a necessary admission that so far his administration had failed. However, to the public it gave the impression that the White House was in disarray. It undermined people's confidence in the president and his administration at a time when what they needed was reassurance. It left people feeling lost and adrift.

Again, it demonstrated perfectly the impact of the RWX strategy of leadership. Instead of taking a strong lead on the front stage, Carter admitted that he, too, was struggling to cope with the situation. He was listening, but he was not pretending that he had all the solutions. The Serving strategy always pushes responsibility firmly back onto the followers. In a sense, the leader refuses to solve the problem for them, rejects their calls to fix it, to make it all better. Instead, he encourages them to attend to the problem, as he is doing, so that they can find the solution together. It is undoubtedly a more honest strategy, and one that in the long run fosters greater maturity, responsibility and understanding in followers; but at the time it is unsettling. It's essential that followers should feel a deep trust that the leader is still big enough not to be overwhelmed by events.

In the end, this was Carter's fatal weakness: he could not show that he was big enough not to be overwhelmed by events. Chief among these, perhaps, was the hostage crisis. On 4 November 1979, the American embassy in Tehran was seized by Iranian students. The overthrow of the Shah by Islamist revolutionaries earlier in the year had led to a steady deterioration in relations between Iran and America, and when the exiled Shah was allowed to go to America for medical treatment, a crowd of about five hundred seized the embassy and the ninety-odd people inside it. Carter applied economic pressure by freezing Iranian assets in America and halting imports of Iranian oil, and at the same time began several diplomatic initiatives to secure the release of the hostages. When all of these measures proved fruitless, on 24 April 1980 the armed forces attempted a rescue mission. That, too, failed. After three out of eight helicopters were disabled or crashed in the Iranian desert, the operation was aborted, with eight American personnel dead. In the end, after 440 days in captivity, the last 52 hostages were released on the day Carter left office. The crisis had been a devastating blow to national prestige.

This apparent weakness in Carter's approach seems to have been one of the factors that prompted a dramatic change of tack in his foreign policy. After the Soviets invaded Afghanistan in 1979, Carter announced what became known as the Carter Doctrine: that America would not allow any outside power to gain control of the Persian Gulf. He terminated the wheat deal that Nixon had made with the Soviet Union to promote détente and prohibited Americans from participating in the 1980 summer Olympics in Moscow. He reinstated registration for the draft for young men, to rebuild America's military power. He also commenced a covert $40-billion programme to train Islamic mujahidin in Pakistan and Afghanistan. Ronald Reagan would later expand this programme greatly as a way to contain the Soviet Union. Today, critics blame both presidents for the resulting instability in post-Soviet Afghanistan, which led to the rise of Islamic theocracy in the region and also created much of the current problem of Islamic fundamentalism.

Reaction to the action

This unexpected switch from Carter's instinctive Serving posture to one of greater aggression and domination illustrates the strange paradox that lies at the heart of the RWX strategy. In the ecology of power, this is paired with the Commanding PSC strategy. The act of serving, if you like, vacates space for others to impose their own control. It allows others to come onto the front stage and dictate events, as both the Iranian students and the Soviets did. At the same time, if the Serving leader feels that things are slipping away from him, he may suddenly conclude that he needs to reassert control on the front stage and often his response is a PSC one. It is rather like the panicky reaction of the driver who, having allowed his child to hold the steering wheel for a while, suddenly finds himself wrenching it back again as the car heads towards a tree; or the teacher who, having given her students a free rein in the classroom, suddenly senses that they are taking advantage and things have gone too far, and she then clamps down much more severely than she normally does.

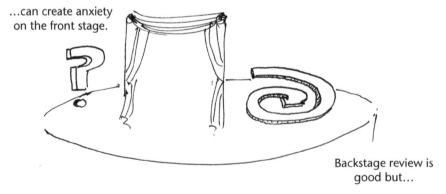

...can create anxiety on the front stage.

Backstage review is good but...

This kind of action and reaction is characteristic of the RWX approach. It explains why Carter's contribution to the political scene after his presidency has met with a mixed reaction. He has campaigned for human rights and other causes, striven to resolve conflict and eradicate disease, and in particular worked tirelessly with Habitat for Humanity, which builds affordable homes in partnership with poor families. Nonetheless, his interventions are seen by some as unhelpful. They object to his criticisms of subsequent administrations and what he sees as their unjust policies, and protest at his readiness to listen to and mediate on behalf of what others regard as brutal regimes. Carter is still a powerful figure, but his power lies as much in what he *failed* to deliver as in what he succeeded in doing. For some, he recalls the confusion and indignity of a president of the United States of America sitting on the floor listening to religious leaders and environmentalists, installing wood-burning stoves in the White House, proving impotent to free hostages. His image, like any other Serving leader, destabilizes our perceptions of power and challenges us to look again at what we really want from our leaders. We play lip-service to the ideals of integrity and authenticity, but in reality we want leaders who are strong. We deride the greed of some business executives but at the same time find

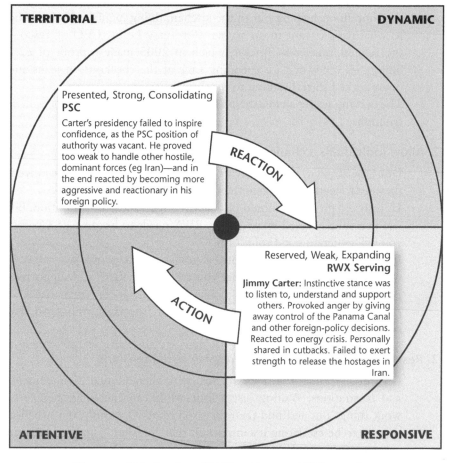

TERRITORIAL

DYNAMIC

Presented, Strong, Consolidating
PSC

Carter's presidency failed to inspire confidence, as the PSC position of authority was vacant. He proved too weak to handle other hostile, dominant forces (eg Iran)—and in the end reacted by becoming more aggressive and reactionary in his foreign policy.

REACTION

ACTION

Reserved, Weak, Expanding
RWX Serving

Jimmy Carter: Instinctive stance was to listen to, understand and support others. Provoked anger by giving away control of the Panama Canal and other foreign-policy decisions. Reacted to energy crisis. Personally shared in cutbacks. Failed to exert strength to release the hostages in Iran.

ATTENTIVE

RESPONSIVE

Diagram 9.1: Serving (RWX) action and PSC reaction

it unsettling if a CEO lives modestly and drives a Ford. There is a disturbing inconsistency in our own attitude to power when we encounter a leader who serves us. And perhaps that is why the RWX strategy is one of the most potent of all for a leader to employ.

How does a leader implement an RWX strategy?

There are four key elements to implementing this strategy effectively:

1. Identify with the situation of those you lead

- The Serving leader accepts that, first and foremost, she must identify with her followers. Instead of remaining detached, she opts to be involved.
- She may do this by physically being with her followers—working on the shop floor, helping out in the kitchen, doing menial jobs, listening to what people want to say to her. (Sir Terry Leahy, CEO of Tesco— the biggest retailer in Britain, which in 2005 made a profit of £2.2 billion—is renowned for spending time at the checkout, in jeans and open-necked shirt, listening to his shop assistants.
- The Serving leader shares the privations of her followers as well as their triumphs.

2. Allow individuals a chance to develop their own solutions

- Don't be afraid of silence. Giving people time and space is imperative if they are to learn to navigate their problems.
- Unresolved problems should be acknowledged and given attention, but not necessarily solved immediately. RWX needs to become RSX before you will generate good solutions.
- In meetings, it's very important that you convey to people by both your words and your expressions that you are being patient and supportive. Be comfortable being silent!
- Aim to resource ideas and initiatives from the background, so that others will enjoy their success.

3. Resist intervening too soon to resolve social tensions

- Give people time and space to deal with their mutual disagreements and frustrations. Waiting just a little while can encourage people to work things out and find their own solutions. Obviously, if a situation appears to be escalating it's important that you should apply a different strategy (for example PSC, if you need to take control in an authoritative way). 'Putting your foot down' straightaway can limit other people's opportunities to try out social skills, such as listening to other points of view, or to see the effect of their unkind words on other people.

- By observing social tensions, you can learn important things about people and the way they relate to others, and on reflection you can see how they are developing socially, and what sort of experiences and personalities challenge them. You will also find it very effective to have specific illustrations to share with the team when it comes to feedback.

4. Negotiate the mess

- Rather than denying and suppressing a messy situation, or trying to fix it while remaining detached, get involved.
- Others may be paralysed by the situation, but you should show confidence that a brighter future is attainable and should offer hope.

Some examples of RWX leadership in action

- An executive taking time to go round the office, listening to his staff or making cups of coffee
- A surgeon visiting her patient late at night after an operation, just to make sure they are settled before she leaves the hospital
- A host clearing up in the kitchen while the guests at his dinner party enjoy coffee
- A golf caddy supporting his player, carrying his bags, measuring distances and so on
- A teacher moving round the class, helping individual children who are stuck on an exercise
- A consultant brought in to address an IT problem, working invisibly in the background to fix it
- A government making a pact with a potential enemy to deal with something inimical to both
- A nurse caring for the patients on his ward
- Two parties reaching a covert deal before formal negotiations begin
- An executive taking a pay cut in lean times, to show solidarity with her workers

When to use an RWX strategy

- When your followers face a steep challenge, for which you must release them but also prepare them

· When you are using the Commanding PSC strategy in a situation. This should be counterpointed consciously and intentionally with a policy of serving, in little ways, to win respect and trust.

· When people are fragile or hurting, as an act of service

· To model authenticity in your own life by matching your words and your actions

· To encourage others to take responsibility and trust themselves rather than depending on you

TEN

Winston Churchill and the Pacesetting Strategy (PSX)

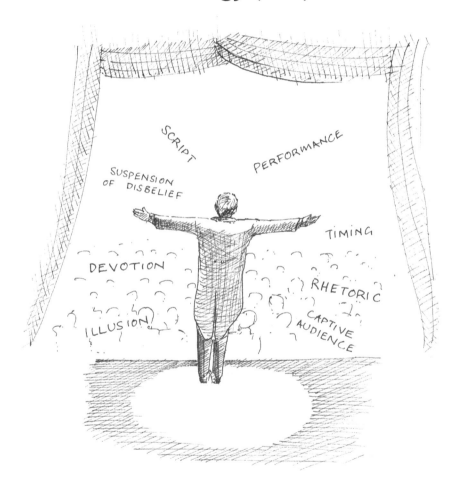

Sir Winston Leonard Spencer Churchill was a man who believed that his destiny was to bestride human history. In total contrast to the humility of Carter, or the modesty of Lincoln, or even the humorous warmth of Reagan, his ego was magnificently dominant. F S Oliver, the Conservative pamphleteer and historian, offered the following appraisal of his personality: 'From his youth up Mr. Churchill has loved with all his heart, with all his mind, with all his soul, and with all his strength, three things: war, politics and himself. He has loved war for its dangers, he loves politics for the same reason, and himself he has always loved for the knowledge that his mind is dangerous—dangerous to his enemies, dangerous to his friends, dangerous to himself. I can think of no man I have ever met who would so quickly and so bitterly eat his heart out in Paradise.'

He was a man of enormous ambition and energy, and yet for a long time the trajectory of his political career was as wide of its target as a misfired shell from one of the great warships he so loved. It was not until 1940, after the outbreak of the Second World War, at the age of 65, with the best part of 40 years in political life behind him, that Churchill was able finally to find his range. (Or perhaps it was that the target itself had moved to where he was aiming.) From that point onward, however, his contribution was immense and extraordinary. Churchill was to leave a legacy unsurpassed in modern prime-ministerial history in Britain—so much so that in 2002 (forgetting perhaps that he was half-American), the public voted him the greatest Briton ever.

Far and away the larger part of his political career had been erratic and often undistinguished. He suffered notable failures throughout his career, not least in the debacle at Gallipoli in 1915–16. Churchill proposed a plan to bring the First World War to an end by opening up a new front in Turkey. Through what appears to have been a combination of miscommunication and misfortune, the campaign became a disaster. In the first, naval attack, Britain had six out of nine battleships put out of action, three of them sunk. The subsequent amphibious assault was followed by nine months of fruitless fighting in which the Allies lost 46,000 dead before they were forced to withdraw, defeated. Churchill carried much of the blame and by the end of the year had resigned from the government.

Throughout his career, his big asset (but also his biggest problem) was that he saw everything in terms of the great global drama of political and military history. After the end of the First World War, his chief anxiety was the rearmament of Germany. Having struggled (and himself experienced battle) against an enemy that had, as he put it, 'almost single-handedly fought nearly all the world and nearly beat them,' Churchill issued what proved to be prophetic warnings during the emergence of Nazism and Adolf Hitler's rise to power throughout the 1920s and '30s. At the time, there was no appetite for such talk. The climate was one of appeasement. The cost of the last war, in both lives and money, was still being counted. Few people had either the emotional or the financial resources to face the threat of another confrontation with a resurgent, belligerent Germany. Churchill, however, always had the stomach for a fight. The image of him as the British bulldog standing up to Hitler that lives in the memory of anyone who witnessed the Blitz or other crucial battles of 1940, epitomizes the pugnacious spirit of this indomitable man.

Domestic politics is, on the whole, not as dramatic as war, nor does it usually call for great heroes. On its more mundane and pragmatic stage, Churchill's larger-than-life performance diminished between the two world wars and he was reduced to minor roles in which he could be more easily managed. He had always used the media to the hilt and he got his message about the state of Europe across through a series of commissioned articles in the *Evening Standard*. He cultivated relationships with newspaper proprietors such as Lord Beaverbrook, and when his opinions differed from theirs he would find other channels through which to express them. In 1938, when his contract with the *Standard* was terminated after a disagreement with Beaverbrook, he managed to get his articles read by millions through the *News of the World*, which was syndicated throughout both Europe and the Empire. At the same time, he churned out book after book about great British figures (including his own ancestors) and famous military campaigns. His approach to history was to write it himself; his approach to his own place in history was the same. Churchill understood the need to manage the story that was told both about world affairs and about his role in them. His instinct was always to intervene and to influence. To leave history to be written by other individuals, or even to emerge by consensus, was alien to his sense of purpose.

His unique character and role illustrate *in extremis* the leader who pursues the PSX Pacesetting strategy. We might note that he was always more at home on the front stage of politics—and the front benches of the House of Commons—than the back. 'No informed person could well deny that Winston S Churchill was probably the most spectacular showman in the history of British politics,' wrote the influential American scholar Harry Elmer Barnes.[7] Certainly, he cultivated an image quite deliberately. The cigar-chewing, victory-sign-waving, growling persona was one he adopted extensively throughout the war—he was aware that he needed to 'put it on' before going out to meet the public. He also cultivated his reputation for sharp one-liners, rehearsing quips and repartees to give him the edge in debate.

He appreciated the need to manage the front stage when communicating with the public, especially in times of high emotion or anxiety. On 4 August 1912, nine Boy Scouts, all from working-class communities in south-east London, were drowned when their boat capsized on a sailing trip down the Thames to the Isle of Sheppey. In a grand gesture, Churchill, then First Lord of

---

[7] From *The Journal of Historical Review*, Summer 1980 (Vol 1, No 1), pp163–68

the Admiralty, immediately ordered that their bodies should be brought back up the river on board a destroyer. As *HMS Fervent* sailed slowly up the Thames, thousands of people gathered on the banks to mourn the loss of innocent life. Churchill understood that working men and women would be touched and comforted more by such a gesture of respect than by any formal act of remembrance.

Perhaps his most famous frontstage acts of communication were in his speeches and his radio broadcasts to the nation in 1940, as the threat of invasion loomed. 'I have nothing to offer but blood, toil, tears and sweat,' he told the House of Commons in his first appearance as Prime Minister. He followed that closely with three more, equally famous declarations. After the defeat at Dunkirk, he assured an anxious nation: 'We shall defend our island, whatever the cost may be. We shall fight on the beaches, we shall fight on the landing grounds, we shall fight in the fields and in the streets, we shall fight in the hills; we shall never surrender.' As the Battle of Britain loomed, he urged: 'Let us therefore brace ourselves to our duties, and so bear ourselves that, if the British Empire and its Commonwealth last for a thousand years, men will still say, "This was their finest hour."' And at the height of the Battle, his bracing survey of the situation included the memorable line: 'Never in the field of human conflict was so much owed by so many to so few.'

...can rescue people from being overwhelmed by anxieties in a crisis.

A magnificent and compelling frontstage presence...

Above all, Churchill had a sense of timing. When he was finally appointed Prime Minister, he recorded that 'all my past life had been but a preparation for this hour and for this trial.' He also understood what people needed to hear and feel, and when. He was at home with the hyperbole of the moment: when the front stage was his and his alone, and the audience was gripped with fear before some mighty threat, he was at his best. In such circumstances, he seemed to grow in stature, rising to the epic occasion. Rather than being crushed by the odds stacked against him, he relished the confrontation. He used strong, rather than weak, power almost exclusively, demanding loyalty, commitment, energy, will and self-belief from those who (very much) followed in his wake. Collaboration, discussion and consensual decision-making were foreign concepts to him. So was moderation. He was notorious for his interference in the details of military operations, finding it hard to cede authority and autonomy to those under him. His 'Action this day!' memos were like a stream of consciousness he wanted implemented without debate throughout the war. He wrote in excess, drank in excess and commanded in excess. Those who served under him at that time could scarcely keep up with him, often despite being many years his junior. His instinct was always to take the battle to the enemy; retreat was rarely an option. Expanding rather than consolidating was his strategy.

These are the hallmarks of the Pacesetting leader, frontstage, strong and expanding: relentless confidence, apparently limitless drive, indomitable will, commanding presence, compelling personality, dominating authority, with vast horizons in a heroic enterprise. In the end, PSX leadership is all about the leader himself; it is his own ego projected onto a social or historical canvas, compelling circumstances around him to conform to his personal will.

What the Pacesetting strategy can achieve

There are, of course, only certain contexts in which such leadership is desirable or even tolerable. In the main, it is needed in a situation where winning is the only acceptable goal. It was necessary for Churchill, confronting the threat of a Nazi victory in Europe. It is necessary also in competitive sport. In both situations, the conflict or confrontation is specific and relatively limited in duration. Events conspire to create a particular window in which victory must be achieved; in this window, one's entire effort, and that of the team, organization, army or country one is leading, must be focused on that goal. You exert every fibre in your body, draw on all your reserves, to resist your enemy's attacks and to win. PSX leadership demands in the leader an unfailing confidence of victory even in the face of defeat.

In 2003, Martin Johnson led England to a famous victory in the Rugby Union World Cup in Sydney. The win was attributed largely to the inspirational leadership of Clive Woodward, the head coach, who had managed the preparations for this tournament over the previous seven years. The character of Woodward's leadership was essentially PSX. He had always said (and believed) that his team would win the World Cup; he never looked back and always moved quickly on from any defeat. He spared no expense on the latest and best training methods, and fostered a culture in which only winning mattered, ruthlessly ditching players who were out of form regardless of their reputation. Some commentators argue that the World Cup was won before a single game had been played: other teams simply wilted before England's ruthless imposition of its will.

Of course, there is nothing moral or good in itself about such dominance. The 'will to power' is entirely Nietzschean, and we know that it can be used as easily to abuse as to liberate. You could argue that Churchill's opponent Hitler was a similarly gifted and driven PSX leader. In fact, as many commentators have pointed out, he was in many ways the more disciplined and focused man, whose ideology opposed drunkenness, laziness and immorality and advocated self-sacrifice in the cause. Like Churchill, however, Hitler used the emotional dynamics of PSX power—in his massed rallies, his epic depictions of the struggles of the Reich after the First World War and the sense he conveyed of the place in history of the Aryan race. The danger of PSX leadership is that it demands of its followers utter loyalty and submission to the cause, whether it is good or bad.

Even when the cause is good, PSX leadership can sometimes leave a mixed legacy. I used to be involved in an organization that ran houseparties to introduce schoolchildren to the Christian faith. Its strategy, devised by its founder in the 1930s, was to concentrate on the top 30 private schools in the country—Eton, Harrow and so on—to target the people who would one day play a strategic part in the leadership of the country. The houseparties were of extraordinary benefit to me and many thousands of others who were nurtured in their faith in adolescence and on into early adulthood. The organization showed many of the classic signs of PSX leadership: it was well run and effective, with a strategic goal, a charismatic and compelling leader, a heroic sense of mission, a belief in its own historic importance and a demand for total loyalty from its staff and volunteers. I recall giving up an opportunity to tour Japan with my university track and field team in order to help out on a week-long revision houseparty for 16-year-olds.

One outcome of those houseparties was to school a generation of leaders who went on to wield influence at the highest level in the church, in education and even in politics. That organization was like an express train speeding towards its destination, and its progress was extraordinary. However, a lot of people have fallen off the train along the way. It doesn't stop for anyone—if you're on board, you're expected to stay on, adhering to everything required of you in belief and behaviour. If you can't keep up with the pace or live up to expectations, you simply go out the window. PSX organizations almost always leave a wake of broken, disillusioned people behind them. Of course, those still involved in them scarcely notice: they have already moved on, too focused on the goal to worry about those who couldn't make it.

The reaction to the action

Personally, I will always be grateful for the impact of those summer houseparties; but I am grateful for the experience of some of the pitfalls of PSX leadership as well as its benefits. It can cause problems not only for the organization but also for the leader herself. Its intensity is rarely sustainable for long. Typically, a PSX leader suffers periods of burnout and collapse. Churchill's life was blighted by a periodic depression, which became so familiar to him he dubbed it his 'black dog'. What such leaders have to fear is that when the spotlight is not on them, they often find it hard to know who they are. Their sense of self is so bound up with their public image and the power associated with it that outside that context anxiety and self-doubt can creep in. Coupled with their exhaustion after their tremendous exertion on the front stage, this means that such a leader

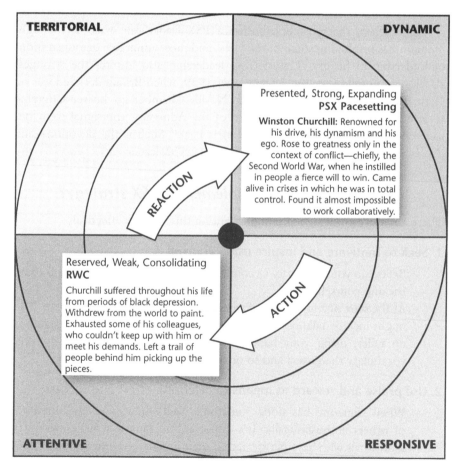

Diagram 10.1: Pacesetting (PSX) action and RWC reaction

may be vulnerable and unstable and may finally withdraw. The reaction PSX generates in the ecology of power is RWC—reserved, empty and passive, the squeezed-out lemon after the juice has flavoured the meal.

PSX leadership is leadership for a season, for a very particular kind of context, where the heightened drama of a confrontation or competition makes the most extreme demands. Leaders who choose to use this strategy need to recognize this—and also need to be aware that the followers of a PSX leader may reject him when the crisis has passed. Churchill experienced just such a desertion in 1945 even before the war was finally over, when, after he had led the country through its 'darkest hour' to victory in Europe, his party was voted out of government. In a similar way, Woodward's demands for even greater control following England's World Cup victory were resisted, and this ultimately led to his resignation. Followers can live with the intensity in times of crisis, but rarely want it in times of stability.

Nonetheless, the rare contribution a PSX leader can make at the right moment has resulted in some of the finest and most admirable demonstrations of leadership in history. This style of leadership also inspires the strongest attachment in followers. On 3 September 1939, when Britain declared war on Germany and the then Prime Minister, Neville Chamberlain, invited Churchill to join his War Cabinet as First Lord of the Admiralty, the signal went out to every naval ship and base: 'Winston is back!' Such is the devotion—and dependence—that can be generated by a great PSX leader.

How does a leader implement a PSX strategy?

There are four key elements to implementing this strategy effectively:

1. Seek to motivate and inspire using yourself

- Believe in your authority to command and lead people—PSX is all about backing yourself!
- At the start of a new piece of work, consciously try to change pace. This might include talking in a more animated and 'projected' way, standing up taller, using your hands as you speak, choosing more dynamic vocabulary than usual and so on.

2. Use praise and reward as means to celebrate effort and success

- When someone has done something well, draw it to the attention of others enthusiastically. It's important to choose a wide variety of individuals who have performed to their limits.

3. Set goals for individuals and groups

· Use a simple 'Next big challenge' sheet to monitor the team's progress. A 'challenge' might be to deliver a report by a deadline, visit a certain percentage of stakeholders or reduce waste by so many per cent.

· Make sure the challenges change frequently. The sense of achievement and momentum is what you are after. Any challenge that lasts longer than four weeks is probably too long.

· Use red, amber and green 'lights' to indicate how confident and how effective the team is in each project. A green light means: 'We're all systems go.' An amber says: 'We're moving, but could go faster.' A red says: 'We're stuck and need help to get going again.'

4. Make your standards explicit and be available

· Show the team what a project should look like when it is finished to a high standard.

· Make it clear how people can come to you with issues and problems. PSX leadership always tends to produce withdrawn, RWC behaviour in some people.

· Spend time 'on the ground' being available. Don't be remote or even absent when you are pursuing a PSX strategy.

Some examples of PSX leadership in action

· A sales department planning how to increase market share through more aggressive marketing tactics

· A coach pushing an athlete with a strict, ambitious training regime before a major competition

· A charismatic leader persuading her community to follow her on a risky path they would otherwise have avoided

· A mother promising a trip to a theme park 'once the Star Chart has been completed'

· A confident and lively child in the playground inventing a new, imaginative game and persuading others to join in

· An executive demanding a 10-per-cent increase in performance from his sales staff in the second quarter

When to use a PSX strategy

- In a competitive situation, to drive up performance
- When faced with a threat that requires self-belief and aggressive determination
- To motivate people to give their best
- To set an example for others to follow
- For short periods of time to inject a sense of urgency and excitement
- To give people experience of winning and losing

ELEVEN

Martin Luther King and the Visionary Strategy (RSX)

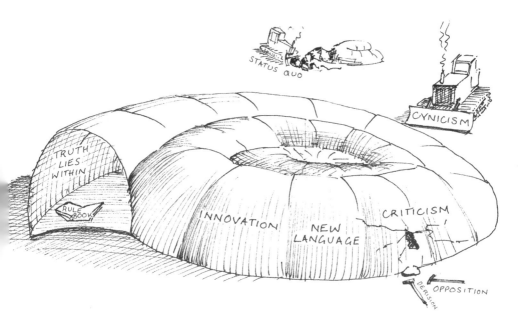

Among those images of the second half of the 20th century most deeply seared into the Western mind is one of an animated young black man with his arm raised, his finger pointing to the sky, as he addresses a huge rally. The man, of course, is Martin Luther King, and the date is 28 August 1963. He is delivering the speech that climaxes in one of the most widely known and quoted lines of modern times: 'I have a dream...'

King's was a life summed up by that one, single phrase. He was compelled by a dream of the end of the racial segregation that had endured in America, and in particular the southern states, since the civil war nearly a century earlier. King had experienced that segregation at first hand. He had been excluded from white educational institutions, been refused service at milk bars that were for whites only, been obliged to give up his seat on a bus for a white person; he had experienced imprisonment and would ultimately suffer assassination for the dream that one day such segregation would come to an end.

What set him apart from his fellow black Americans was three things: the advantage of education, a calling to religious leadership and a deep, burning passion against the injustices suffered by his community. Others had one or two of those attributes, but in King they converged into a vocation that drove him into the centre stage of one of the most momentous dramas in recent American history. He had take his doctorate at Boston University and was by nature a studious man. His knowledge of theology, biblical scholarship and political theory funded a career not in academia or the church but in political activism. His later speeches and, especially, his open letters to his fellow clergy reveal how in those earlier years of study he laid down an understanding of social justice and the rule of God that enabled him to think deeply about them. Like most activists—and all the more because he had a young family and because he was caught up in the stream of confrontations and crises that only grew stronger throughout the 1960s—he had comparatively little time for study and reflection later in his life. You get the sense that he drew heavily on the wells of thought he had bored as a young man. Whether or not they would ever have dried up we will never know, as his life was cut short at the age of only 39.

Second, King was informed by a sense that he was called to the ministry. Though he was to serve for only a short period as a pastor, in a local church in Montgomery, Alabama, his roots in the church and his fellowship with other Christians, both black and white, gave depth and breadth to his vision and filled it with confidence. At the heart of his thinking on desegregation lay a theological conviction, that all human beings are equal: equally created in the image of God, and so equally able to share in the benefits and rights of civil society. It was also his theology that prevented King from embracing the doctrine of black supremacy that some in the Black Power movement were promoting. For him, the Civil Rights movement was never about black domination but about black freedom.

Third, King was a man fuelled by righteous indignation at the injustices he witnessed around him. Perhaps because he himself had had a stable, loving home, he didn't have the slightly cowed mentality of some of his fellow blacks. He had seen how many simply accepted their place in society and made no protest at the way they were marginalized; but he was sufficiently sure of his own dignity not only to resist such treatment but also to believe that it could and should be resisted by others, too.

Most historians date the beginning of the modern civil rights movement in America as 1 December 1955. That was the day when, in Montgomery, an obscure 42-year-old seamstress called Rosa Parks refused to give up her seat on a bus to a white man. Her solitary act of defiance began a movement that was to end legal segregation in America. It so happened that King was the pastor of Dexter Avenue Baptist Church in Montgomery. He had arrived with his family just a few months earlier and was still finding his feet, but as the trial of Mrs Parks on 5 December approached, encouraged by others in the black community, he felt compelled to lead some kind of protest. What developed was the first of many boycotts of the buses in cities across the country. King soon became a mix of organizer and mouthpiece. He was involved in public meetings that rallied support, as it was vital, if the protest was to be effective, that the entire black community took part in it. Otherwise, if even a few had continued to use the buses, the symbolic significance of the boycott might have been lost. The protest depended on the power of collective action—not least in arranging other means of transport, for otherwise black workers who had ridden to work every day on the buses would risk losing their jobs. If you had been in Montgomery over Christmas and the New Year in 1955/6, you would have seen an unusual sight: many black people walking miles to work while others cycled or were ferried by those who owned cars and taxis. The boycott went on for over a year and the immense organization required put a strain on everyone involved, not least King.

The response of the white community was predictable enough. Imaginary traffic offences were invented and people were arrested. One night, returning home from a meeting by car and keeping well under the speed limit, King himself was stopped and taken in on a trumped-up charge. Only a few weeks later, things turned much nastier and, while King was out speaking at a meeting, his home and family were fire-bombed. Mercifully, neither Coretta, his wife, nor his children were injured. The opposition to the dream had started, and it was time to discover whether the vision had any substance.

The struggle that was to follow lasted 12 more years. The key strategies of the Civil Rights movement were devised and orchestrated by King and his close followers and included mass civil disobedience, or 'passive resistance'—the form of opposition first used by Gandhi and his followers in South Africa some 60 years earlier and then developed in the struggle for India's independence in the 1940s. Civil disobedience involved a peaceful refusal to comply with an unjust demand. So, when the authorities banned a protest march, the demonstrators would assemble and walk in peace nonetheless. When the police used batons and water cannons to disperse them, even though they were doing nothing to deserve arrest or provoke violence, their response was entirely peaceful. When they were beaten, they took the blows. When they were arrested, they did not resist. Indeed, part of the idea was simply to overwhelm the bureaucracies that imposed this injustice. The courts and the prisons couldn't cope with the numbers they had to deal with and at times they broke down. Meanwhile, the publicity the strategy was generating in the media was massive and, in general, highly favourable.

Increasingly, King's task was to be a figurehead, standing in front of his people and calling them on to the Promised Land of a desegregated America. It was in this role that he delivered some of his most memorable and visionary sermons and speeches. His rhetoric was highly visual and used concrete imagery to drive home the legitimacy of black people's claims. In 1968, he gave an address that included these words, which illustrate his straightforward use of extended metaphor. 'In a sense, we've come to our nation's capital to cash a cheque. When the architects of our republic wrote the magnificent words of the Constitution and the Declaration of Independence, they were signing a promissory note to which every American was to fall heir. This note was a promise that all men, yes, black men as well as white men, would be guaranteed the "inalienable rights" of "life, liberty and the pursuit of happiness". It is obvious today that America has defaulted on this promissory note, insofar as her citizens of colour are concerned. Instead of honouring this sacred obligation, America has given the Negro people a bad cheque, a cheque which has come back marked "insufficient funds". But we refuse to believe that the bank of justice is bankrupt. We refuse to believe that there are insufficient funds in the great vaults of opportunity of this nation. And so, we've come to cash this cheque, a cheque that will give us upon demand the riches of freedom and the security of justice.'

King drew on traditions of African-American folk preaching in which spiritual and invisible concerns are highly materialized as actual, felt realities. Critics have often pointed out that he was a plagiarist and that large sections of his addresses were taken from other people's sermons. I wouldn't want to condone that, but I think it is an indication that he chose to speak the language of the street, to use rhetoric that would connect with his followers. The real motive force behind his leadership, however, was his sense that he had glimpsed the future of which he spoke. In this respect, he was a seer: a prophet who not only pronounced judgement on the injustice of the structures around him but also foresaw that they could not stand in the face of legitimate protest.

I believe King's life exemplified the use of the RSX strategy and illustrated its power more vividly than anyone else in recent years. It may seem strange to locate his influence on the 'reserved' back stage rather than on the 'presented' front stage. Certainly, King made use of the front stage. Like Churchill, he became adept at public speaking, and his sense of timing and drama was important to the impact of the civil rights campaign. But, unlike Churchill, King didn't speak from a position of power on the front stage of government. Churchill was the central figure in the authority system of his day in Britain; King, however, was excluded from any such position of power. It is only in more recent times that his black successors such as Jesse Jackson, Colin Powell and Condoleezza Rice have found it possible to gain acceptance in the halls of power in Washington. In King's day, he could only protest. However influential, his was a voice from the political margins. In a sense, he lived on and spoke from the hidden-away back stage of American society—the part that many people wanted to be suppressed. He spoke for, and to, the conscience of America about the consequences of its frontstage politics and economics. In this regard, he didn't have at his disposal any of the kinds of power at his disposal his opponents had. He didn't have the authority to impeach politicians or prosecute police officers who attacked peaceful demonstrators. He didn't have the influence to get state legislation on desegregation changed. In this regard, his power lay in more subversive strategies that undermined the moral legitimacy of the regime that he and his followers opposed.

Nor, however, did he accept the status quo and simply empathize with the suffering of his people. Like Churchill, he compelled the black population—some of whom were reluctant to follow his lead—to find the courage and the will to undertake the pilgrimage to that Promised Land. Unlike Carter's Serving strategy, which sought to listen to people's anxieties and support them, King's was a Visionary strategy, which stirred the hearts and minds of those around him.

What the Visionary strategy can achieve

The RSX strategy often has to make use of subversive tactics: without access to the channels of authority, it exercises influence through protest and catalysis. This Visionary strategy offers people another way, an alternative to the one they have hitherto taken as read. It begins by questioning the assumption that things cannot be different, and it asks: 'What would the world look like if we rewrote the script, if we tore up the rule book and started again?' In many organizations, imagination has simply been squashed over years of mundane productivity. Creativity quickly drains away unless it is fed and fostered. Some organizations simply lack the leadership to imagine a different world—to believe there could be another solution to their sales problem, or a different way to tackle the difficulties in their supply chain, or a new approach to 'people development'.

The RSX strategy also seeks to reform the language that followers use about themselves. Most people have an inbuilt resistance to something novel, which destabilizes the old and the familiar. 'Better the devil you know...' 'If it ain't broke, don't fix it'—this is the language of the weary manager, tired and cynical about new initiatives that promise much and deliver little. There has been a growing realization over the past 50 years that the language a leader uses to describe his role, his work, the organization in which he leads, has more power than he may be aware of. If you talk to someone who is depressed, for example, they may talk a lot about things being grey or black, about feeling trapped and powerless, unable to move forward. The language they use doesn't merely reveal how they see and feel about the world they inhabit—it's as if they are actually defining the colour and size and shape of that world.

I can remember a sustained period of depression I myself suffered. If you had asked me then to describe myself, I would have struggled to find positive words. My wife helped me one day to think about the impact of the negative images of myself that I lived with, and in a sense gave life to. She suggested that I needed to put these to death and bring to life instead some new, more affirming ways of speaking about myself. I began to try, writing down some positive statements about myself as a man, a father, a husband, a leader. I found that, gradually, I started to *inhabit* this new language about myself. Instead of being hunched, dishevelled and scowling, I began to walk tall, dress smartly, look people in the eye once more and believe in myself. The language slowly changed me.

King offered black Americans a new language in which to think of themselves. His speeches did more than merely stir emotions: they reinvigorated cowed and crushed imaginations, opening up broad horizons and depicting strong and noble shoulders ready and able to bear the weight of power and responsibility. Churchill, too, had his Visionary side, and his early war speeches provide a powerful and familiar example of this 'world-absorbing' power of speech in leadership. In the dark days of 1940, he used language to redefine the reality of millions of fearful folk gathered round their wireless sets. It was vital that he should project a version of reality opposed to the one that all the evidence set against them, and this he did, not by denying that evidence but by confronting it and also transforming it. The threat of invasion was something not to make them cower but to inspire resilience, resolve and courage. This island was portrayed as the last bastion of hope for the free world, standing alone against a terrible enemy. Churchill knew that ambivalence would be fatal—that if people were to accept the suffering that lay in store, they would need to see themselves in heroic terms, as engaged in a great struggle against dark powers. To create this perception, Churchill drew on the ancient Anglo-Saxon vocabulary at the heart of the English language. Thus the RSX leader sees herself as a storyteller or dramatist whose job is to create, with her audience, a world that is captivating, robust and compelling.

What, then, must a leader do in order to remodel reality for her followers? First, she must see her words as not merely informing but *transforming*. Second, she must invite people to participate in the drama of history. It's not inappropriate to use the word 'drama' in relation to leadership.[8] The leader

---

[8] Paul Ricoeur writes interestingly about the close relationship between metaphor and narrative in *The Rule of Metaphor: Multi-Disciplinary Studies of the Creation of Meaning in Language* (University of Toronto Press, 1977), trans Robert Czerny, pp19 and 24.

is a director who creates a piece of theatre in which she invites her followers to play their parts. She needs to be the one who draws the 'story arc' of the whole community. She may leave it to her cast to develop the script themselves, but she herself takes responsibility for the trajectory of the story. She must understand the characters and the themes and be aware of the moods, the threats, the climaxes. And she must explain to the cast the nature of the current scene, and how it relates to the bigger story.

More and more senior executives are becoming no more than bean counters, ministers of the spreadsheet, exegetes of the financial 'word'. They live in the prosaic language of financial reports, in thrall to the minutiae. This is a terrible price to pay for efficiency, because it robs organizations of the imagination, vision and perspective that characterize all great human endeavours. Many businesses have traded these for the levers of contractual controls, reward schemes and incentives.

When we appreciate the role of language in constructing our worlds, rather than merely reporting them, then it becomes clear that leadership is fundamentally about language. The words a leader uses are not simply a vehicle with which to convey information and deliver orders. Rather, his language itself creates the system of meaning in which the community functions and operates. So, for example:

- George W Bush uses the language of the cartoon strip to construct a black-and-white world of 'good guys' and 'bad guys' that legitimates his foreign-policy agenda.
- A corporate executive may speak in terms of execution, delivery, re-engineering and deployment—imagery derived from the world of systems and mechanics—to construct a system of meaning around the core values of reliability, performance and control.
- A politician may talk of empowerment, sharing, value and vision—metaphors that refer back to the world of the tribe—to construct a system of meaning around the core values of loyalty and responsibility.

A leader who employs the Visionary strategy examines carefully the imagery she uses. Many leaders simply adopt metaphors that are 'given' them by current social discourse, like people who dress shabbily in hand-me-downs or clothes picked up at jumble sales; but genuine progress—let alone transformation—rarely occurs without the adoption of a new vocabulary.

The reaction to the action

In creating a new vocabulary and a new vision, the leader also creates, almost accidentally, a new 'called-out' community, as people start to hear, learn and 'live' the new language. In the ecology of power, the corollary of the RSX strategy is PWC, as followers experience a sense of belonging together. In part, this is because they are distinguished by their differences from the wider community: they believe in a different message, a different gospel. There is always a sense of community when you feel embattled—and when a group of people hold radically different beliefs, the private world it creates often gives them such a sense of identity and security that they're willing and able to do things their opponents would not think possible. Perhaps that's why those people who marched peacefully behind King or under his banner—both black and white—were ready to suffer the batons of the police.

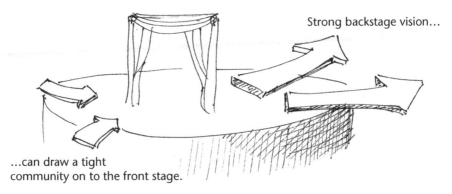

Strong backstage vision...

...can draw a tight community on to the front stage.

This is also why those outside the movement feel so threatened. On 3 April 1968, King told a euphoric crowd: 'It really doesn't matter what happens now. ... Like anybody, I would like to live a long life. Longevity has its place, but I'm not concerned about that now. I just want to do God's will. And he's *allowed* me to go up to the mountain! And I've looked over, and I've seen the Promised Land. I may not get there with you. But I want you to know tonight that we, as a people, will get to the Promised Land. And so I'm happy tonight. I'm not worried about anything. I'm not fearing any man. Mine eyes have seen the glory of the coming of the Lord!'

Those words were to prove prophetic. The very next day, he was shot dead in his hotel room in an assassination that many believe may have been orchestrated by the FBI. His death provoked a wave of riots across America, but it also paved the way for an unstoppable revolution in civil rights for black Americans.

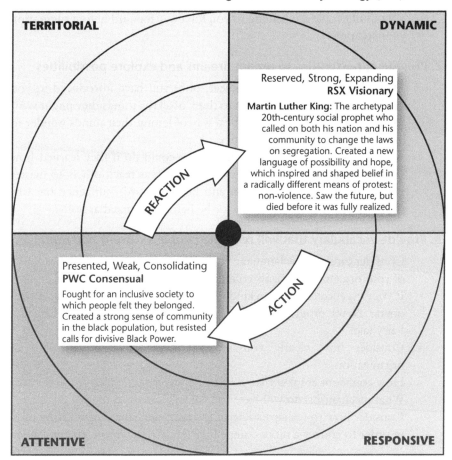

Diagram 11.1: Visionary (RSX) action and PWC reaction

How does a leader implement an RSX strategy?

There are four key elements to implementing this strategy effectively:

1. Highlight the current problems without providing premature solutions

- Most vision is born out of pain and dissatisfaction with the status quo. Allow discontent to brew.
- Help people to focus on current problems rather than simply papering over them.
- Allow unresolved issues to remain so and let others take responsibility for solving them.

- Wait until people are coming to you for a way forward before suggesting your solution.

2. Provide opportunities to dream dreams and explore possibilities

- At the beginning of a new project, once you have introduced it, you might ask members of the team to think of all the things they might want to know by the end. This can be a way of letting their minds wander to big ideas and exciting possibilities.
- Ask them to imagine all the things they could do if they learned how to (for example) run a training course—such as teach others to master a skill, win greater recognition and better rewards, influence the way things are done in the company or be better organized at home.

3. Provide vocabulary that will redefine people's current horizons

- Consider carefully the language you use. Examine the current vocabulary of your organization for its colour, shape and texture.
- If your organization were a kind of drama, what sort would it be? A soap opera? News programme? Factual documentary? Comedy? Tragedy? Fairy tale?
- Consider how clearly you see the overall 'story arc' of your organization.
- How confident are you that your cast appreciate it?
- What mechanisms do you have to communicate it to them?
- Consider how to reshape some of the language your organization uses, in order to convey a more compelling sense of the future you envisage.

4. Provide opportunities to build a sense of community—vision (RSX) is often closely related to belonging (PWC)

- Create a safe environment in which people can say anything without criticism.
- Respect every idea put forward.
- Suggest off-the-wall ideas yourself in order to model risk-taking. Make sure that some of your ideas can be improved on!

Some examples of RSX leadership in action

- A board choosing to double its investment in R&D
- A politician speaking in a campaign to reduce global poverty through fair trade
- A poet writing a ballad of love and remembrance

- A teacher capturing his students' imagination with his tales from history
- An engineer devising a new technology to improve a medical procedure
- A pharmaceutical company developing a new anti-cancer drug over seven years of research
- A priest inspiring followers, through his teaching of the Bible, to greater devotion and love

When to use an RSX strategy

- When more of the same is not going to change things for the better
- When structural forms of power are not available to you
- When people lack vision, hope and momentum
- In the face of a challenge or threat it will take courage and sacrifice to survive

TWELVE

Nelson Mandela and the Consensual Strategy (PWC)

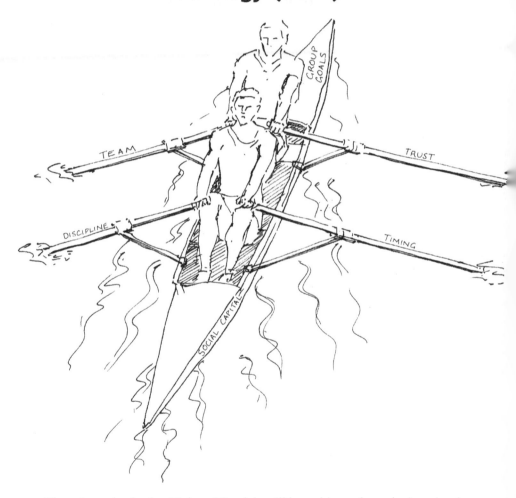

There is no doubt that Nelson Mandela will leave his mark on the imagination of a generation around the world. For many, it's remarkable enough that a man who had endured 27 long years in prison—mostly doing hard labour on Robben Island—emerged unbroken. Others are profoundly impressed by his ability to go beyond recrimination and retaliation to find a more peaceful way. For others, he simply represents a symbol of fortitude and hope in the face of the darkness of human wickedness.

Mandela was born in the black 'homeland' of Transkei on 18 July 1918. His Xhosa name Rolihlahla could be taken to mean 'troublemaker,' a connotation that was to prove prophetic. Like King's, his country was racially segregated, under a policy of apartheid (Afrikaans for 'separation') adopted in 1948. People were classified as white, black, Indian or coloured (that is, mixed-race) and on that basis were kept apart from each other. In particular, black people (who constituted the great majority of the population) were legally citizens of various 'homelands' which were nominally sovereign nations but in fact were more akin to the Native American reservations or Australia's aboriginal reserves. In effect, this deprived non-white people of the vote (and other polical influence), as it restricted their rights to a distant territory they might never even have visited.

Like King, Mandela's political roots lay in protest. Believing that peaceful opposition was the best strategy, he joined the Youth League of the African National Congress and became involved in programmes of passive resistance to the laws that required blacks to carry passes and kept them in a state of permanent servility. However, in 1956 the South African government tried 156 of its principal opponents in the ANC for treason, and Mandela was among them. The trial dragged on for five years and ended in the acquittal of every one of the defendants—but by then the country had witnessed the massacre of peaceful black demonstrators at Sharpeville in 1960 and unrest was spreading. The government was intent on crushing all opposition, and most liberation movements, including the ANC, were banned.

Perhaps this was a turning point for Mandela. In 1961, he became the leader of the ANC's armed wing, which he had co-founded. He co-ordinated a campaign of sabotage against military, government and civilian targets, and planned for a possible guerrilla war if this failed to bring an end to apartheid. Now the most wanted man in South Africa, he was on the run for more than a year, so elusive the police nicknamed him 'the Black Pimpernel'. For a while he went abroad to enlist support for the ANC; but on his return he was arrested and sentenced to five years' hard labour for 'inciting African workers to strike' and 'leaving the country without valid travel documents'.

Within a matter of weeks, Mandela was dragged from prison to be charged with 'complicity in over 200 acts of sabotage aimed at facilitating violent revolution and an armed invasion of the country'. If convicted, this time he faced almost certain death. In the courtroom, he made a statement that would change the way he was perceived throughout the country: 'During my lifetime I have dedicated myself to the struggle of the African people. I have fought against white domination, and I have fought against black domination. I have cherished the ideal of a democratic and free society in which all persons live together in harmony and with equal opportunities. It is an ideal which I hope to live for and to achieve. But, if needs be, it is an ideal for which I am prepared to die.'

Mandela found that this stand gave him moral authority and he began to assume the leadership of the movement. His response to the ordeal of incarceration on Robben Island was to encourage his fellow prisoners to educate themselves. As they left their cells each morning to toil in the quarries, buffeted by the merciless southeaster or broiled by the sun, each team was assigned an instructor, in history, economics, politics, philosophy or whatever. In this way, their minds and spirits were sustained and enriched, despite the privations they were suffering. Two decades later, Mandela began a long and laborious attempt to negotiate directly with the South African regime. Now one of the most famous prisoners in the world, he was escorted, in the greatest secrecy, to the office of President F W de Klerk, where the two men began to prepare for the transition from apartheid to full democracy. On 2 February 1990, de Klerk lifted the ban on the ANC and announced Mandela's imminent release.

What followed was a battle in diplomacy. Mandela first had to secure the support of his own followers, and then had to address the far more difficult task of winning the trust of the white population. In that effort, Mandela's obvious integrity, combined with the wisdom and moral authority he had acquired over the years of suffering patiently endured, gave his voice power and credibility. But he still needed to have a heart that was big enough to forgive injustice, to lay the foundations for a new nation.

One of the key themes to which Mandela returned throughout his own presidency was the country that South Africans of all colours had been given to share. The unity of the nation was based on their common relationship with the land that lay beneath their feet. 'To my compatriots, I have no hesitation in saying that each one of us is as intimately attached to the soil of this beautiful country as are the famous jacaranda trees of Pretoria and the mimosa trees of the bushveld. Each time one of us touches the soil of this land, we feel a sense of personal renewal. ... That spiritual and physical oneness we all share with this common homeland explains the depth of the pain we all carried in our hearts as we saw our country tear itself apart in a terrible conflict, and as we saw it spurned, outlawed and isolated by the peoples of the world, precisely because it has become the universal base of the pernicious ideology and practice of racism and racial oppression.'

These words, taken from Mandela's inaugural presidential address, speak of the land as something living to which people belong in life as well as death. To the European or American mind, the language is quite foreign—we tend to think of land as inanimate, a thing to be owned and exploited. In the African paradigm, people and land are far more closely bound together in a single life. The identity of one people is conjoined with the identity of one land; the rupture of racism caused so much pain because it tore the land apart and violated its fundamental unity.

Such convictions about the very nature of shared society and the bonds that both hold it together and make it distinct, lie at the very heart of the PWC strategy of Consensual leadership—presented, weak and consolidating. This kind of power implies the choice *not* to use strong forms of force: not to exploit or to dominate. It implies a willingness to settle in one place, rather than expand relentlessly wherever you can. There is a commitment in it to the wellbeing, integrity and value of the place you find yourself in. It is in marked contrast to the PSX Pacesetting strategy, which seeks to dominate, expand and possess. It is also in contrast to the PSC Commanding strategy, which seeks to control, contain and conform. It is in contrast, too, to the PWX Affiliative strategy, which seeks to motivate and move on with restless energy.

You might look at Consensual leadership and feel at once how weak and fragile it is. At first glance, it seems to lack the will to dominate, the force to control. It lacks the drive to expand and take more. It feels like a more gentle, self-effacing and fundamentally *collective* approach. In this regard, it is highly non-Western. Fundamental to the Western enterprise, built as it is on the intellectual foundations of the Renaissance and the Enlightenment and shaped by the economic principles of the Industrial Revolution, are the values of ownership, opportunity and growth. Capitalism is merely the economic expression of a more innate human drive to consume. Individual rights (as opposed to collective responsibilities) and personal freedom (as opposed to communal commitment) lie close to the heart of most Westerners' ideology.

In contrast, the essence of the PWC strategy is to build up the strength of the relationships between people. My first boss, the pastor of a sizeable church, used to say to visitors who were wondering whether or not to join the congregation, 'What you need to do is to look at the spaces between people.' They would look at him, bemused for a moment until the penny dropped. Then they got it: the health and strength of the church—and of any organization, for that matter—lay not in the capacity of any one of its people or its departments, or in its vision or its growth, but in the strength of the bonds that existed between people. 'Look at the spaces between people'— that's how you can tell whether this is a community you want to be part of.

What the Consensual strategy can achieve

PWC leadership is all about strengthening the 'spaces' between people. In technical terms, this is what is known as 'social capital'. We are all familiar with the idea of financial capital, and probably know about intellectual capital; 'social capital' expresses the notion that a community's wealth lies not just in people's pockets or their brains but in their relationships—their trust of and commitment to one another.

Imagine, for example, an organization that has little social capital. You would find that people talked to each other only when they had to. Conversation around the coffee machine would be sparse and often negative, cynical and bitchy. This would be a place where rumours flew around and where if people could get out of a job, or get away with a half-truth, or pass the buck so someone else got the blame, they would. Teams would invariably be tense and often ineffectual, because their members were suspicious of each other, distrusting each other's motives and disrespecting each other's skills. At the time, you would sense that the real game was about individuals climbing up the ladder rather than about people working together to make the whole organization more productive and more fulfilling. This is the kind of organization I myself would avoid like the plague. No matter what business it was engaged in, no matter how much money it was making, or what its share value was, or what salary it was offering, it would be an utter misery to work for. My motivation, my concern, my energy would plummet. They wouldn't get the best out of me—and I'm sure they wouldn't get the best out of the rest of their staff, either.

On the other hand, imagine an organization that was the opposite in every respect. When you walked in, you were greeted with smiles and hellos. People enjoyed hanging out at lunch because the company was good and the mood upbeat. It wasn't uncommon to hear of one staff member offering help to another. Ideas were shared and people were valued and respected. Because it had a culture of trust, people took on responsibility because they weren't afraid of failing; and when someone got something wrong, they were helped to get it right next time. At every level, people were learning. In their teams they enjoyed support, exploration and discovery. People took the view that if the organization as a whole flourished, they as individuals would flourish, too. They saw that their interests were not in competition with their colleagues' but in harmony with them.

Now, that is the kind of organization I'd enjoy being part of. I suspect it would also get the best out of me. The difference between the two organizations is the quality of the spaces between people: the social capital of trust, concern and commitment based on the realization that the good of the individual is bound up inseparably with the good of all. This is the kind of organization that would be led by someone who used the PWC strategy. This strategy is not an expression of weakness (in the conventional, negative sense of the word); nor is it the product of a lack of vision, or of passivity and indecision, or of the leader's failure to take responsibility. Rather, it is a deliberate commitment to build the social capital of the organization, whether it be a business, a family, a government or a nation.

Often, such leadership involves considerable statesmanship and largesse: building up the strength of relationships in any meaningful way also involves 'decentring' and giving away power. If the organization is actually to be bound together, it takes more than people just being nice and friendly to each other. It also involves people genuinely trusting others, setting them free. In the days of apartheid, the weakness of South Africa, the drain in its social capital, lay not only in the overt hostility between whites and non-whites but also (and especially) in the legal restrictions that denied blacks both political influence and educational opportunity. It was the structure of power, which privileged a few at the expense of the many, that sapped both the legitimacy and the health of the country. For example, it wouldn't have altered the basic plight of a poor, disfranchised black South African simply to have enjoyed warm relations with a white neighbour; friendly banter, even hospitality, would not in itself have changed the fundamental, structural problem. The solution lay in both the transformation of personal relationships and the reconfiguration of legal and political relationships.

The statesmanship of the PWC leader, therefore, lies in his willingness to cultivate and embed structures that cede power and enable people to trust one another. For F W de Klerk, accepting the ANC and bringing an end to apartheid was to mean a loss of personal power. After he had made those changes, his presidency lost its legitimacy—he couldn't lead the new South Africa. The same can be said of the changes initiated by Mikhail Gorbachev in the Soviet Union: he made himself vulnerable in the process, and ultimately lost his very considerable power. For any authoritarian leader who embraces Consensual leadership, it will involve laying down the autonomy and control he once had and, instead, submitting to the discipline of being just one part of a much bigger, and ultimately stronger, whole.

For people who have suffered under such an autocratic regime, the way forward is the difficult path of forgiveness. When South Africa hosted the Rugby Union World Cup in 1995, it was the first time the country had been invited even to participate in the event, after the lifting of a ban imposed throughout the years of apartheid. The South African rugby team (known as the Springboks) had been made up exclusively of whites; it had a symbol of everything apartheid stood for and as such was hated by the black population. Mandela encouraged non-white South Africans to support the team, and after the Springboks had won an epic final against New Zealand, he wore a Springbok shirt to present the trophy to the captain, Francois Pienaar, an Afrikaner. This was widely seen as a major step forward in the reconciliation of white and black South Africans.

Of course, there are countries whose transformations have been less peaceful and successful than the transition from apartheid government to full democracy in South Africa. In the former Soviet Union, the instability that has ensued in regions such as the Caucasus illustrates graphically (and tragically) how difficult it is for a once dominating PSC government to reallocate power in a stable, non-authoritarian system. Much the same is true of the component parts of the former Yugoslavia. More often than not, factions and ethnic groups, previously bound together by a common hatred of their rulers but prevented from overthrowing it, find it hard, once they are free and empowered, not to see each other as the new enemy. The temptations afforded by the acquisition of power and the opportunity to dominate have proved too strong and have led to civil wars and other catastrophes. Of course, the ecology of power predicts that, when the lid of PSC Commanding power is removed, those who have suffered under its rule, suppressed as an RWX Servant population, tend to adopt the style of their oppressors. The challenge of establishing a culture of forgiveness and reconciliation after decades of violence and abuse is a monumental one that calls on all the resources of human goodness.

The story of post-Soviet Russia is just as distressing in its way as the tragedy now unfolding in Iraq. In the political chaos that followed the dismantling of the Communist regime, a few businessmen managed to seize economic power, taking control of the country's mineral and energy assets through a series of shady deals. The failure of a naive young democracy to create a robust legal structure to safeguard its new open markets allowed them essentially to steal most of the country's wealth before its very eyes. In political terms, democracy is the primary means to make a society strongly Consensual, as it ensures that each individual is recognized and empowered; but in Russia it has not been a success. The country is notionally democratic but the redistribution of power has been very patchy, on account of both the strength of the oligarchs and the readiness of the government to exercise authoritarian (PSC), rather than consensual (PWC), power.

In the West, while we may recognize that democracy is the best way to achieve a fair distribution of political power, we tend to make rather different assumptions about power structures in organizations. We're familiar with the top-down dynamic of control, from the board to the workforce (the trade union is the PWC counterbalance to this). However, more imaginative and collaborative systems have also proved successful. For example, Alcoholics Anonymous is an organization of about two million members, working in many languages and cultures right around the globe—yet it is staffed almost entirely by volunteers. It has, in its own words, 'no real government': every group is self-sufficient and decides its own ways of working, rules and customs. Nonetheless, it is a highly cohesive community. What binds it together, of course, is its members' shared experience of alcoholism, and their common commitment to the 'Twelve Steps' programme.

AA doesn't ask or accept money for its services, but such structures can also generate profitable businesses. I have already told the story of Linux in the first book of this trilogy, *Leading out of Who You Are*, but let me recapitulate it briefly. Linux is an alternative computer operating system, a competitor to the likes of Microsoft's Windows. Unlike Windows, however, Linux is freeware: you can download it onto your PC—or a whole officeful of PCs—absolutely free of charge. The reason is that every single line of its code was written by volunteers. It was the brainchild of a Norwegian called Linus Torvalds, who wrote the first code himself and then in 1991 invited other programmers to add to it. Since then, hundreds of thousands of lines of code have been contributed: none of the authors has been paid, and no one owns the copyright. The way the company behind Linux makes money is by selling support services to the organizations that use the software. By 2008, it is expected that Linux will have more than 37 per cent of the market. The basis of the whole operation is trust—the willingness of Torvalds to trust his contributors and of them to trust him, and of the public to trust both. This is particularly effective because all alike probably share a *dis*trust of (and even hostility towards) the domination of the field by Windows, to which Linux is seen as a radical, subversive alternative. This is the common vision: to create something that works on entirely different principles—technological, social and even moral—from those of the traditional market.

An even more high-profile example of a PWC organization that is both very productive and very profitable is eBay. At first glance, it seems a ludicrous idea to set up an online market in which people part with money for goods they haven't seen and have no guarantee of ever receiving from vendors who may be on the other side of the world and who may not even have the goods they are offering for sale. However, eBay has been a phenomenal success—and it depends entirely on trust. Does this mean, therefore, that all those who buy and sell on eBay are intrinsically more trustworthy than other people? Of course, the answer is almost certainly no: they are just as dishonest, just as willing to abuse the system, as anyone else. The reason they don't is that eBay has put in place a set of restraints that penalize people who have shown themselves to its virtual community to be untrustworthy. It all relies on feedback. Each time a sale is made, the buyer and seller are asked to rate each other's reliability, and in this way regular traders acquire a score that is visible to everyone. The system is thus self-sanctioning: you may find it profitable once to break faith, but you will reduce your credibility as a trader and this will make it harder for you to profit in the future. The social bonds ('the space between people') are so arranged as to discourage deceit and create a market that costs little to participate in and requires very few legal controls.

In all three of these examples, certain conditions were necessary to achieve a profitable distribution of power. A mechanism was needed whereby information and goods could change hands: for Linux and eBay this was the Internet, for AA the multiplication of small groups. The 'product' itself must be 'open-source' (or what has been termed 'copyleft'): rather than being copyright-protected, it must be freely available to anyone both to use it and to develop it. Each of my three examples represented a move away from initiatives driven and controlled by leaders towards leader/follower collaborations. In the former, a 'leader' decides the direction and both the desired and the actual outcomes of an enterprise; in the latter, he creates the conditions for the 'followers' to participate and share control. In order to effect this, a leader must be able to achieve two things that AA, Linux and eBay all achieved. The first is a vital idea that the community will share and safeguard. For AA, this was the Twelve Steps programme. For Linux, it was what Torvalds calls its 'kernel', the core of the code around which all the rest is built. For eBay, it was the profit motive. The second is a 'brand story' that is big enough and compelling enough to motivate those who take part to join in writing the storyline themselves. Finally, the leader must adopt management structures that allow followers to participate in directing the enterprise. The operation needs to incorporate feedback mechanisms that enable it to evolve and allow those who administer it to learn from what its co-creators are saying.

The reaction to the action

The reaction to the use of PWC power that is predicted by the ecology of power is RSX: reserved, strong and expanding, the domain of the visionary. One thing you notice about instances of PWC leadership and the structures rich in social capital they produce is that they are always funded by a powerful vision. Think of the kibbutz, an example of communal living based on sharing and collaboration. Behind this is a vision of what human society could be like—which is why many people enter a kibbutz for a period to have their own vision of society renewed. Again, a monastic community is always based on the spiritual vision of its founder, whether it be Francis, Benedict, Dominic or another 'saint'. Or, again, take a Western democracy such as France, whose social cohesion derives from a secular vision established in the Revolution.

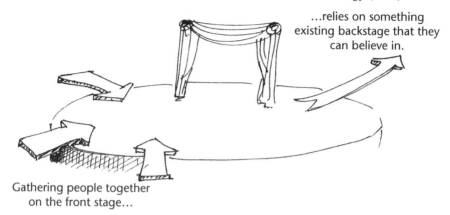

...relies on something existing backstage that they can believe in.

Gathering people together on the front stage...

In other words, a prerequisite for the formation of a PWC community rich in social capital is a deep ideological root that feeds the organization that grows out of it. Those PWC structures that fail to nurture their roots begin to lose the vision that funds them and gradually lose their social cohesion, drifting from social cohesion towards individualism. This is something we are witnessing in the West, where the loss of social and spiritual vision that has followed the decline in influence of the Christian faith has meant that arguably our democracies are slowly withering. Our commitments to social responsibility, freedom of speech and so on are becoming less strongly defended, and this has only accelerated the fragmentation of our societies.

Essentially, the vision that must inform a PWC strategy and underwrite its values is one of a common humanity, that sees people as equally human, possessing equal worth and dignity. No other vision will prove strong enough to withstand our tendency to sectarianism. This was the vision, funded by theology and faith, that inspired Martin Luther King's appeal for desegregation. No less, it was the vision that shaped Mandela's conception of South Africa post-apartheid. One day, when he was asked to comment on the BBC's somewhat unflattering verdict on his performance as a political leader, Mandela replied simply with a smile and a wry comment that expressed his deepest convictions about life: 'It helps to make you human.' At heart, what he believed in was the human spirit that binds us all together.

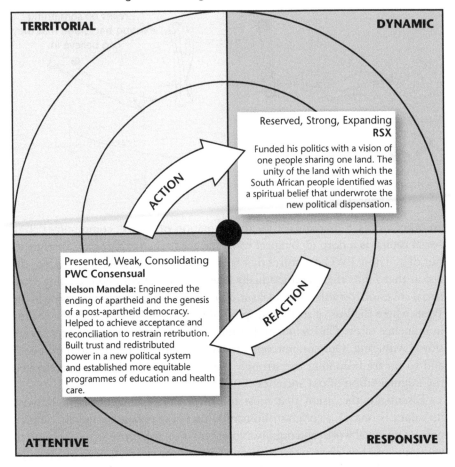

Diagram 12.1: Consensual (PWC) action and RSX reaction

How does a leader implement a PWC strategy?

There are four key elements to implementing this strategy effectively:

1. Work to overcome divisions and build trust

- Pay attention to any experiences of distrust, anger or sectarianism in your organization.
- Address it early by listening to the different points of view.
- Bring opposing sides together and help them to listen to each other.

2. Create a sense of belonging and mutual commitment

- Consider how you can distribute power around the group. This could involve rotating who chairs meetings. Ensure that people are properly briefed on key issues rather than kept in the dark. Put key decisions to a vote.

- Consider how the structure of your organization reflects the balance of power. For example, many shareholder companies offer their employees very little in the way of power. Consider how ownership of the organization could be distributed formally to best accrue social capital.

3. Establish, model and nurture a collaborative learning environment

- You could try pairing people up within departments, with the object of enabling them to work collaboratively. (Think of an appropriate name for the pairings, such as 'learning partners'.) You would find that everyone benefited from this kind of 'peer' mentoring and support. You would also see how gifted some people are in nurturing others in this way, and how well some 'challenging' individuals respond. Remember how effective Mandela's 'Island University' was in engaging and educating so many of the inmates on Robben Island.

- Encourage the sharing of ideas. Most adults learn best when they are actively engaged in a task. When teaching or presenting, take opportunities to enable the group to participate as much as possible. This could include asking people to face their partners to do some of the following:

  Explain to them what *you* have just explained

  Share some ideas

  Test each other on how well they understand what you have just said

  Think of examples to illustrate the point you have just made

  Work out a problem. Have a flip chart available during meetings on which anyone can write any idea or suggestion.

4. Deliberately incorporate some activities that require collaborative thinking or work

- It's very interesting to watch how different individuals respond to collaborative learning experiences. You will see people playing a variety of roles, from taking the lead to opting out. The most valuable part of such an activity is helping them afterwards to reflect on what happened.

- This can help people to learn skills such as listening to another perspective, overcoming difficulties, managing conflict and so on.

- As a leader, your role is not only to enable people to do a task but also to nurture (and equip them to develop) their confidence, independence and ability to learn.

Some examples of PWC leadership in action

- A community or population embracing democratic structures that give political recognition to the value of each individual
- A committee adopting consensual chairing and putting decisions to the vote
- A family sitting around the meal table discussing what they are going to do the next day
- A trade union giving individual workers a more powerful, collective voice
- A peacemaker in the family, who listens and is warm, smoothing over differences and reducing tensions so that warring parties can listen to each other

When to use a PWC strategy

- When faced with an unstable situation, where bridges need to be built and things in common found
- Where trust is low
- As a way of limiting the top-down exercise of power and preventing its abuse
- To spread ownership of a project or organization
- To encourage teamwork and foster a team spirit

THIRTEEN

Jesus and the Self-Emptying Strategy (RWC)

For many, the death of Jesus of Nazareth some two thousand years ago was a tragic martyrdom. They look at the life of this remarkable man and think how sad it was that it was ended so early, while he was still in his thirties. He had so much more to offer: he could have achieved so much more, shared so much more wisdom. Some people also wonder wistfully whether, had he lived a bit longer, his followers might have grown to be a little more like him, for in their experience the church his disciples established seems very different in character from the life and teaching of the man who inspired them.

From the perspective of social history, Jesus was a victim. His execution was ordered by an insecure Roman governor, Pontius Pilate, under pressure from an envious Jewish elite who judged the rabbi from Galilee to be a threat to their leadership and control. It is only those who follow the man as his disciples who see his death in other terms. They agree that those who had Jesus killed were culpable for his execution—which, indeed, was entirely unjustified by the false charges brought against him. However, they also maintain that his death was no accident, no mistake. They argue that Jesus died *willingly*—that he had had plenty of opportunity to escape from those who were coming to arrest him. Moreover, it appears that he consciously and intentionally put himself in the way of death, and predicted it would happen. Not only did he 'volunteer' to die, he also taught from early on in his ministry that his dying would be an act that, in itself, would release power—God's power—and would transform the social and spiritual order. In other words, he saw his death not as an occasion of weakness and defeat but as his most powerful display of strength. He saw it not as the end of his vision but as its beginning. He saw it not as a capitulation to powers he could not overcome but as his overthrowing of them.

Indeed, if you consider the impact of Jesus' life in comparison with the impact of what ensued after his death, there would seem to be some truth in his prediction. In his lifetime, he travelled no more than a few hundred miles from his birthplace; within 50 years of his death, the message he had been proclaiming had reached thousands of miles, to north Africa, Spain and possibly even India. In his lifetime, he addressed an almost exclusively Jewish audience; since his death, his message has been embraced by people of almost every race and has been translated into many hundreds of languages and dialects. In his lifetime, he inspired a few hundred people to follow him; by his death, he has inspired hundreds of millions to do so, thousands of whom have given their lives for their faith.

Many people have regarded Christianity as a death cult—as the veneration of a murdered saint, or the worship of the dying god. This misses the point, however. The power of Jesus' death doesn't lie in some macabre embrace of death itself, in some dark gothic fantasy; rather, it lies in what Jesus' followers say his death made possible: life. Christians see the death of Jesus as an act that brought life. Their celebration of his death is, in fact, a celebration of the life that flows from it. The veneration of Jesus on Good Friday, the day on which traditionally Christians remember his death, is followed two days later by the celebration of Easter Sunday, when they rejoice in what they believe to have been his resurrection from the grave.

This narrative of death and resurrection is a captivating tale of triumph in the face of disaster, of strength in the face of weakness and of gain in the face of loss. It speaks to the deepest needs of the human heart. The one reality from which we cannot escape is death—our own as well as that of those we love, which robs us of all we hold dear. Death represents the ultimate loss, the final confirmation of human impotence. If we are to find a satisfactory account of power, we must try to explain this experience of total weakness. Conventionally, death is perceived as the annihilation of power—both the annihilation of someone *by* power and the annihilation *of* power in the one who is dead. The death-and-resurrection narrative, however, calls this formula into question: it suggests not only that death itself may be robbed of power but that the power available in the life that follows death is greater than that available in the life that precedes it.

How can any of this possibly be true? The burial or cremation of tens of thousands of people this very day seems to confirm the finality of death and its extinction of all that was once alive. This is certainly true. I am not for a moment suggesting that some great cosmic reversal is in train by which, through some magician's trick, all death is turned into life. I do believe in a resurrection, both spiritual and physical; but I am not primarily talking about such a thing here. I am instead talking about how power *within the human sphere* can be released through the sacrifice of life.

Think, for example, of the power of the martyr. When a righteous man or woman gives their life for their cause, it is inspirational. Most religions venerate those who have died for the cause in the face of unjust persecution. If we broaden the term a little, we could regard as martyrs those Indians who peacefully marched in the cause of Independence and were clubbed to the ground. We could regard as martyrs the marchers who endured police brutality and imprisonment during the American Civil Rights movement. We could consider those people imprisoned for their faith in countries that restrict religious freedom: in China, Burma, Saudi Arabia, North Korea and much of the former Soviet Union. We could consider political prisoners who have refused to submit to tyrannous regimes. The word 'martyr' literally means 'witness': one who bears witness to the truth through his blood, his body, his loss.

What all these people seem to have in common is the weakness in which they confronted a system that was both strong and morally repugnant. Now, it appears that, under certain circumstances, this imbalance—the weakness of one against the immoral strength of the other—can bring about a radical shift in power. Without doubt, it was reports of this kind of situation that eroded the moral authority of the British Raj and precipitated negotiations towards an independent India. Without doubt, it was images of such a situation that shook America in the 1960s and turned the tide in favour of desegregation. Without doubt, it was such a situation that drained the moral credibility and political will of the apartheid regime in South Africa.

How can this be? How can power be located in such displays of weakness? How can vulnerability work to change the course of events? Here is one answer: self-sacrifice can draw out the evil of the enemy. As long as Indians resisted the British with force, it could be argued that the British had a right to beat them down. However, when Indians did not use any force and did not resist, when they took the blows of the rifle butts and batons on their heads, any right the British had evaporated. Indeed, the authorities' readiness to use brutal measures to suppress peaceful opposition was exposed for all to see. Previously, it had been hidden. Previously, their desire to dominate had been concealed backstage, while the front stage presented the well-mannered spectacle of tea and cucumber sandwiches. However, the self-sacrifice of the Indian marchers brought it out and revealed it.

Here is another answer: self-sacrifice compels people to take responsibility for their choices. As long as Indians used violence against the British, it was possible—even easy—for their fellow countrymen watching from the sidelines not to take sides. Why should they? Were armed insurgents a good thing? They seemed rather bloodthirsty—perhaps their rule would be worse than the British! Other Indians could remain uncommitted, while in Britain those who felt some pangs of conscience about the rule of the Raj would have been dissuaded from opposing it by reports of the violence of the natives. These people needed to be kept in check, they clearly couldn't rule themselves—they didn't have the moral discipline. However, when rifle butts and staves cracked the skulls of innocent, peaceful, white-clad men, young and old, the picture changed. The horror! The brutality! The unjustified suffering! This needed to be opposed, stopped! From that moment, a choice had to be made. Moral indecision was not an option.

Consider this, too: self-sacrifice compels people to take action. When a leader withdraws, she leaves a vacuum. As long as she is present, we can rely on her: she'll get us through this, we say, she'll come up with a plan, she'll sort this mess out! Strong power encourages complacency and apathy—there is too little incentive to take the reins ourselves. However, when that leader has gone, the issue becomes urgent. Of course we must act—no one else will! Either we do something or we suffer the consequences. Inaction is not an option.

Self-sacrifice is the conscious choice not to use force or to exercise power but instead to allow something to be done to *you*. Inevitably, therefore, it involves a degree of suffering and risk. It may be the emotional suffering of letting a loved one walk away, and the risk they may not come back. It may be physical suffering under persecution or even torture. In this regard, self-sacrifice is the weakest, most powerless course of action: unlike the other seven we have looked at, this final strategy—reserved, weak and consolidating—involves doing nothing, abdicating your right to impose yourself and choosing to allow others to impose on you. The combination of weak force and the drive to consolidate means that this kind of leadership is about leaving space for others to act. When it's employed deliberately, it obliges followers to take responsibility for their choices: there is a genuine withdrawal of the leader's presence that leaves his followers to cope without him. Direction, focus, authority are absent. The situation feels uncertain, tense, vacant—but also pregnant, awaiting a renewal of leadership. The leader allows others to come to the fore, to pursue their own initiatives, whatever the outcome. By renouncing active influence, he allows other leaders to emerge and accepts the risks associated with this lack of control.

What the Self-emptying strategy can achieve

It's important to recognize that I'm not referring here to the abdication of power as a dereliction of duty. The 'absent leader', the one who walks away, is very different from the Self-emptying leader. The former lets people down when they need support; the latter judges that the best and most powerful—and, indeed, most responsible—action is to choose not to exercise influence. The Self-emptying leader is, in one sense, fully engaged, fully present: this is a strategy that requires the utmost courage and determination, to restrain yourself even in the face of provocation.

It's important also to recognize that I'm not promoting suffering for its own sake. I see no good in pain and loss in themselves at all. They are merely tools with which we can achieve greater ends if we use them correctly. They are not an end in themselves—we progress through them towards an end where there will be no more death, or mourning or crying or pain.

What I am advocating is—on occasion—the strategic use of weakness, of self-emptying, in leadership. Just as there are situations in which each of the other seven strategies is appropriate, so there are situations in which the RWC Self-emptying strategy is right. I believe that several conditions need to be met if it is to be used wisely. First of all, the leader must be willing to suffer. You can't coerce someone else to suffer or it becomes an abuse of power. Self-emptying must be voluntary, informed and deliberate.

Second, the leader must be able to bear the suffering without being overwhelmed. King advised his followers not to march if they could not endure being struck by batons or water cannons without lashing out in retaliation It takes an extraordinary kind of discipline and maturity to absorb such provocation.

Third, it is wise to use this strategy only when there is a moral conscience to arouse and an emotional consciousness to be awakened in those who witness it. A recent, poignant illustration of this point was the suicide of the American musician Malachi Ritscher, who publicly burned himself to death during the rush hour in Chicago on 3 November 2006 in protest at the 'mass murder of innocent civilians' in Iraq. In his suicide note, he wrote that his countrymen were 'more concerned with sports on television and ring-tones on cellphones than the future of the world'. Unfortunately, his words proved to be prophetic, as his terrible end was almost completely ignored by the American media. He had expressed the hope that his one death could 'say to the world: I apologize for what we have done to you'—but it seems that no one was listening or had ears to hear him.

The reaction to the action

It is disturbing to think, even for a moment, that vulnerability may have something to contribute to leadership. We have been so indoctrinated with the received wisdom that we can't see past it: being a leader means being in control, being in power, having options, having information, having skills and resources. Leadership is not supposed to be about weakness and fragility and self-sacrifice. But what is extraordinary in the ecology of power is that power can flow through a point of weakness. In the moment of defeat, power can be released. So it was through the self-sacrifice of a few hundred Indian men, when the populace of the whole subcontinent, some 200 million men, women and children, were empowered to take control of their own lives. In the same way, the Christian church which was cruelly persecuted by the Roman emperors in the first and second centuries came to be more powerful than the Empire itself. This is the power of a wizened, bent old lady in the slums of Calcutta to challenge the hard-hearted assumptions of the world's economists. It is the power of Gorbachev to release the grip of Communism and allow a new order to emerge. It is the power of Gandhi to state that 'passive resistance is a method of securing rights by personal suffering.'

Leaders often say they are trying to 'do themselves out of a job'. By that, they are implying that if they do their work as leaders sufficiently well, their followers will be so well trained, equipped and empowered they'll be able to take on everything that needs to be done and they themselves will finally be redundant. This is an ideal of what you might call 'enabling leadership'. Certainly, there is some merit in this approach, which has grown out of the experience of many people that their leaders never relinquish control and so those who follow them never grow up fully and learn to take responsibility. Some leadership is still strongly paternalistic, with followers as dependants expecting their problems to be sorted out by a parent figure. In contrast, the enabling model encourages leaders to see themselves first of all as equippers of others: teachers who train others to be as competent as themselves, if not more so.

In the ecology of power, this kind of leadership is what you would call RSC or Foundational. It involves the laying of foundations, by providing resources, training, support—rehearsing the cast so that eventually the show can go on without the director. The assumption behind this is that independence is a good thing. The logic is that if a team or an organization fails to gain independence from its leader, it will always, in some ways, remain dependent on her—and so will be vulnerable should something ever happen to her. However, I'm not convinced that this kind of independence is ever entirely appropriate. There's a difference between being able to trust yourself and being so self-sufficient you no longer need anyone else. The former is certainly a mark of maturity, but the latter implies a lack of vulnerability, as well as a lack of maturity. No human being ever is, or should aspire to be, so self-sufficient they can do without the support and help of anyone else. That is a recipe for arrogant autonomy. The proper goal for leaders (and this includes parents) is not to make their dependants entirely self-sufficient, simply having no need of them, but to foster self-awareness and the ability to trust themselves as well as others.

There often comes a moment when a leader needs to 'let his followers go'. I have talked at length in the first book of this trilogy, *Leading out of Who You Are*, about the way followers can idealize a leader. Anyone who has led a community, an organization or a country for any length of time, through bad as well as good times, and remained faithful and humane will have formed a strong bond of affection with his followers. Moreover (as I pointed out in Chapter 3 of this book) they will see him as a symbol of their identity. The time will come, however, when this transaction must end—and the leader must help his followers to prepare for this. This is an act of mutual release, the letting-go of a relationship that has supported and sustained them on the journey they have made together. The role of the leader in this situation is to help his followers to navigate this emotional experience without being overwhelmed by it.

In the final months of his life, Jesus spoke often about his imminent death, as well as the resurrection that would follow. His disciples were confused and so he tried to elucidate, explaining why he needed to die and also foretelling what would happen next. The night before his execution, he enacted with his closest friends a ritual that has been imitated by his followers ever since. Sharing bread and wine around a meal table, mindful of the Jewish festival of Passover, which symbolized God's act of liberation from slavery, Jesus offered his disciples a rite by which to remember his own approaching sacrifice to free the world from slavery to sin. Today, Christians all around the world, of whatever denomination, re-enact this ritual: the Eucharist, Holy Communion, the breaking of bread, the Mass. In so doing, they share in those final hours of Jesus' life and prepare themselves to receive the benefits of his death and participate in the life he called people to as his disciples.

Jesus was preparing his followers for his final withdrawal, after which he would no longer be present with them. The time had come for him to 'let them go'—and for them to let him go. 'Don't hold on to me,' he told Mary Magdalene when she met him in the garden after his resurrection. Of course, his physical withdrawal made possible the greater release of his spiritual power, in the gift of his Holy Spirit, who Christians believe empowers the church for a self-sacrificial life of witness and worship.

Many leaders speak of 'enabling leadership', of 'doing themselves out of a job', and yet they fail to achieve this because they're not able to withdraw from their followers when the time is right. A leader can become an obstruction to confidence and growth if he stays too long, if too much is invested in him. The founder of the organization prevents growth after a while because everyone still 'sits under her authority', so to speak, even though they are unaware they're doing so. People defer to a founder and yield to a longstanding leader, and when her authority needs to be outgrown if the organization is to grow further, the only way it can happen is for the leader to withdraw: to empty herself as a final expression of her attachment to the thing to which she may have devoted her life. It is a little death, a loss, a giving-away, a hollowing-out. And yet for the followers she leaves behind, if it is done in a healthy and responsible way, it can lead to both freedom and empowerment.

Withdrawing from the stage altogether...

... may release powerful reactions, both for good and for bad.

The reaction to RWC leadership is PSX. The inverse of self-emptying is transforming. It seems that in the ecology of power an act of great weakness is linked to a release of great power—unexpected, dangerous, often uncontrollable power, power that no leader can teach or organize or buy. The reason self-emptying has such mighty effects is that in the ecology of power it produces the most potent reaction. It can galvanize the strongest of human emotions and drives. It has an energy and life of its own. There was no stopping what ensued in India in the early Forties. There was no stopping what ensued in America in the Sixties. There was no stopping what ensued in the Soviet Union in the Eighties. There was no stopping what ensued in South Africa in the early Nineties.

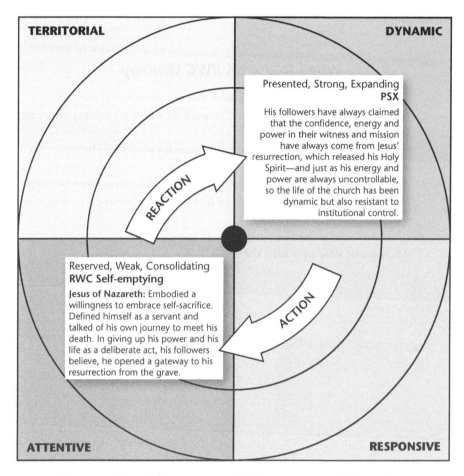

TERRITORIAL   **DYNAMIC**

Presented, Strong, Expanding
PSX

His followers have always claimed
that the confidence, energy and
power in their witness and mission
have always come from Jesus'
resurrection, which released his Holy
Spirit—and just as his energy and
power are always uncontrollable,
so the life of the church has been
dynamic but also resistant to
institutional control.

REACTION

Reserved, Weak, Consolidating
RWC Self-emptying

Jesus of Nazareth: Embodied a
willingness to embrace self-sacrifice.
Defined himself as a servant and
talked of his own journey to meet his
death. In giving up his power and his
life as a deliberate act, his followers
believe, he opened a gateway to his
resurrection from the grave.

ACTION

ATTENTIVE   **RESPONSIVE**

Diagram 13.1: Self-emptying (RWC) action and PSX reaction

Here are some examples of RWC leadership in action

· A chair withdrawing from a meeting to allow the rest of the board to come to a decision without her

- A politician choosing not to defend himself against some accusation or slander
- A mother allowing her teenage daughter to go to a party without saying what time she'll be back
- An army falling back in a show of weakness in order to deceive the enemy into thinking it's defeated
- A founder letting go of the organization she conceived and brought to birth

When to use an RWC strategy

- When faced with an unjust situation that needs to be exposed as such
- When you feel a call to sacrifice yourself in order to achieve a greater good
- When there is sufficient moral consciousness for your act to be recognized, so that it will catalyse change
- As a witness to injustice—which implies that the witness must be visible. For some, this may be simply in the sight of God; for others, it will mean while the world is watching.
- When revolution is called for rather than evolution
- As an act of solidarity with the weak

Part 2C

UNDEFENDED POWER

FOURTEEN

Finding the Holy Grail of Leadership

Eight different leaders, eight different leadership strategies. Each leader exemplifies the characteristics—strengths as well as weaknesses—of one of the strategies. Of course, none of these men was confined to using only that strategy: throughout his life and his career each would at times, in different situations, have used others. I have identified each strategy with a particular leader merely because they demonstrated it particularly powerfully.

It is also true that organizations—and, indeed, societies—go through different phases in which they look for different kinds of leadership. I have seen many organizations that, after the incumbency of one especially driven Pacesetting CEO, have appointed as his successor someone much more collaborative and Affiliative: following PSX with PWX leadership. Often, in such an appointment the organization is adjusting its internal balance after the impact of one particular character. It can also reflect the way that human communities have different needs at different times in their histories and look, often unconsciously, for leaders whose dominant strategies answer the needs they are conscious of at the time.

For example, Churchill's Britain was a country faced by an enemy of seemingly invincible might. His predecessor as prime minister, the emollient Neville Chamberlain, lacked the necessary bloody-mindedness to overcome such a challenge. Churchill's uncompromising personality, his indomitable bulldog spirit—indeed, his appetite for the battle—made him the kind of leader people craved and needed in 1940.

Margaret Thatcher's Britain was a different place. In 1979, this was a society struggling to escape the clumsy grip of the trades unions, which was stifling productivity and economic growth. For her, Britain was a country facing an 'enemy within', and so she appealed not to our common heritage but to our individualism. Thatcher tuned in to the message of the Sixties and Seventies, of the freedom of the individual, and gave it a political and economic interpretation. Her strident, Commanding PSC approach confronted the opposition and legitimated self-interest.

By the late 1990s, the British had had enough of the authoritarianism of Thatcher, the hypocrisy of the Conservatives and the instability of the economy. This was a society that wanted a new Affiliative sense of belonging. Tony Blair's language, manner and approach struck all the right chords to convince people that he offered a fresh start. His rhetoric was classic PWX: 'us' (rather than 'you'), 'our vision', 'our land', 'our time'. It was a positive, optimistic (if ultimately unrealistic) appeal to our sense that we wanted to be part of a vibrant new, emerging world.

Crucially, an effective leader resonates with his society—tuning into the same frequency, humming in the same key—and he exploits this. When this occurs, a relationship forms between the leader and his followers that binds the two together in a contract of trust and, for a while at least, the two become identified with each other. The strongest bonds between leaders and followers usually are formed when the social conditions are acute and so people's need to be made secure is greatest. When the social context is less extreme, the resonance and the bond between leader and followers are, inevitably, less strong.

The transition from one style of leadership to another is prompted, then, when this bond is broken—when the resonance that united leader and followers becomes a dissonance. Perhaps the most dramatic and shocking example in recent political history of such instant dissonance after a period of strong attachment is the effectual rejection of Churchill's government in the 1945 election. Churchill had been bound to the British people over the crucial war years by an emotional tie, because he was the symbol of their dogged resistance to the Nazi threat. However, in the early summer of 1945, following the end of the war in Europe and the break-up of the wartime coalition between Conservative, Liberal and Labour politicians, he called a general election. Despite overwhelming public affection for Churchill (whose approval rating only that May had been 83 per cent), despite predictions of a big win for his Conservatives, the Labour Party under the uncharismatic Clement Attlee was swept to power, winning almost two-thirds of the seats in the House of Commons.

The size of Churchill's defeat matched the strength of the tie that had bound him to the people through those extraordinarily demanding years of war. Once they were over, the need for that bond was past. Indeed, with Britain in ruins, the urgent need was for a government that was not identified with the hardships and sacrifices of the war but instead stood for progress, reconstruction and growth. In hindsight it seems almost inevitable that the man the people had clung to through the storm would not convince them that he could lead them in the aftermath. Churchill was never as great as a peacetime party politician as he was as a national leader and statesmen in wartime. His impassioned PSX rhetoric, drawing on the deep wells of the British spirit, was appropriate to the darkest of days when heroism and sacrifice were required, but was less suited to the moderate optimism of the careful social reconstruction needed after the war. The resonance had gone, and with it the political bond—though the emotional tie remained, and indeed ensured a return to No 10 for Churchill six years later. By 1951, of course, the welfare state (and especially the National Health Service) was well in hand and the reconstruction of Britain well under way, and people could again afford to recall their attachment to their great war leader. Even so, there was never again the same strong bond that had tied them together in the years 1940–45.

What becomes clear is that no single one of the eight leadership strategies is sufficient in itself. Each one achieves a particular effect, creates a particular configuration of power. What is important is whether a leader understands the kind of power she is using and whether it is the appropriate kind to use in that situation. For example, the parent who adopts a Consensual strategy when a child is about to run across the road in front of an oncoming car is using the wrong kind of power for that situation. The executive who employs a Commanding strategy when chairing a board of colleagues of similar status is using the wrong kind of power for that situation. The government that uses a Pacesetting strategy to drive a bill through Parliament is using the wrong kind of power in that situation. Leadership is not about being able to use any one form of power. It's not just about being able to create consensus, or face down opposition, or set a demanding pace. It's a bigger task than that.

Leadership itself must be thought of as a 'meta-activity'—that is, an activity that can see beyond any particular situation and has available to it a range of potential interventions, as well as the capacity to know when and how to implement them. Clearly, what matters is the repertoire of strategies a leader possesses. Each individual's 'signature' (so to speak) is the particular array of strategies he is able to use effectively to shape a situation. Every leader has such a signature, which identifies their presence and their social and emotional impact. Pope John Paul II, for example, used an affiliative PWX strategy very effectively, forming strong emotional bonds with people both through his travels and his displays of courage. He also sought to give the Catholic Church a vision, employing an RSX strategy—and after the attempt to assassinate him and towards the end of his life he also showed himself to be weak and vulnerable, a suffering leader who was pouring himself out for the church. However, he will not be remembered for his Pacesetting or Foundational approach.

Bill Clinton was known for his PWX and consensual PWC strategies. His foreign policy was more affiliative than that of either his predecessor or his successor, and in his own country he fostered a sense of openness. However, he, too, did little to reinforce the foundations of his society, relying instead on a relatively benign period of economic growth to create optimism at home.

George W Bush, on the other hand, has a leadership signature that is strongly slanted towards command and control. His rhetoric renders shades of grey in black and white and reduces complex issues to simple formulas in which the American people are the good guys and their enemies are the bad guys. His concept of international collaboration conjures up images of hospitality on his Texan ranch: 'Come and join me and the boys for a steak and a beer! We'll be rootin' out some cattle rustlers later if you stick around.' Confident, dominant, welcoming on his terms—in his policy he is almost exclusively PSC. It is because he's unable to employ other leadership strategies that his signature appears so perfunctory. It's not that a Commanding approach is inappropriate in itself, but on its own it becomes simplistic and dangerous.

Many leaders other than Bush lack this 'meta-leadership' ability. They are adequate, even effective, in one approach or another—they can practise Consensual leadership or Pacesetting leadership, perhaps—but they lack the mobility to progress beyond this to exercise a different kind of power when occasion demands. Mobility is the most important capacity a leader needs to develop. To some extent, this is something that can be learned—there are certain mechanics involved in moving from using one strategy, one kind of power, to another and you can master them. You can learn how to chair meetings in a Consensual way, for example—walking into the room and taking your seat with an air of confident authority. You can develop the ability to be warm and relational and Affiliative. You can learn, in short, to adopt different strategies as appropriate and use power to achieve different effects.

A very moving story that illustrates the potency of such mobility is that of the Guinea Pig Club. During the Battle of Britain, many pilots suffered appalling injuries when their fighters were hit by enemy fire and engulfed in flames. Reconstructive surgery was in its infancy in 1940, but some badly burned men were sent to the Queen Victoria Hospital in East Grinstead to be treated by the pioneering surgeon Archibald McIndoe, a man known to his colleagues as 'the Boss' or 'the Maestro'. The first batch of pilots decided to set up a club, which only men who had been patients at the burns unit could join, and called it 'the Guinea Pig Club' because they knew how experimental this surgery then was. MacIndoe encouraged this kind of humour as a way to deal with the trauma and stigma caused by their horrific injuries. (He himself liked to refer to these men as his 'boys'.)

Aware that many of his patients were going to spend a long time at the hospital—some of them had to undergo over 30 operations—McIndoe also got the East Grinstead community involved. Heroes or not, he knew that the pilots would not find it easy to mix with the townspeople, not only because of their disfigurement, which others would find it hard to look at, but also because of the intensity of all the experiences they had gone through. However, two good friends of his, Neville and Elaine Blond, managed to persuade some local families to take some convalescents into their homes as guests. Gradually, more and more people agreed to help, and in this way the pilots became integrated into the community. They soon became a familiar sight in the pub, and a number of them even married women they had met at dances organized by the Boss.

Everyone assumed that the Guinea Pig Club would disband when its members left the hospital at the end of the war, but six decades later it is still going strong and it meets every year for an emotional reunion. The Guinea Pigs speak of the way McIndoe restored their sense of dignity, their self-respect and their confidence. An extraordinary camaraderie has developed between them all, and many of these, now elderly, men will say that, despite the horror of their injuries, if they could have their life again they would not want to miss out on the experience of being members of the Club.

Few people can claim to have pioneered a new medical technique like McIndoe (who was knighted in 1947). Perhaps even fewer can claim also to have pioneered a kind of group therapy, long before the psychological revolution of the 1960s and some 60 years before such practices were to be used to address cognitive disorders in the NHS. McIndoe combined technical skill and imagination with an extraordinary insight into the emotional needs of men. At the same time, he had the vision to initiate, and the social skills to foster, a fellowship of humour, courage and adventure in a situation of terrible suffering and loss.

Sir Archie McIndoe was a man whose leadership signature was admirably fluent.

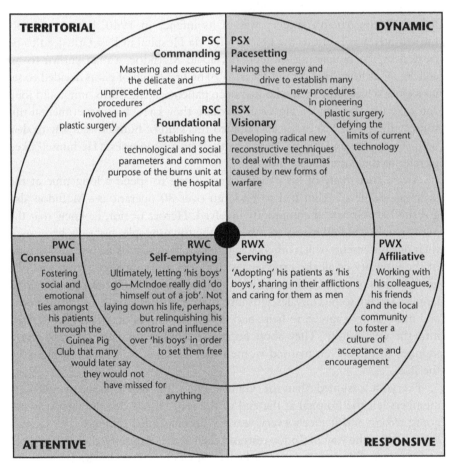

Diagram 14.1: The characteristics of McIndoe's leadership

The skills that enable mobility in leadership

1. Master each strategy

You can't employ a strategy unless you know when to use it. This is entirely a matter of competence. If we are not willing to train ourselves to be better leaders, we may as well give up now.

Using strong force. For example, you can't execute the PSC Commanding strategy unless you know how to gain and keep people's attention and respect, project authority and issue orders. This may be a matter of attending to your body language, your tone of voice and your behaviour around people. If we simply lack awareness of how we come across, we will need to enlist the help of others to give us some feedback about how we are thought of. Like mastering a new sports skill or a part in a play, this is to some extent a matter of learning the behavioural mechanics. When I first began to speak in public, I was nervous and tense, tied to my script. It took a while for me to learn the rhetorical and performance skills to practise Commanding or Pacesetting leadership from the front.

Language: An interesting exercise is to go through a talk, speech or presentation you're going to give and replace polysyllables with simple words. Illustrate often. Stick to the point, don't digress, be direct.

Symbols: Consider what symbols are associated with your 'message'. When you are speaking, the symbols around you will probably be speaking even louder: your clothes, your gestures and expressions, your poise, the way the room is set out, the lectern you lean on, the notes you give people, the welcome they received at the door, even the location of the venue. These things are not extra to your message, they are integral to it: they express it more powerfully than your words will, and they do so subliminally. How do you as a leader use symbolic language?

Gesture and movement: Do you have an understanding of gesture? Are you aware of how you stand, how you hold your papers when presenting? For example, the action of standing up in a group can indicate the taking of authority. Simply by standing up to seize people's attention as you introduce a new idea and then sitting down again to invite feedback and discussion, you can manage the emotional dynamics in the group. In the course of a meeting, I aim to stand up and then sit down five or six times. Or, again, I will employ some arm gestures to reinforce my point—for example, bringing my fingertips slowly together in front of me if I am talking about bringing a problem to a resolution, or throwing my arms wide to say that this idea is big enough to encompass the whole situation.

Often, I will try to use the whole room as a theatre, walking down from the stage to illustrate a point. If you begin making a proposal on one side of the room and slowly walk across to the other side as you fill in the detail, the gesture says: Here is something that can move you from A to B. I often look back across the room to my starting point and draw attention to how far I have come, step by step. I will always aim to make eye contact with each person in an audience of up to 20 or so as I talk. A speaker's task is to make people feel they are being addressed personally, and even momentary eye contact achieves this. I will always exaggerate my actions on stage, as if in a pantomime, because subtle gestures tend to be lost.

Resonance and the use of visual media: I personally believe that an active, energetic presentation, using gestures to echo meaning, is much more effective than PowerPoint. The latter restricts you to a linear flow and often reduces the theatre of the occasion. They are suitable for financial reports, where clear, informational charts are needed, but not good for other contexts.

The reason for this is that a good speaker achieves a resonance with her audience, so that the flow of her talk is determined not by a preset script but by the emotional connection between her and her audience. She becomes aware as she speaks of whether they are with her. When this point is reached, they are captivated and the atmosphere changes: an environment has been created in which her audience are sensitive to her. Their ears and hearts are open, they trust the speaker and she can begin to connect with their emotional needs. There is no foretelling exactly what language she will need at this point—she could not have prepared a text. All she can do is 'be still and listen to the space'.

Dramatic climax and timing: To be able to go off-script like this requires experience—I don't recommend that anyone with less than 200 talks or presentations behind him attempts it. A moment comes when there is nothing more to be said, and then the speaker needs to be able to 'hold the silence' in the room, instead of filling the air with more words. What is called for then is simply stillness and quietness while what has just been spoken hangs in the air, resonating in the audience's ears like the deep note of a bell. It takes confidence and authority to stand on a stage and hold a silence like that—perhaps to invite people *into* that silence—for as much as five seconds. It takes confidence and authority and experience to be able to manage the emotion in the room through pace, rhythm, volume, vocabulary and timing.

A powerful leader is skilled in creating dramatic moments that capture people's attention. He constructs such events as a theatre director might, manipulating the audience so that they notice the climax and are affected by it. He pays attention to his props and stage settings and (as I observed above) every aspect of his front stage, not merely the script. In mastering these things he acquires considerable power, of course, which can be misused; and it behoves him to use it with self-awareness, responsibility and restraint.

Using weak force. Learning to use weak force is no less of a challenge, but once again we can work to develop the necessary skills.

Emotional space: Using weak power—for example, in order to practise Consensual or Serving leadership—involves having sufficient emotional space ourselves to 'contain' other people's emotions. We choose to open our own emotional selves, like a garden without walls, so we can welcome in other people and the feelings or issues they may have, rather than keeping them outside, detached and managed. A good example is when a child has a tantrum and his father resists his own feelings and becomes a container to hold the child's feelings. Some key prerequisites for this are:

- Keeping the posture of your body open, rather than closed or aggressive
- Reflecting the other person's emotions back to them ('I can see you're feeling very angry about this...'). Tone as well as content is important in doing this—so that you echo that anger (say) in your voice rather than merely commenting on it in a detached and neutral way.
- Inviting the other person to say a little more about the situation ('Could you say a bit more about that?')
- Exploring their feelings ('And how does it make you feel when I do that?')
- Asking them to help you change the situation ('What do you feel I could do now to make things better?')

Emotional containment: The psychotherapist Margo Sunderland explains what goes on chemically in the brain when a person is 'emotionally contained' in this way. Asking an angry man (say) to express his feelings provides a release for the pressure that built up while he felt no one was listening to him. When he feels a resonance with another person and believes he has been heard and accepted by them, his need to be defensive or aggressive diminishes and the adrenaline that flooded his body during his outburst begins rapidly to subside. Offering to help him stimulates the flow of positive-attachment chemicals such as serotonin and creates a virtuous cycle of positive emotions rather than a 'stress cycle'.

Finally, Sunderland suggests, physically touching him will reconnect him to others and make a dangerous situation safe again. One of the things that will have triggered the release of adrenaline is that during his outburst he knew he had crossed a boundary and was out of control and that felt dangerous. The adrenaline flows and aggravates both his defensiveness and his aggression. Making him feel safe again is important to break this cycle.[9]

2. Learn when to use each strategy

There is obviously no point in being able to use different strategies but not knowing *when* to use them. This is a matter of reading a situation accurately. A former aide to Henry Kissinger recalls that three questions would be asked when Richard Nixon's administration addressed any issue at its daily conferences. They were these:

· What is actually happening right now?
· What is likely to happen next?
· What will A do if B does X?

Those three simple questions highlight what good strategy is all about: knowing what is actually going on (rather that guessing, or being content to be ignorant), being able to predict where things are likely to go and being able to forecast what kind of reaction any action will provoke. This is basic systems thinking. It works because it is not too complicated. Of course, what it requires is both experience and a predictive model—experience of what has happened in the past and a model that enables you to predict the effect of doing X. This is the value of the concept of the ecology of power: it gives us a model that explains the fundamental structure of power in any social system. This enables us to identify, almost in a clinical way, all the different forces that could be brought to bear and it puts us in a strong position to predict how the system will react if B applies force Y to A.

Sadly, in our specialized age it is increasingly rare to find in any one single individual the mobility demonstrated by Archie McIndoe. One reason for this is that today we are encouraged by our educational curriculum and culture to divorce the social and the emotional from the intellectual. While we are still young, we are taught to think of these realms as entirely separate. Mathematics and the sciences on the one hand are 'hard', intellectual studies; the arts on the

---

[9] Margot Sunderland has created, with the aid of the artist Nicky Armstrong, the most engaging, delightful yet powerful set of resources for adults working with children who have emotional difficulties. Using stories and pictures, her books explore metaphors that enable children to express the feelings they have been repressing, and help adults to manage these feelings (as well as their own). See, for example, *Helping Children who Bottle Up Their Feelings/A Nifflenoo Called Nevermind* and *Helping Children who Have Hardened their Hearts or Become Bullies/A Wibble Called Bipley (and a Few Honks)* (Speechmark, 1999 and 2001 respectively)

other hand are 'soft' and expressive and engage the emotions. Doctors are not enabled to develop 'people skills', while nursing is regarded as a profession for the non-academic. Caring is removed from strategy, humour from execution, fellowship from delivery. By impressing this division on the young we polarize knowledge and may prevent children from developing the ability to 'know and lead' in a richer, more holistic way.

Leadership is one of the very few disciplines in which the *dis*integrated need to become reintegrated. The leader operates *not* within any one discipline but across the whole range of human encounter and meaning. The leader and her followers perform a kind of dance. At times, this is structured and disciplined and set moves are rehearsed, refined and co-ordinated. At other times, the dance is fluid and the dancers invent their own steps. Sometimes the dance breaks new ground, at other times its moves are familiar. At times it is fast, at other times stately, or even sombre. The dance can be both intimate and clinical, precise and fluid. The leader is not the leader of the dance but a partner in it—because it is something beyond us, in which (as T S Eliot put it) we 'must move in measure'.[10] Paradoxically, it is an experience in which time becomes timeless and movement becomes stillness.

Eight tips on how to develop greater mobility as a leader

1. Learn by experience. Take a leadership role—you will learn most about leadership by practising it.
2. Practise using different strategies. If there are some you know you have not developed, consciously create opportunitites to try them out.
3. Reflect on what happens when you use different strategies. The more you notice, the more you'll be able to change and develop.
4. Assemble a council of wise friends around you—a small, trusted group of people who know you well, are on your side and can help you to identify your blind spots. Give them permission to point out your areas of strength and weakness.
5. Serve. Every leader needs, as good practice, to have an area of her life in which she is not leading but being led. This might involve serving on a voluntary body (but not as leader!), taking on some menial tasks or helping out some people in need who have nothing to offer you in return.
6. Practise being still and 'attending to the moment' at different times in the day, rather than always looking ahead to the next step. You will notice more about what is actually going on.

---

[10] T S Eliot, 'Little Gidding', *Collected Poems 1909–1962* (Faber and Faber, this edition 1963)

7. Lay down your power at major junctions of your life. It's tempting to move from one high-powered role straight into another. Consider taking a sabbatical, when you will be out of the system and no one will call you. Only in this way will you discover whether you are truly free of the *need* to be powerful.

8. Be patient. You will probably find that, as you become more undefended, so your influence will grow. However, now may not be the time when you can use it most significantly. Often we need to wait quietly, learning to be content with what we have, before we are given the opportunity to make our greatest contribution (think of Churchill, Mandela and Reagan, among many others).

FIFTEEN

Leading with Nothing to Lose: the Key to Mobility

You might think, from the previous chapter, that the freedom to be mobile is simply a matter of acquiring the skills and experience to do so. You might be forgiven for concluding that this is just another book offering yet more tips on how to be the most competent and effective leader possible. You might also feel confused. The title of this book is *The Undefended Leader: Leading with Nothing to Lose*, but am I not simply providing another set of arms so that leaders can be better defended, not less?

If the skills I have talked about were to make us more potent and less vulnerable as leaders, then yes, that would be true. However, if those skills are not for *our* benefit, not to defend *us*, but instead are acquired for the benefit of the people we serve, the answer is 'No'. Then they are not assets we exploit but gifts we give to others. The difference here lies in the fundamental freedom of the leader as a person. Every single one of us has emotional needs. The message of the first book of this trilogy, *Leading out of Who You Are*, was that unless those needs are met in the context of a relationship with an Other who accepts us unconditionally, we will seek to meet them from human relationships around us. When a leader does this, she starts to exploit her followers as a surrogate source of affection, power, control, belonging or whatever it may be she needs. Her followers cease to be people she is freely serving and instead, to some extent, become commodities she needs and uses. The transaction between leader and followers becomes corrupted and, rather than freedom, it results in a kind of collusion.

The undefended leader is the one whose needs are met through an unconditional attachment to an Other, in which she finds identity, belonging and affection. This source of approval gives her such security that her sense of self is not defined by her success as a leader. Who she is is not determined by the response of the audience she is performing in front of. As a result, she is free to play the role of leader without having any personal interest in earning applause. Instead, she can act generously, both in attending to the needs of her audience and in serving them freely, with courage and commitment.

Anyone who is attached to success and results, for example, may be unable to practise the reserved, weak strategies of leadership, Self-emptying (RWC) and Serving (RWX), which require an attitude of service and a readiness to relinquish control. I remember working with the leader of a large church. He had been in post for about a year and had followed a pastor who had nurtured the congregation so well over the years that it had grown considerably. However, now that growth had stopped and many of the church's activities were slightly tired and dry. People desperately needed a fresh start and a renewed vision. However, this would have involved discontinuing some of the activities. 'I can't just stop them,' the new pastor said to me one day as we were discussing the options. 'If I did that, what would people think? That I wasn't as good a leader as my predecessor?' His fear of damaging his image, of being seen as less effective, prevented this man from adopting the Self-emptying and Serving strategies the church so desperately needed. The result was that it did not begin to grow again.

Likewise, anyone who is frightened of failing may be unable to practise the presented, strong strategies of leadership, Commanding (PSC) and Pacesetting (PSX), which require a willingness to run the risk of missing the targets they set. I recall another leader who consistently failed to impose the controls on the front stage of his organization that were necessary for it to be as productive as it could have been. The reason for this was that he felt more comfortable using the Visionary strategy, inspiring a vibrant, imaginative community, and was unwilling to take control of the front stage. He feared that if he did, the organization would lose some of its authenticity and creativity. The result was frequent conflict with his board. They wasted energy and money, and he didn't receive the trust and support he wanted.

Ultimately, it is not a matter of competence that enables a leader to become mobile but a matter of inner security and personal freedom. I remember a conversation I had with the head of a large school in London as we discussed a problem of leadership one day over a drink after work. 'But, Simon,' he said, 'how possible really is it to change? I mean, you maintain that each of us can learn to use other strategies, but, given that we have all been using the same old, familiar strategies for years, and given that they have worked OK for us and we feel safe with them, is it really possible to change them, now at my age? It's a great idea, but is it realistic?'

This is a crucial question. If it is not possible actually to change, why should we bother at all? The answer is this: I think it is possible to change, but it's not just a matter of being willing to learn or developing new skills. Certainly, these are both important factors, but they are not the most important. In fact, the most important thing is stillness. 'You see, Ben,' I told him, 'the only way I will possibly let go of my strategies, which I know so well, which I'm so comfortable with, which give me a sense of safety and also—let's be honest—power and control, is if I reach that point of stillness where what I needed to achieve by using them no longer matters to me like it did. It's a matter of letting them go. You see, most of my day I am busy focused on my task, trying to get my jobs done, running frantically from one thing to the next. I don't notice what's really going on around me—I've got a hundred things in my head, I haven't got time to stop and reflect about how I feel, let alone how others feel. Of course, I carry on doing the same thing, day after day. The only way I will change is if I am able first to stop. Before change comes stillness.

'Imagine', I went on, 'what would happen if you were still for a moment—truly still. Not just inactive, but still in your heart. You let go of your ambition, your desires and personal hopes, and instead paid attention to the situation in front of you. You allowed yourself to become open to what was going on around: the moods, the fears, the energy of all that was happening around you, in the office, at home, wherever you were. You paid attention to it. And now imagine that, instead of reacting in fear, you acted in freedom—freedom then to intervene in that situation and do whatever was needed.'

'But', Ben replied, 'how could you ever achieve that stillness in the first place?'

'You can only find that stillness if your own needs have first been met. If I'm still worried about my own success or reputation, then I'm dominated by fear—fear of what I might lose or suffer. I need to have that fear quelled, and that anxiety assuaged. And that can happen only if I'm confident of being loved: secure in a relationship in which I know who I am, and which can't be jeopardized by anything I may do or not do. Then I am safe enough to be still.'

The upshot of all this is that the freedom to move anywhere, to use all of the leadership strategies, is available only to those who can freely face personal loss without fear. Or, to use the language of the ecology of power, only those people who have themselves experienced self-emptying, who have reached the point where they lay everything down and let go of power, and have accepted their vulnerability and sought security instead in another kind of relationship, only these are truly free to lead.

In terms of power, Christians have tended to regard the death of Jesus on the cross as a mystery. They recognize it as a sacrifice through which their sins are forgiven, and appreciate that it is at the heart of the Christian message. They know, too, that it is the mainspring of their own response to God of gratitude and faith. However, they can't make out how it might impinge on their understanding of power. As a result, they continue to exploit power in much the same way as they did before they become followers of Jesus. They believe that churches should be well organized and managed. They advocate the use of the best resources to promote church growth and send their pastors on training courses to become more effective evangelists, teachers and executives. They read books on executive leadership and want the church to learn from the business world how to be more successful, how to grow faster. They pore over strategies that promise greater church growth much as a CEO might pore over books that promise an increase in corporate profits if he just follows this system or that.

Jesus used many leadership strategies in the course of his ministry: he could be Commanding when confronting his opponents, Consensual when nurturing his group of followers, Foundational when expounding the Law and establishing the basics of his message. In fact, he could and did use all of the eight strategies—if you wanted, you could easily make an analysis of how he used each one in different circumstances and for different purposes. However, in the moment when he achieved his greatest triumph, in the act that changed the world, he brought to bear not competence or strength or force, but weakness. He emptied himself of power and died on a cross.

Some Christians would like to see God as the Great Executive in the sky. Many church leaders regard themselves as eager junior managers, running his operation for him; as a devoted salesforce, racking up the converts; as a committed customer-care department, providing superlative pastoral oversight; as a forward-thinking training-and-development division, improving staff performance. What they fail to grasp is that God chooses not to work through executive strategies without first going through the suffering of death and resurrection. The death of Jesus on the cross was not a one-off, an out-of-character gesture by God, like a heavenly curve ball. No, it was the very paradigm of how he acts. Giving up his life in an act of self-emptying, so that it could be given back again, more powerful than before—this exemplifies the way that God continually chooses to act. Yes, he can use other strategies of power. Yes, he knows all they can achieve. Yes, he understands that a healthy human society needs foundations and commands, social capital, vision and drive. However, he also knows that unless people are willing to participate in death and resurrection, they will remain trapped in a system that is based not on freedom but on fear. The process of self-emptying is not merely one of the eight different leadership strategies: it is the foundation of all the others, the key that unlocks them all, the sacrifice that consecrates them all.

A willingness to embrace weakness is utterly characteristic of the God that is portrayed in the Bible. In contrast to how other world religions conceive him, the distinctive Christian understanding of God is that his priority is for the underdog: the poor, the meek, the broken, the outcast. It seems that the depth of his love is revealed most fully not in power but in the brokenness of Jesus, on a cross. And it is for that reason (and that alone) that any leader seeking to 'lead as Jesus led', seeking to implement a vision of leadership informed by faith—whether in the church or in business, in the family or in government—must be equally willing to embrace weakness.

Again, I need to make it clear I am not talking about weakness as an end in itself. Self-emptying, laying down power, is merely a channel through which a great power is allowed to flow—but it is power that enables others to flourish, not power to aggrandize us. Peggy Noonan observed how crucial Reagan's own experiences of weakness and failure were in forming him as a man and as a leader. 'I like to remember this: Reagan played Vegas. In 1954, when demand for his acting services was slowing, Reagan emceed a variety act to make money and keep his name in the air. He didn't like doing it. But it was what he had to do, so he did it. The point is he knew what it was to be through, to have people not answer your calls. When I thought about this time in his life once, I thought, All the great ones have known failure, but only the greatest of the great use it. He always used his. It deepened him and sharpened him. ... He didn't become President to reach some egocentric sense of personal destiny; he didn't need the presidency, and he didn't go for it because of some strange vanity, some weird desire to be loved or a need of power to fill the empty spaces within. He didn't want the presidency in order to be a big man. He wanted the presidency so that he could do big things.'

Freedom is the jewel that is shaped by such self-emptying, and it has three beautifully-honed facets. The first facet is *freedom from the need to be great*. Almost all leaders have a desire to be great—to dominate their world and leave their mark on history. Such atavistic drives spur us on and summon from us the sacrifices that are often required to achieve such goals. However, the greatest glory remains for those who have conquered such ambition. Only when you are content to be used or not used, wanted or not wanted, can you truly serve others without at the same time exploiting them. Only then can you truly enable others to flourish and become great without regarding them as a threat.

The second facet is *the freedom to be fully available*. One of the greatest gifts a leader can give to others is the space within herself to contain their feelings. This is a matter of listening, of taking into ourselves the needs of others, absorbing them and sharing in them without being overwhelmed by them. This kind of listening is the basis of true friendship, if not of all human relationships. We pay therapists billions of dollars a year to do just this—and yet at heart the role they play is only what is properly human. Listening to someone else without jumping in with our own answers, being still enough to hear without being distracted, being patient enough to give them time to untangle their confusion, being open enough to accept them wherever they are, being wise enough to see their situation in the context of a wider narrative—these are the greatest gifts one person can give to another. They lie at the heart of what it means truly to lead another person.

If we ourselves have unmet emotional needs, we are, paradoxically, 'full up' with our own emotions—and in that event we won't have room for anyone else's. I know all too well that when I come home from leading a course all day I am pretty full emotionally: I have spent the day 'containing' the emotions of many other people and haven't paid attention to my own. If my children start fighting and hurting each other, I have very little space to contain their feelings and often just want to put the lid straight back on them. If we are to listen to others in the way I have been describing, we ourselves need a container in which to place our own feelings. This relationship may be a human one, but it is my contention that a relationship with a divine Father who himself is 'emotionally big enough' is the only thing that can securely contain all our feelings.[11]

The third, and perhaps most wonderful, facet of the jewel of freedom is *the freedom to lead with nothing to lose*. Think back to the time when you did best something that you love doing—perhaps singing in a choir, or acting on a stage, or giving a piano recital, or sailing a boat, or playing in a sports team. I would bet that your finest performance was when you were most free of the fear of failure. This is certainly true for me. When I was free to concentrate totally, to be completely absorbed in what I was doing, to give myself to it, with abandon, with no anxiety about the outcome, those were the times when I have given my most noteworthy performances. When we lead with something to lose, whether it be our reputation, our position, our salary or whatever, we

---

[11] Walter Brueggemann, *Spirituality of the Psalms* (Augsburg Fortress, 2001)

lead with our guards up. Of course, this may mean we are totally focused—I would not deny that—but always some of our energy is being consumed by the self-protective self-monitoring that goes on when we are trying to evaluate our performance even as we give it. Leading with nothing to lose liberates us from fear and gives us an abandoned freedom to give everything we have to what we are doing.

Paradoxically, when we reach this position we achieve a kind of stillness in which we are free to pay attention to what is really going on around us. Stillness in the eye of a storm results in a deeper awareness, an ability to listen to the moment—and this in turn enables us to join in with what is truly important, right and good. And when we do this, we have the necessary mobility to lead appropriately—whether to act with strength or weakness, on the front stage or the back, to expand or consolidate. In this way, our freedom does indeed become manifest in our supremely enhanced performance, as we are able to choose to do whatever needs to be done, in whatever way is called for.

SIXTEEN

The Hospitality of the Undefended Leader

YOU AS HOST

DRAW YOUR OWN PICTURE

Mark and I were discussing current ideas about leadership. Like me, Mark worked with leaders, helping them to become more aware of their effect on others around them.

'On the one hand,' he said, 'there's the idea of the leader as hero, strong, capable, brave, who takes problems on and overcomes them. And then, on the other, there's Greenleaf's idea of "servant leadership". They seem to be at two ends of a scale. One is about power, the other about passivity. One is about dominating, the other seems to be about letting others dominate. Neither quite seems to capture what leadership is all about.'

I agreed. 'Neither concept is quite full enough or rich enough, is it?' I suggested. 'Leading others involves more than either of those two polarities. Of course, there are times when you do both of those things, but you do a lot more, too.' We had met up to talk about a possible new way of thinking about what a leader really needs to be, which we believed might be a better model than either hero or servant. We were exploring the idea that, at its heart, leadership is really most a matter of being a host.

You see, one of the problems with the model of hero or servant is that it focuses attention on the nature of the leader and her fundamental assets. Yet leading other people is actually about the space between the leader and her followers. It's about the relationships she creates and manages. If you think of a leader not as a hero or a servant but as a host, you immediately think in terms not of her fundamental assets but of the space she creates around her. You can't think about a host without thinking about a party, or a home, to which guests are welcomed. You start to think about the relationships that already exist, the friendships that may be formed. You start to think about leadership in terms of encounter and conversation.

This book has explored eight different leadership strategies, each of which 'does something' to the space around you. Used in concert, they offer a repertoire of social and emotional skills that allow a host to create and sustain a healthy, enriching, dynamic and (most importantly) humane space in which people can grow and give of their best. There are several basic ingredients in this task of hosting:

· Creating a safe space in which people can relax, confident that they understand what is going on and what is expected of them
· Facilitating encounters between people in which genuine listening can occur, and encouraging conversation, laughter and the exchange of ideas and possibilities, so that people leave enriched
· Giving the occasion meaning, structure and a sense of significance through sharing in rituals and traditions (playing games, saying grace, drinking toasts, asking people to sign a visitors' book...)

Each of these elements is important if the guests are to enjoy the experience and be enriched by it. They all fit into the eight strategies of leadership, which underlines how close the parallels are between the role of host and the role of leader. Each of the eight strategies provides ways in which the 'leadership host' can create the right social and emotional space around himself. Ideally, they are used in concert by a leader who is fully attentive to their effect, and the character of the space they are helping to create. He takes responsibility for shaping the overall character of this space and brings out the best in other people by making them feel welcome and at home.

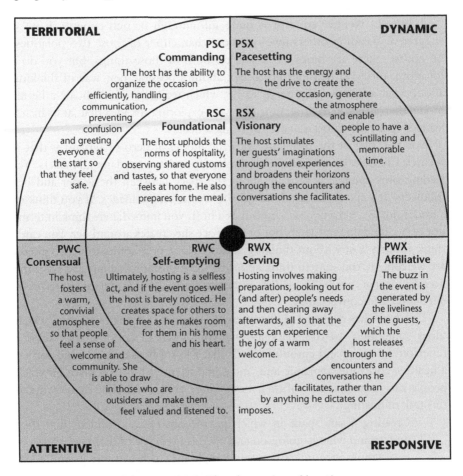

Diagram 16.1: The dynamics of hosting

Arguably, a leader can rarely offer genuine 'hospitality' if she insists on retaining control over everything that is going on. How miserable it is as a guest to feel that you can't walk where you like in the garden, you have to do exactly what your host has planned for you and you're going to be watched the whole time. A hospitable leader 'creates space' for others to express themselves and their gifts in shaping the 'landscape' of the occasion. She trusts them, and enjoys seeing them involved in this way—it's a source of delight to her that this is a collaborative endeavour. The greatest leadership always establishes freedom rather than control and is not too worried about results. It measures success not in terms of output or productivity but of the freedom others have to contribute—the way guests are drawn out of themselves and into the community.

Undefended leadership is about that kind of generous hospitality: a giving of ourselves to the world that transforms it, an opening-up of space in our lives in which the 'other' is welcomed and, indeed, utterly changed. As such, it is a task that depends on the 'space' available within the leader that others can be invited into. The quest to become undefended leaders is a quest to cultivate this interior space within ourselves, as well as the fluency to become welcoming hosts who can enrich our guests.

We've come to accept an idea of leadership in which the character of the leader is virtually irrelevant to his task as leader. The concept of undefended leadership contradicts this and insists that the right character is the primary attribute required. We've come to accept an idea of leadership in which the leader is strong and powerful and 'does things' for her followers. The concept of undefended leadership, however, says that first of all the leader must be led. Leadership is not a primary activity but a secondary one. A leader is not a leader first but a follower. First and foremost, she must be focused on the source of the love and grace that gives her security and sets her free.

Undefended leadership subverts expectations of power and self-sufficiency in favour of a life of vulnerability and dependence. It declares that the first steps taken by the undefended leader may not be on the metalled road to the training school but on the rough path of personal discipleship. It is on that journey that the process of formation is begun. Undefended leadership begins not with the amassing of skills and the acquisition of power but with the humility of learning to trust and to receive. It insists that the leader must begin by receiving. Only then can he go on, enabled to give to others. It is only out of this kind of life that the freedom and power to act greatly can come.

The language of hospitality draws our attention beyond issues of personal leadership towards wider horizons. How hospitable is the society we live in? To what extent does it create safe space in which very different people can not only enjoy a resilient coexistence but can also trust each other? How far does it protect the vulnerable? How far does it enrich the human spirit by promoting the highest virtues? To what extent is it founded on principles of generosity, trust and collective and personal responsibility? To what degree are those same qualities exhibited in its citizens?

Our exploration of the nature of power in undefended leadership has brought us to the frontiers of social and political leadership. Now we must ask the question: What would an undefended *society* look like? This is the territory I cover in the final book of this trilogy: What if the same parameters of hospitality were applied to a state? With such an ideal in mind, perhaps we could ask ourselves what sort of political, economic and even military choices we might make. Perhaps we could approach the major, pressing issues of our day with the same questions to help us: How could a principle of hospitality inform our country's policy on immigration? Or climate change? Or intervention overseas? Or education? Or the arts and media? Or business and private enterprise? Or religion and faith? Or medical ethics? Or civic responsibility?

If it's good to live in a home or work in a company that shows hospitality, perhaps it may also be good to live in a society that is founded on the same principles. Of course, such a proposition needs to be thought through very carefully. Families, and even companies, are relatively simple communities, but a society is far more complex and variegated. We would need to consider, for example, what it might mean for wealth creation and ownership. We'd need to look at the political mechanisms that distribute power, at the role of the constitution, written or unwritten, and the foundations of the state. We'd need to think about the nature of education, the principles underlying the formation of socially responsible adults. We'd need to reflect on the issues of rights and responsibilities, freedom and duty, and on how our society gives permission and approval. We'd need to examine all of these, and many other, facets of our society in order to try to understand how it functioned as a whole, as a social *system*.

However, we should be confident that principles that have proved true and good and strong at both a personal and an organizational level will also prove true, good and strong at a societal level. It has been worth taking pains to understand the nature of power in the simple transactions between an individual leader and his followers, because we may be able to apply our knowledge also to more complex situations. For example, we could analyse not just individual behaviour but that of a whole society in terms of the front stage and the back stage. We could differentiate the use of strong and weak power not just by individuals but by whole demographic groups, and could assess whether different sectors of the population were driven to expand or to consolidate. Indeed, it might be possible to build up a dynamic and yet coherent picture of our whole social system in these basic terms.

And if this were possible, the rewards might be great. Many of the big, unresolved and urgent questions of our day require just such a systemic analysis. We need to look at the whole, rather than just individual parts. We need to understand, for example, the impact our country's trade policy has right across society—on the 'underclass' as well as on the business elite. Likewise, we need to understand how its education policy affects the nation's economic future as well as our own children's welfare, and how its security policy impinges on our social cohesion as well as on our personal safety. Each individual thread is part of a much bigger picture, and if we try to pull it out we risk spoiling the whole tapestry.

As we come to the end of this second part of the trilogy, we turn our attention from questions of personal and organizational leadership to questions of social and political leadership—questions whose answers are going to determine the context for all our lives for years, if not decades, to come.

Appendix: Troubleshooting Problems in Leadership and Other FAQs

Now that we understand a little more about the mechanics of power in any social system, we may be able to apply these insights to different circumstances to achieve the results we need. Some of the most frequently asked questions about building organizations, teams and communities we can address effectively simply by following the principles suggested by the ecology of power and using the right strategies at the right time.

Here are some of the FAQs I have encountered, both in leading my own organizations and when advising others.

Q. *I'm trying to build a new business, and it seems to me important to establish the right culture at the outset. How do I do that?*

A. Your new business needs foundations. You've probably got a business plan to lay out the financial and commercial foundations, but what you also need is a 'culture plan' to lay out the social and emotional foundations. This is NOT the same as an organizational map that shows who is managed by who. It's a plan you draw up to establish the culture of the organization over the coming months. It must address the following questions:

· What are your foundations going to be? You need to establish core values, expected behaviours, standards, goals, routines and rhythms. Are you clear about yours?

· How are you planning to build these foundations so that they're all agreed and owned? You need to begin by creating opportunities to speak to all your teams face-to-face. Put a presentation together. Get their feedback. Make yourself available for comments. Check that everyone buys into them—get them to sign up! Train your managers to implement these foundational principles and practices with absolute consistency.

· How are you going to reinforce these foundations over time? Invent ways to remind everyone of these principles and practices every year. Think about how you integrate new staff so they are familiar with them—use a buddy system to teach them.

Don't over-manage your staff! If they're not doing what they should, don't do it for them—and don't axe them. Instead, get them to look again at the charter they signed up to, identify where things have gone wrong and put it right.

A final point: you will probably find you have to reinterpret your basic principles for every new phase of your business's growth. Be flexible—but remember the foundations you said the business was built on in the first place. Then you will have a business you can be proud of.

Q. *I'm in a real battle for survival. The market has turned down, sales have fallen and my staff are getting anxious about their futures. What should I do?*

A. There may be ways in which you need to look at the market and see where it's going in the future. If you can't adjust the service you provide to fit the new demand, you may be in trouble.

However, in the short term you need to hold your nerve *and* help your staff to hold theirs. This is a matter of Commanding leadership. Imagine that you're Ernest Shackleton leading an Antarctic expedition: the weather has turned against you, your rations are low and people's lives are in danger. You need to plot a course for survival. What do you do?

· You give people confidence that you can make decisions and can protect them. Now is the time to stand tall, look people in the eye and tell them the truth.

· Explain the sacrifices you're all going to have to make to survive (job cuts, reductions in expense accounts, other cutbacks, consolidation). Explain why they need to make these sacrifices and the benefits of doing so.

· Explain very clearly the next immediate task—that is, what you all need to achieve today in order to survive till tomorrow. And the same tomorrow. And the same the next day.

· Explain the route you're plotting out of the mess, step by step, so they know exactly what is happening and when.

· Keep close to your troops—remember that Commanding PSC leadership needs to be supported by a Serving RWX style. Spend more time face-to-face with them, be present in the office and be seen to be making sacrifices yourself. Make people coffee. Find things to celebrate. Little things like that keep people's spirits up.

· Build camaraderie by encouraging people to share ideas, resources and so forth. Consider buddying people together so no one feels alone. In these situations, you will either develop tremendous camaraderie or run the risk of mutiny or desertion. Use your instinctive team-builders to create the former and prevent the latter!

Q. *We have a team that needs to perform really effectively over the next 12 months. If they can rise to the challenge, we have a real opportunity to break into a new level of business. What should I be doing to ensure they achieve that level of performance?*

A. Developing teams that perform exceptionally well is all about creating a virtuous circle of energy, drive, discipline and self-belief. The key is to get the circle started. Here's how to do it:

- Teams work best when they are fired up by a vision that motivates them. You need to use RSX leadership to find the critical thing that will excite your team—it may be the pride of achieving something unprecedented, it may be financial success, it may be new opportunities that flow from success, it may be a higher purpose they would be fulfilling. Find the vision, focus it and project it—and refer to it consistently as the mountaintop to which you're all heading.

- The vision will create a sense of community. Use a PWC strategy to capitalize on this. Create a sense of privilege, intimacy and camaraderie in the team. Mark them out as different, so they know it. Foster a culture of mutual encouragement and community by getting them to talk to each other every week, sharing ideas and thoughts.

- Give them team incentives, in Affiliative style. That is, instead of individual incentives, reward the whole team when one of them does well. This motivates them all to help each other to succeed.

- Their energy, drive and discipline will inspire the hope that the vision can be realized, and thus a virtuous circle is created, for as the vision gets stronger, so does the sense of community and so does the energizing sense of self-belief.

One warning! Once you have created a team like this, you'll find it hard to separate them and they may become a maverick unit in your organization. You need to think about how you are going to integrate them with other teams in the future to avoid them becoming potentially rebellious.

Q. *For years, we've been asking for more independence from our parent organization. They are so controlling and refuse to recognize our desire to take responsibility and have greater autonomy. The effect is demoralizing. What should we do?*

A. If things are as bad as that, it sounds as if you're reaching the point where a more radical approach is called for. First, though, you need to make sure there really is no way your parent organization could cut you some slack. Have you found out why they won't do this? Have you demonstrated that you could manage on your own?

Once you have clarified this, you need to gauge just how strongly your staff want the change. How desperate are they? What are they prepared to do? And to give up, perhaps? In other words, how much would they really hate it if things remained as they are? Many people talk about change but in reality lack the fight to make it happen. This is about using an RWX approach that listens to your staff on the ground.

If you are clear that there is sufficient support, you have two options. Both of these employ RWC force, and both are inflammatory and entail risk.

First, you could simply cease to comply with your parent organization. This is the equivalent of passive resistance or civil disobedience. You're not downing tools, you're not going on strike, you're simply refusing to recognize their authority over you. You get on with your work, deliver results, but you do it outside their jurisdiction. Expect things to get hot! It will provoke a reaction and you'll find you're forcing your parent organization either to clamp down or to start negotiating. Either way, they will realize you mean business. You keep the moral high ground by continuing to work, and you hope that ultimately this will make them see sense.

Your other option is to withdraw. If you really feel you can make a better job of it alone, go and do it! Take the staff who want to go with you and start up a rival company. As long as you abide by the restrictions in your contracts, there's nothing to stop you doing this. Maybe it's time to put your money where your mouth is.

Q. *I'd like help with general troubleshooting. Often, I'm faced with teams that seem a bit stuck: they're demotivated, apathetic, just kind of run out of gas. Mostly they become cynical, and then bitchy at the same time. As a result, they're not only unproductive but also a negative influence on others in the organization. What should I do about such teams?*

A. Most problems with teams lie with their foundations. If you build a house and give it only one-foot-deep foundations, pretty soon you'll start to notice cracks in the walls as it begins to subside. The problem is not in the walls, or in the architecture necessarily: it's in the structural engineering—what has not been done underground. Teams become apathetic when they have no clear sense of where they're going, why they're doing what they're doing and whether it can be achieved. They may be worn out, they may not think their work is worthwhile, they may not think it is doable. All you can do is embark on the messy and time-consuming work of digging up the foundations of the structure and underpinning it.

· You need to examine your expectations of the team. Do you have strong foundations?

- If so, to what extent do the team know about them and consent to them? If you have never communicated those values, expectations, boundaries and so on, they won't know about them. If you simply imposed them at the outset as 'This is what I want to happen,' they may never have given them their consent.

- Get the team together and broach the subject of the problem. Admit that something is wrong and see if they acknowledge it, too. Tell them what the problem is on your side—that is, how it is affecting you, the organization, productivity and so on—and let them tell you what the problem is on their side.

- As you start to understand the problem, get them to reflect on the foundations—the shared expectations—that underlie your enterprise and their team. Do they still agree with them? Do they matter to them any more?

- You may find that at this stage some people say these foundations no longer matter to them in the same way. Fair enough, people change—but in this team you ONLY have people to whom the agreed objectives really matter. Thus, you make it clear to the dissidents you need to work with them to find them a role they do believe in, because they can't remain in this team. This is a team in which everyone agrees to aim towards the specified goals in the ways agreed. Otherwise, they're letting everyone else down.

- Then, having strengthened the foundations of purpose and expectations, removed any cause for further subsidence and dealt with the rubble, you have to establish whether there is anything YOU need to do differently to support them better. 'What do *I* need to change to ensure you can get your work done?' It may be to provide more direct support, or more training, resources or time.

- Finally, you all agree the new basis on which you're going to work. You make a commitment to it, and agree to review it in a month, then in three months, then a year.

If things don't improve, it may be time to think about winding the team down. Every group has a natural lifespan, and this one may just have reached the end of theirs.

—3—

Leading with Everything to Give

Lessons from the Success and Failure of Western Capitalism

Preface to the first edition of
Leading with Everything to Give

These are difficult days. The collapse of Lehman Brothers on 16 September 2008 marked the beginning of a period of economic collapse that, at the time of writing, is still unfolding day by day. My own business suffered the immediate effects of the crisis: clients promptly cancelled projects and deferred all non-essential investment, as they took measures to cut costs—including lay-offs and sell-offs—that are now becoming only more severe. None of us knows how deep, or prolonged, the downturn will prove to be, or quite what the world will look like when we emerge from it. Our financial models are simply not sophisticated enough to cope with the unprecedented complexity of these global events. The truth is that most of us today are scared.

At the same time, however, we should be absolutely clear that nothing that is now taking place is either surprising or unexpected. I wrote the first draft of this book more than two years ago, and the thinking it is based on was done well before that. I am not alone in the opinion that the factors that have caused this collapse were evident to anyone who had eyes to see them. The truth is that most of us, including our financial and political leaders, chose not to.

The broad thrust of this book is that Western civilization is nearing the end of its current life-cycle. If we locate its intellectual origins in the European Renaissance in the 15th century, we can trace from there a line of cultural development and flourishing that is now coming to an end. The industrial expansionism, the economic models of capital ownership, the organization of political power, the structure of our societies, all have lost their intellectual, practical and moral purchase. It is not that they are bankrupt in themselves but that our expression and application of them have become corrupt. The present economic crisis is merely a manifestation of a wider, more systemic breakdown in our civilization.

Thus, though it is economic turmoil that fills our foreground, we must not look for an answer that is purely economic. Our problems go far deeper. Our self-analysis must be more rigorous, more ruthless. It is incumbent on us, as the immediate dust settles, to ask how we got to this position, what impelled us to be so irresponsible and why our leaders failed to prevent it. Such questions insist that we explore our wider sociological, psychological and intellectual footings for an answer.

In fact, this is a time of great opportunity—of opportunity, in fact, on a scale not seen for several centuries perhaps. Over the next 50 years we have the chance to bring about a new Renaissance, with a new vision of what it means to be fully human. The glories of Venice, Florence, Sienna and other cradles of that cultural renewal in the 15th century remind us of our legacy in the West: architecture of extraordinary beauty and exquisite craftsmanship, art and music of sublime sensitivity. That period saw the birth of both modern science and modern literature, and the careful construction of a theology and philosophy robust enough to bear the weight of systems of governance that have brought forth arguably the greatest progress in political history.

Once again, we need a cultural rebirth, from which will grow a new social, economic and spiritual landscape. We must be aware, however, that such a rebirth cannot precede, let alone prevent, the demise of what has stood before. The shattered colossus of Shelley's Ozymandias reminds us of the inevitability of the death that must come first. We need courage to face our present loss, severe and painful as it is. We must take the first steps towards the future with a deep humility, aware that (as T S Eliot put it in 'Little Gidding') we come at night like a broken king, not knowing what we came for, in the hope that the purpose will break forth even as it is fulfilled.

Simon Walker

Part 3A

DECONSTRUCTION:

LESSONS FROM THE FAILURES OF WESTERN CAPITALISM

ONE

Laying Out the Map

In the first two books of this trilogy, I have used the model of the 'ecology' of power to illustrate the interactions of power and personality. Rather like a map, I have used it to set out the different regions (as it were) in which we might venture to exercise power, so that each of us can chart how and where we do so. It also helps us each to understand the impact of our actions on others (because if you choose to exert power in one region, it will also have an effect in another region). This 'ecology' functions as a whole: no one part of it can be separated out in isolation. The model shows us how we are interrelated, the character of the 'space' between one person and another.

This same idea will form the basis for our observations of society as a whole in this third and final book of the trilogy. We are interested in the interrelations not just between individuals but between whole populations. We are concerned to understand the flow of power between people(s). We want to know, if one population does this or that (spends its money in this way, for instance, or restricts freedom of speech in that way), what will happen to another population within the same social system. We want to understand how societies are connected as wholes, how they relate within themselves and between themselves. And to help us in this endeavour, I will be using a specific model of social ecology that I have developed over the past five years.

This particular model envisages three dimensions in which social interaction takes place.

Presented and reserved
(also known as 'frontstage and backstage')

'Presented' (or 'frontstage') and 'reserved' (or 'backstage') describe the two ways in which a social system can be perceived and experienced. On the one hand, a society has elements in it that are explicit for all to see—which might include the image it chooses to project, the way it portrays itself, the 'visible landscape' of its culture, its overt industries, occupations and trades, its apparent rulers and authorities. All these are things that are 'presented' by that society to the wider world. They can be contrasted with those things that are 'reserved' by that society from such exposure—its underclass, most obviously, but also (for example) those values, beliefs, traditions and tales that express its history and character but are not always recited publicly. Every society has assumptions, attitudes, mores, taboos, ideas and stories that shape and inform it profoundly but are not apparent to the average tourist. You have to dig for them.

Presented
(What is visible)   **Reserved**
(What is hidden)

Strong and weak

'Strong' and 'weak' differentiate the two kinds of power that groups in society exert over others. Strong power is a force that is directive, shaping or determining the response of others. Weak power is a force that is responsive, reacting to or following the action and direction of others. So, for example, *haute couture* fashion exerts strong power, setting a direction in design that the high street then follows. When scientists create a new drug that revolutionizes the treatment of cancer, they apply a strong force to medical practice as doctors change how they do things accordingly. If they don't comply, legal sanctions can be applied. On the other hand, if a man goes to the doctor about a lump or a bump in his body that is worrying his wife (however much, being a typical male, he might prefer to ignore it), she is exerting weak power over him. His love and respect for her oblige him to go, even though she has no (strong) power to compel him to.

Strong power
(What is directive)   **Weak power**
(What is responsive)

Expanding and consolidating

'Expanding' and 'consolidating' refer to the two directions in which a force can move the society. An expanding force moves it on onto new ground, resulting in new ideals, new ideas, new aspirations, new enterprises. For example, immigration breaks up old social structures and exposes society to new cultures and new possibilities (as well as, potentially, new problems). On the other hand, a consolidating force establishes society on familiar ground. Conventions, traditions, institutions, governance and compliance with government are all examples of this. Families exert a cohesive force within a society, binding individuals into older, 'familiar' patterns of life, exerting discipline, nurturing emotional stability and health. So do strong local communities, voluntary organizations and schools.

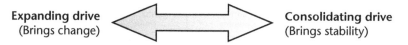

Expanding drive
(Brings change)

Consolidating drive
(Brings stability)

Of course, these three 'dimensions' are not isolated from each other, but rather they interact with each other. In fact, they combine in eight different ways, which I denote by eight different three-letter 'codes'.

	Strong/weak	Expanding/ consolidating	Legend
Presented or frontstage	Strong +	Consolidating	(PSC)
	Strong +	Expanding	(PSX)
	Weak +	Consolidating	(PWC)
	Weak +	Expanding	(PWX)

	Strong/weak	Expanding/ consolidating	Legend
Reserved or backstage	Strong +	Consolidating	(RSC)
	Strong +	Expanding	(RSX)
	Weak +	Consolidating	(RWC)
	Weak +	Expanding	(RWX)

We could represent these eight different combinations as sectors on a map that represents a society. We would expect the character of each sector to be different and distinctive, as it expressed the particular dynamics of visibility, power and stability that governed that part of society. The diagram on page 6 illustrates what those distinctive characteristics might look like.

The model of social ecology gives us, as it were, a map with which we can make sense of our current political and economic landscape. Only when we can see our particular situation in the context of the whole will we be able to find the way ahead.

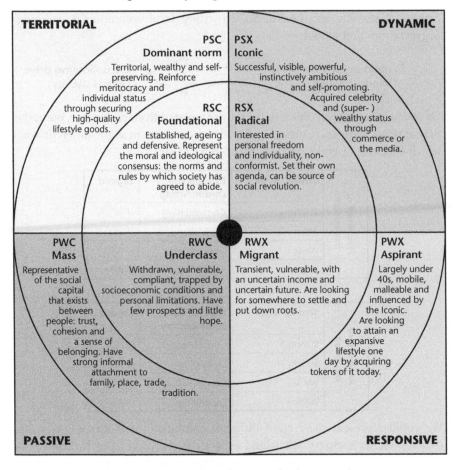

The model of social ecology applied to a society

TWO

The Crumbling of Our Foundations
(RSC)

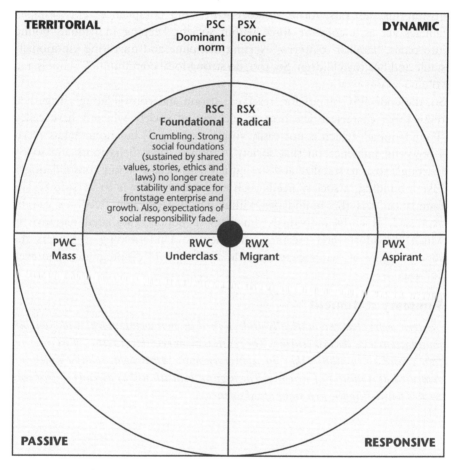

The current weakening of foundations in the West

Chapter summary

In this chapter, we explore the Foundational aspect of Western society. The code for this sector is RSC, with each of these letters referring to a basic aspect of the social system.

The R stands for *'reserved'* (as opposed to P for 'presented'). Reserved elements of a society include its traditions, beliefs and values and the stories that express its history but may not always be told publicly. The S stands for *'strong force'* (as opposed to W for 'weak force'). Strong force is that which is directive and shapes or otherwise determines the response of others. The C stands for *'consolidating'* (as opposed to X for 'expanding'). Consolidating force anchors society to familiar ground—time-honoured habits, ways of relating, institutions, festivals, forms of governance and compliance. For example, families act as a cohesive force within society, keeping individuals bound into older, 'familiar' patterns, exerting discipline and nurturing emotionally stable and healthy children. So, too, do strong local communities, schools and voluntary organizations.

So, the code RSC stands for 'reserved, strong and consolidating'. Together, these three characteristics form an element of society which I have called 'Foundational': which is not easily visible ('reserved') but nonetheless exerts a powerful influence on that society's cultures, laws, behaviours and so on ('strong') so as to stabilize and strengthen that social system ('consolidating'). Like a building, a society needs such a foundation if it is to be secure. The foundation sets the boundaries within which acceptable freedoms can be expressed. It curbs individuals' impulses. It supplies a shared narrative in which individuals find meaning and identity. Undermining it renders the superstructure of that society unstable and at risk of disintegration and even collapse.

Summary statement

Western society has systematically undermined its own social, moral and economic foundations over the last century. The result is an inevitable fracture of its internal fabric, and an instability that threatens even more catastrophic collapse unless it is remedied as a matter of urgency. The ground beneath us has already shifted and we are witnessing the first signs of subsidence.

Let's be clear: the economic crisis that exploded in the early autumn of 2008 was not caused primarily by bad banking practices. Certainly these resulted in an unbearable weight of bad debt, but the fundamental faults that led to the accumulation of that debt lie further back in the past, and are much less easy to see. The problem lay—indeed, still lies—with a crumbling of our social, moral and political disciplines that began about a century ago.

A few years back, my wife and I were house-hunting. One of the properties we viewed was a lovely old Victorian gabled house, now 'in need of some modernization' (as the real-estate agent's notes euphemistically put it). We could see at once that it needed total redecoration and some internal reordering, but some other, more fundamental problems soon became apparent. The wiring was 70 years old, the plumbing and boiler were archaic and there was no central-heating system at all. The infrastructure was looking dodgier all the time. And then we spotted the crack. Over a bay window on the side of the house that was built above a steeply sloping bank, a nasty-looking fissure had opened up. One look at that and we knew that if we bought the place we would be in for a whacking bill, simply to stabilize the building. Its foundations on the slope had sunk, and that entire side of the house had dropped.

The house had a fault line only one centimetre wide—not a lot, you might think. However, it pointed to bigger structural problems below the surface, problems that could threaten the entire building. Moreover, the cost to fix these problems would be immense. It's relatively cheap to lay deep and strong foundations when you put up a building, but to underpin an existing one that is sinking is an entirely different matter, requiring complex and expensive engineering work. It's always extremely difficult to reinforce foundations that are too shallow once the building has been erected on top.

Social foundations provide stability

Human societies are not unlike buildings. Just as a building needs to have strong, deep, stable foundations hidden away underneath it, so the establishing of strong, consolidating patterns of power on the 'back stage' of a human social system is essential to give it stability. Thus, for example, the Roman Empire was built upon the training and organization of its legions. Without the agreements, sanctions, rewards and resources required to assemble and then manage a highly cohesive, disciplined army, the governance of that vast territory would have collapsed. Again, the British Empire was built upon the strict hierarchy shaped by the class system and the Christian religion. Respect for authority, dutiful obedience to God and Monarch and the Protestant work ethic were all crucial components in Britain's ascendancy from the 16th century onwards. Likewise, the extraordinary capacity of the Japanese to make tremendous sacrifices in the Second World War was the product of a highly ordered society in which devotion to the Emperor was paramount and surrender was a disgrace worse than death.

Social foundations allow freedom

The foundations that support social systems and give them stability and resilience have to be laid down and reinforced consciously and deliberately. They do not come about by accident. The great freedoms set out by Thomas Jefferson in the American Declaration of Independence in 1776 laid down a philosophical and ideological foundation for the legal structure of the Constitution to be agreed in 1787. They represented fundamental shared beliefs about the nature of human life and civic responsibility: 'We hold these truths to be self-evident, that all men are created equal, that they are endowed by their Creator with certain unalienable Rights, that among these are Life, Liberty and the pursuit of Happiness.' On them was to be built the entire commercial and cultural civilization that developed over the following centuries. The Constitution is the American family's agreement on how things are going to be done, what is shared in common, what citizens are responsible for and what membership of the United States involves for each and every individual.

It is no coincidence that such fundamental principles should have been laid down at the beginning of the 13 states' new-won independence. Just as with a house, the foundations must come first before the walls and roofs can be constructed. Indeed, it is the strength and solidity of those foundations that will determine how stable the social structure will be that is built upon them, and how long it will last. Nation-building is much like any other form of building: problems arise if you can't lay deep enough foundations at the outset—which is arguably the basic issue in the current attempt to bring peace to Iraq. It is also much more difficult to prop up a shaky edifice at a later date.

Like a well-established set of architectural rules, which everyone assents to and upholds, the American Constitution has defined the shape and set the style of the great national 'home' that has been built over the past two centuries: a house of liberty, in which individuals are encouraged and empowered to take the opportunities available to them—and to create more. It has fostered a diverse commercial competitiveness, welcoming enterprise and innovation without any fear that they might threaten the security it has created. Indeed, it harks back to the Declaration of Independence and the fundamental rights and ideals that that expressed, which provided Abraham Lincoln with the ideological and political resources to dismantle the institution of slavery in the 19th century and gave King's Civil Rights movement the leverage to overturn racial segregation in the 20th. It was the thinking in those first, foundational statements that was the scaffolding in which the 'architecture' of America took shape in the centuries that followed. Likewise, the feeling of confidence and cultural 'belonging' that these foundational ideals engender, as well as the festivals and rites of passage associated with them, endow Americans with a strong sense of national identity. In no British city (and few European cities) will you see the national flag hanging in school yards and the windows of private homes— except during the World Cup—or find schoolchildren beginning their day singing the national anthem or reciting the national civic constitution.[1] Outside Switzerland and Scandinavia, 21st-century Europeans lack the same sense of collective national identity.

Social foundations create limits

What foundations provide for the building above them—whether it is a suburban home or a shopping centre or a skyscraper—is a basis on which people can live safely and securely, without anxiety. Belief in the liberty of the individual, freedom of expression, the right to happiness, these values have supported and sustained an economy that has dominated the world since the Second World War. The economy of Europe, while not as powerful, is built on the same values of individual enterprise, the free flow of capital and the right of the individual to create and amass personal wealth. The free-market capitalism of both America and northern Europe owes much of its character to the Protestant work ethic that underlies it and, with its emphasis on hard work, self-discipline and the renunciation of immediate pleasure for the sake of profit to come, gives it spiritual and moral strength. The same ethic asserts both the responsibility of the individual to learn, grow and make the most of their God-given opportunities and gifts and, at the same time, the subordination of the individual to the authorities set over them, whether church or state, which it sees as agents and instruments of God's ordering of this world. Western industrial society is built on the twin premises of the capacity of the individual to create wealth and the authority of the state to constrain behaviour. The result has been dynamic economic growth but within the bounds of shared moral and cultural values—in other words, freedom within limits.

The weakening of our social foundations

However, over the past century there has been a concerted and quite aggressive attempt on both sides of the Atlantic to undermine the social and moral foundations that have sustained our societies. This endeavour owes its origins

---

[1] 'Whilst some nations promote the national flag and other symbols of nationhood through education, there has been no recent tradition of flag flying and the singing of a national anthem in schools in England' Hugh Starkey, Jeremy Hayward and Karen Turner, 'Education for Citizenship', *Reflecting Education*, 2 (2) (2006), p2. Retrieved on 8 March 2008 from http://reflectingeducation.net/index.php?journal=reflecting&page=article&op=view&path%5B%5D=31&path%5B%5D=31

to many things, but one that has almost symbolic significance was a debate that took place in 1863 in my home city of Oxford. This event had such powerful intellectual consequences, it could be compared to an earthquake that shook the very foundations of a whole society— an earthquake whose aftershocks are still being felt to this day.

In 1859, Charles Darwin published his book *On the Origin of Species*.[2] In it, he set out the hypothesis that all the diversity of life on earth could be accounted for by a process he called 'natural selection'. While he himself did not suggest that such an explanation debunked or even doubted the idea that the world and everything on it were made by an omnipotent, divine Creator, the church at the time understood it as an attack on the biblical account of creation in the Book of Genesis. Instead of seeking to understand the new theory, the church tried to demolish it. In June 1860, Samuel Wilberforce, the then bishop of Oxford, invited the biologist Thomas Huxley to debate Darwin's ideas with him. Their encounter took place in a room on the top floor of the University's museum of natural history and, though many accounts are clearly mythic, undoubtedly resulted in a decisive victory for Huxley. It became clear that no good case could be made against Darwin's theory on the basis of scientific evidence alone.

This controversy contributed to an emerging consensus in our culture that it might be more expedient to regard hard, empirical science and matters of faith as existing in different epistemological worlds. In one, truth was established by rational research; in the other, by personal experience and belief. The crucial outcome of the debate was the detachment of science from any foundations of religious faith. Science, people began to think, offered a more comprehensive account of the world than Christianity and did not need the support of religious dogma. Indeed, religion was in competition with truth, not an avenue to it. One almost immediate result of this development was that the church began to retreat from intellectual life, wounded by this and other experiences of its authority being questioned. If you visit Oxford today, you will see that opposite the University's natural history museum stands Keble College. Built just a few years after the debate between Wilberforce and Huxley, it was founded by and named after John Keble, who, with others in the so-called Oxford Movement, mounted something of a religious resistance to the 'secularization' they saw around them.

However, this resistance was not primarily intellectual, nor did it seek to re-enter the debates, scientific, literary and historical, that had already been lost. Instead, it tended to define religious faith in terms of a personal, experiential

---

[2] Charles Darwin, *On the Origin of Species by Means of Natural Selection: or, The Preservation of Favoured Races in the Struggle for Life* (London: J Murray, 1859)

moral piety and inner spirituality that need have no connection to the outer, intellectual world. In essence, it defended the sacred by removing it from the secular. The Christian faith had been protected, but at great cost—closeted away in a safe corner where believers could hold on to their own personal faith and morality without having to engage in the turmoil of debate going on in the commercial, cultural, intellectual and political life of the nation.[3] Meanwhile, science steadily became established as a new quasi-religion, and with evangelistic zeal its ministers of truth began to reform school and university curricula up and down the land.

As a graduate in biological sciences from Oxford myself, I come down firmly on the side of Huxley in the debate with Wilberforce, whose arguments I believe were false and unsustainable. However, I believe that something crucial was lost when Huxley demolished the church's credibility, and that was the link between the market and morality. If the church and its notion of individual responsibility but subordination to church and state were no longer to guide public life, what else was going to? What was to emerge over the next hundred years was a new principle: the freedom of the individual subordinated only to the limits of technology. In the absence of any moral rule derived from theology, British society rapidly began to explore novel social mores. Permissiveness—legal, sexual and intellectual—became an essential element of modern liberal democracy. In the market, a new breed of entrepreneurs and 'captains of industry' emerged who lacked any overriding commitment to social cohesion. In science, debates about genetic modification, IVF, embryo growth, human cloning, abortion, euthanasia and the environment have been conducted by technocrats who have lacked a coherent moral framework to shape their decision making. Consequently legislation made by one body contradicts that made by another. Because there is no agreed view on the value of human life, the right to an abortion is promulgated alongside the right to IVF—with one hand our society takes life, with the other it gives it. Because we have no shared perspective on death, demands for the right to have our lives extended by medical science if the means are available are mingled with calls for

---

[3] The major initiatives of the Christian church in the West in the last century have focused on either social or personal mission. The former has usually been conducted through agencies designed to support those who have fallen out of society's safety net—drug users, homeless people, sex workers, people who have been abused. Often, this has involved remarkable (and unsung) commitment outside the structures of politics and government in what is now called the 'third' or 'voluntary' sector of our economy. Personal mission has taken the form of initiatives, large and small, to communicate the message of the Christian faith and demand a personal response. Examples are the Billy Graham 'Crusades' of the 1950s and '60s, the Church of England's 'Decade of Evangelism' in the 1980s and the Alpha movement of the 1990s onwards. Their 'call to conversion' has always focused on personal piety but has rarely emphasized either the need or the means to contribute to the reshaping of our culture. As a result, three generations of Christians have been involved largely in saving individuals in one sense or the other but not in transforming nations.

euthanasia to be legalized as more and more of us limp on into advanced old age. Because we have no common understanding of the nature of personhood, we are busily creating designer embryos even as we seek to protect our rights to personal privacy and integrity. Our law-making is pulled in contradictory directions by our commitment to individual rights and freedoms as opposed to any social or religious commitment.

Freedom without limits

To be simplistic, the West in the 20th century could be summed up in one sentence: 'Because we can, we will.' Given the fantastic ability of our technology to open up, it seems, ever new sources of power, whether medical, military or commercial, we appear to have found no way of saying 'No'. Because we can, we will. However, just because we can does not mean that we must. Because we can does not mean necessarily that we want to. There is a moral choice. We don't have to develop the technology. But, now we have detached morality from the marketplace, the reality has been that whenever a commercial case can be made for some technological advance, sooner or later that advance will be exploited. Sometimes it has taken a while before we have gone through the opened door, but almost every door that has been opened, in medicine, entertainment or whatever, we have gone through in the end. The same is true in other areas of human endeavour—for example, in artistic expression.

The West has almost no moral mechanism for saying 'No' any more—and that is a terrifying situation for a society to be in, because it is only a small step from being unable to say no to breaking down completely. Émile Durkheim coined the term 'anomie' for the condition of a society in which social and moral norms are confused or missing altogether.[4] He argued that, whereas traditional societies managed to teach people (primarily through religion) to control their desires and aspirations, modern industrial societies tend to separate people and so weaken social bonds, and this has the effect of removing such constraints. Whereas people's desires and aspirations previously were curbed by social order and morality, now they seem to know no limit.[5] Inevitably, cracks have begun to

---

[4] 'Anomie springs from the lack of collective forces at certain points in society; that is, of groups established for the regulation of social life': Émile Durkheim, *Suicide: A Study in Sociology* (this translation, J A Spaulding and G Simpson, London: Routledge & Kegan Paul, 1952), p382. See also p258. The book was published originally in 1897.

[5] 'The third sort of suicide ... results from man's activity's lacking regulation and his consequent sufferings. By virtue of its origin we shall assign this last variety the name of anomic suicide. ... In anomic suicide, society's influence is lacking in the basically individual passions, thus leaving them without a check-rein': Ibid., p258

'Religion has lost most of its power. ... Industry ... has become the supreme end of individuals and societies alike. Thereupon the appetites thus excited have become freed of any limiting authority': Ibid., p255

appear in the social edifice that was once supported by a foundation of shared values, and it has started to collapse.

It is the lack of such a constraining 'architecture' that has allowed the unprecedented, unregulated growth in our industries and our exploitation of the world's resources. Take, for example, our energy consumption. Five years ago, the average American was using nearly 24 times as much energy as the average Indian.[6] It has been estimated by some researchers that it would take at least six Earths to support the current global population at such levels of consumption.[7] The situation is simply unsustainable, and there is no question that within 30 years we will all have to reduce our consumption—not least because the global population is projected to have risen by another two billion by then!

Similarly, the systemic failure of the 'architecture' of our financial regulatory structures has allowed the unprecedentedly irresponsible leverage of global debt. What was needed to hold our personal freedoms in reasonable check, as Durkheim stressed a hundred years ago, was the constraint of foundational shared values that would have governed our individual appetites for comfort and convenience.

Social foundations reduce the burden on the individual

In dismantling the morality of our society, and allowing unbounded individual freedom on what I have called 'the front stage', the liberal capitalist agenda has inadvertently created a social system that has no mechanism of self-regulation. Ultimately, the individual consumer has to regulate herself if any capitalist system is to be sustained. What our economy requires is not just financial capital, or a more robust structure of financial regulations, but the social capital of self-restraint and a morality that considers the consequences of our actions for others, even if they are invisible to us on the other side of the world. It requires a willingness to curb our appetites, as well as confidence in a self-identity that is not defined simply by how much we own and how much we consume. Without these personal, psychological foundations in place, the Western edifice was always going to become unstable. The sheer scale of the

---

[6] 'India's per capita annual energy consumption was 594kWh in 2003 compared with 14,057kWh in the US': Amy Yee, 'Flood Threat to Bangladesh a Warning to the World', *The Financial Times*, 2 February 2007, p9

[7] 'It is only fair that other nations would want access to the same types of homes, education, cars, health and luxury consumables that we enjoy. The problem is that this type of global consumption is not possible. It would take more than six planets with the same resource supplies as [E]arth in order to sustain a global suburban lifestyle': *Peak Oil News*, 6 November 2006 (http://www.peak-oil-news.info/north-american-energy-consumption)

global economic crisis bears witness to the yawning holes that for the past 30 years have been opening up under many Western economies and societies.

Social foundations locate and support society

One of the ways in which the crumbling of our society's foundations has affected us is in the collapse of our shared cultural disciplines and patterns. The loss of daily, weekly and annual rhythms of life, both personal and national, has been a feature of the past two decades, accelerated by the opportunities of our globalized economy. In a market operating across time zones, diurnal rhythms necessarily become less marked. The same is true for annual rhythms as supermarkets offer us strawberries in January and clementines in June and cut-price air travel makes the summer sun accessible all year. Television—in particular, satellite TV—lets us watch seasonal sports at any time of year, while all-weather pitches and floodlights have lifted the restrictions on when we can watch games live. Urbanization has reduced our contact with the rhythms of nature, and our air-conditioned cars remove us from the vagaries of the weather. In Britain specifically the Sunday Trading Act of 1989 abolished the one day off a week that everyone had shared, while European Union regulations now insist on an indiscriminate 48-hour week. Shift work, flexitime, overtime and home working all have the effect of flattening the demographically shared rhythm.[8] Meanwhile, 24-hour news channels, all-night television and the 'omnitemporality' of the internet mean a world always on the go. We have become trapped in an accelerating treadmill of economic expansionism from which we are unwilling to escape.

In addition, the benefit of the old rhythms lay in giving a sense of shape to our lives. For example, the discipline of not buying anything on a Sunday reminded us that shopping is not all there is to life. Instead, that one day a week could be reserved for other activities as a family, a community or (for some) a church—a practice that more secular but arguably more family-orientated European societies such as France and Germany retain.

The foundations of a society include a shared rhythm and a shared calendar. Feast days and fast days tell a shared story and both express and reinforce a society's self-identity and sense of cohesion. They also inculcate personal discipline and foster a sense of anticipation. However, the West has lost confidence in the legitimacy of celebrating Christmas, Easter, Whitsun (or Pentecost) and All Saints' Day as specifically Christian festivals (for fear of alienating adherents

---

[8] 'Organisation of Working Time (Basic Directive)', directive 2003/88/EC of the European Parliament and the Council of 4 November 2003, retrieved on 10 March 2008 from http:// europa.eu/scadplus/leg/en/cha/c10418.htm

of other faiths) and instead these occasions have been exploited merely as commercial opportunities. Our sacrifice of a shared religious story has created not a richer cultural environment but a poorer one—except in financial terms. The same can be said of the erosion of social conviction about other cultural markers (such as Remembrance Sunday) and their historical origins by the guilt we feel about our nation's past. When such shared stories are forgotten or disregarded, society fragments. It is difficult to resist the impulse towards individualism—an individualism that increasingly has defined itself through insatiable acquisition and consumption.

Loss of social foundations inspires contempt

In 1964, while living in America, the Egyptian scholar Sayyid Qutb was provoked by that 'open and free' land to write *Milestones*.[9] We should take notice of this, because the book inspired the modern jihad movement. Qutb had devoured Oswald Spengler's *Decline of the West*, Arnold Toynbee's *A Study of History* and T S Eliot's *The Waste Land,* which all portrayed the West as degenerate and profane, lacking any direction. He found in this a parallel to the state of depravity and godlessness that had existed in Arabia before the arrival of the Prophet Muhammad, and he called on his readers to destroy 'this rubbish heap of the West'. Critics will say that Qutb misread those writers and that the West was neither degenerate nor profane. However, when we consider the dynamics of social ecology we see that there is more truth in his perception than we would like to admit.

A society that has no shared values, a market that has lost touch with morality, is a terrifying place to be in. It is fundamentally unsafe, like a building without firm foundations. Its collapse is only a matter of time. Technology cannot itself provide the foundational limits because it has no limits itself. Science will continue to advance, and ever more powerful cures will be invented because the market will demand them. It is also true that ever more powerful bombs will be invented, because the market will demand them, too. Technology, always and only morally neutral, takes no account of its social consequences, good or evil. It can only—and must be—constrained by a moral discourse that lies outside the realm and the control of the scientist and the technocrat. The only alternative is to put our fate entirely in the hands of those who simply hold most power.

Technology was sufficient to overcome the chaotic forces of nature; it could impose its own order on the disorder of the world. The myth of technology as a means of government and social order is always seductive: we are captivated by

---

[9] Sayyid Qutb, *Milestones* (this edition, Beirut: The Holy Koran Publishing House, 1980)

the extraordinary, mesmeric promises of a better and brighter future in a world free of disease and poverty—if only we can make this or that technological breakthrough. We in the West readily subordinate ourselves to the authority and the promises of the technocrats and the free-market economists who want to build and govern our world on the basis of 'Because we can, we will,' who believe that the market will regulate itself. My concern is that we won't stop until we can't go on—and then it will be too late.

Study questions 2

1. What are some of the deepest foundations in your own society?
2. In what ways are these currently being eroded or undermined?
3. What are the implications if that continues?
4. What lessons about social foundations can we learn from recent Western history?

THREE

The Insatiable Hunger of the Well-Fed (PWX)

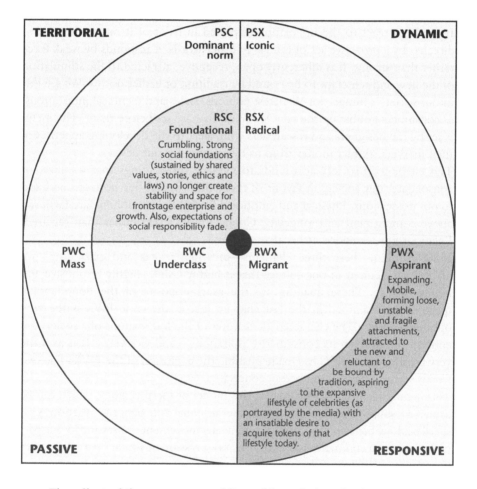

The effect of the current crumbling of foundations in the West on aspirational behaviour

Chapter summary

In this chapter, we explore the Aspirant sector of the social ecology model, which I have given the code PWX. These letters stand for *'presented'*, *'weak'* and *'expanding'*.

'Presented' refers to an element in society that is visible, explicit and on public view, and perhaps no aspect of our society is so obvious, so 'presented', as our aspirational consumerism! Almost the first thing that most people see when they arrive in the West is the shops in the airport terminal—and their drive from the airport will then take them past out-of-town shopping precincts and 'retail parks'. We live surrounded by opportunities to purchase and consume.

At the same time, our consumption is highly responsive to the market's leading. It tends to react to the opportunities placed in front of it rather than being directed by a proactive set of values. In other words, it responds by weak force rather than strong. It is inherently open, receptive, attracted to the stimulation of the new and reluctant to be bound by tradition or earlier norms. We see this in our society's hunger for the latest fashions, styles and technical innovations, as consumers gobble up the new 'goodies' that are set before them. The menu is set by the designers and researchers who, alert to the developing appetites of their markets, extract money from us by catering for our desires.

This element in society also tends to sacrifice those things that stabilize, or consolidate, our society in favour of those that expand our horizons and add to our possessions. Physical and emotional flexibility and mobility are favoured above commitment and longevity. Goods are discarded rather than repaired. Relationships are ended rather than endured.

If we combine these three elements—presented, weak and expanding—we identify an element in our culture that is highly visible, highly responsive and highly mobile. These qualities are the exact opposite of the Foundational qualities we examined in the last chapter, just as the code PWX is the very opposite of RSC. The characteristic features of the foundations of a society are entirely absent from its consumerist aspirations – and vice versa. It is as if the very erosion of the RSC has made possible the explosion of the PWX. The two trends seem to have developed in concert.

This highlights a crucial dynamic of this model of social ecology, which can be expressed simply like this: any action has an equal and opposite reaction. Our social ecology behaves like a closed system: any movement or pressure in one part of it produces a commensurate movement or pressure in another part. It's rather like a balloon half full of air—when you squeeze it at one end, it tends to bulge at the other. Your inward pressure at one point applies an outward force elsewhere. This feature of the model of social ecology is one of its most important and illuminating, as it enables us to predict what the response will be to any pressure we apply. In this instance, the two related sectors of the model are PWX and RSC. As the RSC foundations of our society have been eroded or have crumbled, so its PWX aspirations have been expanded.

Summary statement

Detached from the constraints exerted by strong foundations, our aspirational behaviour has become insatiable and unregulated. The consequences of this are psychological fragility, social insecurity, financial debt and a lack of cultural resilience.

....

Building sandcastles may be a peculiarly British pastime. The vicissitudes of our weather have made us experts at making the most of a grey and sometimes rainy outing to the beach, and building sandcastles is something you will find countless families doggedly engaged in on a typical summer day by the sea. One reason why it is so satisfying, of course, is that it can take only a few minutes of furious digging, piling and moulding before you have a respectable structure in front of you. And not just a castle keep: there may also be a moat and a drawbridge, turrets, battlements, even lookout holes and booby traps and other features of an embattled community.

Of course, the enemy you are fighting is not a raiding force from another castle but the sea itself. For while the whole edifice can be constructed in an hour or so, it may take only a matter of minutes for the returning tide to wash it away entirely, for all the industry and imagination that went into it. In the end, building sandcastles is an exercise in futility. However, that very fact only spurs the builders to greater effort, and even as the tide is remorselessly coming in, they are devising ingenious and optimistic schemes to divert it with walls and ditches in order to preserve the castle for as long as possible. They know the inevitable outcome, but they choose to suspend their disbelief and think that they might, miraculously, against all odds, find a way to defy the elements. Building sandcastles is an exercise in fragility. By definition, it is building without foundations. The advantages are that you can build quickly and expansively—and can 'make it up as you go along'; the downside is that, inevitably, all you construct lacks solidity and strength—a few waves will wash it away.

If it is true that over the past century the West has assiduously undermined its own social, moral and cultural foundations, it will also, worryingly, be true that the edifices that are now standing stand on sand and not rock. One would expect to see alarming signs of fragility at various levels: in the emotional and psychological well-being of individuals, the social and relational health of marriages and communities, the energy and engagement in political life and the resilience of the economy.

Psychological fragility

One of the key foundations of our society in the past was the accepted permanence of marriage. Regarded as both divinely ordained and the appropriate environment within which to bring children into the world and nurture them, this was one of the strongest sources of social cohesion until the middle of the 20th century. Since then, this part of our social foundations has been systematically deconstructed. To many people today, it is no more than a quaint—and deeply restrictive—convention. Similarly, many people see the idea that 'sexual union' is a sign to society of the formation of a new, discrete and permanent social unit as archaic and irrelevant. Finally, the notion that it is healthier for children to be raised in such an environment has been attacked ferociously for the last three decades by many intellectuals who argue that any number and variety of sexual attachments, long or short, are good enough—or even preferable.

Once we had lost the conviction that sexual union, accompanied by responsibility and commitment, is integral to social cohesion, it was inevitable that social bonding was going to become more fluid and fleeting. This was facilitated, of course, by the invention of the Pill, and given extra impetus by a reaction in the 1960s against the repressive mores of the post-Victorian era. As a result, whereas once most people, adults and children, enjoyed strong and stable attachments, today, with their sexual and emotional boundaries largely open, people experience each other as available, as convenient and expedient. Any people who see themselves in this way become insecure, unsure of the reliability of relationships. Commitment becomes increasingly difficult; unattached sex becomes an anxious surrogate for intimacy, a panacea for loneliness—and yet it cannot provide the social or emotional 'anchorage' of an enduring relationship. In purely medical terms, there is a dramatic rise in the incidence of both sexually transmitted diseases (STDs) and, some evidence suggests (as a result of delayed childbirth and multiple sexual partners), infertility.[10] However, the most profound effects have been on children.

---

[10] 'Between 1991 and 2001, the number of new episodes of sexually transmitted infections (STIs) seen in Genitourinary Medicine (GUM) clinics in England, Wales and Northern Ireland doubled from 669,291 to 1,332,910. Young people, in particular females under the age of 20, bear the burden of sexually transmitted infections. ... The sexual health of adolescents in the UK is poor. It is likely that an increase in risky sexual behaviour has contributed to sexual health outcomes such as STIs and unwanted pregnancy among young people': 'Sexual Health: Teen Infection Almost Doubled during 90s', National Statistics, 30 March 2004. Retrieved on 27 March 2008 from http://www.statistics.gov.uk/cci/nugget.asp?id=721

A growing social cost

After two generations of children have experienced the open boundaries of emotional and sexual mobility, we have a legacy of growing emotional dysfunction.[11] Developmental psychologists agree on the cause of this: when a child is unable to trust the relationship between his caregivers, he will, inevitably, find other ways to cope with his lack of security. Emotional 'self-holding' (which manifests itself in anxiety, depression, self-harm and aggression) and emotional incontinence (attention seeking, lack of impulse control, proneness to distraction) alike are, unsurprisingly, characteristic of an 'unboundaried' population.[12] This is what we must expect, increasingly, from children who have experienced adult relationships as both unpredictable and fragile. The incidence of such dysfunctions has risen dramatically in the past decade.[13] The extraordinary rise of ADHD (attention-deficit and hyperactive disorder) in recent years, though caused by a mix of factors from processed foods to patterns of parenting to the advent of TV remotes and game consoles, suggests that the context in which children now grow up is essentially one in which change is the only thing that is predictable.[14]

---

[11] 'Nearly a quarter (24 per cent) of children in Great Britain were living in lone-parent families in 2006, more than three times the proportion in 1972': 'Changing Lives of Today's Children', National Statistics 2007 news release regarding the 37th edition of *Social Trends*. Retrieved on 10 March 2008 from http://www.statistics.gov.uk/pdfdir/st0407.pdf

[12] 'Half those children with a mental disorder had at one time seen the separation of their parents, compared with 29 per cent with no disorder': 'Mental Health of Children and Adolescents', ONS (2000) 118. Retrieved on 27 March 2008 from http://www.statistics.gov.uk/pdfdir/mhc0300.pdf. 'Family stability is positively related to child and young adult behavior (Hao & Xie, 2001; Hill et al., 2001; Wu & Martinson, 1993)': W D Manning and K A Lamb, 'Adolescent Well-Being in Cohabiting, Married, and Single-Parent Families', *Journal of Marriage and Family* 65 (2003), pp876–93. However, other authors consider other factors that contribute to social problems: 'Poverty, abuse, neglect, poorly funded schools, and a lack of government services represent more serious threats to the well-being of adults and children than does marital instability': P R Amato, 'The Consequences of Divorce for Adults and Children', *Journal of Marriage and the Family* 62 (2000), pp1269–87

[13] 'A recent study based on information from the GP Research Database found that between 1991 and 2001, the rate of British children prescribed antidepressants rose by 70%. In the US, a pandemic is already in progress. One out of every six American children, according to a recent declaration of the House Committee on Energy and Commerce, is taking a prescription antidepressant such as Prozac': John Cornwell, 'Prozac for Eight-Year-Olds?', *The Sunday Times*, 12 November 2006, p14

[14] 'Of the disturbed 10%, half have behavioural problems, 40% anxiety or depression, 15% attention-deficit hyperactivity disorder (ADHD), and 8% autistic spectrum disorders (some children have multiple problems). ... Everyone has their pet explanation—lack of fish oil, TV-watching, illegal drugs, lack of exercise. Likely candidates in [Professor Robert] Goodman's eyes are widening inequality, family breakdown, school pressures and a materialist, consumerist society. ... "Both behaviour and ADHD are much worse in Britain. Norwegians live in a much more equal society, with shorter working days, more time spent with families, particularly on outdoor sports at weekends, public values publicly shared. They eat lots of oily fish, too!"': Victoria Neumark, 'Education: Wellbeing and the Web', *The Guardian*, 15 January 2008, p29

The British government has implemented a raft of initiatives to try to tackle such problems: basic training in parenting, school counsellors, an entire curriculum of 'emotional literacy' in schools across the country.[15] In essence, it is trying to teach adults skills they never learnt from their parents, and to use schools to nurture their children because their families are so fragile and dysfunctional. It seems that the cost of undermining our society's moral foundations has been high. Has it been worth it? The argument has always been that those sexual and domestic morals were restrictive and denied individuals freedom of choice; people were unhappy being stuck in marriages after love had died. But has the removal of those old 'Victorian' constraints made us happier? Sadly, it seems not. Measures of overall well-being in Britain suggest that people are no more content today than they were 50 years ago.[16] In other words, our society is no happier despite its new freedoms. However, it now sees a far higher incidence of mental-health problems: depression, anxiety disorders, stress-related problems and suicide, in particular among young males.[17]

Social mobility and social fragility

We are now physically mobile to a degree the world has never known before. The mass manufacture of cars and motorbikes, increases in oil production and cheap air travel have all given us the ability and opportunity to roam far afield. At the same time, we have witnessed a corresponding change in our cultural attitudes that has made it acceptable, and even desirable, to leave behind the place you grew up in in pursuit of employment—or fulfilment—unfettered by local attachments.

In Britain, this mobility was greatly encouraged in the 1970s by the social policy of Margaret Thatcher's Conservative government. Social housing, which the state had owned in the inner cities through local councils, was sold off at the insistence of an ideology that believed that people would aspire to improve themselves only if they owned their own homes. The results have been nothing less than spectacular. The average price of a house in Britain has gone

---

[15] 'Respect Drive Targets Troublesome Families', Department of Health news release, 10 January 2006 (http://www.dh.gov.uk/en/publicationsandstatistics/pressreleases/dh_4126269); 'Better Support for Emotional Wellbeing in Schools—25 Pilot Areas Announced', Department for Children, Schools and Families news release, 24 January 2008 (http://www.dcsf.gov.uk/pns/DisplayPN.cgi?pn_id=2008_0016)

[16] 'Britain's Happiness in Decline', Mark Easton, BBC News, 2 May 2006 (http://news.bbc.co.uk/1/hi/programmes/happiness_formula/4771908.stm)

[17] 'Mental Health: Mental Disorders More Common in Boys', National Statistics, 30 March 2004. Retrieved on 1 April 2008 from http://www.statistics.gov.uk/cci/nugget.asp?id=853

up 3,900 per cent between 1971 and 2007,[18] while monetary inflation has barely exceeded 900 per cent.[19] The early consequence of the policy was that large parts of many British cities were emptied of their indigenous populations as people sold their recently acquired council flats and houses and moved out (and up) into the suburbs or newly-built towns.

The mass ownership of cars has opened up a far larger landscape that has been exploited by commerce in several ways. Large, cheap out-of-town stores and shopping centres have proved very popular, but take us away from our local shops. The fragility of employment contracts means that people's working patterns are necessarily more fluid—and precarious.[20] Often, people will commute long distances, returning home only late in the evening. Indeed, 'home' is arguably a misnomer—T S Eliot's references to a 'homeless' city and suburb in which God therefore finds no home now seem not only apt but prophetic.[21] This increase of our physical mobility has corresponded with an emotional and cultural mobility, as people are no longer so tied to a particular world view, set of values, aspirations and economic prospects.

Social mobility and social isolation

In emotional terms, family roots have never been so confused. In 1995, there were 165,000 divorces in Britain, 280 times the number in the first year of the century.[22] Today, over half of the population under 40 has been affected by divorce, whether as parents or as children. According to the social psychologist Oliver James, the consequent emotional havoc has been appalling.[23] The arrival on the scene of further partners after a parental break-up increases a child's confusion and is likely to affect her emotional development badly.

What has occurred demographically has been legitimized intellectually. Individualism was a hallmark of Enlightenment thinking,[24] and postmodernism, though it rejects much of the modernist agenda, is perhaps better referred to as 'hyper-modernism' when it comes to its approach to the

---

[18] http://www.communities.gov.uk/housing/housingresearch/housingstatistics/housingstatisticsby/housingmarket/livetables

[19] http://www.measuringworth.com/ppoweruk/result.php?use%5b%5d=cpi&year_late=1971&typeamount=1000&amount=1000&year_source=1971&year_result=2007

[20] See David Harvey, *The Condition of Postmodernity: an Enquiry into the Origins of Cultural Change* (Blackwell, 1989), p303 on the economic drivers of, and postmodern confusion about and quest for, roots.

[21] 'Choruses from *The Rock*', T S Eliot, *Collected Poems, 1909–1962* (Faber and Faber, 1968), p162

[22] Oliver James, *Britain on the Couch* (Century, 1997), p152

[23] Ibid., p157

[24] J Richard Middleton and Brian J Walsh, *Truth Is Stranger Than It Used To Be* (SPCK, 1995), p47

individual. Psychologically, we find ourselves playing roles, not rediscovering our roots. As the social psychologist Kenneth Gergen put it: 'Since there is no essential me, I can be whoever I want to be.'[25] Postmodern Man is 'able to be anything so long as the roles, costumes, and settings have been commodiously arranged.'[26]

A mobile society quickly becomes a society in which people are isolated and find they lack neighbours, friends and family nearby who they can turn to when in need. Isolation then turns to anonymity, as people feel less and less 'known' by or 'connected' with their local communities. Their sense of belonging diminishes and, rather than gaining a sense of identity and well-being through social ties, people turn to acquisition and consumption as ways to define themselves and 'belong' to some group. In this way, we are commoditized and lose our sense of depth, place and history as we focus instead on the brand of clothing we wear or the car we drive. Economically, our society's fragmentation puts unprecedented pressure on the housing stock as the total number of 'housing units' spirals to meet the needs of people living more and more solitary lives.[27]

Growing economic fragility

Perhaps the single biggest economic change over the past three decades has involved the financing mechanisms now available to the consumer. We now borrow money not within the local community (or the family) but outside it, unconstrained by social ties. Before the Second World War, debt was socially stigmatized. Generally, people borrowed from a member of their family or the local community—perhaps a pawnbroker or a loan shark—and in such a system it was seen as an expensive last resort that could eat up both capital and reputation. The social pressure to repay a loan was often immense. Today, in contrast, huge, remote, impersonal banks provide 'credit' without any stigma attached—in fact, often they offer it unsolicited and present this as a compliment! There is usually no pressure to settle your debts—indeed, repayment even of large unsecured loans can now be spread over many years, something unheard of only 20 years ago. Vast amounts of credit are now available as a result, and all without social stigma.

With the means to finance aspiration now in place, the full-scale swelling of this sector of the population can take place. A population insecure about

---

[25] Ibid., p53
[26] Ibid., quoting Kenneth Gergen, p53
[27] 'In 2004 there were 7.0 million people living alone in Great Britain, nearly four times as many as in 1961': 'Households: More People Were Living Alone in 2004', National Statistics, 2005 (http://www.statistics.gov.uk/cci/nugget.asp?id=1162&pos=&colrank=2&rank=672)

personal identity seeks fulfilment in the acquisition of branded 'lifestyle' goods, which act as surrogates for tradition and a sense of social identity. We can now invent and reinvent our own stories through our clothes and accessories. In effect, the easy availability of credit furnishes the 'front stage' of our personal theatres with costumes, props, narratives and scripts—all of which are disposable. We now have a plethora of lifestyles from which to choose, and when we become bored we can simply move on to a different costume, a different drama, even a different cast of co-actors. Our physical, emotional and social mobility mean we can now give our technologically-navigated virtual lives whatever shape or form we need to pull the illusion off.

And in all of this we consume. Our ever-expanding storylines get through enormous quantities of goods. The fashions we embrace literally label us amidst the chaos of fleeting encounters in which we now engage. Brands are now deliberately promoted as the new traditions, which help to give us a shape to our narrative and a sense of community.[28] Our appetites are insatiable simply because the function for which we buy each costume or prop in the first place—to set ourselves within some bigger drama devised by other people—is itself only transitory and illusory.

And of course such consumption is unsustainable. Britain's consumer debt (including mortgages) now totals £1.4 trillion.[29] America's (excluding mortgages) is nearly $14 trillion,[30] or over $20,000 for every household, and its trade deficit is now $58 billion.[31] We dress our lack of identity at a terrible and unsustainable price not only to our social ecology, our economies, but also to our planet. And it does not lead to a happier society. The market works by creating desires that are fulfilled only briefly, in order to sustain relentless demand. As Durkheim observed in his work *Suicide*, 'To pursue a goal which is by definition unattainable is to condemn oneself to a state of

---

[28] 'Material goods are important to us, not just for their functional uses, but because they play vital symbolic roles in our lives. This symbolic role of consumer goods facilitates a range of complex, deeply engrained "social conversations" about status, identity, social cohesion, group norms and the pursuit of personal and cultural meaning': Tim Jackson, 'Motivating Sustainable Consumption: A Review of Evidence on Consumer Behaviour and Behavioural Change' (draft version), 1 August 2004 (http://portal.surrey.ac.uk/pls/portal/docs/page/eng/staff/staffac/jacksont/publications/jacksonsdrn-review.pdf)

[29] J Charles, 'Debt Watch', *The Times*, 22 March 2008, p16

[30] Paul Harris, 'Living on Borrowed Dimes', *The Guardian*, 4 May 2006. Retrieved on 1 April 2008 from http://www.guardian.co.uk/business/2006/may/04/usnews.comment; 'American household debt reached $13.8 trillion at the end of 2007, or more than double the amount in 1999': 'America's Coming Garage Sale', *Time*, 24 March 2008 (http://www.time.com/time/magazine/article/0,9171,1725094,00.html)

[31] 'Goods and Services Deficit Increases in January 2008', US Census Bureau, 11 March 2008 (http://www.census.gov/indicator/www/ustrade.html)

perpetual unhappiness.'[32] Thus, we find that the incidence of depression and mental disease in our society has never been higher.

The sheer fragility of our financial system is now being exposed. The scale of the collapse of the real economies of some countries will be so great simply because the tolerances in people's domestic finances are so tight. Leveraged to the hilt with both secured and unsecured debt, a steep rise in unemployment or fall in property values will plunge millions into financial crisis. Retailers, reliant on consumer spending, will go into liquidation. Brands will disappear. Whole economies may become bankrupt. Future generations will look back at us and ask how we ever could have believed we could carry on consuming the way we have done.

Political fragility

Tragically, one reason is that in Britain and America—and perhaps in the West more generally—there has been a systemic failure of political leadership over the past 20 years, caused specifically by a dereliction of the basic, essential contract between governments and the people they govern. In a democracy, political leadership is based on a social contract. Citizens willingly submit to the laws made by their elected representatives and, in so doing, recognize that they are responsible participants in the social system, not simply individuals at liberty to do what they please. However, as Durkheim suggests in the observation quoted above, this requires us to rein our appetites in. The problem in the West is that our politicians have increasingly seen themselves as corporate managers and us as consumers of their 'products'.

Politics is increasingly concerned with offering us a range of 'choices' as consumers, rather than with presenting us with our responsibilities as citizens. Pollsters and focus-group researchers have done their work and have found that when you ask people they will always demand greater freedom of choice in their own lives. But a politics that expects governments simply to satisfy the demands of consumers in order to win another term in power is a politics not worth having. The result is that politicians are afraid to demand any genuine personal sacrifice in the interests of greater collective good. It is tragic to see education and health policies designed to offer us greater choice rather than greater commitment to our neighbourhood and its resources. Why should anyone commit themselves to improving their local schools and hospital if they can just choose to go further afield to get treatment or education somewhere else? What will happen to the schools and hospitals that those who can afford to go elsewhere abandon?

---

[32] Op. cit., p248

A less resilient society

Detaching a society from its historic foundations is a costly business. Although it may seem to offer individuals freedom and opportunity to express themselves, ultimately it exposes them to powerful forces they will be unable to resist. The population in general becomes more fragile psychologically as each generation of broken families leaves a growing legacy to the next. The social fabric becomes thinner and more tattered; individuals become more isolated and more anonymous as they become more mobile, and increasingly define their sense of identity through the brands they wear rather than the families, communities and friendship groups they belong to. Economically, such a society slides into a debt culture in order to finance its over-consumption. Aspiration ceases to have any social worth because people aspire to have things that can neither satisfy them in the long term nor help to build a cohesive society. Politically, people regard themselves increasingly as consumers rather than citizens, and politicians offer the electorate a choice of products rather than privileges on the basis of shared responsibilities. Political discourse descends into arguments about rights and becomes increasingly litigious.

Those who benefit from these changes are the people who finance consumer debt, negotiate legal contracts and sell consumers the goods they demand in order to define themselves. The economy grows rapidly—just as a sandcastle can be built with ease. However, every sandcastle is threatened by the rising tide, and our fear must be that the fabric of our society will lack the strength and resilience to cope with the growing crisis. The resilience we need is not only financial (which we manifestly lack) but also societal: the ability to nurture our children and care for the vulnerable and elderly. Likewise, we must fear that the psychological health of our nation will prove too fragile and will burden the state with ever more mental illness and chronic sickness, as well as antisocial behaviour, sexual promiscuity and the catastrophic costs associated with STDs and unwanted pregnancies. We must fear that the economy, having tipped from production and growth towards consumption and debt, will depend too exclusively on the financial and professional services sectors for recovery and growth—sectors that can provide employment for only a small proportion of the population. An economy so narrowly based is highly precarious in a global downturn. We must fear, too, that the political contract will break down and democracy will become little more than focus-group consultations and news management, offering scant leadership to make the longer-term and increasingly costly choices that now face the whole human race.

Study questions 3

1. Why does the erosion of social foundations create greater social fragility?
2. In what ways have Western societies become fragile?
3. What psychological role does consumption now play in the 'developed' world?
4. What are some of the potential negatives of a wealthier population?

FOUR

Bowing the Knee: the Ascent of Money (PSC)

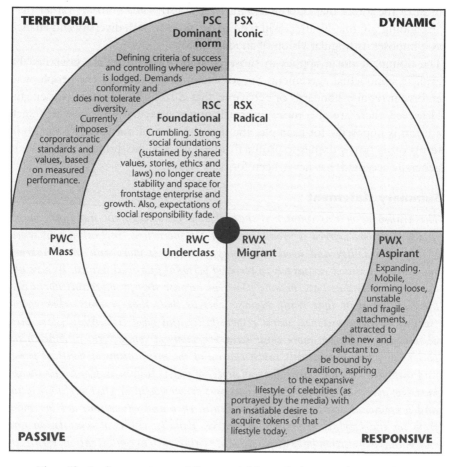

TERRITORIAL	**PSC** **Dominant norm**	**PSX** Iconic	**DYNAMIC**

Defining criteria of success and controlling where power is lodged. Demands conformity and does not tolerate diversity. Currently imposes corporatocratic standards and values, based on measured performance.

RSC Foundational — **RSX Radical**

Crumbling. Strong social foundations (sustained by shared values, stories, ethics and laws) no longer create stability and space for frontstage enterprise and growth. Also, expectations of social responsibility fade.

PWC Mass	**RWC** Underclass	**RWX** Migrant	**PWX** Aspirant

Expanding. Mobile, forming loose, unstable and fragile attachments, attracted to the new and reluctant to be bound by tradition, aspiring to the expansive lifestyle of celebrities (as portrayed by the media) with an insatiable desire to acquire tokens of that lifestyle today.

PASSIVE — **RESPONSIVE**

The effect of current crumbling social foundations and expanding aspirations in the West on the dominant norm

Chapter summary

In this chapter, we explore the Dominant Norm sector of the social ecology model, which I have labelled 'PSC'. Every society has an image (explicit or not) of the ideal citizen, and this represents a 'norm' against which individuals can be measured. Everyone aspires to match this ideal, whether it is expressed in economic or ideological terms, and those who succeed in doing so are invested with power as a result. Those who are seen to have failed are disregarded, while everyone else continues to strive to attain the standards this dominant norm demands.

This element in society is *'presented'*, in that it is highly visible. It also exerts *strong* rather than weak force, in that its thrust is relentless, without regard for most of the forces that oppose it. Finally, it is also *'consolidating'*, rather than 'expanding', in that its effect will tend to be to resist both diversity and change as it imposes its singular vision of an ideal life.

The dominant norm applies in those areas of society that are governed by explicit, contractual agreement. So, for example, the law and the people who enforce it require standards of behaviour that citizens by and large consent to. However, there are also more informal, non-contractual ways in which such a norm is imposed—for example, the measurement of our society's wealth in terms of its 'gross domestic product', or GDP, is a PSC principle that, while generally accepted, has never been formally agreed.

Summary statement

The argument of this chapter is that, though historically the dominant norm in the West has covered a broad range of considerations, including conscience, social responsibility and good citizenship, today it is more and more narrow, being defined almost exclusively in terms of personal financial wealth. As a result, the institutions that have become powerful because they promote this norm are, increasingly, those that trade money, whereas those that promote other values (such as moral conscience, social responsibility and good citizenship) have been disempowered. A new, more constricted hegemony of commercial and financial power has slowly but steadily taken control of the mechanisms of political power and intruded into the way that every aspect of society functions. Consequently, the models of governance and management that are now used in what were once social and professional occupations, such as health care and education, are borrowed from the marketplace of private commerce. Equally, values of competition and individual acquisition have displaced other values such as consideration, creativity and the common good.

The tools you need for the beach, to build your sandcastle, are buckets and spades. There is little in life that gives more instant gratification than packing a bucket with damp sand, turning it over, giving it a couple of pats and then lifting it off to reveal a perfectly moulded tower underneath!

Of course, the only way to keep your sandcastle standing in the long term is to keep the bucket over it. If you can't build on foundations, you need to build inside a shell. Rather like an insect, which lacks an internal (or *endo-*) skeleton and instead supports and protects the soft parts of its body with an external (or *exo-*) skeleton, a sandcastle must be encased in something strong if it is to endure.

Government as the imposition of control

It would hardly be surprising, therefore, if a society that had consistently undermined its own foundations and moreover had recklessly built with sand then found itself resorting more and more to dropping a bucket over its crumbling ramparts to restore their shape. The structure is essentially unstable and increasingly needs to be held together from the outside because it lacks internal cohesion. When this starts to happen in social systems, it becomes almost inevitable that some forms of control will have to be imposed.

The interventions of an ever more intrusive 'nanny state' have become the cause of increasingly loud complaints in Britain as people feel that the authorities are interfering in their private lives and taking away their civil liberties. New 'anti-terror' laws greatly extend the police's powers of arrest and restraint, and the courts can now restrict our freedom with 'anti-social behaviour orders'. CCTV cameras monitor our every move, while the roads are watched by ever more speed cameras, and we are being threatened with ID cards. These and other mechanisms of top-down social control are a response to anomie, the absence of those 'backstage' forces (such as respect for elders and for institutional and parental authority) that used to hold society together. They are inevitable, and may even be necessary, now that our communities have lost their self-discipline.

This application of strong state power on the front stage is akin to someone patting down their sandcastle with a spade to try to prevent it collapsing. Unsurprisingly, it is restricted less and less to the actually criminal or antisocial as the government treats every citizen with suspicion. Public services such as education, health and social services are increasing dominated by bureaucrats. In state education, a national curriculum is now dictated by civil servants in Whitehall. The freedom of teachers to be spontaneous, to follow their own instincts and go off at a tangent is now virtually eliminated.[33] Moreover, the targets now set by central government treat both the health and the education service like a factory assembly line. Units of production are counted, and quality is assessed against a set of national criteria with no local variation permitted. Penalties are imposed when productivity falls below the required measure and the results of regular inspections are made public for all to see.[34]

Government as customer service

As the foundations of our Western societies have given way, so our sense of identity as responsible citizens has also disintegrated. We are no longer citizens enjoying the privileges of our social system, we are aspiring consumers. We judge our public services in the same way we judge Tesco or McDonalds. We see it as our right to demand all the treatments we want and expect the state to provide them for us. In response, the government has increasingly over the past two decades tried to impose on the public sector the mentality of private-sector industry. It has applied the same measures of performance to its healthcare providers that the private sector applies to a factory or to a company listed on the stock market. For economic reasons, it has sought to manage the public sector like a private enterprise, and indeed has privatized much of it, from our coal mines and steel foundries to our buses and trains, our prisons, our postal service and, increasingly, our hospitals—and soon our state schools as well. Patients and pupils alike are referred to as 'customers' or 'clients'. In a society in which people see themselves not as citizens but as consumers, the politicians who get elected are the ones who understand what the market wants and (promise to) deliver it.

The result is that we have allowed the flow of financial rather than social capital to dictate the shape of our civil society. This has happened in two ways. The first relates to government spending. In the private sector, there is an assumption that if you want better services you have to pay for them, and the government has bought into this and 'invested' huge amounts in (for example) our health service. This extra spending inflates the market, however: doctors' salaries soar, and so does the cost of equipment and resources, while only comparatively

---

[33] 'There is now a torrent of evidence emerging that Britain's rigid, centralised approach to teaching has utterly failed in what it set out to do. ... Teachers had lost much of their autonomy and discretion, and were frequently obliged to follow pre-prescribed lesson plans laid down by Whitehall, rather than engaging with the children in front of them': Jenni Russell, 'The NUT Has Cried Wolf Too Often, But This Time It's Right', *The Guardian*, 26 March 2008, p29

[34] 'Since the first Conservative management "reforms" on the NHS in 1973–4, a bewildering number of procedures that derive from commercial models of management have been relentlessly demanded by both political parties within a system that is quintessentially professional (non-commercial) in its outlook and ethos': Professor Paul Brown, unpublished article, 2006

modest gains have been achieved in terms of patient waiting-times, for example. Nonetheless, the government is able to point to its investment strategy, as well to incentivize the health-care providers to reduce patient-doctor time and rack up greater productivity. Health care is transformed from a professional, public service into a private industry, assessed against the same financial benchmarks. Thus, the second way in which we have allowed capital flows to shape our society is that the culture of the national health system (for example) has become that of the private market, where performance is judged by a set of criteria that are ultimately all financial, concerned with reducing costs, maximizing revenue and hitting productivity targets rather than improving patient well-being and the quality of care. It is, after all, much easier to measure progress in monetary terms.

Government by the market

In this way, as a nation, we in Britain have found ourselves being governed by the rules of the market in areas that were previously the domain of social responsibility. And this highlights the fundamental shift in our social ecology, which has destabilized the delicate balance between freedom and responsibility. We have changed the 'social game' we play from one about citizenship and participation into one about the market and consumption. The ultimate object of any civilised society must always be the well-being of its members and their safe, meaningful, creative, energetic and peaceable interaction. However, since the end of the Second World War, this overriding purpose has increasingly been supplanted by another: the generation and management of financial capital.

The economy as a system of markets is a derivative of a social system—a mechanism for trading goods and services. It is not an end in itself. It serves an end, which is the well-being of people within that system. The benefits it offers include employment and the chance to improve their lot for those who are fit to work and welfare for those who are not, and opportunity for those who are creative and entrepreneurial. As long as the economy serves that greater end of human flourishing, it can function appropriately. However, over the last few decades we have seen a subtle but hugely significant change in our social discourse that indicates that it no longer serves the common interest but rather subordinates it.

Listen to any report on the health of our or any other country and the measure that is generally used is GDP. This expresses the size of the economy, being the sum of the financial transactions that occur in a year within its boundaries. It takes into consideration only how much is sold and bought and at what price. It takes no account of what goods are used for, for example, or of how wealth is distributed through the population. GDP could grow and yet the gap between rich and poor could widen. It could grow and yet 90 per cent of the population could get poorer. It could grow and yet the happiness, security and mutual trust within the population could diminish. GDP is now regarded as the basis of social health in the West and accepted without question as its proper measure, even though (as the Greens point out) by this measure an ecological disaster counts as a positive because it boosts economic activity. Recession—dread word!—is no more than the contraction rather than continuing expansion of an economy, and yet it is regarded as an object of terror, which governments must prevent at all costs, the cause of all kinds of evil, from rising unemployment to falling pensions.

Human life becomes less human

What this represents is the domination of financial capital that we have come to accept as axiomatic in how we value ourselves as a society. There are four implications that flow from this change. The first is a dehumanized vision for human life. The moment we start to value people in terms of how much they earn, we begin to see them as mere utilities. It is dismaying to see how we now identify celebrity almost exclusively with financial wealth—not that all rich people are famous, but that everyone who aspires to be famous does so because they believe it will make them rich. As a society, the people we put on pedestals tend to be those with financial assets. It is a national disgrace that we hold activities such as academic research and teaching in such low esteem that we seem to be content with a market that pays a footballer in a couple of weeks as much as such public servants, who are building the intellectual and social capital of the next generation, may earn in a year.[35] Moreover, we have convinced ourselves that we are getting richer as a nation because our GDP has grown so massively over the last two decades, and there is increased investment in education and ever more technological advances—regardless of the fact that in other terms, such as social cohesion, trust, happiness and security, we have seen either no progress at all or an actual regression. In fact, research suggests that average levels of individual happiness in Britain have not risen one inch in the last 20 years,[36] while we have witnessed the continuing disintegration of our communities and family structures.

---

[35] The starting salary for teachers in London was £25,000 in 2008, according to the Association of Teachers and Lecturers (retrieved on 2 April 2008 from http://*www.tda.gov.uk/recruit/ becomingateacher/startingsalary.aspx*). The average basic salary of a footballer in the English Premiership in 2006 was £676,000 a year, or £13,000 a week, according to a survey of professional players by the *Independent* published in that paper on 11 April 2006.

[36] 'Happiness pundits cite the lack of any connection over time between recorded levels of happiness and material wealth (GDP), both in the UK and across the developed world. GDP in the UK has

The emergence of the 'corporatocracy'

The second implication is that we have created a new master to toil under: a 'corporatocracy'. In a democracy power is (in theory, at least) distributed across the population, but in a corporatocracy it resides with neither the people nor the leaders they elect but an uneasy coalition of government and industry, whose interests become conflated. For example, it is no secret that America's post-war foreign policy involved forming alliances with countries across the Middle East (such as Egypt, Saudi Arabia and Iran), the Far East and Latin America (such as Ecuador, Panama and Colombia), which involved 'helping' them to develop their economies.[37] Typically, American energy consultants advised the governments of these countries on how to assess and plan for the construction of the infrastructure they needed in order to exploit their natural mineral resources, and the governments then borrowed from the World Bank the huge sums of money required.[38] Many commentators have criticized the cosy relationship between the Washington-based World Bank, Wall Street and the American Treasury. The debts that were run up were so vast they were virtually impossible to repay. Usually, these governments awarded the construction contracts to one or more of America's massive firms, which ensured that the capital they'd borrowed flowed back into America's economy, and to its Treasury. Moreover, sometimes America took a controlling stake in their state-owned industries, or else it took advantage of their indebtedness at a later date, perhaps by requiring them to vote a certain way at the United Nations or to allow its armed forces to use their territory or airspace. Politics, finance and big business were fused into a single axis of self-sustaining power.

The gap between rich and poor widens

Such a strategy ensured that America attained an unprecedented position in the world, in terms of both political dominance and control of resources and industry. It also meant that globally financial capital flowed from the poor to the rich. We are always told that the justification for the capitalist system is that, however unequally the 'cake' is divided, nonetheless capitalism makes it bigger and so everyone gets a larger slice. However, the evidence suggests that the opposite is true. This is the third implication of the domination of financial

---

doubled since 1973 yet ... happiness has hardly changed at all': Paul Ormerod, 'Sorry, You Won't Find Happiness This Way', *The Sunday Times*, 8 April 2007, p4

[37] Robert A Rosenbaum, *The Penguin Encyclopedia of American History* (Penguin Books, 2003), p128

[38] *Confessions of an Economic Hit Man* (Berrett-Koehler Publishers, 2004) offers one account of such dealings from the personal experience of one American agent, John Perkins.

capital. Ultimately, it has not closed the gap between the haves and the have-nots but has actually widened it. This is the case not only in America but also in many of the 'developing' countries it has 'helped'. Sadly, the effect of loans from the World Bank has often been to line the pockets of corrupt politicians in majority-world countries while the rest of the money flows straight back into Western bank accounts.[39]

Rising global aspirations jeopardize sustainability

Fourthly and finally, the domination of financial capital makes it very difficult for the world to respond to challenges that require any kind of multinational co-operation that involves a reduction in GDP growth. The aspirations of the 'developing' world are focused on catching up with the levels of wealth and consumption enjoyed by the 'developed' world. India and China's new middle classes aspire to the lifestyles of their European and American counterparts—and what right do we have to deny them the opportunity? However, the reality is that such equality, even if it could be attained, could never be sustained—the planet simply does not have the resources to allow it. Indeed, unless the West itself changes course, it will be responsible for leading the rest of the world into very perilous waters.

Challenging the notions of ownership

If the fundamental problem is the domination of financial capital, the solution must lie in the subordination of that capital to other measures of wealth and health. This can be achieved only if our understanding of ownership is changed. Many large businesses are now talking about 'the triple bottom line', which recognizes profit or loss in environmental and social as well as financial terms. This kind of language is an attempt to bring into the valuation of profit-making business some other criteria than purely financial profit. However, as commentators have pointed out, while it is very easy to draw up a balance sheet to gauge a firm's financial performance, it is far more difficult to measure the 'social profit' or 'environmental costs' it has generated. How much should a sexual harassment lawsuit be worth, for example? What value should be attached to more just terms of employment for factory workers in the Philippines? The measures become too slippery, too vague and too subjective to be useful and may only allow companies to claim they are taking responsibility for their impact when actually they are not.

---

[39] Nick Cohen, 'When Giving to the Poorest Just Lines the Pockets of the Richest', *The Observer*, 17 September 2006, p11

The alternative is to accept that we have a perfectly good system for putting a financial value on things and we are best to stick with that. What needs to happen is that a larger constituency of people owns shares in each publicly listed firm than is currently the case. In the new terminology that is now gaining currency, 'stakeholders' would need to become shareholders. We all broadly accept the idea that suppliers and customers are to some extent 'stakeholders' in a business, but we have not gone so far as to recognize that their 'stake' should actually constitute a 'share'. Until this is the case, the notion of a stakeholder is a con that counts for nothing. There are a few models of business ownership based on such principles that look promising, and we shall examine them in the second half of this book.

These, then, are the four implications of the domination of financial capital:

· a dehumanized vision for human life that ultimately reduces people to commodities fulfilling a commercial function
· the emergence of a new structure of power: a corporatocracy which is neither elected by nor accountable to the people, which conflates the interests of government and big business
· a growing imbalance in the distribution of wealth
· a lack of any real means to make financially costly decisions internationally

Like a bucket over the top of a sandcastle, financial capital has dictated the shape of the post-war global economy. The 'hard' measures of financial value have subordinated all other, 'softer' measures of social value and environmental impact. The unregulated global free market advocated by Milton Friedman has prevailed as the only viable system, and has been accorded its own moral authority. Political decisions are now determined by the rules of the market alone. A financial 'mould' can be pressed onto every element of social life—be it health, education, the arts...—to impose the same shape upon it, and this uniformity gives governments an easy measure to assert and assess their targets for improvement and justify their policies and budgets. Our social system has changed from one that is built from the bottom up on the concrete of moral consensus, social responsibility and political participation to one that is formed and held together by the impositions of an unelected but increasingly powerful alliance between politicians and businesspeople, who may have scant regard for their social, environmental or moral impact. Commerce shapes society and imposes its values on citizens, and in allowing this we have allowed ourselves to become merely consumers, defined by our purchases.

And besides the 'buckets' that determine our values and direct our spending, our fragile, aspiring populations must increasingly be 'patted down' by the force of laws and regulations and the threat of the penalties attached to them. We no longer internalize our social boundaries as psychological norms and so increasingly they are imposed as legal constraints. Inevitably, society is ever more monitored and restricted and the police are given more and more powers to curb antisocial behaviour. The nanny is given the tools to keep her charges in check.

Study questions 4

1. When the foundations of a society are eroded, what sort of top-down control tends to be exerted in their place?
2. What role does the market now play in controlling politics in the West?
3. How has the social contract between citizens and the state been altered in the West over the last 30 years?
4. Is there any alternative to either the public or the private ownership of business (and therefore capital)?

FIVE

Buying the World Cheap (RWX)

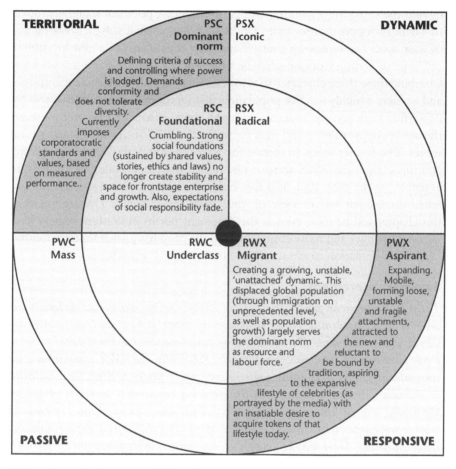

TERRITORIAL	**DYNAMIC**

PSC Dominant norm

Defining criteria of success and controlling where power is lodged. Demands conformity and does not tolerate diversity. Currently imposes corporatocratic standards and values, based on measured performance..

PSX Iconic

RSC Foundational

Crumbling. Strong social foundations (sustained by shared values, stories, ethics and laws) no longer create stability and space for frontstage enterprise and growth. Also, expectations of social responsibility fade.

RSX Radical

PWC Mass

RWC Underclass

RWX Migrant

Creating a growing, unstable, 'unattached' dynamic. This displaced global population (through immigration on unprecedented level, as well as population growth) largely serves the dominant norm as resource and labour force.

PWX Aspirant

Expanding. Mobile, forming loose, unstable and fragile attachments, attracted to the new and reluctant to be bound by tradition, aspiring to the expansive lifestyle of celebrities (as portrayed by the media) with an insatiable desire to acquire tokens of that lifestyle today.

PASSIVE

RESPONSIVE

The effect of the powerful dominant norm on the growing migrant sector

Chapter summary

In this chapter, we explore the Migrant sector of the social ecology model. I have labelled this 'RWX', and it is the reaction within the system to the action of the PSC dominant norm. It is *'reserved'* as opposed to 'presented' because it is largely hidden beneath the surface of society. If the PSC represents what people aspire to, the RWX represents that which the PSC sector controls.

The force this sector exerts is weak rather than strong in that those within it have migrated in response to opportunities that are created by powerful economic systems elsewhere. They do not themselves create the market, but they do serve it. And the sector is *'expanding'* in that the Migrant population literally moves to where the opportunities arise. This is what migration involves: breaking free of your roots and removing yourself and your dependants to a new location in the hope of finding work or safety or whatever.

Combine these three characteristics together—reserved, weak and expanding—and we have a highly reactive population that serves the needs of those who are powerful in our society. Indeed, we might observe that the PSC sector creates the market opportunities and structures that the RWX sector then reacts to and serves. The former tends to dictate the terms on which the latter can operate, and this obliges the RWX sector to be highly flexible, mobile, responsive and available. At the same time, it is the *'hidden'* sector, providing support, service relied on by, but out of view of, the 'front stage' buyer. The argument of this chapter will be that, even as the dominant norms in Western society have become stronger and more controlling, so the need has grown for a responsive, 'migrant' population to service those normative PSC expectations.

Summary statement

The growing financial power of the PSC corporatocracy has meant that the legitimate broader social needs and rights of those from whom it buys goods or services are increasingly overlooked. The imbalance of power means that traditional forms of trade have become intolerably inequitable. Politically, the RWX population is an uncomfortable fact that many governments would prefer to deny. Economically, it represents the less affluent and therefore less influential members of society. Physically, it often lives in areas that are hidden away, quasi-ghettoes or enclaves where ethnic minorities become concentrated, rather isolated from the surrounding neighbourhoods. There may be long-term consequences of the social disruption their migration causes that have yet to be addressed.

Is there limitless sand? On holiday last year on the south coast of England, I observed several major operations in progress as beaches whose sand had over time been washed away were replenished by the local authorities. Trucks would dump their loads in huge piles at one end of the beach, and diggers and earth-movers would then spread the sand across, covering the eroded areas and building them up against the action of the sea. Presumably, there was another beach somewhere that had a surfeit of sand and could happily spare it. Strictly speaking, no sand is ever lost, it is merely moved from one location to another. Perhaps that movement is global and the little patch of beach I was watching on the south coast of England once lay under the palm trees in Borneo. Who knows?

Borrowing to buy sand

In much the same way, the 'sand' from which our society has built its metaphorical castles has all come from somewhere else. One feature of globalization is the ability to transport goods around the world. Supply chains grow ever longer. One region of the planet, the West, lacks enough raw materials to go on building but can buy them from elsewhere. In 2007, America (for example) had borrowed nearly $700 billion against its national bond in order to continue this redistribution.[40] It had a monthly running trade deficit of $64 billion, of which 20 was with China alone.[41] At the same time, the British treasury had run up a record debt in relation to overall GDP.[42] Moreover, at £1.4 trillion, consumer debt in Britain had reached unprecedented levels. The availability of credit with minimal down payments had become an endemic problem for Western society.

I wrote this chapter originally in 2007, but since then the world has changed. What has happened has exposed the utter absurdity and irresponsibility of the consumptive borrowing that has sustained global economic growth for the past 15 years. It has become clear that the entire global financial system

---

[40] US House of Representatives Committee on the Budget, 24 July 2007 (http://budget.house. gov/doc-library/2007/foreignhelddebt_hearingsummary.pdf)

[41] 'Remarks by Treasury Secretary Henry M Paulson, Jr. before the Economic Club of Washington', US Treasury press release, 1 March 2007. Retrieved on 2 April 2008 from http://www.treas.gov/press/releases/hp285.htm

[42] 'Provisional estimates show that for the calendar year 2007 the UK recorded a government deficit 43.8 per cent of GDP': 'UK Government Debt and Deficit', National Statistics (2008) (http://www.statistics.gov.uk/cci/nugget.asp?id=277). This represents an increase on previous years, according to 'Euro-indicators', a press release from Eurostat dated 17 August 2007: 'Reported data ... show ... a government debt to GDP ratio of 42.5% in 2006/2007 compared with 41.6% in the previous year' (http://64.233.183.104/search?q=cache:qAhY1BMlVhUJ:epp. eurostat.ec.europa.eu/pls/portal/docs/page/pgp_prd_cat_prerel/pge_cat_prerel_year_2007/pge_cat_prerel_).

was built on a parcelling-out of bad debt in ways that were fundamentally unsecuritized. The collapse of the financial markets represents nothing more than the inevitable (and entirely predictable) results of consuming more than the world can sustain and, in effect, fabricating money as a means to negotiate the trade of real commodities. It makes little difference whether we are talking about borrowing in relation to retail spending, or spending on real estate, or government spending on services and capital building projects: the financial markets had evolved to allow unprecedented levels of expenditure, in order to maintain unsustainable levels of acquisition, both personal and public. We may blame the bankers, but arguably the real culprits are the politicians who based their electoral mandates on increasing their country's GDP (and the tax revenues that went with it)—GDP that, in effect, consists of nothing. Their guilt is only underlined by their eagerness to reinflate their shrinking economies with yet more borrowing. Their addiction to inflated tax revenues has driven them to inject yet more poison into the system, the toxin of 'buy now, pay later', encouraging the public, too, to go on buying and consuming insatiably.

Of course, this trade in goods has been fuelling tremendous growth in Asian and other economies; but how long can it go on? What social consequences are those countries suffering that are supplying the demands of the West? And how stable are those demands? From the perspective of the suppliers, there are some basic questions to be asked about the relationship in terms of power and control.

The growth of the migrant class

The growth in the Asian 'tiger' economies has largely been balanced by a decline in the corresponding sectors in the West, mainly in manufacturing industry and agriculture, which have been replaced by low-level service industries. The coal mines of Nottinghamshire and the steel works of Glasgow have closed, and the employment they used to provide must now be sought in the range of low-level service industries that serve the dominant brands that feed our consumption of goods: construction companies, call centres, supermarkets and superstores. One thing these have in common is the flexibility of their working hours. However, working '24/7/365' means that people become divorced from the rhythms of wider society. Moreover, employment contracts are typically short-term and temporary, allowing employers to assemble a flexible labour force to which they are less committed. The result is a kind of migrant working class, detached from their local communities and at the beck and call of their corporate masters.

Squeezing the supply chains

However, it is not only their employees who are in servitude to corporate masters: their suppliers are under relentless pressure to reduce supply costs. The fair-trade movement may represent an ethical protest against the exploitation of the labouring class around the world, but global free markets mean that every supplier has to cut his costs if he is to compete—otherwise, the purchaser can simply buy coffee from Colombia instead of Kenya, their bauxite from Jamaica instead of Australia. One of my Indian students from Bangalore tells me that his friends are giving up their careers as engineers, health workers or teachers because they can get better pay working in the call centres of a Western bank. The threat to his country is very great: talent and training are lost and vital professions are deprived. The stability of the economy is being undermined— and, moreover, it is becoming vulnerable to the same forces that brought it the bank's custom in the first place. What will happen when it is cheaper to relocate the call centre to Indonesia or Brazil?

What price unrenewable resources?

It is not only people who are exploited as a global commodity: so are the resources of the planet. The fierce competition in the global market and the pressures corporations can apply drive down the price of goods as well as encouraging unethical practice and the despoliation of the environment. Illegal logging in the Amazon Basin, for example, feeds the insatiable demand for hardwood garden furniture in Britain, while great swathes of rainforest are burnt down so that cattle can be grazed or soya grown to supply the Western market—even though the thin Amazonian soil will support them for no more than a few years before it is exhausted. In the 1970s, there were dire warnings about the growth of the global population and the planet's limited ability to produce food. Those fears have proved to be unfounded, so it seems, because we have developed more intensive farming techniques—and yet there is now not one agricultural region of the earth where the soil is not seriously depleted or eroded and unable to sustain the yield we now expect from it.[43] Water, too, is a growing problem—for example, in the rice-growing bowl of India, where wells have been sunk ever deeper (often financed with Western aid) in order to irrigate the land as modern agriculture demands. In many regions, the aquifers

---

[43] Matleena Kniivila, 'Land Degradation and Land Use/Cover Data Sources', working document from the Department of Economic and Social Affairs' statistics division dated 31 December 2004 (http://unstats.un.org/unsd/environment/envpdf/landdatafinal.pdf); Keith Wiebe, 'Will Land Degradation Prove Malthus Right After All?', *Amber Waves*, June 2003 (http://www.ers.usda. gov/amberwaves/june03/pdf/awjune2003resources&environmentfinding2.pdf)

these wells tap into have already sunk from six metres to 150 metres below the surface.[44] Australia's recent drought was a result of the excessive demands made on its principal rivers—a catastrophe for one of the world's breadbaskets.

What is an acceptable cost to a country to supply the demands of the developed West? The loss of talent? The loss of control? The loss of social cohesion? It would seem that the risks involved in the deal are overwhelmingly borne by the supplier and not the buyer, and their partnership is very unequal. Power is not distributed equitably, or even humanely. Once again, it comes down to a question of ownership. Is it right that suppliers should have no share in the firms they supply? Is it right that consumers should have no obligations to those who produce the goods they consume?

Mass urbanization

One consequence of all this is increasing migration from the countryside to the city, to create ever larger metropolises, where vast factories can produce goods at lower cost through economies of scale. The displacement of communities in the majority world is a result both of voluntary migration and eviction. Plans to dam major rivers, whether to generate electricity or to deal with some problem in water supply, require the removal of whole communities to burgeoning urban sprawls. In China, for example, the government is rehousing huge numbers of people in distant cities to make way for massive dams.[45] It is estimated that as many as 15 million farmers will lose their land in the years ahead, and already riots have broken out over compensation. In Europe, meanwhile, national and urban infrastructures are struggling to cope with the integration of large immigrant communities, not least from Eastern Europe. The ability of a country to absorb outsiders in a healthy way, which breeds goodwill rather than suspicion and gives people opportunities for growth and social mobility rather than trapping them to run-down ghettoes, depends not

---

[44] 'In Tamil Nadu, a state with more than 62 million people in southern India, wells are going dry almost everywhere. According to Kuppannan Palanisami of Tamil Nadu Agricultural University, falling water tables have dried up 95 percent of the wells owned by small farmers, reducing the irrigated area in the state by half over the last decade. As water tables fall, well drillers are using modified oil-drilling technology to reach water, going as deep as 1,000 meters in some locations. In communities where underground water sources have dried up entirely, all agriculture is rain-fed and drinking water is trucked in': Lester Brown, 'Aquifer depletion' in The Encyclopedia of Earth, 12 February 2007. Retrieved on 2 April 2008 from http://www.eoearth.org/article/aquifer_depletion

[45] 'Nowhere have the costs of dam-building been more visible than at China's Three Gorges, the world's largest—and perhaps most notorious—hydropower project. Begun in 1994, the dam forced the migration of millions and led to high unemployment in the region, deadly landslides, pollution and other environmental problems': Andrew Batson, 'Rising Tide: Dissent Slows China's Drive for Massive Dam Projects', *Wall Street Journal* (Eastern edition), 19 December 2007 (http://online.wsj.com/article/SB119802214926737977.html?mod=googlenews_wsj)

on its luck or (primarily) the national temperament but on its social capital. Inevitably, migration and displacement fracture the bonds of the social ecology in those host communities. Families lose their sense of attachment to land and place, exchanging it for a shiny new life hundreds of miles away. The benefits of established social structures are traded for a few white goods. The change is inevitable, but it poses all kinds of questions for societies as the stories and ties that have traditionally held them together are replaced by something new.

Mass migration

Migration within countries mirrors migration from the 'developing' to the 'developed' world. In Britain, we have recently been experiencing an influx of immigrants from Eastern Europe. Since the EU expanded to include a number of these former Eastern Bloc states on 1 May 2004, an estimated 585,000 people have migrated to Britain from this part of the world.[46] Government estimates had put the number at around 13,000. In 2007, incomers to Britain totalled about one million. This is immigration on an unprecedented scale, which looks set to increase the population of this country by 20 per cent by 2050. Often, these migrant workers have several, very low-paid jobs, as builders, labourers, cleaners, waiters, nannies, au pairs, fruit-pickers or farmhands. Go into any bar in London and, as like as not, you'll find it staffed and maintained by Poles and Romanians. The availability of so much cheap labour has kept costs down and some analysts estimate that without it interest rates in Britain would be 0.5 per cent higher. It is clear that the Government regards economic migration as an expedient way to prevent the economy from stagnating.

However, throughout the 'developed' world, such populations of migrant workers are vulnerable and easily exploited. They do not enjoy all the same rights as the citizens of their adopted countries and can expect low wages and poor working conditions where their health and safety are inadequately protected. It is difficult for them to protest against their treatment and face the continual pressure that others will replace them if they are unhappy with their work. Moreover, alongside so much legal immigration, there is now the global problem of illegal immigration. In America, the border with Mexico is now a place of danger, policed not only by state guards but also by vigilante groups trying to stem the flow of illegal immigrants. Estimates put the number of illegal immigrants in America at over 11 million[47]—who, again, offer cheap, easily exploited labour that boosts the economy.

---

[46] 'Migration: Net Immigration 191,000', National Statistics (2007) (originally found at http://www.statistics.gov.uk/cci/nugget.asp?id=260)

[47] 'In summary, there were an estimated 11.6 million unauthorized immigrants living in the United States as of January 2006. Nearly 4.2 million had entered in 2000 or later. An estimated 6.6 million

In Europe, the points of entry from Africa and Asia are similarly policed. Thousands of people are encamped on the coast of Morocco hoping to make a desperate crossing to Gibraltar or Spain just a few tantalizing miles away. The scale of human trafficking is immense, and the fate of the people who are 'imported' in this way is often appalling. The drowning in 2006 of 21 Chinese cockle-pickers who were working for a Chinese gangmaster on the coast of northern England drew attention to the virtual slavery in which many illegal immigrants live. Meanwhile, many vulnerable girls and young women who agree to be smuggled into Britain or other affluent countries in the belief that well-paid jobs await them end up trapped in prostitution.

In part, this flow of migrants is a result of the flow of capital from the countryside to the cities and from the 'developing' to the 'developed' world. In part, it is caused by the wars all over the world that are making huge numbers of people homeless. In part, it is a consequence of our continuing failure to address the deep problems of Africa in particular. The outcome, in any event, is instability and lack of cohesion.

Exploiting the desperate

Desperation energizes anyone, man, woman or child. The deeper you dig down through Abraham Maslow's hierarchy of needs, the more primal the sources of energy you find. In all of us, the drive to survive is strong, and although our experience of prosperity in the West may have made us apathetic, those in the majority world who lack it hunger for it. Uprooted from their places of origin, they live as temporary aliens in a foreign land. They have no sense of connection or belonging to the places where they now live and work, which lack the traditions of home for them. They have lost their sense of identity. The desire to be 'at home' runs deep in all of us: we crave a place where we can settle and feel safe and establish a relationship with our environment. Human communities have always made up stories and traditions about the places they live in so as to give them a shared sense of identity, belonging and history. When people groups are displaced, as refugees or exiles, they lose these 'psycho-geographical' attachments and markers. They become vulnerable and unsettled—easy to exploit, easy to influence but hard to predict. Globally, migrants are a volatile population, disempowered and yet energetic, without any proper place or voice and yet craving for their lot to be improved.

---

of the 11.6 million unauthorized residents were from Mexico': Michael Hoefer, Nancy Rytina and Christopher Campbell, 'Estimates of the Unauthorized Immigrant Population Residing in the United States: January 2006', *Population Estimates*, August 2007, p1. Retrieved on 3 April 2008 from http://www.dhs.gov/xlibrary/assets/statistics/publications/ill_pe_2006.pdf

It is worth noting that it is often such social conditions that result in revolution. In the end, slaves so resent their slavery that they seek to overthrow their masters. It is only a matter of time before the cauldron of anger and desire and the energy they generate can no longer be contained by the social 'lid' that is put on it and that anger, desire and energy start to boil over. What ensues will be spontaneous and chaotic, impossible to predict and extremely hard to manage or contain. Ultimately, it is futile to try to make the lid tighter or more secure. The only way to subdue the volatility is to improve the circumstances that have caused it in the first place. As long as their circumstances drive them to desperation, people will resort to desperate—and even suicidal—measures. Only when they believe they have something worth preserving will they begin to show a proper concern for their own safety, prompted by a proper sense of dignity. The current policies of America and Britain in response to the global threat of Islamist terror are catastrophically flawed, in that they are designed simply to contain the contents of the cauldron while the West continues with the strategies of political and economic domination that lit the fire under it in the first place. As long as we persist with those strategies, the resistance will still bubble away—and unless we turn the heat down, sooner or later it will boil over. It's basic physics, and basic social ecology. Let's hope there is no explosion.

Study questions 5

1. What is the link between the dominance of the corporatocracy and increasing migration?
2. Who is in control in this situation?
3. What are the dangers for economies built on a migrant class?
4. What are the long-term implications of long-term migration for a country's social capital?

SIX

Celluloid Slavery: the Economics of the Celebrity Class (PSX)

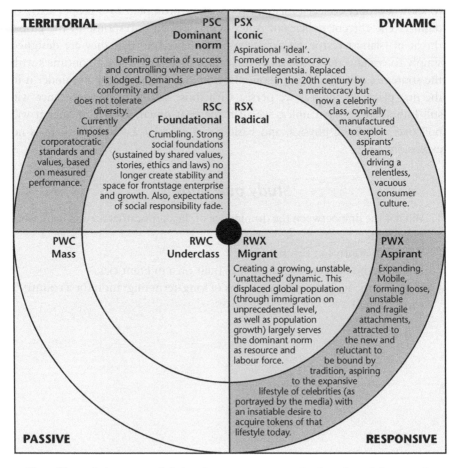

TERRITORIAL ... **PSC Dominant norm** ... **PSX Iconic** ... **DYNAMIC**

PSC Dominant norm
Defining criteria of success and controlling where power is lodged. Demands conformity and does not tolerate diversity. Currently imposes corporatocratic standards and values, based on measured performance.

PSX Iconic
Aspirational 'ideal'. Formerly the aristocracy and intellegentsia. Replaced in the 20th century by a meritocracy but now a celebrity class, cynically manufactured to exploit aspirants' dreams, driving a relentless, vacuous consumer culture.

RSC Foundational
Crumbling. Strong social foundations (sustained by shared values, stories, ethics and laws) no longer create stability and space for frontstage enterprise and growth. Also, expectations of social responsibility fade.

RSX Radical

PWC Mass

RWC Underclass

RWX Migrant
Creating a growing, unstable, 'unattached' dynamic. This displaced global population (through immigration on unprecedented level, as well as population growth) largely serves the dominant norm as resource and labour force.

PWX Aspirant
Expanding. Mobile, forming loose, unstable and fragile attachments, attracted to the new and reluctant to be bound by tradition, aspiring to the expansive lifestyle of celebrities (as portrayed by the media) with an insatiable desire to acquire tokens of that lifestyle today.

PASSIVE ... **RESPONSIVE**

The effect of the powerful dominant norm on who has 'iconic' status in the West today

Chapter summary

In this chapter, we explore the Iconic sector of the social ecology model, which I have labelled 'PSX'.

This element in society is, obviously, highly visible, and so is *'presented'* rather than 'reserved'. It exerts a *'strong'* (as opposed to weak) influence over the direction that others will take—not least, the Aspirant sector of society, who tend to imitate the iconic classes. It determines the fashions and styles and influences the values to which we aspire. It is also *'expanding'*, in that it takes us into new territory: the novel, the exotic, the exhilarating, the risky. That is its appeal—the glamour of it all!

Put together, these three characteristics—presented, strong and expanding (PSX)—define that element in society that lights the way to a brighter, more confident future, captivating those who follow it and inducing them to look and dream.

Summary statement

In this chapter I will argue that over the last century the nature of what is iconic in our society has changed dramatically. Historically, it used to consist of the social elite, the so-called upper classes. The 20th century saw a gradual shift to a meritocracy, in which we looked up instead to people who, through some virtue, skill or effort, had accomplished something out of the ordinary. However, recently a further shift has occurred whereby we now admire people who have little, or even no, discernible talent or achievement. The label 'celebrity' fits this new aristocracy better than 'icon', and an individual can win it almost regardless of any merit. This chapter will explore how and why this change has occurred, and the function celebrities have in our social ecology. I will maintain that the creation of this new aristocracy is neither accidental nor surprising, but rather represents the extreme of the control exercised by the PSC dominant norm. The consequences of allowing our icons to be manufactured to reflect such values back to us are profoundly damaging to the well-being of our society.

....

In my family, building sandcastles is always a competitive business. At some stage in any day on the beach, one of us will throw down the gauntlet to the others. It doesn't really matter what the challenge is, as long as there is one: to build the tallest, the widest, the strongest, the most intricate, the most lifelike—or simply the one that will last the longest against the returning tide. Then we all set to, and for 40 minutes or so nothing can be heard but the sound of happy hands scraping, piling and patting sand.

There is something instinctive, and even atavistic, in the human desire to compete. Few societies have emerged that have not offered some kind of prize for the best fighters or runners or riders or wrestlers. We seem to have a basic need to push ourselves to our limits, and an urge, too, to identify those in our society who have performed supremely well. We honour them with titles and medals and reward them with money, prestige and even adulation. The desire to build the best sandcastle on a blustery day on the English coast is just one small expression of a universal urge that drives human endeavour at the highest social, industrial and economic levels around the world.

And it leads to the creation of the social elite.

The reconstruction of the iconic class

Every society has its elite, who determine the horizons and the aspirations of the rest. In Britain at the start of the 20th century, this would have included royalty, the nobility and the gentry, who lived a life apart in terms of wealth, power, status and culture. As their titles were inherited, they created dynasties. It was in these 'upper-class' circles that fashions were dictated—in clothing, pastimes, decor, education and travel. The social elite was also associated with pushing back the intellectual and political frontiers. It is no coincidence that in Britain both the Fascist party and wartime traitorous spies emerged from within the ranks of the nobility. Of course, political and military power rested disproportionately with the aristocracy.

A hundred years ago, our society revered the wealthy, landed elite. It revered the intelligentsia. It revered its political and military leaders. It deferred to them, accepted their authority and followed their ideological lead. However, over the course of the past century we have gradually transferred this esteem to others. Tragic failures of leadership perhaps contributed to this development, not least in the First World War. Up to that time, all army officers were drawn from the gentry, regardless of ability, and they commanded such little respect that it was not uncommon for their men to shoot them in the back when they were ordered to advance from the trenches. In response to this, after 1918 the British Army became the first institution to develop psychological tests so that it could recruit officers who had genuine leadership skills rather than mere breeding. This was a significant move towards meritocracy. At the same time, the growing availability of education to the wider population gradually disseminated social, political and intellectual power from the elite to the 'lower' classes. By the 1960s, the intellectual agenda itself was to denounce the hegemony of the wealthy 'upper' classes and deconstruct the traditional and institutional forms of power in our social system. The iconic influence of the aristocracy was fast being eroded.

The role of the media

Who replaced the aristocracy in our social ecology in the role of social icons? A key factor in the rise of a new breed was the influence of the media. The media provided the means whereby the attention of the whole population could be directed towards particular individuals—by the broadcast not only of words (for example, in radio talks given by the members of the elite) but also of images. The celluloid celebrity was born. The shift from an essentially verbal culture to a visual one marked the end of a culture based on thoughts and ideas. Ideas cannot really be conveyed successfully high profile through images: they can be illustrated, they can be animated and made more compelling, but they always rely in the end on the logic of words, the sense of the sentence. The visual as the basic media form upon which the second half of the 20th century was to be built ensured that ultimately our icons would be visual, sensual and aesthetic in nature.

Unimaginable wealth now flows into the hands of those who the public wants to look at. In 1992, the average salary of a soccer player in the Premier League was £75,000.[48] Compared with the incomes of most other people, that was substantial but not exorbitant. Nowadays, such a player would be earning on average more than £1 million a year, as a result of the huge television audience (not least on subscription TV) and the very high prices people will pay to go to a game.[49] A similar story can be told of stars in both the film and the music industry. Tom Cruise earned $75 million from *Mission Impossible*. Madonna is reckoned to have grossed over $260 million from her single 2006 tour, in addition to all her other revenues that year.[50]

The fame and attention such icons enjoy is no less extraordinary. They can be assured that they will be invited to every premiere, every gala, every party that matters. Moreover, their endorsement of clothing or other branded goods will earn them enormous fees. We will wear what they wear, get our hair cut like theirs; we will buy the magazines that offer them to us. The influence some of them have appears to be limitless. Where the world's politicians and diplomats have failed, they can get debate going within the G8 about lowering trade

---

[48] 'In 1992–93 the average wage for a Premiership player was £75,000 per year. In 2001–02 the average wage for a Premiership player was £600,000': Vivek Chaudhary, 'Forty Factors Fuelling Football Inflation', *The Guardian*, 31 July 2003 (http://football.guardian.co.uk/comment/story/0,9753,1009392,00.html)

[49] 'On average, the league's players each earn more than £1m a year; a top player like Liverpool's Fernando Torres can cost £20m or more': Theo Leggett, 'Foreign Owners Boost UK Football', BBC News, 9 August 2007 (http://news.bbc.co.uk/1/hi/business/6938866.stm)

[50] 'Paramount: Cruise is Risky Business', CNN, 23 August 2006 (http://money.cnn.com/2006/08/22/news/newsmakers/cruise_paramount/index.htm); http://www.billboard.com/bbcom/yearend/2006/touring/top_tours.jsp)

barriers, cancelling international debt and increasing aid to the majority world. Bono and Bob Geldof command more attention on the global stage than all but the most senior of the world's political leaders. When they champion a cause, the world listens.

The role of the celebrity

However, there is a trade they make with the public in return for such wealth and influence, and that is their lives. They sell us themselves, their appearance and their persona. They become publicly owned goods and as such must dance to the tune the public demands. Of course this must be the case: in the economy of this market, what such people provide is more than simply an image of glamour, style and beauty, it is availability. As we observed in Chapter 3, what the aspirant population lacks is emotional rootedness—and it looks for this, and for meaning and identity, through celebrities. The celebrity industry first and foremost provides a social avenue for identifying yourself in society, but in addition it provides an emotional avenue for understanding yourself. We demand not only availability from our celebrities but also intimacy, as we crave to know all about their inner lives, their messy stories and secrets. We demand those paparazzi shots of Jennifer Aniston or Britney Spears emerging from their apartments, baggy-eyed and bed-haired, to pop down to the gym. We long to see what they look like behind the mask. We have a desire to feel emotionally connected with them. In this way, we see our own imperfections and insecurities mirrored back to us. We discover, ultimately, that we are not alone in the universe and someone else shares our mess. In the absence of a family in which we can find a sense of self, intimacy and belonging, we reach out to the remote-but-intimate celebrity. They become our emotional comforter, reassuring us when we feel lost. They show us a life we can only dream of, perhaps, but they also console us in the life we actually live.

The role of the 'puppeteer'

People have always been inspired by heroes and heroines. It is essential for the health of a nation that its people aspire to the qualities of men and women of remarkable character or achievement, who excel in their courage, compassion, energy, skill or artistry. However, danger arises when such role models no longer promote values that are good for society as a whole. In the corporatocracy of the West, the worth of our idols is defined increasingly not by their character or achievement but by their commercial leverage. Behind every 'star' is a promoter—whose eyes are fixed on the bottom line. The dark secret of our celebrity culture concerns not the public or the performer but those who manage the show. The fact is that the whole structure has been built and maintained by people from another part of the social ecology, in order to extract vast sums of money from desperate aspirants. Celebrities are celebrities only because the media pay them attention, and the media pay them attention only because it is profitable to do so. And that profit comes from two streams of revenue: direct sales of media products and advertising. Sky Sports will pay clubs multi–million-pound fees for the exclusive right to televise Premier League soccer because it can sell the broadcasts to its subscribers for an enormous profit. Manchester United and others will happily sign such a deal because it ensures that they can make huge profits from the sale of club merchandise to their now global audience.

When Real Madrid bought David Beckham from Manchester United in 2003, it did so less for the sake of his footballing prowess than because it wanted to break into the market in the Far East, where Beckham already had a huge following in China and Japan. The thinking behind the transaction came from the club's accountants, who were interested in only one thing: increasing its share value on the stock market. The star player himself was merely a commodity, a utility expedient for their purposes of generating greater financial power and reward.

The cultivation of celebrity has been a collusion between brand manufacturers, the media, aspirant consumers and the celebrities themselves, to create a circle of consumption and desire. In this transaction, the flow of financial capital runs from the aspirant consumer to the brand manufacturer, the media, the celebrity and, of course, the financial services that supply the loans on which the purchases are made. In return for their money, the aspirant consumer gets a sense of emotional intimacy and surrogate social identity, which makes up for their lack of any authentic emotional and social attachments.

The role of the non-celebrity

The final twist in the tale of celebrity is the emergence of the non-celebrity. For the last decade, it has been a running joke that the quality of today's 'celebs' has plummeted. It's often said that you used to need to have achieved something in order to be famous but nowadays you need to be famous in order to achieve anything. The causality seems to have changed. Indeed, this is what you would expect: if the celebrity is merely the cipher of the brand/media conflation, their actual quality becomes increasingly unimportant. We pay attention to them simply because we are made to pay attention to them, not because they have any merit that commands our attention. Celebrity shows present us with a succession of 'C-', 'D-', and 'E-list' nonentities.

Consider the ironic story of Chantelle in the British version of *Celebrity Big Brother* in 2005. The usual very minor celebs were planted in the Big Brother house to be scrutinized for a few weeks—but included in their number was an ordinary young woman from Essex who had no celebrity 'credentials' whatsoever. The production company behind the programme called her 'Chantelle' and gave her a cover story about being a member of a girl band. As no one in the house had heard of any of the other 'celebrity' contestants anyway, no one twigged that they were being set up. And, of course, she won the contest, having similarly fooled the viewers. Since then, she has, in her own words, been 'living the dream', with TV appearances, fashion shoots and the whole media circus making her the celebrity she never was. Obviously, the media's motivation is to make money, which means they must be selling something to someone. But who is actually buying Chantelle when she really does have nothing to offer—and we know it?

The answer is: 16 per cent of Britain's teenagers for a start, who (according to a survey in 2006) believe they will find success as a celebrity. The odds against making the big time through a show such as *Big Brother* are, in fact, about 30 million to one, yet the same poll found that one in 10 of the teenagers surveyed would be willing to give up their education to appear on TV.[51] Here is the rub. A hundred years ago, the iconic PSX sector of our society was an all but closed group that outsiders could not aspire to join except perhaps through marriage. Since then, the terms of membership of the social elite have changed: from being inherited to being earned by merit to being won today by anyone who has the good luck to flash her body or land in bed while the cameras are rolling. The truth is that the non-celebrity is the most cynical of all media/brand creations. Whether or not Chantelle has qualities lacking in millions of other young British women—many of them lost and emotionally dysfunctional, all craving attention and looking for an identity, all aspiring to escape their present lives, all believing the dream that money and publicity would give them fulfilment—it now appears that they need no expertise, no discipline, no effort to make it into our social elite. Instead, they can get there, with a bit of luck, just as she did—as long as the cameras keep rolling and the audience remains interested. In the meantime, all they can do is to prepare themselves for the call: watching the right shows, buying the right products, drinking the right drinks, frittering their lives away without ever taking responsibility for their choices. And in the end they can

---

[51] 'Fame hungry teenagers are planning to ditch education and live in dreamland. More than one in 10 (11 per cent) young people would drop out of education or training to be on TV, according to new research from the Learning and Skills Council (LSC). And more than one in six (16 per cent) young people believe that they will actually become famous. However, the odds of being picked for a *Big Brother* style reality TV show and being successful afterwards are around one in 30 million': LSC press release 336 (2006), 'Kids Seeking Reality TV Fame instead of Exam Passes' (http://readingroom.lsc.gov.uk/lsc/2006/externalrelations/press/kids-seeking-reality-tv-fame.pdf)

assuage their inevitable disappointment by acquiring things that at least remind them of Chantelle's glittering Essex palace: the HD plasma screens, the white leather suite, the satellite TV, the holidays, the boyfriends.

And the cash they will need for these acquisitions? Well, there's always another credit card deal, always another six-month interest-free balance-transfer offer, always another way to pay off their debt in the future—and with only a £1 downpayment who can refuse? Meanwhile, the corporatocrats driving the machine press the buttons and pull the levers, create the brands and exploit the celebrities, finance the loans and squeeze the supply chains around the globe to manufacture the products, pocket the money and add another property to their portfolio of country residences.

Nobody builds yet another sandcastle unless they want to. The fuel of economic growth is discontent with what we already have. Capital expansion depends on aspiration. Encourage one and you encourage the other. And one of the key ways in which aspiration has been encouraged in the West has been through the cynical manufacture of a new 'celebrity' class. Crucially, members of this class are valued primarily not for their skills but for their potential financial leverage—that is, how effectively they and whatever brands they endorse can be sold. This has been a key means corporations have used to enlarge their markets. However, in the process they have created social icons who are not admired, let alone held to account, for their values and principles. Those who idolize celebrities and seek to emulate their lifestyle therefore adopt ideals and aspirations that are at best socially neutral and at worst socially damaging. The net impact of this new aristocracy on our society is to have encouraged aspirant consumers to aspire to wealth and fame (or, indeed, notoriety) rather than more noble attainments that require self-discipline, self-sacrifice and commitment as well as good manners. As a result, the dreams of the rising generation are being squandered and the vital energy that is needed to sustain a vibrant, creative, fertile and mature civilization may be waning.

Study questions 6

1. How has the composition of the ruling classes in the West changed in the past century?
2. What is the psychological function of the new celebrity class?
3. Who is controlling it and profiting from it?
4. What is the social legacy of this situation?

SEVEN

The Rending of Our Social Fabric (PWC)

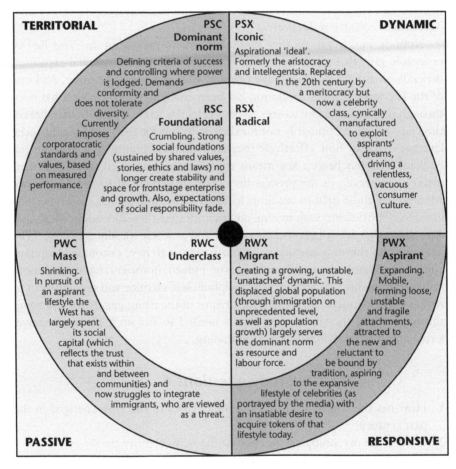

TERRITORIAL			DYNAMIC
PSC Dominant norm		**PSX** Iconic	

Defining criteria of success and controlling where power is lodged. Demands conformity and does not tolerate diversity. Currently imposes corporatocratic standards and values, based on measured performance.

Aspirational 'ideal'. Formerly the aristocracy and intellegentsia. Replaced in the 20th century by a meritocracy but now a celebrity class, cynically manufactured to exploit aspirants' dreams, driving a relentless, vacuous consumer culture.

RSC Foundational / **RSX** Radical

Crumbling. Strong social foundations (sustained by shared values, stories, ethics and laws) no longer create stability and space for frontstage enterprise and growth. Also, expectations of social responsibility fade.

PWC Mass

Shrinking. In pursuit of an aspirant lifestyle the West has largely spent its social capital (which reflects the trust that exists within and between communities) and now struggles to integrate immigrants, who are viewed as a threat.

RWC Underclass

RWX Migrant

Creating a growing, unstable, 'unattached' dynamic. This displaced global population (through immigration on unprecedented level, as well as population growth) largely serves the dominant norm as resource and labour force.

PWX Aspirant

Expanding. Mobile, forming loose, unstable and fragile attachments, attracted to the new and reluctant to be bound by tradition, aspiring to the expansive lifestyle of celebrities (as portrayed by the media) with an insatiable desire to acquire tokens of that lifestyle today.

PASSIVE

RESPONSIVE

The effect of the expanding iconic, aspirant and migrant sectors on social capital in the West

Chapter summary

In this chapter, we explore the Mass sector of the social ecology model. By this (which I have labelled 'PWC') I mean that which gives cohesion to any social system.

This element in society is visible, and so is *'presented'*, but the force it exerts is weak in that, by and large, the bonds that hold society together consist of trust, respect, compassion, social proximity, shared interest, a shared heritage and so on, rather than contract and obligation in any legal or economic sense. This effect of this element in a society is to consolidate it rather than expand it. It creates cohesion rather than mobility; it represents the roots people put down rather than the acquisitions they take with them. It is fostered by shared stories, community events, festivals, traditions and local practices and customs—all those things that bind people together at a subliminal level.

Summary statement

This chapter will argue that in most societies people belong to wider collective groups: families, clubs, teams, communities and so on to which they have some kind of attachment. The strength of such bonds has been diminishing over the past 50 years. As a result, our society has been losing its resilience, as well as its ability to foster talent. Moreover, the social roles people used to play informally, such as policing their neighbourhoods and protecting the vulnerable, now have to be carried out formally and contractually by the state, which will increasingly place an unsustainable financial burden on the economy.

....

There is sand that is great for building castles with and sand that, despite all your efforts, just won't do the job. The ideal sand for building is neither too fine nor too coarse. Too fine and it gets cloggy and sticks to the bottom of the bucket; too coarse and it lacks coherence and behaves like mere grit. However, the most crucial ingredient in a good sandcastle is the right amount of moisture. You want to be working with sand that was under water a few hours before: not saturated, but not dried out by the sun, either. If the sand is too dry, it is best to have a partner who can bring water back from the sea to wet the sand so you can work with it.

The essential function of social capital

What is it that gives the 'grains' of society coherence? What binds individuals together to form a cohesive community? The magic ingredient is the glue of social capital. Like financial or intellectual capital, this is an asset or form of wealth that can be exploited. Some of this capital is 'spent' when 'costs' are incurred in absorbing outsiders, for example. If a society has enough in the bank, as it were, it can generally afford to pay the costs of integration—and there always are costs. However, if its bank balance is low, it may quickly run into the red. Unlike financial or intellectual capital, you cannot amass social capital by selling or buying things. It cannot be grown through a government programme. It cannot be borrowed, or multiplied through the markets and strategic investments. Nor is it the preserve of an institution, organization, government, company or any other collective body that can own it. And for this reason it is both more fragile and more precious than other kinds of capital.

At its simplest, social capital is the trust that exists between people. This is what makes it unownable. It is a commodity that is present in the space between human beings: between one human being and another, between individuals in a community and between communities; between the elderly and the young, between the rich and the poor. Social capital is the bonds that hold the social fabric together, the transactions that bind the social ecology into a stable whole. If financial capital is the monetary wealth of a society and intellectual capital the wealth of ideas that it possesses and can exploit, then social capital is the wealth of trust it can rely on. It is the richness of the spaces between people, the unpaid-for, invisible ties. It is the soil of society in which each individual plant grows. Social capital therefore consists in the closeness, integrity and reliability of relationships in any community.

Nurturing potential

A society rich in social capital can do a number of things. First, it is able to cultivate, direct and mentor talent. Small, local, family-run businesses act like a net to catch the potential of the rising generation. When 16-year-olds leave school and don't go on into further education, they need to find employment; and such a society can channel this stream of potential informally into useful occupations. When I worked in the East End of London, it was expected that a young man would learn his father's trade, or another relation's, and end up in his workshop or office. Uncles took on nephews in the family building firm and trained them on the job, or often there was someone in the extended family who owned a garage, who would take an apprentice. In this way, young men (in particular) who had no future in white-collar professions were able to find a place in society and a way to make a living.

Self-policing

Second, such a society can police itself. In close-knit communities, the behaviour of any individual youth is always seen by someone else who knows their mum or dad or an aunt or uncle. A neighbour of ours has lived in this part of our city most of her life, as have her mother and her children and grandchildren. Mary knows most people locally simply because she has been around; she is connected to almost everything that goes on. One day, she was on a bus when two youths began swearing and abusing other passengers. She marched straight up to them and said: 'Right, I know who you are. Let me tell you that I know your uncle and if I see you carrying on this kind of behaviour, you'll have him to deal with.' Of course, their misconduct stopped there and then. It is not just ordinary people who are connected: there is also the network of local public servants, from the bus conductors to the park keepers to the refuse collectors to the local postmen and women who, simply by being around and being familiar with people, prevent society from becoming anonymous and unaccountable.

Caring for the vulnerable

Third, a society rich in social capital is able to care for the elderly and the vulnerable in its midst. In 2003, France discovered how depleted its social capital was when a drought caused the deaths of some 15,000 elderly people across the country, and in Paris especially. Many died in their own homes, unremarked. No one knew these old folk were there; no one visited them.[52] They were not members of church congregations or lunch clubs or voluntary organizations that would have noticed their absence. They were, in effect, invisible. Much the same could be said of the population of New Orleans, similarly left to their fate in the wake of Hurricane Katrina. Here in Britain I recall one local doctor telling me that when she prescribed a course of treatment to an elderly or vulnerable person, she would ask them whether they had any relatives nearby. If they did, she knew they had a much better chance of completing the course of treatment, as she would ring the relative and ask them to visit her patient regularly to check that they were taking their medicine. Social capital underpins a society's ability to care for its elderly and vulnerable members at an informal level, through the exercise of compassion, goodwill, generosity and 'other-person-centeredness'. It reflects the extent to which each member of that society looks beyond their own individual life, or that of their nuclear family, and feels a sense of responsibility for others around them.

---

[52] 'Paris Continues to Feel the Heat from a Deadly Summer', Jo Johnson, *The Financial Times*, 24 December 2003, p6

Welcoming incomers

Fourth, such a society is able to befriend outsiders. Both Britain and America have strong traditions of welcoming immigrants in the belief that their societies will be enriched by their cultural and economic contributions, and as a result both countries are richly multiracial and multicultural. However, in both cases the relationship between the host culture and those of the immigrants has not always been easy. Distrust can easily build if it is seen that newcomers are receiving preferential treatment (in terms of housing, for example)—which is often the case when immigrants have larger families than other people locally—as well as taking jobs and helping to drive down wages. Usually, it is the perception of socio-economic injustice that lies at the root of ethnic tension in urban areas rather than race per se. Broadly speaking, though, in both Britain and America the social integration of people of other races has been possible because of a set of values and practices shared by the host nation: toleration of expressions of faith and ideology other than your own, confidence in your own national identity, a clearly defined set of social conventions and norms, festivals and rhythms that enable immigrant communities to understand and participate in the host culture, a market which incomers can enter and where they can prosper on the same basis as anyone else if they work hard, and, finally, an interest in the rich and colourful cultural diversity that is expressed on the 'front stage' of that society as a result.

Raising the next generation

Fifth, such a society is able to nurture healthy, well-adjusted children. Crucial to the development of emotional stability in any individual are sound relationships with primary caregivers who are consistent in imposing their values and norms. In such conditions, children grow up learning to trust both themselves and other people. They also learn social responsibility within the context of the family as they witness the effect of their behaviour on those around them and see themselves within a wider set of relationships. Families also provide the context for intergenerational learning, as experience, tradition and wisdom are passed on over the meal table or while walking the dog or sharing a story at bedtime. The young learn to appreciate the contribution of the old, and the nature of vulnerability. They learn to see themselves within a historical tapestry of society and are exposed in a healthy way to the realities of both birth and death. Moreover, institutions such as the churches and historic faith-based organizations can help children and adults alike to develop a sense of the sacred and of the rhythms of the year, and to exercise the disciplines of self-restraint and thankfulness, generosity and compassion. All this can have a profoundly humanizing effect on our emotional and social formation.

The web of relationships we are talking about—with families, local small businesses, schools and congregations, neighbours and doctors and other public servants—form the very fabric of any society. None of these relationships are established purely by contract. These are not bonds between employers and employees, masters and servants—they are what we call 'weak' social bonds that rely upon trust and respect rather than financial or legal obligation. Even the marriage contract is based less on legal commitment than on the promises of the individuals concerned. The strength of such relationships lies in the ties between people and their willingness to help one another out.

When this pattern of relationships is widespread, society is healthy and stable and functions well. When it is not, other kinds of power tend to be exerted, which are either less accountable or more formal and dominating. Post-Soviet Russia is an example of a society afflicted in this way. Power and wealth there are concentrated in the hands of a tiny minority of the population. Access to the market is available only to a few. Power is exercised either negligently or oppressively by the state. Levels of alcoholism and other addictions are rising catastrophically, and many observers are predicting an associated Aids crisis in the years to come, as the bulk of the people become relegated from the 'front stage' of their society, where they had status, purpose, opportunity and hope, to its 'back stage', where they languish as an underclass. Any society that is poor in social capital will similarly be seriously weakened. Essentially, it is able to do far less to help itself than a society that is rich in social capital, as each of the capacities we have discussed above are undermined or diminished.

The loss of social capital

When we examine the evidence, we begin to see that one of the consequences of the growth of our financial capital and the subsequent domination of Western societies by monetary wealth has been a catastrophic loss of our social capital. The social bonds that in the middle of the 20th century were strong have since been seriously eroded. As a result, first of all, we are failing to nurture potential. There are fewer trades open to young adults, fewer small local businesses, fewer apprenticeships. In their stead, they may have to find employment in temporary shift work stacking shelves or staffing call centres, where young men in particular will not gain any sense of identity and self-respect. Moreover, the links between each generation of men and the next are weakened, as the old hands no longer act as mentors to the novices. The wisdom of experience is not passed down but instead leaks out of the system and goes to waste. Given that

80 per cent of crime in Britain is committed by disaffected young men aged between 18 and 25,[53] this is a serious problem.

Second, we are less able to police ourselves. Whereas in 1959 a British poll found that 60 per cent of respondents said that basically they trusted other people, by 2005 that percentage had fallen amongst younger people by over a third.[54] There may be good reason for this, of course. Crime—whether it be mugging, burglary or murder—is increasingly related to drug use, and criminals under the influence, who cannot to be reasoned with, are chaotic as well as lawless. We learn that the use of knives is rising, and hear too many stories of responsible citizens stepping in to prevent violence and only getting stabbed and killed themselves—and it discourages us from either trusting or caring for others. Moreover, as we break up our families and communities, we all become more anonymous and less accountable. Incidents such as Mary's intervention on the bus become rarer, and in some parts of our cities people do not dare to venture out after dark for fear of the gangs that roam the streets. My wife works as a behavioural adviser in schools, helping them to deal with dysfunctional adolescents, and she witnesses the problems first-hand. So often the means that are needed to constrain behaviour are simply not available. Fathers are absent. Parents are suspicious and angry and themselves offer violence to staff. Children who are excluded from school simply go out on the streets—while their schools employ bouncers to keep them out. It is a bizarre and tragic indictment that in a First World country with an economy of the size of Britain's some children cannot enjoy even basic safety at school, let alone an education.

Third, our ability to care for the elderly and the vulnerable has gradually diminished. Instead of this care taking place in the community, it has to be provided increasingly by the state. Today, 30 per cent of people who go to see a doctor in Britain do so in connection with psychological problems: depression, anxiety, loneliness and stress.[55] Perhaps it is no coincidence that, at the same time, recruiting for voluntary organizations such as the Scouts and the Guides has never been more difficult.[56] Meanwhile, instead of getting support

---

[53] 'Crime: 4 in 5 Offenders are Male', National Statistics, 8 January 2004. Retrieved on 27 March 2008 from http://www.statistics.gov.uk/cci/nugget.asp?id=442

[54] Paul Haezewindt, 'Investing in Each Other and the Community: the Role of Social Capital', *Social Trends* 33, National Statistics (2003). Retrieved on 6 April 2008 from http://www.statistics.gov.uk/articles/social_trends/socialtrends33article.pdf

[55] Undated survey of GPs conducted for Mind (originally found at http://www.mind.org.uk/Information/gpsurvey.htm)

[56] 'The age of philanthropic volunteering is gone. We need to produce things of interest and benefit to volunteers to make us appear an enticing opportunity': Simon Carter, head of communications and marketing at the Scout Association, quoted in 'Finding the Need', NCVO (n.d.), (https://www.ncvo-vol.org.uk/?template=1&template=1&id=2417)

through local clubs, associations, churches or the like, isolated individuals are increasingly having to turn to formal agencies, in the private or public sector, to meet their basic social needs. More often than not, my local doctor cannot rely on a local network or extended family to support a patient. Instead, he has to get in paid help in the form of home nursing funded by the state. The loss of social capital always results in more expense for the state, which has to step in as a surrogate to prevent people slipping down into an underclass.

Fourth, we are less and less able to welcome outsiders, but instead perceive them as threats. The open borders of both Britain and America are fast being closed, and tolerance is becoming a thing of the past. In part, this is a consequence of the devastating psychological impact of '9/11', which has made Americans feel vulnerable on their own soil and suspicious of others. The growing popularity of the re-emergent far right in mainland Europe demonstrates that this less open, less trusting and more defensive perspective on society is not limited to Britain and America. Part of the problem is the erosion of the shared values that give cohesion to our own cultures, into which we hope to integrate newcomers. Ironically, in our efforts to make room in our society for other cultures, we have damaged the very features that made our society attractive to them in the first place. Britain's liberal tolerance is rooted in a particular set of values, and you will find no such tolerance in Saudi Arabia or Afghanistan, which lack the same ideology of human life. Those values are fostered by and expressed in not only our secularism but also our spiritual traditions, which are unavoidably Christian. Our laws, which seek to protect the weak and offer asylum to refugees, which guarantee the rights of others and a fair trial, are all specific to our culture and history. They cannot be sustained without that context and that narrative—they do not exist in a vacuum. When we discard the religious basis of the festivals of Christmas and Easter, for example, so as not to discriminate against ethnic minorities of other faiths, we do them no favours. We are in danger of undermining the very things for which they came here.

Fifth, we are making the next generation increasingly dysfunctional. The proportion of marriages in Britain that end in divorce will soon reach one in two. At least one in two people has been affected in some way by a fractured home, whether as a child or as an adult—and everyone learns to parent from their own experience of being parented. More deeply, the formation of our own emotional well-being and sense of self and the development of our ability to trust others are related directly to our experience of reliable, stable relationships with significant others. Like seeds growing in soil that is continually disturbed, children who endure emotional disruption suffer damage in their emotional and social formation.

The social price of liberal morality

Of course, the impact of technology has also had a deleterious effect on children. The average time an American adolescent spends in front of a computer or game-console screen is 21 hours a week. The effect of this is to reduce the influence of both their parents and their peers on their socialization. Children learn social skills through social interaction—primarily, through playing in groups and teams. Isolated individuals, interacting with a screen for hours each day, do not learn these skills or acquire emotional literacy. Not only this, but the content of the programmes they watch is often negative. A recent study on the effect on teenagers of watching soap operas—not video nasties!—found that they reduced their patience, trust and goodwill towards others and encouraged aggression and intolerance.[57] TV shows, no less than action movies and computer games, often reduce human interaction to a level where problems are resolved through hostility and violence, or else the abdication of responsibility; and such are the attitudes and behaviours that children learn, internalize and are given permission to exhibit.

Considering that in 2005 the biggest-selling computer game in the teenage market was Grand Theft Auto,[58] in which drug lords rob and kill and pick up prostitutes, is it any wonder we are seeing a rise in aggressive, antisocial behaviour and a lack of self-restraint in our young people? One of the truths of our day that has been most thoroughly and damagingly suppressed in the name of the free market, tolerance and individual rights is that engaging with such negative images and roles does indeed have a damaging effect on the behaviour of those who play these games. Of course, without a shared moral framework within which to discuss the issue, we seem impotent to regulate the market that generates such material. Thus, we find that our children fall victim to the pernicious, amoral operations of a gaming world that aspires only to make money, as well as to the boundary-free world of the internet.

Trust, respect, compassion, a sense of responsibility and a sense of belonging that has nothing to do with contracts are the glue that holds any society together

---

[57] Alison Motluk, 'Blame It on the Box', *New Scientist*, 6 April 2002 (http://www.newscientist. com/article/mg17423372.200); 'Dr Aric Sigman, an associate fellow of the British Psychological Society and author of a book on children and television, said: "It is the greatest unacknowledged health threat of our time. ... The key stages of development are language acquisition and social skills and if they're displaced at this time they may be irreplaceable." He added: "Television is isolating. Children end up spending years in front of a screen instead of speaking and socialising with real children. As a result, they don't learn how to get on with other people. At the same time, faster editing with colours, zooms and a constant stream of images has been linked to a lower attention span"': Steven Swinford, 'Kids Behaving Badly After Just Two Hours' TV', *The Sunday Times*, 30 September 2007, p21

[58] 'GTA: San Andreas Toasts Success', BBC News, 4 November 2005 (http://news.bbc.co.uk/1/hi/technology/4404088.stm)

and enables it to absorb and integrate immigrants. The West is discovering that the sand it is building its castles with is losing all its cohesion. Why, we may ask, has there been such a catastrophic loss of our social capital? It turns out that we have paid even more for our consumer lifestyles than the price that was exacted at the checkout, and it is a social cost we have largely overlooked, or else have chosen to ignore. We may be dangerously in the red in financial terms, but we are so, too, in social terms. We have spent our social capital with no thought for the future, and only now may be starting to recognize the scale of the investment we have squandered.

Study questions 7

1. Why is social capital so important to the well-being of any society?
2. What can a society rich in social capital do that a society poor in social capital can't?
3. What are the factors that have caused the loss of social capital in the West?
4. Who benefits commercially when a society is poor in social capital, and who pays?

EIGHT

The Swelling of the Underclass (RWC)

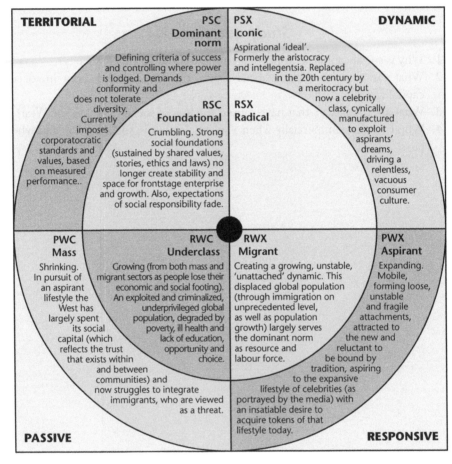

TERRITORIAL

PSC
Dominant norm
Defining criteria of success and controlling where power is lodged. Demands conformity and does not tolerate diversity. Currently imposes corporatocratic standards and values, based on measured performance..

PSX
Iconic
Aspirational 'ideal'. Formerly the aristocracy and intellegentsia. Replaced in the 20th century by a meritocracy but now a celebrity class, cynically manufactured to exploit aspirants' dreams, driving a relentless, vacuous consumer culture.

DYNAMIC

RSC
Foundational
Crumbling. Strong social foundations (sustained by shared values, stories, ethics and laws) no longer create stability and space for frontstage enterprise and growth. Also, expectations of social responsibility fade.

RSX
Radical

PWC
Mass
Shrinking. In pursuit of an aspirant lifestyle the West has largely spent its social capital (which reflects the trust that exists within and between communities) and now struggles to integrate immigrants, who are viewed as a threat.

RWC
Underclass
Growing (from both mass and migrant sectors as people lose their economic and social footing). An exploited and criminalized, underprivileged global population, degraded by poverty, ill health and lack of education, opportunity and choice.

RWX
Migrant
Creating a growing, unstable, 'unattached' dynamic. This displaced global population (through immigration on unprecedented level, as well as population growth) largely serves the dominant norm as resource and labour force.

PWX
Aspirant
Expanding. Mobile, forming loose, unstable and fragile attachments, attracted to the new and reluctant to be bound by tradition, aspiring to the expansive lifestyle of celebrities (as portrayed by the media) with an insatiable desire to acquire tokens of that lifestyle today.

PASSIVE

RESPONSIVE

The causes and effects of a growing underclass

Chapter summary

In this chapter, we explore the Underclass sector of the social ecology model, which I have labelled 'RWC'.

The underclass is typically *'reserved'*, in that most societies will try to hide this section of their population away. These people are, to some extent, its shame, or at the very least its awkward nuisance: the costly leftovers when their economic productivity has diminished. The power the underclass exercises is *'weak'*, in that it does not have political leverage or financial clout, educational privilege or career opportunities.

Moreover, it is *'consolidating'* rather than 'expanding' in the sense that these people are afraid that their world is being taken away from them and they try to cling on to it. They have lost the vision to make a positive contribution to society or to climb up the social ladder. In some ways, their behaviour is marked by despair. For some, as hope has died, so too have faith and goodness, dignity and self-control. For them, only a life of violence awaits. Others retain their sense of humanity but are so crushed in spirit they are unable to see beyond the task of surviving another day. They are characterized as RWC by their passivity, emptiness, impotence and vulnerability. Decisions are made for them by others.

Summary statement

The chapter will argue that in the social ecology model the RWC underclass represents the opposite of the PSX elite. The rise of the former parallels the rise of the latter. For a society to be healthy, its most powerful members need to show compassion to its most powerless, something that seems to happen less often today than in the past. There are more routes into poverty now than there have been since the advent of the modern welfare state, and there are fewer routes out.

....

As sand dries out, so its cohesion diminishes. Grains that previously were incorporated into a structure begin to separate and fall away. In a similar way, the underclass consists of people who have become detached and lost their place in the social structure and fallen away, no good to anyone.

Every society in history has had an underclass. This is that section of a population that lacks the economic, social or political power to choose. Such people have no opportunity to change their own future. They are essentially vulnerable and passive, dominated and dictated to, their fate decided by the actions of other social groups above them. Both isolated and crowded at the same time, they are impotent to influence the shape of the game, and soon become dispirited, lethargic, cynical and hopeless. In India, the so-called 'untouchables', who are supposed to be the lowest caste, are ignored, or else treated with contempt, by higher-caste society. Below them, however, there is yet another caste, the 'invisibles', who are so ashamed of themselves that they come out only at night so as not to be seen. Their role is to wash the clothes of the 'untouchables'. For Gandhi, the mere existence of the caste system and the injustice it represented was an appalling affront to his civilization. Other societies may not have such an explicit underclass as India, but they have them nonetheless: 'ghettoes filled with bums', 'the long-term unemployable', 'the mentally ill', 'the criminalized', 'the homeless', 'addicts and vagrants'. The names we call them may differ but the social reality is the same, and so is their place in the ecology of power, whether in Beijing or Berlin.

Compassion and welfare: the pride of the West

There are two questions concerning the underclass in any society: What are the factors that put people there? And what measures are in place to prevent that happening—and, indeed, to enable those already there to escape? In Victorian Britain, life was grim for the underclass, and frequently short. The most vulnerable people in society—the young and the elderly and infirm—often ended up there, in the workhouse or the debtors' prison. Street children and those who were no longer able to support themselves and had no relatives to look after them were swept up and dumped in a convenient dustbin. Given the harsh realities of this past, the last hundred years of Western civilization have seen a remarkable shift in attitudes, with far more resources now available to those at the bottom of the pile. Great social revolutions such as (in various countries) the abolition of slavery, the universal provision of education and the introductions of a welfare system, a state pension and a public health service represent enormous advances which have prevented many people slipping into the underclass. The post-war years have been a golden age of social support in Britain, which has attracted many outsiders to this country to enjoy its benefits. There is no question that this generosity towards the underclass, expressed through both individual philanthropy and public provision, represents a high point in Western civilization. Indeed, there are those who argue that the health of any society can be measured in terms of its attitude to the weak and vulnerable—and on that basis we must celebrate the health of our own society.

The growing global underclass

However, even as we acknowledge this, we may also question whether the same social compassion (not to mention political energy) still exists today to maintain that generosity. What is more, we understand better now than ever before that there is a link between the operations of the global economic system and the fate of those groups that end up at the bottom of the pile—and with greater knowledge comes greater responsibility. We also have to acknowledge that, while the underclass in our own, Western societies has benefited from their increased wealth, we now have a global economic system and so have to consider the global underclass within the same moral landscape as the domestic underclass. Both are intractable, because they belong to one global economy.

In the past, the factors that put people into the underclass were a mixture of birth, education, finance, health (or, rather, the lack of them) and, sometimes, war. These same factors operate today. If you are born in Sierra Leone or northern Uganda, you are born into a civil war. Not only your life but also those of your parents are under threat—not only from war but also from Aids, malnutrition, water-related diseases, even curable conditions for which your community lacks the cure. You have few educational opportunities, and they are precarious and may be destroyed by an enemy raid. You are surrounded by systemic corruption, which is part of your very culture. Work is scarce and the cattle your parents own could be lost if there is a drought. The mortality rate of under-fives in your country is 15 per cent. If you survive past the age of five, you may be abducted and forced to fight as a child soldier, to see and commit atrocities that might traumatize you for life.

If you are born in downtown Detroit, you may suffer from lack of nurture—maybe your mother never knew your father, who raped her and (while he was about it) infected her with Aids. Perhaps you are brought up by your grandmother, who hits you. Perhaps you drop out of school, along with your friends, and descend into gang life, drug use and crime. You could have your first stretch in prison at the age of 16 and learn there a way of life (or, at least, survival) from which you will see little chance of escape. You feel that you owe society nothing and society owes you nothing.

These two scenarios, which are so familiar to us, could be recast in different social contexts around the world, from Washington to Wellington. Some people, of course, slip into the underclass from the migrant sector. If, over time, the energy and drive that caused them to migrate in the first place fail—because their resources are exhausted, or their spirits are broken—they may sink into a passive resignation and despair. One wonders, for example, what will happen when the very large numbers of economic immigrants in Europe, grow old. Instead of boosting the economy, as they do at present, they will become an additional drain on the state's resources, requiring benefits, pensions, health care and so on. In exploiting the endless supply of imported cheap labour, the minority world is storing up serious trouble for itself in the future. There seems to be little long-term thinking behind current policy. And one can expand this observation to consider the future of migrant populations in the majority world. Moving from the countryside into megacities may fuel an economic boom for a decade, but the impact of 20 million human beings, crowded together but separated from their extended families, has yet to be seen. This is an unprecedented situation for humankind.

The true cost of losing social capital

Furthermore, healthy societies have always relied to a great extent on their social capital to contain their underclass; but if that capital is reduced, more people—young, elderly, sick, unemployable—slip down, into the 'nether world' inhabited by the likes of Paris's invisible old people in 2003 and the poor of New Orleans in 2005. As I have argued above, in the absence of the informal social care provided by our social capital, the state has to take responsibility for policing, supporting and caring for the community. It is inevitable that, for both financial and logistical reasons, it is not going to be able to do so. Imagine how complex—and how unlikely to succeed—an intervention by the state would have been if my friend Mary had not been able to stop that antisocial behaviour on that bus! Someone would have had to call the police, and then perhaps there would have been a chase, an arrest, a prosecution, a trial, a community order overseen by the social services. The cost to the public purse would have been vast—and to what effect? Little good would be achieved, and it would generate resentment and hostility. Project that across the entire country and the task of trying to prevent people slipping into the underclass through the agencies of the state becomes simply unmanageable.

Likewise, the task of caring for an ageing population is becoming increasingly problematic. In the past, the elderly were cared for by their relatives, but our growing individualism and aspirant mobility have fragmented families and broken up local communities. They have also reduced the birth rate, which means that the working population is likely to shrink. Unless these trends are reversed and families again come together to care for their older members, the state will be faced with unsustainable costs. The effect of losing our social capital will ultimately be to decimate our financial capital. The purely economic arguments for rebuilding it are overwhelming.

An unsustainable financial burden

If it is true that the underclass in the West is being swollen both by the dispirited migrant communities and as a result of the loss of our social capital, we are in trouble—for two reasons, one economic and the other to do with security. First, our society will not be able to afford the cost of care for all those who need it. Second, it will become increasingly difficult (as well as expensive) to police the global underclass, which is the primary source of the growing criminal population, dehumanized by a mix of cynicism, boredom, hopelessness and anger. Dealing with this population worldwide will be far costlier than addressing the causes. However, the really insurmountable obstacle to containing the global underclass is that it now wields an unconventional power of its own.

Ironically, the very technology that so often we have assumed to be accelerating our progress towards a more humane society is also enabling the forces of chaos to work towards its destruction. Mobile phone technology, for example, allows al-Qa'ida's loose network to coordinate its activities and to manage its funds. Technology is morally blind, and the opportunities the Web provides for invisible, untraceable flow of information helps a group of terrorists to operate just as much as it helps a group of social entrepreneurs. Already, it is clear that 'dirty bomb' technology is available 'out there', beyond the control of any single government. A global underclass that had access to such means of devastation and the desperation to use it could never be simply 'contained'.

The West has bought the world cheap. Ultimately, the problem of the global underclass is not a matter of too little aid or trade, or too much debt: it is a matter of too much consumption. It is impossible that wealth could become so concentrated in the hands of the shareholders of the multinationals with any other outcome. We have bought the world cheap and the price we have paid is not enough to sustain the dignity and hope of people who have sold almost everything they had. The poor may have always been with us, but now with a handful of 'box cutters' they can bring down the trade towers of the world.

Study questions 8

1. Why is welfare the pride of the 'developed' world?
2. In your own society, who constitute the underclass and how does society deal with them?
3. In your opinion, is the world a more or less compassionate place than it was 20 years ago?
4. What are the financial implications of little social capital in relation to the underclass?

NINE

Death, Grief and the Changing Cycles (RSX)

TERRITORIAL | **DYNAMIC**

PSC Dominant norm
Defining criteria of success and controlling where power is lodged. Demands conformity and does not tolerate diversity. Currently imposes corporatocratic standards and values, based on measured performance.

PSX Iconic
Aspirational 'ideal'. Formerly the aristocracy and intellegentsia. Replaced in the 20th century by a meritocracy but now a celebrity class, cynically manufactured to exploit aspirants' dreams, driving a relentless, vacuous consumer culture.

RSC Foundational
Crumbling. Strong social foundations (sustained by shared values, stories, ethics and laws) no longer create stability and space for frontstage enterprise and growth. Also, expectations of social responsibility fade.

RSX Radical
Growing and inspirational. Possible source of new vision to fund social renewal. With Islam resurgent, the West is under pressure to formulate its own moral and spiritual footing again and develop an undefended vision of society.

PWC Mass
Shrinking. In pursuit of an aspirant lifestyle the West has largely spent its social capital (which reflects the trust that exists within and between communities) and now struggles to integrate immigrants, who are viewed as a threat.

RWC Underclass
Growing (from both mass and migrant sectors as people lose their economic and social footing). An exploited and criminalized, underprivileged global population, degraded by poverty, ill health and lack of education, opportunity and choice.

RWX Migrant
Creating a growing, unstable, 'unattached' dynamic. This displaced global population (through immigration on unprecedented level, as well as population growth) largely serves the dominant norm as resource and labour force.

PWX Aspirant
Expanding. Mobile, forming loose, unstable and fragile attachments, attracted to the new and reluctant to be bound by tradition, aspiring to the expansive lifestyle of celebrities (as portrayed by the media) with an insatiable desire to acquire tokens of that lifestyle today.

PASSIVE | **RESPONSIVE**

A profile of the current distribution of the global population in the West using the model of social ecology

Chapter summary

In this chapter, we explore the Radical sector of the social ecology model, which I have labelled 'RSX'.

This element in society is *'reserved'* because it acts subversively, working behind (and even against) the explicit ('presented') values of the system. It wields *'strong'* power in that, while it may not have institutional authority, it does have a compelling influence over the imaginations of the wider population. In a sense, it influences the direction of the future. And certainly it is *'expanding'* rather than 'consolidating': this element in society longs for change and seeks to bring it about. It believes in a new order that will be better than the present one.

Summary statement

This chapter will argue that Western society is coming to the end of an era that began with the Renaissance in the 15th century. A founding vision of human life that produced five centuries of cultural, intellectual and industrial productivity has been lost. In its place there is a profound absence of any compelling ideology of what it means to be fully human. There is an urgent need for the West to rediscover its own moral and spiritual roots, so that it can enjoy a new growth of cultural, intellectual and, arguably, spiritual life.

....

Most sandcastles do not last even a day. One of the pleasures of a visit to the seaside is to walk along the beach early in the morning when it has been washed clean and smooth by the tide. Perhaps a few rounded contours remain of the biggest ditches and ramparts of yesterday, but otherwise all sign of its labours have vanished. The sand is laid out again by nature pristine and ready for fresh acts of creation, fresh statements of defiance against the inevitable, with only the memory maybe of what stood there before to inspire today's builders.

Of course, most human civilizations have left traces that time has not yet erased, but the fact remains that civilizations, like sandcastles, inevitably fall. As the poet Shelley wrote of the imagined ruin of one ancient monument:

> *...On the pedestal these words appear:*
> *'My name is Ozymandias, king of kings:*
> *Look on my works, ye Mighty, and despair!'*
> *Nothing beside remains. Round the decay*
> *Of that colossal wreck, boundless and bare*
> *The lone and level sands stretch far away.*

Theorists of social history divide into two camps: there are those (such as Spengler and Sorokin) who see history as cyclical and those (such as Hegel and Marx) who see it as trend-based and evolutionary. There are many in the West today who retain the prevailing optimism of the 18th-century Enlightenment that the human race is, broadly speaking, launched on a trajectory of self-improvement and progress. Often, advances in technology are cited as evidence for this. Some point to advances in medicine (such as the discoveries of penicillin, anaesthetic and antiseptic), health (sanitation and water purification), agriculture (intensive farming and genetic modification), communication (the personal computer, the internet, the mobile phone) or education. However, it is a mistake to confuse advances in technology with advances in human well-being and civilization. Sometimes, indeed, a step forward in one area of our social ecology is countered by a step back in another. For example, the intensive farming methods developed since the 1970s have indeed sustained a global population explosion of nearly two billion, but arguably at an unsustainable cost to the quality of our agricultural land and the health of the water table. In parts of Africa, it has merely prolonged the habitation of otherwise uninhabitable desert margins through food aid given by the UN.

The panacea of technology?

Instead of solving our problems, technology has often merely deferred them to the next generation. The discovery of nuclear fission made possible nuclear power, but also nuclear war (not to mention the dirty bombs I have referred to above). We now have the ability to kill more people at a single blow than any previous generation in history. The advent of the internet has opened the doors of knowledge, but has also made it easier for paedophiles to groom children and has arguably facilitated and accelerated both a new global traffic in human beings and informal, supranational terrorist networks. In fact, technological advances merely change the context for human behaviour. Technology is no more than a tool which can be used just as effectively by the murderer as by the doctor. The real measure of human progress is what we choose to do with it: whether humankind—worldwide, not just in the West—is more just, more fair, more humane and more compassionate than it was even a century ago. On this measure, the evidence is far more ambiguous.

Revolution, not evolution

The model of social ecology suggests that human history follows neither an evolutionary nor a cyclical path, but instead describes an expanding and contracting spiral. Here we come to the final sector on the chart of our social ecology: RSX. The combination of these characteristics—*'reserved'*, *'strong'* and *'expanding'*—suggests that this area of society will be source of visions, ideals and dreams that catalyse and energize the drive into the future.

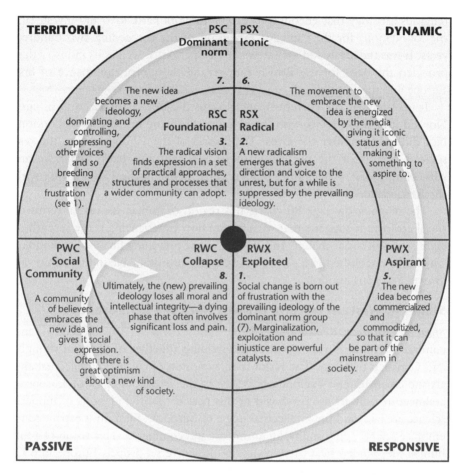

The model of social ecology applied to the general way in which social change takes place

This final sector of any social system marks both the beginning of the end and the end of the beginning: the death of the old and the birth of a new society. History never repeats itself exactly, never returns to quite the same point: the parameters change and different civilizations, cultures and populations become involved as the spiral turns. The spiral dynamic is shown in general principle in the diagram above.

The end of the current cycle

If what I am saying is true, Western history seems to be coming to the end of the current cycle of its social ecology, which began properly with the Renaissance. Western manufacturing, facilitated by technological advances and fuelled by a religious ideology that encouraged people to work hard, save and invest, laid the foundations for the capitalist expansion of the succeeding two hundred years. It was the ideals and aspirations of that period, as well as its industry that provided the basis for the British Empire and the global dominance of first Europe and then America.

It is clear that the current financial crisis did not begin 12 months ago. Nor did it begin in 1986, with the so-called Big Bang in the City of London. Nor did it begin after the Great Depression of the 1930s. In fact, the real societal origins of the present crisis lie five centuries back. What we are witnessing today is the ending of an era that began in the 15th century with the Renaissance.

The diagram on page 80 charts this period of human history in terms of social ecology. It suggests that what we are now experiencing is the seventh of eight stages of social change: the collapse of the prevailing financial orthodoxy, which was established in a period of ultimately unsustainable industrialization, growth and consumption.

Stages in Western cultural growth since the Renaissance

Stage 1: Radical Renaissance (RSX, 15th Century). An intellectual and cultural revival in Europe involves the welding together of Classical thought and Christian theology. The result is an explosion of cultural, intellectual and artistic creativity and exploration. Many of the finest examples of European architecture and art are produced in this period; the foundations of modern science are laid, and the intellectual scope of European thought is expanded to embrace science, philosophy, literature, art and commerce. This vision of a full human life, funded by a theistic view of the universe, propels Europe into its richest period of intellectual flourishing.

Stage 2: Reformation Foundations (RSC, 16th Century). This intellectual liberation leads to a shift in power from church to laity, and from church to state. In due course, the principles of 'the good life' are to become the foundations for political governance across Europe: notions of law, state and civic power, individual freedom and also commercial obligations. A Reformed theology full of gratitude for Christ's sacrifice and a strong sense that human beings are stewards of Creation produces the so-called Protestant work ethic, with its emphasis on hard work, duty and productivity, while belief in a better world to come—that is, heaven—encourages self-discipline, self-denial and investment in the future as key principles of the economy. The foundations for capitalism are laid.

The model of social ecology applied to Western cultural growth since the Renaissance

Stage 3: Social Equality and Democracy (PWC, 17th–19th Centuries). The shift of power from church to state is paralleled by a shift from a single ruler to collective rule. Monarchies topple. The establishing of democratic forms of government across Europe is built on the theological belief in the inherent, equal value of every human individual. Democracy fulfils three intellectual convictions: to preserve individual freedoms, protect the vulnerable and prevent tyrannical abuse of power. The political outworking of the theology of the past two centuries leads further to radical reforms in education and health care and the abolition of the slave trade, child labour and, in due course, racial inequality. At the same time, people start to forget the RSX theistic world view that funded all these developments.

Stage 4: Aspiration (PWX, 1900s onwards). Increased personal freedom and better access to education produce a meritocracy. Aspiration funded by the Protestant work ethic, liberated by social meritocracy, accelerated by educational opportunities, driven by a belief in the goodness of progress brings in a hundred years of acquisition and consumption. However, the theological and moral anchors of the RSX world view have by now been lost. Progress is seen as something good in its own right, rather than as a preparation for another, heavenly life, and is understood in entirely materialistic terms. The RSC sense of moral obligation to state, neighbour and spouse is weakened as it comes to be regarded as intellectually indefensible; the RSC moral foundations of society collapse, leading to psychological dysfunction and social fracture.

Stage 5: Iconic (PSX, 1950s onwards). A new iconography, no longer religious but commercial, further fuels aspiration. Devotion to the new icons—celebrities— results in unprecedented growth in spending as people try to acquire the same lifestyle. A new psycho-spiritual orthodoxy based on consumption develops in the second half of the century, in which brands, like new traditions, provide identity and meaning in an ideologically empty society. Brand-makers use increasingly sophisticated means to manufacture consumer hunger through advertising and product placement.

Stage 6: Dominant Orthodoxy (PSC, 1980s). The consumptive orthodoxy is funded by an increasingly sophisticated mechanism of markets and finance. This makes possible unprecedented levels of capital lending, leading to an explosion of consumer and commercial debt. Increasingly, politicians define well-being in purely financial terms (GDP) and predicate their manifestos on economic growth. This in turn liberates corporate taxes to fund public spending, resulting in an insatiable corporatocratic monster that needs to feed itself with spending, debt and taxation. Addicted to spending and unable to define well-being in broader terms, governments irresponsibly promote consumer spending, leading to unsustainable levels of debt.

Stage 7: Collapse (RWC, 2008). The first collapse occurs. The corporatocracy inevitably begins to consume its own innards, borrowing from itself and inducing its own collapse. This is sharp and brutal but not, at this stage, necessarily final. Governments rally to prop up the system by nationalizing banks and pumping money back into the system. The final collapse may be deferred for a later generation to deal with as countries sink ever deeper into debt and, in the West, manufacturing industry continues to decline. It remains to be seen whether our addiction to consumption itself will, or can, be addressed.

Stage 8: Exploitation (RWX, 1990–2050?). Consumption relies on the increasing worldwide exploitation of raw materials. People migrate around the world into massive conurbations as human resources are redeployed to feed the appetite of global industry. However, the unrenewability of mineral resources, as well as the ever-growing global population, means that this appetite can never be satisfied, and the breakdown of the system is only deferred to some point in the future.

The pain of the current collapse is acute. It is a bereavement, to which we will respond with the usual stages of the grieving process: first of all denial, followed by anger, then bargaining, then depression, then acceptance. Our loss is complex—it is financial only in the most obvious and superficial of our experiences. Losing wealth wrecks lifestyles, damages health, causes anxiety, fear, confusion and stress. It may destroy families. We will go through cycles of personal grief as well as collective, societal grief. We will deny what is happening, pretending that recovery will come in three years. We will get angry with our politicians and leading financiers, who failed to prevent this reverse. We will bargain, trying to find some way to get back what we have lost, on whatever terms. We will probably also become depressed as we begin to realize that the kind of lives we have lost, we truly have lost. They will not come back.

Grieving is an inevitable process of life, an essential dimension of our human condition. It is not to be feared, but rather embraced with courage and compassion. It is also an opportunity for learning, a chance to question ourselves more deeply. However, it needs careful navigation—and now is a time for leaders who will help us to make that journey well. Of course, the temptation is to short-circuit the process, in an attempt to avoid the pain. This is my fear in these times. I am not convinced that we or our leaders have the courage to embrace our loss as deeply as we must. I'm afraid that they will seek (as they currently seem to be seeking) some way to prod the dying mule back into life. In fact, I'm afraid that they may actually manage to get the old beast back on its feet again, by some artificial means of resuscitation, but only to prolong its demise until a final, more painful collapse in the next few decades.

My hope, on the other hand, is that our leaders will recognize the times we live in. Death is the opportunity for a renewal of life. However, birth is never easy or painless: labour involves struggle and risk. We should bear in mind that bringing new life to birth can be difficult, protracted, even violent.

The birth of the new?

What, then, are the seeds that may fund a new birth in our social ecology today? It is clear where one such vision may come from: the West finds itself dealing with a new power in fundamentalist Islam which it does not seem to be able to hold in check. There is no doubt that for many Muslims the idea of an *ummah* (the worldwide Muslim community) ruled by shari'ah law is an appealing one. However, we must understand that appeal in the broader context of our current social ecology, in which most Muslims see themselves as migrants and members of a global underclass. The presence of 'infidel' foreign troops in the holy land of Saudi Arabia throughout the 1990s and into the 2000s inflamed Muslim sensibilities. The backwardness of the economies of many Muslim countries in comparison with those of the West suggest a subservience that many Muslims find intolerable. The fundamentalist understanding of the global situation is of a territorial war between the forces of Christendom and those of 'the house of Islam' in which for three centuries the latter has been humiliated. The poor living standards of even moderate Muslims mean that, sadly, they are easily manipulated by the rhetoric of radical mullahs.

And here's the rub: those displaced, migrant populations are easily radicalized. Extremism flourishes wherever people are marginalized. It is no coincidence that a state such as Chechnya produces suicide bombers, women as well as men, who are willing to murder 340 schoolchildren. It is no coincidence that the recruitment of radical young Muslim men to radical versions of Islam is rising rapidly in our prison population. It is no coincidence that growing numbers of people at the poorer end of our society are converting to Islam. In certain Muslim communities around the world, there seems to be an endless supply of would-be suicide bombers. Their hearts and minds are so easily won over by rhetoric that promises revolution, power, authority, justice. Such desires are common to all those who occupy those positions in the social ecology—and when they are married with a religious ideology that glorifies martyrdom and promises an instant transfer to Paradise, it is not difficult to see how a death cult arises.

The Islamist vision is enjoying a strident and violent resurgence around the globe. It is a response to both the decline of the vision of Christendom and the ascendancy of the vision of a secular world. It is a response to a vision of humankind dominated by the market. Ultimately, however, as a territorial ideology, it is informed by a sense of fear rather than a sense of trust. And it is for this reason that it must be resisted, even as we look about for an alternative vision. Perhaps the greatest problem that faces the West is simply this: we no longer have a compelling ideological vision of our own.

Our liberal democracies and capitalist economies were products of the theological vision of the Renaissance. Such theological assumptions as that all people are created equal, as individuals with inherent creativity and the ability to work productively, provided the impulse for European civilization. And yet it has been the misapplication of those assumptions that has led us to the point of collapse: productivity without rest, aspiration without restraint, rights without responsibilities, freedoms without limits, ownership without stewardship. And the church has lost its voice as a critic of or contributor to our social health. It is seen either to be irrelevant to society or to be acquiescent to the status quo, giving its blessing to those already in power. For many, its theology has gone dry, its language cold; it is perceived to be just as territorial and political as radical Islam.

And yet human beings are spiritual beings. Whatever the materialist humanists may say, there is more to us than flesh and blood, brain and bone.

You are at liberty to disagree with me, and I will not try to prove that point. What I want to maintain is that there is an urgent need for the people in the West to rediscover this dimension of life. When we lack a spiritual perspective, we tend (with some notable exceptions) to become baser: less able to make sacrifices for others because our lives lack that sense of the eternal that makes sacrifice in this life possible. Our art, poetry, music and fiction tend to become more mundane, because the themes we have to explore are narrower and less deep. Our morality becomes more volatile and more opportunistic, because it is not anchored to any absolute values, and as a result it can easily be diverted in directions that are less costly to us. Our emotions become an end in themselves, and 'feeling good' becomes our ultimate goal, reducing the chances that we will persevere and grow through tragedy, loss and pain, or that we will aspire to act with courage in the noble cause.

Of course, these are generalizations: there are notable exceptions in every culture, men and women who have shown remarkable humanity even though they have rejected the idea of the human spirit in any theological sense. However, my observations are broadly true, and they make sense.

Contemporary spirituality, too, must not be completely separated from the tradition of practice and belief or else it becomes emptied of meaning. For example, it's increasingly fashionable in the West to combine elements of a variety of different spiritual traditions: a little Buddhism, a little Confucianism, a little shamanism, a little Christianity and so on. This pick'n'mix approach appeals to the liberal mind, but what it creates is something fragile and ultimately fairly worthless. The difficult bits of each spiritual tradition—and each of them has uncomfortable insights and disciplines—tend to be eliminated, and what remains is like a fruitcake composed entirely of cherries, a sickly self-indulgence. It has neither intellectual, emotional, moral nor historic rigour. It speaks of the worst kind of Western consumerism, for which spirituality is just another product to stick in your basket and enjoy at your leisure.

Human spirituality is not a sweet counter from which we can select whatever catches our eye. Such a creed of personal indulgence bears no relation to any of the ancient wisdoms that inform our major spiritual traditions. Nor can our spirituality be conceived simply as 'that which fulfils us'. Many spiritual traditions would contend that the fulfilment of our potential as human beings is a by-product of our spiritual journey, not the goal we struggle towards. We strive for something beyond ourselves—and, incidentally, in so doing we find ourselves becoming more human, more alive. However, to seek that as an end in itself (like searching for happiness as an end in itself) ultimately makes us less human, less alive, rather than more.

The Western spiritual tradition is derived predominantly from Christianity. It is clear that historically (whatever revisionist historians might want us to believe) the noblest ideals of our culture and its greatest achievements, both compassionate and creative, have been inspired by the life and teaching of Jesus of Nazareth. His followers have largely not lived up to his ideals, but Western society in all its aspects desperately needs to rediscover him and hear his voice again. This is true not least of the church, which in Europe continues to decline both in numbers and social and political influence. That said, the media have generally been hostile to the church in Europe and have been discrediting it for many decades—but that may soon change!

Is what we need, if we are to see a rebirth in our society, a renewed source of theology that is robust enough to fund an entire vision of life? A theology that can weave together the many different threads in the complex fabric of our society: the cultural and the aesthetic, the industrial and the economic, the social and the communitarian, the personal and the political, the emotional and the psychological, the traditional and the contemporary. To accomplish this will demand the commitment of people of faith in many different disciplines throughout our society.

Study questions 9

1. What are the signs that the most recent cycle of social ecology is coming to an end?
2. Can technology save us? If not, why not?
3. Is the Western malaise due to a lack of ideology?
4. Why is spirituality fundamental to healthy human society?

Part 3B

RECONSTRUCTION:
LESSONS FOR THE FUTURE OF SOCIETY

TEN

The Future Before It Unfolds

At its most basic, we in the West have to choose to live more interdependent lives. Our recent post-industrial history has seen the transformation of our society from one that promotes interdependence to one that promotes independence. Advances in technology, as well as the changes in outlook that have accompanied them, have encouraged us to look after ourselves. Almost every household is now self-contained, with its own water supply, its own means of transport, its own 'entertainment centre' and its own equipment for washing clothes, cooking, mowing the lawn and so on. We have all but completed a journey from the communal life of the medieval village to the extreme privacy of a modern home managed from a computer terminal, with minimal contact with people outside.

It is biology that has allowed this social isolation. Species that live in colonies or groups tend to be found in environments where resources are scarce: when there is little to go round, cooperation makes life easier. Living alone is a luxury usually affordable only to those who live in the midst of plenty and don't need others. In the last two hundred years, technology has given people in the West access to sufficient resources to mean that generally we do not need to cooperate with others in order to survive. Two centuries ago, entertainment might have involved singing folk songs together around a jar of ale; today, I can access all my hedonistic pleasures from the isolation of my computer screen. Transport generally involved sharing a vehicle; today I sit alone in my car, sealed off from other commuters around me. In the past, only the odd ascetic could survive living alone; nowadays, we are all adept at it.

A blip in the history of the world?

However, people may one day look back on this period when we developed such isolated and independent patterns of living as a brief aberration. It is clear that the abundance of resources that made such a lifestyle possible is coming to an end. It is no coincidence, therefore, that the new movements that are developing in the West by and large have a collectivist vision. Groups promoting sustainable lives and renewable energies almost invariably encourage collaboration. For example, for economies of scale to make solar or wind power affordable, local housing communities may need to commit to building something communal. Some new housing developments share waste energy to heat everyone's houses and recycle everyone's used water to flush the toilets. As the resources available to us dwindle, so we will find ourselves looking for more cooperative ways to maintain our standard of living together. Our natural human response to the environmental crisis will be to become more social and cohesive again. 'Interdependence' will be the new buzzword, not 'independence'.

A growing number of 'eco projects' are beginning to emerge, in everything from housing (including community living) to schooling to manufacturing to energy production to the arts, and to be seen as an acceptable alternative to the mainstream. Indeed, increasing numbers of ordinary people will find that these developments appeal to something inside them, a growing desire for a life that is more authentic, more holistic, more honest, more simple, more connected. Here is the germ of a new, compelling, radical collectivist vision which, once it is sown in our hearts, will begin to take root there.

Warnings and lessons for 'developing' economies

While Western societies are concerned with halting the disintegration of their civic structure and the loss of their social capital, those of the majority world are in the grip of increasing individualism. It is almost as if as the West comes down from the peak of its individualism, the East is climbing towards its own peak—and at some point they will reach parity. Certainly there will be terrible costs if the majority world follows the same path as the West. These would be incurred primarily by the peoples of the majority world, in terms of their social cohesion and well-being. This book is a health warning to all those who imagine that all is well in the West and want to emulate it.

The appeal the Western model has for people in 'developing' economies is not hard to understand. All kinds of desire come into play:
- to attain economic parity with the minority world
- to enjoy the status and prestige associated with being a First World economy
- to make the most of your country's talent and capital
- to improve yourself and your country
- to reduce poverty
- to possess the advantages and opportunities available to people in the West
- to offer your people a better life

However, these very proper aspirations all entail costs. Let me spell out, by way of a summary of the argument from the previous eight chapters, what these might be.

- increasing political domination by a corporatocracy
- a breakdown of the extended-but-local family
- an increase in dependence on the state and a growing unemployable underclass
- a decline in trust and informal community, and no increase in popular participation in democratic politics
- a decline in mental health and an associated rise in costs
- no discernable increase in the 'gross national happiness'
- an increasing burden on the state to care for a growing proportion of the unemployable or elderly
- a fragile economy dependent on a small sector of the population and vulnerable to shifts in macro-economic patterns
- a loss of professional talent to service-sector employment (call centres etc)
- increasing materialism, and an associated decrease in spiritual awareness
- increasing social instability, resulting in a growing sense of insecurity among the better off and of injustice among the rest
- a long-term crisis as more and more basic foodstuffs and other resources are imported rather than being produced locally
- the selling-off of the country's assets to foreign businesses
- growing inflationary pressure, reducing the buying power of the (growing) average wealth
- growing pressure to manage the size of the population
- a loss of indigenous culture, replaced by a homogeneous global McCulture shaped by corporate brands

The benefits are clear, but so is the evidence from Western experience that they do not come without their attendant costs. Is there, maybe, a way of enabling economic development that avoids those costs? If there is, perhaps it offers a vision and a direction not just for the 'developing' economies but also for those that are 'already developed'. Perhaps there are lessons to be learned by the leaders of the West as well as those of the East.

Key questions for global society

The second part of this book is a response to the analysis in Part I. The danger in attempting to offer specific suggestions for action is that, on the one hand, if they are too specific they begin to sound like a political manifesto, but, on the other hand, if they are too general they are open to the criticism that they are too imprecise. I want to try to avoid both traps. This is not a political manifesto, in that I believe that each society will have to work out the relevance to its own particular situation of the principles I set out.

Part II, then, returns to the structure of the social ecology that has shaped my analysis in Part I. Using the same methodology, I will ask how each of the eight sectors of a social ecology can be deliberately managed to ensure the good of the whole. The goal is to describe a way in which a social system can grow for the benefit of all, stable and sustainable, offering opportunity to all with justice, compassion and generosity. There are eight key questions we must ask ourselves:

1. RSC: What are the key elements that ensure strong moral and cultural foundations?
2. PWX: How can you direct consumers' aspirations so that they invest in social as well as financial capital growth?
3. PSC: How can you create a thriving private-sector economy that participates responsibly in the wider society?
4. RWX: How can you enable migration while preventing instability and exploitation?
5. PSX: How can you make sure that people who excel in disciplines that are important for society are properly celebrated, in order to encourage aspiration in those disciplines?
6. RWC: What key policies ensure that the underclass receives compassionate support without becoming dependent on the state?
7. PWC: How do you foster social cohesion in an aspirational society?
8. RSX: What is the role of faith in social well-being, and what are its dangers?

It is the responsibility of the leaders of societies around the world to address all eight of these questions and find an answer to them. If they fail to do so, they are culpable for whatever harm ensues. Everyone has the right to expect that their society's leaders—economic and political, in education and in the community—have reflected hard on each of these questions, because they relate to the basic components of every society's health.

Global questions, local applications

Although these questions are applicable worldwide, their application can only be worked out locally. I have written this book largely from a Western perspective—my home is in Western Europe. Many of the applications I suggest in the chapters that follow are relevant only to that particular context and are not intended as universal to all other societies. It is simply impossible for any one book to provide applications across many different cultures and societies.

My hope is that what follows will stimulate you to work out your own local answers. The website hosts a forum, on which are posted substantial responses from leaders in different parts of the globe. If we treat this forum as a smithy, where we can all bring our best ideas to be heated up in the fire and then hammered into shape, I hope it will produce many worthwhile and effective instruments of social change.

Study questions 10

1. Why has Western society been able to foster such independence, in contrast to all other human societies throughout history?
2. Is such independence sustainable?
3. What are the costs associated with it, to society and its members?

ELEVEN

Culture and Nationalism

(RSC, Foundational)

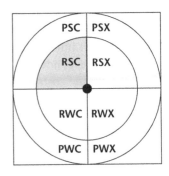

Key question: What are the key elements that ensure strong moral and cultural foundations?

Key principle:

Rebuilding a strong and resilient social ecology begins with reconstructing its foundations. This is a matter of identifying the values and beliefs, the stories and traditions, that underpin the society and strengthening them. This is not something that can be done by government—though legislation can create favourable conditions for such an endeavour.

There are two elements that are essential to the establishing of strong moral and cultural foundations. One is a sense of attachment to a particular time and a particular place. The other is a sense of belonging to something that is bigger and older than we are in being part of a community that shares the same pattern of life. These two ingredients need to be present throughout the mix of society. We feel a sense of belonging when we observe the same rhythms as everyone around us—and those rhythms also draw attention to the things our society values. If everyone is allowed to do whatever they like with their own time, it implies that there is no such thing as society.

Strengthening the family

Children learn how to behave morally by watching how adults behave, chiefly in their own families. The family is the crucial milieu where social and moral norms are passed on. If it breaks down, these norms have to be transmitted through the education system, which is more (and more) expensive, involves the state and is not such an appropriate environment as the family. When children enjoy consistent relationships in their early years with caregivers in the family, it give them a sense of identity and enables them to grow up into emotionally stable adults. Maintaining and strengthening those relationships is arguably the most important task any government has to perform.

A society could assess its own general well-being by examining how stable its family structures were. The key indicators of the strength of its foundations are the resilience of family bonds, the status of marriage and how long relationships between parents last.

Financial incentives, including tax breaks, are essential to support the family and promote lifelong monogamous relationships.

Encouraging common stories

People also need to feel that they belong within a tradition and a history. 'Who am I?' is a question that cannot be answered fully unless you know where you have come from and what your family, your community and your nation all say about themselves. Having such stories passed down to them gives people a sense of security in the uncertainty of the present. However, every society needs to encourage us to tell these stories constructively and responsibly. Stories about the family or the group can become exclusive and divisive, promoting a kind of tribalism, unless they are contained within a bigger, national story, a story in which everyone has a commitment to common values and practices, submits to common laws and accepts the limitation of their own personal freedom for the common good.

Multiculturalism has to be tempered by a recognition that every nation needs a dominant cultural story that its members can find a role within. That doesn't mean there will be no room for individuals to be different in their beliefs and tastes and dress and so on, but nonetheless the nation should be like a huge family and there should be a recognizable family likeness between all its members and each individual should have a sense of belonging and commitment to it. Like any family, it offers privileges—affection, security, opportunity—as well as responsibilities.

This implies a degree of loyalty to the national 'family', a willingness to see other members of the nation in terms of 'us' rather than 'them' and an acceptance of the disciplines that membership of that family entails (which includes recognizing its authorities and limiting our dissent to 'the proper channels'). Our membership of that national family is rarely under threat—but it can be.

At the same time, the national family celebrates the differences between its members and encourages them to learn from each other, to regard each other as friends and to work together on common tasks.

Encouraging local commitment

Arguably, it is essential also to discourage excessive mobility and encourage people to make a long-term commitment to their local communities. This would have an impact on town and city planning, with regard (for example) to the location of shopping, leisure and essential facilities to enable people to work, shop and socialize close to where they live. It should also affect public housing policy, as tenants who have no stake in their state-owned homes have less commitment to them and their neighbourhoods. Schemes that enable people to own or part-own their homes encourage them to put down roots and get involved in the local community.

Investing festivals with meaning

Festivals and national holidays give us an opportunity to 'remind ourselves who we are'.

If a particular religion plays a part in a society's story, there should be an explicit (though maybe not exclusive) role for its festivals in that society's life. They should be offered sensitively to every member of that society, whether or not she follows that faith herself; but they should not be 'fudged', or their meaning or origin obscured, simply to avoid giving offence to non-believers. Once again, if a society is dominated by one particular religion, it should expect everyone to celebrate its festivals, whether that be Christmas, Diwali or Ramadan.

If we allow businesses to determine how a whole society celebrates its festivals, we imply that buying and selling are our top priorities. If we allow the state to dictate how individuals should use their time, we imply that ordinary people can't be trusted. What we want to promote is the idea that people should participate in the dominant culture because it is part of the foundations of their society. The rhythms of public life in any society should be determined not by commercial interests or government say-so but by the bigger common cultural stories that inform that society.

TWELVE

Consumption and Citizenship

(PWX, Aspirational)

Key question: How can you direct consumers' aspirations so that they invest in social as well as financial capital growth?

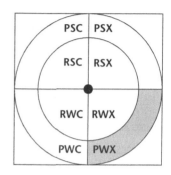

Key principle:

Human beings are by nature aspirational. Our desire for more or better will not abate, but rather needs to be channelled so that we seek to acquire more of the right kind of things. This involves an understanding of the psychology of desire and fulfilment, so that as a society we can encourage people to aspire to that which is, in social terms, sustainable and healthy.

There is no doubt that ultimately the challenge that faces humankind is to reduce our total consumption—and that this must begin with the West. All but the wealthiest Westerners will, almost certainly, have to reduce their consumption of energy and other resources over the next 40 years, if not voluntarily, because we are compelled to by rising prices. However, no elected government is likely to introduce substantial 'green' taxes or a system in which we trade carbon credits like money, or legislate for fair trade internationally or enforce other major changes in our lifestyles. Certainly it is inconceivable that any democracy will embrace the idea of a shrinking economy. All of these may be necessary to secure the future of our civilization, if not our species—and yet it would be electoral suicide for any government to propose them.

In order to build up our social (as opposed to financial) capital and to develop the will to discipline our own lifestyles, we need to take account of the way human beings make decisions at an emotional level. We make choices that make us feel better. We act to reduce our feelings of guilt and sadness, confusion and fear and to increase our happiness and our sense that we have meaning and are loved and are secure. For the past century, our societies have believed that we can achieve all this through amassing financial capital while cheerfully sacrificing our social capital. We need to turn this around so that we expect to attain those same goals by amassing social capital even if it means losing financial capital.

Given that over the coming decades we have to manage a reduction in our consumption of the world's resources, the role of politics will be to enable civic society to adjust to the new constraints while maintaining order, confidence and a sense of shared identity. The change needs to be negotiated rather than revolutionary. At present, this message is as unwelcome as the news that you have won a million dollars would be thrilling. The trick—and it is a trick—is to work out how to help people to adjust to what at first sight looks like a painful future they will want to avert.

Our ideas about happiness are largely mistaken, as recent research has found. We often believe that things will make us happy which actually will not. Some research suggests that the part of our brain that registers desire (for money, sex, power or whatever) is disconnected from the part that registers pleasure. This may explain why we continue to pursue things in the belief that they will fulfil our desires, only to be disappointed. Of course, this fallacy is the whole basis of consumerism! The aim of every advertisement and every product placement is to excite desire in us, to make us want something we don't yet have: it trades on the apparent disconnection between those two parts of the brain. If they were hardwired up to each other, we would feel genuinely satisfied once we had bought the thing we desired, full stop—and that would spell the end of fashion, of 'product lifecycles', of brand marketing, of advertising. The entire capitalist edifice is, in a sense, built on the lack of communication between two different parts of our brains, and a misreading of ourselves and our world.

Given that we are never going to be able to rewire our brains, however, we have to learn to live with this problem and deal with it as best we can. Studies such as the one cited above should help to guide us as we consider how to prepare Western society for less financial wealth and lower consumption.

Managing expectations

Reductions in overall salary levels may not hurt us as much as we fear at first, but our sense that we are getting less than our peers will demoralize us. In other words, our sense of disappointed hope and even injustice will create negative emotion.

If, however, we were hearing from our politicians now that incomes are likely to fall and we need to start saving now, I believe we would adjust to this new prospect fairly rapidly and well. We would tighten our belts and get on with it, I suspect—and when the hit came we would be ready for it, and might even be pleasantly surprised if we ended up a little better off that we had expected. It is our expectations, in other words, that need to be managed.

There is no evidence to suggest that a population living on less will be any unhappier than we are now, or that the political party that presided over that change would be punished at the polls. What matters is how expectations about that change is handled. What we need now is greater honesty about what lies in store for us, rather than desperate prevarication in the hope that some other politician or government will have to break the bad news.

Changing the consensus on consumption

There may be a case for extending the regulation of the advertising and marketing we are all exposed to. Most of us are comfortable with this in relation to products that are now considered to be toxic or otherwise a danger to health. The health warnings on cigarette packets are placed there to dampen our desires; product and warning happily coexist within a free market. Warnings against unprotected sex and drink-driving serve the same function.

Likewise, government warnings about the cost in carbon emissions of unnecessary journeys by car or plane, for example, or of food that has travelled thousands of miles to reach the shop where we buy it, might not change our behaviour necessarily but would help to alter public perceptions of what is and is not socially acceptable. They would bring into play such feelings as shame and respect, which Western governments have rarely appealed to in recent decades.

Redeploying taxation

The most effective and realistic way to control the market generates revenue to pay for public services while at the same time imposing a heavy financial cost on the consumer. It's appropriate in a free society that, within reasonable limits, we can choose how to use our own resources, and yet none of our choices are consequence-free. How we use water, energy, food, fuel and so on has an effect on everyone else. Those resources are limited, and the limits are now being reached. Taxing personal spending rather than personal wealth generation may be a more precise way to control consumption while maintaining people's motivation to work and be productive. Taxation should also reflect the fact that we are taking resources from a finite system—for example, by taxing us on the 'carbon footprint' we leave on our global ecological system.

Rewarding those who build up social capital

At the same time as managing the reduction in our consumption, we need policies that will foster and reward the building-up of social capital. If those positive feelings of affection, fulfilment and happiness are no longer focused on the act of consuming, there needs to be some reward mechanism to give people an incentive to promote social cohesion. For example, it is still shocking that in Britain if you are a married parent and you are staying at home to bring up your children, current taxation policy will make you worse off than you would be if you were an unmarried parent doing the same—and worse off than you would be, married or not, if you hired a childminder and went out to work.[59] The taxation system needs to favour those who make a commitment to their family and their local community—and hence to social cohesion—rather than penalizing them.

Recognizing and rewarding voluntary care

I remember a newspaper interview of a feminist author in 2006 who said that one unexpected consequence of feminism had been its negative impact on elderly people. As a boy, I used to accompany my mother while she took 'meals on wheels' to people who were infirm and housebound. We used to visit old folk in the village every week as a matter of course, just to check that they were OK (and stay for a chat). Sunday lunch in those days was more often than not shared with someone in need from the village. For all my parents' compassion, this kind of local care (replicated by others all over the country) was possible only because my mother had no paid employment. Instead of generating financial capital for her family, she generated social capital for the local community. For this, the state was in her debt. She greatly reduced the burden on the health and welfare services, as well as teaching me the responsibility of those of working age for the elderly.

Sadly, examples like that of my mother are rarely seen these days and are hardly valued. Of course, she paid a price: in later life she was unable to get back into the career she was pursuing before she got married, and she also found herself excluded by the 'professionalization' of all the skills she had to offer. She lived through the transition from a society that believed in and encouraged informal social care for the needy and the old to one whose subservience to a rapacious growing economy has meant that more and more vulnerable people

---

[59] Stuart Adam and James Browne, *A Survey of the UK Tax System*, Institute for Fiscal Studies briefing note 9, 2006 (http://www.ifs.org.uk/bns/bn09.pdf); John Elliott and Claire Newell, 'Why Can't They Be Left Alone?', *The Sunday Times*, 17 June 2007 (http://www.timesonline.co.uk/tol/news/politics/article1942935.ece)

struggle alone, their relations spread out all over the country, while most of the female population is at work. Though overall standards of living have risen as a result of this change, 'gross national happiness' has not—and, given the colossal inflation we have seen in the housing market especially, most of the money has simply gone to the Exchequer.

Without the foresight to see the impact on our social ecology of such economic policies and the ideologies behind them, we have suffered the inevitable consequences of losing the attitudes that led people to practise compassion and promoted social cohesion. Now we have to pay for the care they used to give out of the (inflated) public purse. Help from the state has tended merely to replace private charity rather than supplementing it, and is certainly not an improvement on it. Once again, we could hope to produce some social change through the mechanism of the market, by creating a tax system that rewarded stable families, rewarded those who stay at home to bring up their children and rewarded those who are voluntary carers.

THIRTEEN

Capital

(PSC, Dominant Norm)

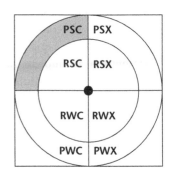

Key question: How can you create a thriving private-sector economy that participates responsibly in social commitment?

Key principle:

We urgently need to restructure the relationship between private and collective ownership. We have seen them almost exclusively as antithetical alternatives, and this polarization has allowed the private sector to become detached from suppliers, stakeholder communities and even the environment. There are other forms of ownership that need to be properly explored. Corporate social responsibility needs to become a universal and central element of business models and practice rather than being just a sideshow.

Since the Second World War, the politics of the West has been dominated by the drive for economic growth. Given the state of the European economies in 1945, such a priority then was understandable. However, this has come at a cost to our larger social and spiritual welfare. Broadly speaking, the growth in our GDPs has been facilitated by the spread of an individualism that has allowed an unfettered expansion of the free market, encouraged enterprise and boosted spending. This has had a number of unforeseen consequences:

- a narrow view of what we value (assessed almost exclusively in financial terms)
- a narrow understanding of corporate ownership, exclusively in financial terms
- the detaching of the supplier from the customer, so that the transaction between them is merely functional and contractual

- the unlinking of corporate salary levels from any meaningful sense of appropriate scale
- a reluctance in governments to impose regulations for fear of being seen as hostile to free-market economics
- an excessive confidence in the market's ability both to regulate itself and to address social ills
- a false polarization between capitalist and collectivist ideas of ownership
- an unfortunate and inappropriate transference of private-sector methods and measures to the public, not-for-profit and professional sectors

Exploring alternative models of corporate ownership

It would be a mistake to think that we can solve the problem of the dominance of capital through either centralized control or radical socialism: neither autocracy nor communism has shown that it can foster more just social structures. However, what needs to be addressed here is the question of who actually owns a company. Clearly, its shareholders are among its owners—but so, surely, do the local communities in whose neighbourhoods the company operates, so do the suppliers who provide it with materials, so do the employees who make its products or deliver its services, so do the consumers who buy them and represent the company's brand to the world. The notion of ownership is complex—far more multifaceted than our current shareholder system suggests. We have to challenge current assumptions about it and get the debate going.

This will immediately strike a chill of fear into the heart of every corporate executive and share owner in the land: fear of losing their financial worth, fear of losing control. It will be argued that to redefine company ownership would inevitably make a company harder to direct, less efficient, less productive, less able to compete in the global market. However, there are examples of different models of ownership that have not only survived but actually thrived in the commercial world. Think of the British retailer John Lewis/Waitrose. Its founding principle is that every one of its employees is a partner in the firm. Every one, from the chair to the most junior cashier, receives the same percentage of their salary as their end-of-year bonus. As a plaque on the wall of the firm's central offices reminds them each day: 'In 1914 John Spedan Lewis laid the foundations for a different kind of business. His vision was of a great commercial enterprise whose success would be measured by the happiness of those working in it and by its good service to the general community.' In 2006, John Lewis/Waitrose had 64,000 partners and turned over six billion euros.

Think, too, of the radical example of ownership of intellectual capital presented by the software company Linux. Its software is written by volunteers and is not sold but 'given away'—an example of 'freeware', observing the 'copyleft' principle of intellectual ownership. The firm generates profits through service contracts and relies on the personal enthusiasm of its contributors, whose reward comes from being part of a creative enterprise. Wikipedia operates on similar principles, and both enterprises are challenging assumptions that products such as theirs will suffer from poor quality if their authors are not contracted, managed and paid along more familiar commercial lines.

John Lewis/Waitrose and Linux present models of ownership that intentionally capitalize on trust and partnership; they build up social capital as well as amassing financial capital. Nor are they alone. There is the Co-operative group of businesses, which includes a chain of supermarkets, a bank, a travel agency and a funeral business. More controversial is eBay, which exploits the way the internet facilitates feedback to create a community of trust without the usual contracts. Meanwhile, the microfinance industry is an astonishing way in which financial capital can be wedded with the building and developing of social capital in the developing world. Perhaps the emergence of social entrepreneurship heralds the dawn of a new era of capitalist endeavour.

- There are undoubtedly models available in which social and financial capital are enabled to grow together rather than competing against each other.
- Business schools must do more thinking on models of capital ownership so that such approaches can become mainstream management practice rather than something alternative on the fringe.
- What we need is a sea change in thinking that will leave behind the instinctive individualism that has marked the West since the Enlightenment.

Collectivism cannot be simply another reaction to individualism: it needs to become the prevailing paradigm within which we understand currency, value and growth.

Reconnecting business with the local poor

Many successful Western firms are now recognizing that their commitment to integrity (whether ethical or financial) is strengthened as they deepen their relationship with their local community and its concerns. This fosters affection, compassion and a sense of common humanity that crosses boundaries. How much easier it is for a business to make a commitment to reducing its energy consumption, or to paying its suppliers a fairer price or to setting up a mentoring scheme for local teenagers, if its employees vote to do so as a result of their own encounters with poverty and deprivation in the local (or global) community! If we can find ways for companies to reconnect with the wider social ecology, it will initiate a virtuous circle that will in time help to make possible a variety of policy shifts and structural changes that currently are unthinkable.

· Increasingly in the West, younger people in the workforce are motivated not by money alone but by a desire for authenticity: they want to believe that what they do makes some contribution to society, that it has meaning and value beyond the stock market. Increasingly, businesses recognize that 'employee engagement' means that the firm itself needs to engage in meaningful activity.

· For some companies, corporate social responsibility, or CSR, seems to be little more than a PR exercise at present—there is little evidence that, if it came to the crunch, it would be allowed actually to affect their strategic objectives or their share value. However, the very fact that they feel the need to pursue CSR for PR purposes shows they are aware that the wider society sees the commercial world as exploitative.

The best way to 'develop' employees: CSR

Some CSR projects involve businesses releasing employees periodically to help in local social projects. Think of the skills there are in the City of London, in Canary Wharf, in other commercial centres around the world! A small fraction of those skills lent to local communities would have a significant effect in terms of creating trust, imparting knowledge and empowerment. Think of the mentoring that could be offered young black and Asian entrepreneurs! Think of the talent that might be saved from going down the drain if those young men and women were given direction and training and role models worth imitating—and not by some government scheme but by a commitment to the community made by the private sector! Think how much more enriching it would be for middle managers to be involved in a leadership development programme alongside local community, religious or business leaders, rather than doing yet another team-building exercise in some dull hotel suite! The evidence is that the rising generation is a generation of pragmatists and activists: people who want to get on and do something. Their talents are best developed by engaging them in some cause.

· There is a tremendous opportunity, as traditional voluntary organizations find it harder to recruit, for businesses to benefit from releasing their own employees to community service. The 'benefit flow' will be far from one-way. Indeed, it may well be that it is the companies' staff who are most enriched by such encounters. The broadening of their horizons may give them 'out-of-the-box' experiences worth 10 traditional management-training events. Moreover, this is not aid, or patronage, or the company 'giving away' the percentage of its profit it can afford to lose in a tax-efficient PR stunt (though it will no doubt include all of those things as well). Fundamentally, it is an investment, not in financial capital but in social capital. What is being built up is trust, that precious commodity that binds human beings together; that almost always reduces the cost of human transactions, changing contracts into covenants; that simply begins with people talking and listening to each other, discovering common ground, finding that they can be friends and not strangers.

Ultimately, if the City were to commit itself to this kind of enterprise, both in London and around the world, within a decade the benefits would be enormous. Private capital would be 'tied' once again to social responsibility. The opposite poles of our social ecology, PSC and RWX, which are currently in opposition to each other, would be brought closer together. Goodwill would be generated, common concerns would emerge and all kinds of small projects that would benefit both the local community and the company would spring up. The loss of 'office time' would be amply repaid by the energy, motivation, creativity and humanity that such initiatives would generate in the office. Businesses would find themselves better able to solve their own internal problems of lack of trust because they had gained experience of trusting other people with very different backgrounds and perspectives.

Defending corporate assets from private collectors

Publicly listed companies are subject to financial audit and regulation. Recently, however, the development of private equity funds has allowed such companies to escape public scrutiny by enabling them to be bought by small consortia of investors who are not subject to the same rules. These funds are inimical to the broader health of the economy because they remove wealth even further from public accountability. Many commentators suggest that these funds make a very small number of people very rich while stripping companies of their assets. It is fairly clear that the owners of private equity funds don't want to buy up public companies in order to make them more open, responsible and socially committed.

FOURTEEN

Control and Capacity

(RWX, Migrant)

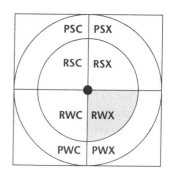

Key question: How can you enable migration while preventing instability and exploitation?

Key principle:

Large numbers of immigrants can be absorbed successfully only by a society that has a robust and resilient culture. Without this, the host society will be damaged and the very things that attracted the migrants in the first place will be destroyed.

There is a crucial difference between a multiracial society and a multicultural society. In the former, people of several different races coexist within a single culture; in the latter, two or more different cultures coexist within one society. In the West, we have come to accept the ideal of a multicultural society, but I suggest that we should, in fact, embrace the ideal of a multiracial one. I believe there are negative consequences to trying to create a multicultural society, which has no single host culture but only a number of equally valid cultures, all competing.

In Britain, we have made the mistake of supposing that giving people freedom from rules and boundaries is a generous act that will liberate them. Instead, it has left them bewildered and insecure. Many people from ethnic minorities fail to find their way out of the RWX migrant niche—which breeds resentment and prejudice and arguably has helped to light the fire of radical Islam. The power structure is completely unstable.

Make the host culture a cohesive force

What is urgently needed now is for Britain's host culture to recover its self-confidence, so that it can redraw its boundaries and rebuild its walls, setting out its values and beliefs so that immigrants can orientate themselves. It must have a distinctive form in which everyone participates positively.

Part of this involves making clear the conditions (RSC) for belonging to the host culture. Such conditions create expectations, create security for the vulnerable and the innocent; they keep out those people who would vandalize or otherwise spoil the environment, and welcome in those who want to make a positive contribution. They provide a stable power structure, as all reserved, strong, consolidating (RSC) elements do. Imposing conditions of entry for asylum seekers and other immigrants and deciding the number of immigrants the country will accept are measures concerned not with exclusion so much as with the protection of those who genuinely want to participate in the society, and a healthy balance of power.

Don't exploit immigrants for short-term gain

Western Europe is suffering a demographic crisis: birth rates are falling and so populations are ageing, obliging people to work harder to maintain economic growth and to retire later. In some countries, the 'deficit' is being met by immigration and imported labour. However, such policies are dangerously short-term, storing up problems of social integration, pressure on the infrastructure and burdens on state services, benefits systems, the education system and so on. Merely the cost of providing translation services to local authorities for hundreds of thousands of immigrant families is unsustainable. Immigration itself is not a problem—but integration is. Our leaders must consider what conditions we impose on immigrants to foster a social system that is stable in the long term without embedding injustice and abuse.

Diversity can flourish only on a foundation of conformity

Only when a society has a strong cultural foundation can it entertain and accommodate alien cultures, which find themselves secure and respected because they enjoy a relationship with the dominant, foundational (RSC) culture, not because they have supplanted it. Without that relationship, they become insecure, volatile and vulnerable. The ideology known as political correctness, which favours the minority as an end in itself and maintains that any majority is self-evidently oppressive and discriminatory, is specious and dangerous. It undermines the very resilience of the host culture that originally attracted the immigrants. In truth, minorities are made secure when they appreciate the foundational host culture in which they have found a safe space (RSC). They are not allowed to develop in isolation, without reference to that culture, or in contradiction of its values. They answer their host's generosity with their own generosity, sharing their own good life just as they have received the good life that exists within the host culture. They recognize that the freedom they have to live and act on the front stage (PWX) of society is guaranteed to them, as to us, only by the foundations that exist 'backstage' (RSC).

FIFTEEN

Celebrity

(PSX, Iconic)

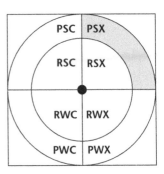

Key Question: How can you make sure that people who excel in disciplines that are important for society are properly celebrated, in order to encourage aspiration in those disciplines?

Key Principle:

Celebrity fulfils an important aspirational function within society. That being so, it cannot be left to the market to define the character of cultural icons. Society must exert some control over the kinds of people who are given the status of icons.

We in the West have been consumed by the aspiration to own more, and by that we mean to own more money and then buy more goods with it. This aspirational drive relates to how we experience happiness. The recent research I have cited indicates that, inasmuch as people find happiness in how much they possess, it is not because they are rich per se but because they are richer than others around them. Being human, we compare ourselves with others in our group—and we see wealth and property merely as signs that indicate social ranking. An inflation of consumption occurs when some members of a small group see others 'getting ahead' and, temporarily, feeling better about themselves as a result while everyone else feels slightly worse. Those who have been 'left behind' then acquire the lifestyle accessories that indicate that they have caught up in the social rankings. Thus, the sum of the group's possessions increases but the sum of its members' happiness does not. Happiness is related not to our possessions themselves but to the messages they convey to us about our social standing within a community, a company or a society.

Happiness is a fairly basic human emotion, and one we cannot fundamentally change. We need instead to employ it to create not consumptive but social inflation—in other words, an inflation of social capital that in turn generates a rise in social standing. To a degree, we see this among the super-rich, when (for example) they become involved in 'philanthropic game-playing', competing to see who can give away the most millions. At this level of wealth the giving is largely cost-free, but it offers the giver a certain status within the social economy of the elite. Much more could be done by both the state and the media to encourage such aspirational generosity.

An essential tool for fostering social aspiration

It is for this reason that I believe passionately in the value of a national broadcaster. One of the most widely celebrated services available to the global community is the BBC World Service. Alongside this, the British Broadcasting Corporation provides four television channels for its domestic audience, and a large number of radio stations. As a national broadcaster, it has both an obligation and the resources to broadcast material that promotes the good of society rather than the good of shareholders. It has the potential to inform the nation's consciousness and to be a powerful agent for the development of social capital. All this is beyond commercial broadcasters, who will always produce material designed to sensationalize, entertain and sell.

It is no coincidence that the BBC is still regarded around the world as a model of good broadcasting or that it has a highly effective consultancy arm that assists other countries (and, in particular, majority-world countries in the process of establishing a democracy) in developing their own national broadcasting services. These states understand the value of a public service broadcaster in supporting a healthy social system. It is my contention that if we bind the RSX (visionary and artistic) and PSX (iconic and celebrity) elements of our society to its RSC foundations, we can build a robust, self-reforming society that is open to change and innovation and yet has strong roots. When this connection is broken and instead the PSX element of a society is linked to the market, it acts like a disease, infecting and weakening society.

Imagine if television shows spotlit the lives of people who were living both elegantly and efficiently, committed to their local communities and causes. How much more enriching than the endless drivel of talk shows featuring social delinquents, D-list celebrity reality-TV shows and makeover shows! Imagine if we began to create a culture of celebrity icons whose fame rested not on their talent alone but on their good citizenship: if we promoted sporting heroes who committed a significant proportion of their time and money to the community, and artists who were funded by public money to produce art that dealt with the real issues of our day rather than the often vacuous and largely obscure stuff that fills most of our contemporary galleries. The state has a role in fostering responsible icons—the days when we could allow the market to determine the character and type of our social icons are surely over. It may be an axiom of the free market and the media that the market generates its own heroes, but why should we let the market dictate the rules of our society? We all pay a price when our celebrities live empty, mean-spirited, financially-inflated lives—our own souls are suffocated and our aspirations are reduced to mere greed.

Society, not the market, must fashion our heroes

We must encourage the emergence of a new kind of hero: a PSX who is valued for what they achieve and what they give, not for the size of their augmented breasts or the way they kick a football. We have allowed the market to dictate whom we idolize. The market is responsible for the grotesque salaries paid to Premiership footballers (obeying the simple economic law of supply and demand). The market is responsible for the idealization of celebrities. The market is responsible for the craving we have for a lifestyle like that of the rich and famous, and for our own five minutes in the spotlight on some reality show. The market defines our heroes, and in the process renders them worthless.

Society, rather than the market, must fashion our heroes. It is in sports such as football, in which there is little incentive to perform for one's country, that the greatest inequities lie. In contrast, the Olympic Games link the performance of the individual to their nation—and those sports in which the funding athletes receive is related to their performance in the great international competitions, rather than in private and commercial club competitions, often produce the more dignified, modest and impressive competitors. When sport relies largely on state rather than private funding, it can demand a certain level of discipline, performance and behaviour from its practitioners and, in so doing, can produce worthy heroes who are dedicated, unassuming and possessed of a proper sense of self-worth and gratitude, and who exhibit values that a nation's youth need to aspire to. In contrast, for example, the pampered footballers of the Premiership lack virtually any values to which I would want my children to aspire.

Arts funding should favour the life-enhancing

Much the same can be said of the arts as of sport. Britain's experience has shown that when the state under-invests in artists, we remove any incentive for our artists to produce work that is of social value, so that it is often what is radical, sensationalist and, frequently, destructive that is applauded. A society needs storytellers, writers and artists who will produce work for which society will be thankful.

SIXTEEN

Compassion

(RWC, Underclass)

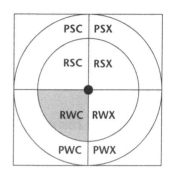

Key Question: What key policies ensure that the underclass receives compassionate support without becoming dependent on the state?

Key Principle:

The contribution of the third sector, and in particular of faith-based voluntary organizations, needs to be recognized in the provision of welfare. Resources should be directed through such channels, while the public should appreciate that welfare is finite and not unconditional.

One might measure the health of a society by its generosity and the protection it affords the vulnerable. However, compassion can easily encourage dependency. Support for those in need needs to be allied to programmes of rehabilitation. State-funded schemes also run into problems unless they find local partners. Nonetheless, a broader culture of compassion for the vulnerable must be fostered.

The crucial contribution of faith-based communities

The most important contributors to social care are local voluntary bodies, and the most important of these are drawn from faith communities. Some people will find this statement provocative. Yet, problems the state is unable to solve are best addressed by just such communities. Many social issues in deprived areas can be dealt with only by agencies that are there for the long haul. The problem with government-funded social initiatives is that their funding is always vulnerable to changes in the political agenda. Usually money is made available for specific purposes and has particular conditions attached to its use, regardless of whether or not those conditions are relevant locally. Moreover, it may be withdrawn if social policy changes—as it so often does—because politicians need to demonstrate commitment to another 'hot' target.

Faith-based community schemes—whether to help the homeless or care for the elderly, provide youth services, run soccer teams or mentoring programmes or give advice about debt—can work much better, for two reasons. First, they are not generated from money from central or local government, and the people who fund them do so out of a long-term commitment to the area. That means such initiatives are best placed to make an effective contribution to social cohesion. Second, such communities can direct their resources at particular local needs rather than those dictated by some national target-based government initiative.

Invest in faith-based schemes that serve unconditionally

In the past, people have voiced the suspicion that faith-based local services are merely a cover for evangelization, and as a result funds have been withheld that would most justly and efficiently have been allocated to their work. Such decisions have been unnecessary and short-sighted, influenced by the dogma of political correctness, which maintains that service providers should have no vested interest, no convictions, if they are to warrant funding. This fails to recognize that every organization has a vested interest and a conviction that drive their mission, not least the Government's own politically motivated work. The question is not what beliefs a particular group has but whether or not it is able and willing to serve the whole community without discrimination on ethnic or ideological lines.

The Government desperately needs to foster and support faith-based schemes that will serve the whole community unconditionally. Often, such projects are run on a shoestring by volunteers, while the state-funded youth work down the road (for example) is lavishly funded but often misdirected by people who do not live in the area and are committed to it only as professionals, not as citizens. The Government needs to work in partnership with faith-based groups to ensure that the best of the training, resourcing and support that can be provided by the state is given to non-partisan, non-ethnically-aligned services. There is no contradiction in a mosque receiving funding from the Government to run a debt-counselling service or a mentoring programme as long as it is available to everyone in the local community, whatever their religious or ethnic background—and that is the crucial point. The same holds true for a synagogue, a Sikh or Hindu temple or a church. If their congregations benefit from the scheme because people are drawn to their faith as a result of the contact they have had with it through using the service or programme, so much the better. A confident society should regard such funding as an investment.

Restrict welfare to a limited period of time

One of the radical, controversial but ultimately successful policies that Bill Clinton introduced was to set a two-year limit on continuous welfare payments and a five-year limit on all payments over a mother's lifetime. The impact of this innovation has been to reduce the number of recipients of welfare and to encourage people to make the transition back from welfare to work.[60] Tough-love policies such as this may be needed to prevent people from becoming welfare junkies, passive and dependent on the state. It also encourages families to take more responsibility for their members rather than relying on the state to do so.

Teach children to get involved in the community

Children develop many of their social values through education and this provides a vital context for them to be exposed to the needs of the vulnerable in the community. It is relatively simple to establish schemes in which schoolchildren get involved in visiting the elderly or the sick, helping to dig gardens or clear rubbish, repaint public buildings or work alongside single parents in playgroups.

Reintroduce a period of National Service

National Service is just that: service to the nation, for the good of society. It need not be military. It can have a social function and focus, which is much more suitable to an age when military investment is diminishing, not growing. Given that the highest proportion of crimes are committed by young men between the ages of 18 and 25, this is the key stage when a period of national community service could have an enormous impact. Many young men do not feel they are part of any enterprise that involves self-discipline, but they need a strong, supportive structure around them and role models they can aspire to. A strong code of conduct, belonging to a group or team, learning to work under leadership as well as to take on leadership, developing the capacity to think of

---

[60] Frank Field, 'Less Carrot, More Stick', *The Daily Telegraph*, 6 March 2007. Retrieved on 6 April 2008 from http://www.telegraph.co.uk/opinion/main.jhtml?xml=/opinion/2007/03/06/do0602.xml

others and not just themselves—these are among the many potential benefits of a period of national service.

SEVENTEEN

Cohesion

(PWC, Mass)

Key Question: How do you foster social cohesion in an aspirational society?

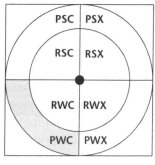

Key Principle:

Many of our current aspirations (for health, fitness and well-being, to name just a few) can be met in more socially constructive ways than at present. Employers and local and national government can all adopt policies that help to encourage people to become more committed to their own communities.

Human beings have a wonderful, powerful drive to improve their lot, and this needs to be harnessed rather than suppressed. Socialist forms of capital ownership have tended to deny this drive in individuals and, as a result, come unstuck. Some people will always seek to stand out from the crowd, and simply organizing people into crowds does not take away that impulse—those with an entrepreneurial streak simply find a way to work round the system to get ahead. Collectivist structures of ownership will always fail unless they also harness people's drive to improve their own circumstances. The trick is to promote the betterment of the individual and the betterment of society at the same time. It requires some imagination and innovation, but it is not impossible.

First exploit natural opportunities for self-improvement

It is often observed that if only we chose to walk or cycle to work or dug our gardens and planted vegetables, rather than sitting in our cars or in front of our TVs, we wouldn't need to spend hours pounding treadmills and lifting weights in the gym. Our ecology very often contains within it the most natural and efficient ways for us to remain fit and healthy. It is only when we abuse that ecology that we have to devise artificial and expensive (and tedious) substitutes. The same, I suggest, holds true for our social health. If employers looked around them for the natural opportunities for enterprise partnerships with the local community and exercised their minds on those, they would find that the need for artificial social-training programmes, 'emotional intelligence' courses and the like would plummet. The most powerful learning (as practitioners of adult education are always saying) comes from our engagement with our environment. For the sake of economy and efficiency, if nothing else, we should be seizing such opportunities with both hands.

Here are some initiatives that corporations could start with:

- Encourage your employees to talk to someone on their journeys to and from work each day
- Encourage your employees to stop on their way to work and help someone who is in need, even if it might make them late at the office. This would involve teaching managers to see the value in members of their teams offering services outside the walls of the office. To be effective, it would require trust and responsibility from all concerned.
- Invite the staff of nearby stores into your offices to look around and see what went on behind your doors. This would make a connection between different sectors of business and the community and would cost almost nothing. In addition, during a festival you could even serve drinks.
- Hold some 'partners events' from time to time, where you invited your employees' partners to come for lunch or drinks after work to see what their other half got up to all week
- Second someone to sit on a local committee set up to improve the look of the street, the road layout or other local environmental concerns
- Hold an 'unusual transport day', when everyone was encouraged to find a different way to come into the office than the usual, just to see the world from a different angle
- Get your senior executives to accompany the cleaning staff or the amenities team around for half a day and help them in their work, so that they gained an understanding of the people who do the apparently less important jobs in the organization
- Begin every Friday in the office with a '10-minute think before you start' routine. From 8.30 to 8.40, say, the computers and PDAs would be turned off and phones set to silent. A room, or rooms, would be set aside where everyone could gather and just sit and think quietly—about the stress of the journey to work, about the day ahead—and acknowledge the 'stuff' they had brought into work that day. It would take some time

to make this part of your corporate culture, but it would dramatically change the way the day began.

· Make space on your premises for a garden, where your staff could grow some flowers and vegetables or fruit. I know the manager of a pig-iron-smelting works who planted a strawberry field on his site. His men loved to spend half an hour digging and hoeing instead of smelting iron. The same could be said for drafting corporate law contracts or doing company audits.

From such immediate, direct and local experience of social responsibility, I believe that deeper emotions and concerns would begin to flow. All of us tend to act on fairly basic emotional responses: for example, if I myself have recently been made redundant or bereaved, I am likely to feel far more compassion towards others who have suffered a similar loss than someone who doesn't know how it feels. Those who are most motivated to help others, and most active in caring for others, are often those who themselves have suffered and have also received care from others. A virtuous circle is created in which people in pain who choose to be compassionate then foster compassion in others. As someone has put it, a 'cascade of grace' begins to flow.

I believe we will see the same effect as we address the bigger problems that face our world, whether we are tackling global poverty, or seeking to change the economic system so that we value social capital as highly as financial capital and GDP, or trying to regulate supply chains and ensure fair wages. These challenges are too remote, too huge, too insurmountable for any one person, however well placed they may be, and their good intentions will come to nothing. However, if even one person is changed, even if the change is felt only locally, quite often it can precipitate something that will build into an ever-bigger 'cascade' of changes.

Discourage hyper-mobility through taxation

As long as it is cheap for people to travel large distances to their work, to the shops, to their holiday destination, they will; but, as we now recognize, all our travelling is having a negative impact on both the built and the natural environment. Not only does it consume resources, it also distances us from each other, reducing our sense of cohesion. In dormitory towns, the daily commute has affected the life of the local community like a slow anaesthetic. However, people will work, shop and holiday more locally only when it is too expensive to do anything else. What we need is a radical approach to taxation on fuel and travel, which is quite practicable. For most of our societies it will be somewhat painful, but we are addicted to hyper-mobility and weaning anyone off an addiction usually hurts. Excessive travel is a luxury whose full costs could and should be paid for, and it will encourage most of us to work, rest and play closer to home. The incentives for people to invest once more in their local communities will grow.

EIGHTEEN

Conviction

(RSX, Radical)

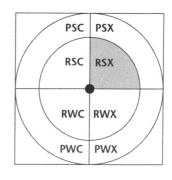

Key Question: What is the role of faith in social well-being, and what are its dangers?

Key Principle:

Faith is an essential dimension of any healthy society. However, it gets corrupted when it becomes associated with any particular territorial expression. Faith will, and must, engage in dialogue with politics as a potent, prophetic and subversive voice, but it must not itself become politically manifest in a controlling system.

At its most basic, being undefended is a matter of being able to trust yourself and others. Most defensive actions on the part of a state or society, whether military, political or economic, arise from a lack of trust. If I am able to trust both myself and you, I can believe the best of you rather than being suspicious of your agenda. I can find ways to share with you, in the belief that we may both benefit more from working together than from competing. I can offer you my culture, as well as receive yours.

This is a radical and idealistic vision for a nation. To be honest, it is only in fairy tales that nations actually do treat each other like that; and yet that should not stop us proposing the ideal or considering how our own nation could move towards it. Historically, we have seen grace, trust and freedom triumph more often in specific matters than in general throughout a culture. For example, in the abolition of the slave trade and then slavery we saw Europe and the Americas become less defended and more trusting and free, and the same goes for the ending of child labour, the regulation of working conditions, the establishment of the welfare state, the ending of segregation, the establishment of freedom of worship without risk of persecution and the enshrining in law of protection for unborn children. All of these developments represented advances into a less defended way of living together, in which threads of trust were woven into the social fabric.

Every generation needs the conviction that flows from shared ideals if it is to raise its eyes from its present situation towards something more noble. The ascent towards values that are more humane, more just, more liberated and more undefended requires an impulse to reach the top of the mountain. Often, that idealism has an explicitly spiritual dimension, which takes it out of the merely human, the merely material, into the transcendent. It is the spiritual that historically has proved to have the greatest capacity to inspire our noblest acts. However, many critics of its influence would argue that religion causes at least as many problems as it solves. Certainly it would be one-eyed to ignore all the ways in which faith and its social expression, religion, have led to more rather than less defendedness, and we need to reflect on why it is that religion fails to be a humanizing force and can actually become inhumane.

Territorial faith allied to political power is dangerous

The problems associated with the impact of religious faith on human society have often arisen specifically when it has become allied with political power. The emperor Constantine in AD 312 embraced Christianity after seeing a vision in the sky before winning the battle of Milvian Bridge. His 'conversion' meant that Christianity became the official religion of the whole of the Roman Empire, and the persecution of Christians, who had once been thrown to the lions in the Colosseum, ceased. From that point on, the church in the West was hand-in-glove with the power of the state.

Although, looking back, we can see many ways in which Christianity had a civilizing influence on Roman rule, by the Middle Ages the church's grip on education, knowledge, authority and the laity's spiritual destiny was restrictive and oppressive. Moreover, in the 12th and 13th centuries it funded the Crusades that aimed to take back control of Jerusalem from the Muslims. The monasteries kept the keys of eternal life and death locked away in their scriptoria, where the monks copied the Bible out in Latin, as the church maintained its authority even over kings by preventing the laity from reading holy writ for themselves in their own language. The church's wealth grew as it sold spiritual favours and blessings through a system of penances and 'indulgences'. It was this systemic corruption and abuse of power that provoked the Reformation in the 16th century, under the leadership of the German theologian Martin Luther.

Luther insisted that the church should not control access to the scriptures, or to the remission of sins. The Reformers' cry 'By faith alone, through grace alone' expressed the conviction that salvation was available to everyone through a direct and personal act of faith in Jesus' death on the cross, rather than through the intercession of priests and through sundry acts of atonement performed by the church on the laity's behalf. The Reformation recognized that for many people the church had become a barrier preventing an encounter with God, and Luther argued that this 'good news' had always lain at the roots of the Christian message. Sadly, the reformed church failed to escape from its entanglement with institutional and state power—and indeed the English Reformation only consolidated its crucial role in the government of England and Wales.

The modern history of the church is tragically punctuated by the martyrdom of hundreds of so-called heretics, both Reformed and Roman Catholic, in waves of persecution. Like the Crusades, such shameful episodes arose out of a fundamentally mistaken alliance between the church and civil government. The Western church was infected with a territorialism that was entirely alien to its founder, Jesus: a territorialism that imposed a dogma, of creed, of uniform, of ethnicity, of culture and of education. Having come to identify itself with the physical territory of Europe, the church began to give its blessing to the defence of that territory by force. The religion it propagated provided the ideological basis for war and domination in the name of truth, justice and God. The Western church displayed a growing pattern of defendedness, rather than undefendedness. Its lack of trust led it to seek to control knowledge, power and money, and even the state, as well as to keep hold (as before) of the keys of eternal life and death. It also created a perspective that saw outsiders as threats rather than potential friends and justified both aggression and violent defence. Finally, it bred a culture of suspicion that insisted on top-down authority, which the Roman Catholic Church struggles to escape to this day.

If the story of the Christian church in the West is one of the entanglement of faith with political power and the territorialism that inevitably accompanies it, it is in this respect little different from that of some traditions of Islam, which is theologically susceptible to territorialism. Beginning with a doctrine of the universal rule of God, to which the *ummah* (the worldwide 'nation' of believers) must live in obedience, Muslims have at many points in history and in many places found they could only fulfil Islam by giving it physical and political expression. Many believe that the *ummah* cannot live rightly under God until they live in a theocracy, where God's law is enshrined in the laws of the state and everyone is required to submit to it. Like Orthodox Judaism, Islam considers that certain ground can be holy, which is why the issue of Jerusalem is so central to the various crises in the Middle East. Both Jews and Muslims claim its Temple Mount as holy in their own traditions, but more than that: many of them feel that it is defiled by the presence of the others. And since there is no practicable way to carve those few square metres of ground in two, the conflict may never finally be resolved.

When faith is territorial, or insists on being enshrined in the laws that govern the state, and as a result is allied with the structures and forces (including governments and armies) that rule human society, it becomes no more than another ideology whereby people can live lives defended from each other. Indeed, there is no one more defended than the religious zealot determined to stand on holy ground.

In Britain, the alliance between the Church of England and the state has been eroded and undermined systematically over the last century. Many in the church feel a great sense of bereavement as a result, seeing the demise of Christendom (created by Constantine 17 centuries ago) as a tragedy. Certainly the church has lost much of its power, but whether that is tragic is another matter. For some Christians, it presents an opportunity to establish a new and more appropriate relationship with the state, in which the power of God is understood non-politically.

Such a rift is less apparent in America. The rhetoric of the current 'war on terror' was initially religious, and even messianic, in tone, and it certainly seemed to be the case that George W Bush's neoconservative foreign policy was shaped by theology as well as politics. At a time when the Muslim world is all too ready to identify the West with Christendom and to see its political and economic domination as something to be opposed, Bush's language has merely heightened the antagonism, polarizing people and legitimizing territorial warfare on both sides. As is always the case when this happens, it is impossible to tease out how much of the resulting violence is informed by faith, how much by politics, how much by economics and how much by simple hatred, fear and desire for revenge.

Does God take political sides?

As things stand, the territoriality of both these forms of Christianity and Islam is deeply problematic for the global population. There are those who argue that society is indeed best governed according to Christian principles, just as there are those who argue the same of shari'ah law. However, when you look in the Bible, the source of authority for the church throughout the ages, you find a distinct and striking ambivalence on the question of whether God can be identified with any human form of power. The fifth chapter of Joshua records an interesting encounter between the leader (and commander) of the Israelites and a man who is referred to as 'the commander of the Lord's army'. Joshua is on the brink of the land promised by God to his people; before him stands the defended city of Jericho (interestingly, a city that has been taken and retaken many times in its very long history). When he meets this angelic figure, 'standing in front of him with a drawn sword in his hand',[61] Joshua asks him whose side he is on, his or the enemy's. Given the story so far, in which God has led his people to this point so that they can take this land, you would expect him to align himself with the Israelites. However, he does not. 'Neither,' he replies, 'but as commander of the army of the Lord I have now come.'

This statement is deeply revealing. It highlights a truth found throughout the Bible: that God, even in his covenants with people, does not fight on one side or another in human battles. It seems he does not divide humankind along ethnic or national lines, as centuries later the apostle Paul made clear.[62] Instead, God assesses each individual according to the state of their heart.[63] He observes which of us seeks to live out our lives trusting him, and trusting in his servant Jesus, and which of us seeks to impose their own will and authority on their own life and others'.

Time and again, the Bible tells stories of people who would have been excluded on ethnic grounds but who are welcomed into God's grace and love, precisely to make this point: Rahab, the prostitute living in Jericho,[64] Naaman, the Syrian general,[65] Ruth the Midianite, the woman from Syrian Phoenicia,[66] the centurion in Capernaum[67]—each one disqualified by their race but included by grace. Indeed, the New Testament writer Matthew drew attention to the fact that Jesus, who he understood to be the Messiah, God's anointed, was descended not only from Jewish royalty but also from outsiders to the Jewish people, including Ruth.[68] He wanted us to grasp that Jesus himself represents God's merciful and generous hand reaching outside the territorial and ethnic limits of the people of Israel.

In fact, it is the message of scripture, abundantly clear throughout the Bible but made most explicit in the New Testament in the life and teachings of Jesus, that God's blessing is not conferred on ethnic, physical or geographical grounds. Rather, it is given to those who relinquish their own means to defend themselves and instead trust in the goodness of God to defend them. It is clear that God draws a single line through humankind, and it is not Bush's 'axis of evil': it's the line that divides those who are defended and those who are undefended, those who secure their own safety and those who trust God

---

[61] Joshua 5.13
[62] Galatians 3.28
[63] 1 Samuel 16.1–7
[64] Hebrews 11.31
[65] 2 Kings 5.1
[66] Mark 7.24–30
[67] Matthew 8.5–13
[68] Matthew 1.1–17

to make them safe, those who seek to justify themselves through their own worthiness and those who acknowledge their own corruption and depend entirely on the forgiveness available in Jesus Christ.

According to the Bible, God's hand is on the side of neither America nor al-Qa'ida. Those who say otherwise represent neither the freedom nor the undefendedness that are truly godly but, rather, the manifestations of defendedness and idolatry that have so distorted God's message that they have twisted it to meet their own ends of domination, fulfilment and control.

Is God undefended?

In contrast to such ideologies, when we read the accounts of Jesus' life and teaching in the Bible we hear a voice that subverts the structures of power and authority in this world. In a well-known parable recorded in Matthew 22.1–14 and Luke 14.16–23, Jesus tells of a banquet laid on by a king for guests who are themselves rich and noble. However, each one finds an excuse not to attend. In frustration, the king instructs his servants to go out into the streets and alleys of the town, and even the country lanes, and bring in the poor, the crippled, the blind and the lame, 'both good and bad', to come and enjoy his banquet. Jesus tells this sharp and subversive parable to the Jewish rulers of his day in order to highlight the fact that God's invitation, though it does not exclude the powerful and the wealthy, is also extended to the weak and the poor. Not only so, but the latter are in fact more likely to accept it and be welcomed in, rather than the proud rich, who can think of better things to do.

Jesus tells many such stories to illustrate the fact that it's not that the powerful and the wealthy per se are barred from entering God's kingdom but that their power and wealth often make it very hard for them to be willing to do so. The reality is that for many of us our assets—be they assets of power, prestige, connections, riches or whatever—defend us: they enable us to feel in control, able to cope with whatever life throws at us. In contrast, God's kingdom is a place that is open to those who are willing to relinquish their defences and instead allow themselves to be defended by God alone (Matthew 5.1–9). In this way, they mirror the character of the King himself, who is himself undefended, who generously makes his world available for people to enjoy, who makes his love and forgiveness available through the death of his Son, Jesus, on a cross, who makes his life, potent enough to overcome death, available to those who will give up their own lives in service to him and his world (Mark 8.35).

Genuine spirituality is a spirituality of undefendedness, of generosity, which enjoys the resources we have but also freely gives them away. It lays down our 'territorial' claims to the ownership of our land, our money, our rights or even our lives. This is possible because ultimately we are secured by relationship with

God, which is strong enough to survive all of life's losses and privations, even death (Romans 8.38–39).

The hunger for transcendence

The West desperately needs to find once again a source of spiritual life which can fund a more exalted vision of society. For too long the church has colluded with the state in a comfortable marriage, and as a result it has become assimilated into Western culture, almost indistinguishable from the wider society in its attitudes, ethics and message. It has ceased to be the provocative and prophetic voice it once was, speaking with conviction and compassion. Because until the middle of the last century it was allied with that society's historic structures of power, it has suffered the same fate as them: the influence of the church has declined along with those of the monarchy, institutional authority and political ideology. As George Santayana once observed, if you marry one generation, you are widowed in the next. It is for this reason that the church finds itself bereft of power and, almost, of title. Its language and its spirituality have little meaning for people today, and less appeal.

For its own sake and that of society, the church needs to find a new language in which to express its vibrant spirituality. Our society needs a distinctive spiritual voice to inform our moral narrative. There is nothing quite so depressing as a typical Sunday morning in Britain. By 11 a.m., out-of-town retail parks are filling up with shoppers who drift from garden centre to furniture store in a state of emotional numbness, their appetites dulled, robbed of anticipation yet drawn onwards, through sheer boredom, into the netherworld of shopping. This dystopian monoculture is a realization of the virtual world we are shown throughout the week via daytime satellite TV, where banks of shopping channels vie for a diminishing 0.01% market share.

My own experience is that many people in our society are crying out for an experience of transcendence. They have never known what it is to walk on holy ground, to enter a sacred space in which prayer has been offered for centuries and take off their shoes in the heavy silence of reverent awe. They have never been awakened to their own soul; they do not know what it is for that soul to touch the Other, to encounter what is beyond, what is older, deeper and more mysterious. They do not know the discipline of waiting, in stillness and denial of self, and paying attention to the Other. We are truly a generation of 'hollow men', superficial, thin, transparent, rootless, substanceless, weightless, in danger of being swept away by the slightest puff of wind. The church will be doing us all a fatal disservice if it offers us no more than another serving of spiritual retail therapy.

NINETEEN

Where Do We Go from Here?

London is without question the financial capital of Europe. Its two great financial centres are the City, the historic location of the Bank of England and the stock market, and Canary Wharf. They lie just three miles apart. The river Thames, that old artery of trade that made London the capital of England in the Dark Ages, snakes its way eastward, out to the North Sea. Passing St Paul's Cathedral, the City and Tower Bridge, it cuts its widening course towards the Isle of Dogs and the brilliant steel-and-glass towers of Canary Wharf. River taxis carrying suited businesspeople ply their way from City to Wharf, and the Docklands Light Railway whisks many another to their polished destinations, without ever touching the ground beneath them.

The land in between the City and Canary Wharf is a part of London once built on trade, when the Thames was deep enough for wooden ships laden with cargo to sail up that far. However, nowadays the redundant docks and basins of Shadwell and Wapping (their business having long gone east to the estuary mouth at Tilbury) are merely playgrounds for the wealthy, and expensive gated developments have sprung up along a narrow strip hugging the river. However, the wider landscape between the city's two centres of financial power is very different. Here, you will find what remains of the indigenous white working-class population. Shrunk to no more than a few thousand, mostly ageing folk, they have watched their livelihoods decay before their eyes. Ask them for their memories of the Blitz or the old London docks and they will tell you stories of almost pure regret: regret at the loss of their industry, regret at the intrusion of ethnic minorities, regret that their families have long since left for Epping, Basildon and Billericay (encouraged by Margaret Thatcher's sale of council houses in the Eighties), regret that the community clubs and the tea dances are things of the past.

This part of London has always been a first port of call for immigrants, from the Huguenots who moved into Whitechapel during the persecutions of the 17th century to the Jews, who established their sewing workshops, and now to the Bangladeshis. However, while once for such newcomers these streets were just the first rungs on the ladder to social status and prosperity elsewhere, the more recent arrivals seem to have become stuck there. The area is now

80-per-cent Bangladeshi and looks set to stay that way. Housed in large, run-down blocks in their own little world, hemmed in to the west and the east by the glittering towers and gleaming spires of the City and Canary Wharf, their situation is a living illustration of the planet's social ecology.

Within that five miles square you will see in miniature the global social landscape: the juxtaposition of two communities separated by a gulf in their ideology, opportunity and power. The City and Canary Wharf represent the interests of the domination of capital, the management of money that (as we have seen) has shaped the planet's social ecology. It represents the exercise of power through financial transactions which determine social and political reality. It exists now, on the very edge of its own cliff of aspiration, compelled by its own rules to seek to grow continually, relentlessly, unsupportably, to dominate and outdo all opposition. Thus, the physical geography of the area has come to reflect the psycho-geography of the planet: the sealed isolation of the West, working and travelling as if in a parallel world, fearful of intruders, trying to insulate itself from the influence, let alone the participation, of the rest of the global community. It justifies its existence with the arguments of capitalism, insisting that it will enrich the whole global system and that even a small slice of a bigger cake is better than a big slice of a small one. There is no trust and only inability to feel for another.

The reality is that unless London takes notice of this growing gulf, its own security and success will be jeopardized. How attractive a proposition for new investment will it be after a few more suicide attacks and a hundred more dead, with no prospect of containment? Global markets sail on confidence, and such waves of panic can swamp them instantly. The day for wilful negligence is surely over. We have to find an alternative—and that alternative must be rooted in the opposite commitments to those of fear and greed that sustain the current system. And the most important of these is trust.

Participation, not domination

Trust entails the amicable sharing of resources. It chooses to believe the best of the other person and welcome them as a friend rather than suspect the worst and see them as a likely enemy. We might begin with the way we share this planet with other species. The Victorians recognized that nature was 'red in tooth and claw' and felt a sense of awe at the power of the biological world. With the afterglow of a creationist world view still imbuing the evolutionary theories of Darwin with light and hope, the natural world was a spectacle of incredible complexity and beauty. Rousseau's romantic vision of a primitive Arcadia saw human life connected indissolubly to the texture of the planet.

For the last century, however, we have set out not to admire our environment but to dominate it, severing ourselves from our biological roots and context as we strive to break the constraints of agricultural, genetic and ecological givens. Only now, in the early years of the 21st century, are we able to see that this project of the last hundred years was merely a brief (and unprecedented) transition between two ages, an interregnum in which we lived out a myth of our independence from the planet. Our technological 'mastery' of the biosphere will not deliver us from its fate, any more than the incantations of the Maya were able to stave off their demise.

Instead, we must accept once again that our future lies not in our domination over but in our participation in the natural world. We must trustfully share the resources we have been given to steward. We must entrust ourselves to the world around us, aware that finally we cannot subdue and control nature but instead must accept a providential relationship of mutual trust and respect. And this relationship must, and can only, begin with humankind. How can we respect the environment if we cannot respect each other? Living trustfully in relation to the natural world will be possible only if we begin to live trustfully with one another. And in the end our ability to take this path depends on our willingness to respect not just our environment, not just other people but our very selves. Choosing to respect our own dignity as marvellous, mysterious but dependent and fragile creatures will lead to us to treat others, and our world, in the same way.

Personal initiatives

Once, *The Times* invited a number of eminent authors to write an essay on the theme 'What is wrong with the world?' G K Chesterton sent in his contribution in the form of a letter. It read:

> Dear Sirs,
> I am.
> Sincerely yours,
> G K Chesterton

His response provides us with a crucial insight into the human condition. The root of our problems in society, whether nationally or globally, lies not in society itself but in the individuals who make up society. This book has focused intentionally on the social mechanisms that constrain and shape the behaviour of human populations and has sought to understand the nature of the social problems facing us all. As such, it has addressed the systemic problems more than the problems of the individual within the system. However, it is the third of a trilogy of books, the first two of which set out the responsibility the individual has within the system. Although it is vital to understand the patterns of the whole, I cannot personally escape an evaluation of my own life. Indeed, it is my own life over which I have some degree of control, and so expediency if nothing else dictates that this is where I should focus my attention.

Let me be honest: I have not enjoyed writing this book. I do not like the implications that its arguments and conclusions have for me and my lifestyle. I am anxious about the hypocrisies in my own life. I feel concerned and guilty about the footprints I have left—and continue to leave—on the planet. I am sceptical about my own willingness and ability to live a more responsible and less defended life. I am fully aware that I am a part of the system I am critiquing, and that I use its machinery to promote my own ends and perspectives. I need also to be honest that I do not know all the answers. I do not see an easy or clear set of choices in terms of how we should buy our goods, travel to our work, pursue our interests or raise our children. I find there are more questions than answers.

Idealism and pragmatism

I am torn between idealism and pragmatism. The idealist inside me points to a distant yet beautiful horizon where the human race experiences a deep and genuine inner reformation and a renewal of its cultural, moral and spiritual life. The pragmatist whispers that such ideals lead only to disappointment and disillusion, that politics is a matter of compromise and accommodation, that you must trim your sails and tack slowly and realistically into the wind towards some more achievable, modest and ultimately acceptable goals. However, I have come to see that idealism and pragmatism are not incompatible and that perhaps we must seek to hold the two together, the one speaking to our hearts, our souls and our imaginations, the other to our minds and hands. We are, after all, human beings with all of these components. I am content, then, that I must create within myself room for the idealist and the pragmatist to sit together and converse with each other. A lively and creative, if at times unsettling, dialogue must be sustained. I hope this book can achieve a similar balance of idealism and pragmatism: enough of one to allow us to contemplate the better horizons that humankind must aim for, enough of the other to ensure we are not disregarded and to offer us some reasonable steps that every one of us can take.

In the spirit of this tension, which I accept I cannot resolve (and perhaps if I were able to, my energy and passion would dissipate anyway), I intend to cultivate both my idealism and my pragmatism. I intend to sustain, and deepen, the spiritual intensity and vision for life that fund my idealism. At the same time, I commit myself to active, realistic, engaged participation in the problems of the world as we encounter them, seeking whatever ad hoc solutions we can find.

I appeal to you to do the same. On the one hand, I want to encourage you to consider practical ways in which you can start to make a difference to your own world. There are all kinds of changes you can make this very day. Here are a few suggestion, which I offer just to stimulate your own thinking...

What we consume

Let's start with the way we travel. Are there ways we can cut down on our use of our cars? Could we walk or cycle, use public transport or share a lift? Some of us can save money by cycling to work (not least by cancelling our subscription to the gym, as we'll no longer need it). Some of us might be able to get a car-sharing scheme going at work. And then there is the issue of air travel...

Then we might consider our use of energy. Simply changing light bulbs to low-energy types, turning equipment off rather than leaving it on standby, washing the dishes by hand rather than using the dishwasher, hanging your laundry out to dry rather than using the tumble drier—these simple changes to your lifestyle will reduce your consumption of electricity, and water, dramatically. Then there is the option of renewable energy: switch to a renewable-power supplier, or find out whether you can harness wind or solar (or even geothermal) power yourself at home. Many people have cut their energy bills almost to zero by such means. Consider wearing a lovely, warm sweater indoors in the winter, rather than turning up the central heating so you can live at 25°C all year round. Consider sharing the bathwater with someone else in the family, or taking a shower instead.

Then, consider what you buy. Reuse the plastic bags the supermarket gives you, or take your own. Buy vegetables loose rather than washed and packaged. Put pressure on the supermarkets to stock more goods loose, or find out whether you can buy more local produce from a farm. Consider pick-your-own, which children usually enjoy (they get to stuff their faces with strawberries or blackberries, and also learn where food comes from). Of course, that would mean buying fruit when it's in season, which means you can't have apples and berries all year round—but then when they come, you'll appreciate them twice as much! It's a simple and practicable bit of self-discipline that will reward us with greater pleasure.

Where we work

How about your place of work? You may be able to assemble a working party to consider how your office or school can reduce its consumption of both energy and material resources. You might consider if you could switch to renewable energy, recycled paper, low-energy light bulbs. Simple education can also help to create a culture of awareness and sensitivity to our impact on the environment:

turning of the lights when leaving a room, shutting down the computer instead of leaving it on standby, putting only as much water in the kettle as you need, driving to your meeting with the windows down rather than using the air-con.

Where we live

As well as reducing our consumption (and saving money as well as resources in the process), there are immediate ways we can choose to improve our human ecology as well as our environment. As an exercise, think about your immediate neighbourhood for a moment, wherever you happen to live. Imagine that the people in that place are connected by a network of invisible threads, which represent the social bonds between them. Think about the people who are joined by the thinnest, weakest and perhaps fewest threads. It might be the elderly people who rarely go out, it might be the young family on benefits, isolated and carless, it might be the teenage boys who live in their own world of gaming and texting, it might be the immigrant family who have different clothes and a different rhythm of life, it might be the disabled woman or the young man suffering from a mental disorder who is very difficult to talk to. Each of us lives in a neighbourhood where someone (at least) is in danger of becoming detached altogether from the social fabric. Think about what you could do to strengthen the connections between them and the community. It might begin with little more than an intentional conversation next time you pass them on the street.

- Maybe you have a garden and can invite a few people round for lemonade and biscuits.
- If you have a Christmas party, maybe you could invite all your neighbours rather than just your friends.
- Maybe you could pop into the local old people's home and offer to visit, with your children, once a fortnight; or maybe you could volunteer to work at the local homeless shelter.
- Maybe you and your children could do up a garden once a year.
- Maybe you could find out whether there is a local scheme you could volunteer for to mentor a teenager.

Some of these ideas are simple and personal; others, which concern our work or communities, may be more structural and formal. Both kinds are needed and neither kind needs to be very costly.

Sponsoring someone else

One of the most enjoyable ways to connect with issues further away from home is to sponsor a child or a community in a majority-world country. Organizations exist that run well-executed and effective schemes, with projects that reliably deliver education, finance and support. There is nothing more rewarding than corresponding with your 'adopted' child in Bolivia or India, and building that relationship over the years. I know people who have 'adopted' dozens of children in this way. And your kids, if you have any, will love to do so, too. They may also enjoy buying their grandma a nanny goat for Christmas—only, the goat will be given to a family in Mozambique rather than standing in grandma's backyard! This kind of scheme, which is rapidly growing in popularity, is a fun way to celebrate Christmas while recognizing that often there is really nothing we are lacking ourselves.

How we invest

If you want to go one stage further, consider ethical investment. In this case, the vehicle you invest in supports a set of ethical values and aspirations as well as financial ones. There are plenty of ethical funds setting up in which money is invested in community schemes, social enterprises or just industries that are looking to benefit people and not harm them. The attraction is that your money grows at the same time as the causes you want to support. Why support causes you don't believe in?

Perhaps the most exciting kind of investment there is at the moment is microfinance. This involves a range of financial services available on micro levels to local communities in the majority world who don't have access to conventional banking. The most important of these services, perhaps, are capital investment loans, which often amount to less than $50 per client borrower! A tiny loan like that can be all that a woman in Sierra Leone needs to buy a sewing machine and set up a business that can in time earn enough to not only feed her family but also send her children to school.

'Microloans' are administered through local 'trust banks', which are essentially collectives of 20 or so client borrowers in the neighbourhood who agree to give security for each other's loans.

The members of the trust bank, all of whom receive loans to run their businesses, ensure that none of them default on their loan repayments, as otherwise the whole group will have to carry the can. In this way, the bank empowers its clients (very often all women), builds social cohesion and achieves remarkable rates of repayment (over 99 per cent). Thus, the donated funds can be recycled many times, which makes the system far more efficient and productive than aid-based projects.[69]

Many Westerners are sceptical about giving money to the majority world, aware that often it simply disappears in bureaucracy, mismanagement, waste

---

[69] For further information, see the UNCDF's *Microfinance Matters*, issue 17 (October 2005), found on 6 April 2008 at http://www.uncdf.org/english/microfinance/pubs/newsletter/pages/2005_10/Microfinance_Matters_Issue_17.pdf.

or corruption. Microfinance doesn't offer aid; it fosters trade. It gives people a leg-up rather than a handout and sets in motion a virtuous circle of trust, empowerment and opportunity.

It costs a mere $8,000 to set up an entire trust bank and transform a community.

I know of several schools in the affluent suburbs of Oxford that have raised the money to do just that, several times over, and now have vibrant, robust, continuing relationships with village communities in Ghana.

Investing our financial capital so as to generate social capital is an example of undefended leadership.

Where we worship

Faith communities at their best provide examples of authentic undefended relationships, as well as being catalysts and engines for all kinds of mission or outreach that demonstrates compassion and creativity both locally and globally. For many people, the confidence and conviction to give themselves in such a way can only have a spiritual source. I know it is indispensable for me.

Living the undefended life

On the one hand, then, I want to be pragmatic: to take small, immediate, achievable steps to make some kind of difference. They may not change the world in one go, but they are at least heading in the right direction. On the other hand, I want to hold on to my deeper aspiration to live a more radical, undefended life. This is an ideal that demands that I see others not as hostile strangers but as potential friends, that my thoughts and actions are not concerned with my own advantage but authentically and freely address the needs of others. In the undefended life, another person is regarded not as a threat to be dealt with, a rival to be beaten or a commodity to be exploited but as someone with whom you should share yourself in trust. Moreover, you see yourself not as an agent that needs to be defended from danger but instead as a potential gift to others.

To live an undefended life does not at all mean being a doormat for others to trample over. Being undefended is not incompatible with (at times) being strong, assertive, authoritative, even dominant. I have set out as clearly as I can in the first two books in this trilogy, *Leading out of Who You Are* and *Leading with Nothing to Lose*, the levers of power and structures of authority that are available appropriately to the undefended leader. It is an act of undefended love to reach out and grab a child who has stepped out in front of an oncoming car and yank them with all your might back to safety. Indeed, to be passive in that moment would be a demonstration of heartlessness that had nothing to do with the kind of life I am advocating. It is undefended concern that ensures that we have laws that protect the vulnerable from those who would otherwise try to exploit or hurt them.

An undefended life is one in which you set aside your own personal interests for the sake of others. There are a few well-known examples in recent history that can inspire us today. Mother Teresa of Calcutta is one, who opened her heart to the plight of the 'untouchables' and lived among them. Mahatma Gandhi is another, who was willing to embrace sacrifice and suffering in order to identify himself with the people of India and empower them. Jimmy Carter is another, who as president of America pursued generous and humanitarian policies at a cost to his own reputation, and then went on not to do something glamorous and lucrative and high-profile but to build houses for the homeless with his own hands. Gordon Wilson, whose daughter, Marie, was killed by the IRA in the Enniskillen bombing, said he '[bore] no ill will ... no grudge' towards her murderers and would pray for them 'tonight and every night'. He is another. Maximilian Kolbe, the Polish priest in Auschwitz who volunteered to be starved to death instead of another man who had a wife and children, is another.

Countless others have suffered similarly as they confronted the evil in the world—Dietrich Bonhoeffer, resisting Nazism, Martin Luther King, resisting racism, thousands of others resisting oppression all over the world. Countless more have at some point in their lives made undefended choices, often unrecognized. When Bill Gates made a commitment to give away most of his billions before he dies, that to me was an undefended act. The example of such people presents a noble alternative to the celebrities who parade before us, and we would do well to fix our eyes on their virtues. Few of us will be called to such heroism, and fewer still to martyrdom (though, of course, some may); but what we see in such women and men is that they did not love life so much that they shrank from death. For them, life had such deep roots that it could not be cut off by mere physical death.

In the West, we have long lacked such convictions, and their confidence seems to us extreme and perhaps unsettling. In recent years, we have understood a willingness to sacrifice your life only in the case of the destructive and immoral work of the suicide bomber who chants: 'You love life, we love death.' Suicide that embraces death as a justified and noble way to execute warfare and destruction of the enemy must not be confused with the generous sacrifice of your life to preserve the lives of others. A man such as Father Kolbe did not trade his life for the broken bodies and severed limbs of children, men and women, destroyed in the name of victory and domination.

The undefended life may be full, fulfilled, creative, long and productive as well as difficult, opposed and misunderstood. Ultimately, it involves relinquishing control over your own powers and assets and holding them lightly. It is about seeing ownership—of our money, our time, our skills, our power—in a different way. Instead of viewing these things as possessions to exploit to our profit, we choose to regard them as things entrusted to us for the benefit of others. They are gifts to humankind, not us alone. We are their stewards, not their owners.

We are free to accept and enjoy wealth, but we are also at liberty to let it go and give it away. We are not the slaves of our status or power, but are free from them. Not that we regard these things as dangerous or wrong in themselves— such asceticism is itself not free—but instead we receive with open hands and give with open hands. The richest man in the world, as well as the poorest, may be undefended—though if they were to meet, the encounter might alter their relative wealth!

It's important to emphasize that an undefended life is not necessarily one that is financially poor: it does not involve always denying yourself and missing out on the pleasures of life. That is asceticism, which is something else altogether. The undefended person is free to enjoy and receive the good things around her, as well as to give them up. Ultimately, she does not see herself as an environmental crusader, who ends up condemning enjoyment in order to save the planet. Rather, her goal is to live out an undefended life in the confidence that, if the whole of humankind did the same, we would find ourselves receiving and enjoying the goodness and generosity of the world in a sustainable way.

Worship—which is what I believe I am created to offer—is a matter of living a fully human, undefended life, receiving God's resources, rather than justifying my own pious existence through self-discipline and self-denial. As Irenaeus wrote, 'Gloria Dei vivens homo' (which is usually glossed as 'The glory of God is a human being fully alive').[70]

Ultimately, I believe that our goal is not to be frugal, ascetic or poor: it is to be free, and undefended in that freedom. Free to receive and enjoy, free to give away and lose ourselves. Such undefendedness can be ours only if we do not need our assets to secure us. I am able to receive as well as to let things go only if my deepest needs for identity, meaning, affection, belonging and intimacy are already provided for.

You may not agree, but it is my conviction that we inhabit a generous universe, made so by the liberality of the One who created it and continues to sustain it. We encounter that generosity in our lives through the food we eat, the love and approval we receive, the opportunities we enjoy and so on. All 'good' things we experience are gifts to us, expressions of God's care. They are also invitations to us to live like children who trust the providence of a divine Father, rather than fearfully storing up goods to ensure that we have enough.

---

[70] Irenaeus, *Against the Heresies*, 4.20

As we learn to receive such gifts with open hands, we begin to find that the world becomes a more generous place.

The person we live next to becomes a true neighbour, who we can choose to bless every day in simple ways, with a greeting, a warm smile, an offer of help, a willingness to listen rather than rush on.

- The elderly person living opposite ceases to be a 'crabby old nuisance' peering from behind his net curtains and instead becomes a friend who has much to give us—reminiscences, insights, even regrets—as well as reminding us of what we ourselves are going to become.
- The glass of orange juice in the morning is no longer a gulp before we run out of the door but a simple delight, first anticipated and then savoured.
- The flight on the plane is transformed from a tedious and exhausting haul to a wonderful opportunity—and, indeed, a privilege future generations may not have—to travel above the clouds and see the curve of the Earth from the edge of space.
- The world around us is teeming with life, generous life, from which we benefit and in which we participate. We have so much—and yet, so often, we appreciate so little. Again, the myth of desire robs us of enjoyment, making us unsatisfied with what we already have, persuading us that we must acquire more. Not so! We must acquire less and enjoy more—and as we do so we will find that there is plenty to go around, that we do not go short when we are generous to a stranger. We will begin to receive life rather than grabbing it. We will find that grace replaces whatever we give away.

This may be a fantasy, but even if it is, it's an intriguing one, isn't it? If only for the sake of the adventure, and the slightest chance that it may be true, perhaps it is worth giving it a go. Why not? What is stopping us from making a change, trying out something different for a week? It would be something to put in the Christmas letter, at any rate… What a shame it would be to die without trying something that, if it were true, would revolutionize your life—and not just your life but the lives of many others, too. What is stopping you? It may just be worth a whirl. And if you have come this far in the story, maybe you are willing to go just this little bit further…

The rule of life

Many faith traditions have recognized the value of a clear set of stated principles for life. Sometimes these are referred to as a code, or a discipline, or a pattern, or a rule. One of the best-known Christian rules is that of Benedict, who recognized the need for human beings to live stable, committed, earthy lives.

The danger of any such rule is that it becomes a set of rules—and we all know what rules are used for: as pretexts to punish us when we break them. If we think of a rule of life like that, it will quickly become oppressive and counterproductive.

The Latin word from which we get 'rule' is regula, which can also mean a straight line or a benchmark. This might suggest that a rule of life is simply a way of drawing a straight line for us to aim at. I tend to think of myself as a climbing plant, whose stem lacks the strength to grow in a straight line unless it is tied to a frame of some kind. A rule of life is like such a frame: it helps me to observe and adjust how I am living and it keeps me aiming in the right direction.

Those who take part in my course on undefended leadership are invited to use a rule of life that encapsulates the principles both of the course and of this trilogy of books. It is structured around three values: receiving, welcoming and stewarding. I include it here in the hope that it may be of benefit to any reader who wants to live an undefended life themself.

Receiving

Our attitude to the world is primarily that of receiving the goodness and generosity of the created order (and therefore the Creator). This is in contrast to a posture of 'giving to' or 'taking from', which implies the priority of our initiative, power and action. As those who receive, we accept our contingency and our codependence on the world, on our fellow humans and on the Creator. We also presuppose that the world, as created, is essentially a generous gift to be received with gratitude.

Welcoming

Our commitment is to see others around us as friends whom we choose to welcome rather than as threats we have to avoid or protect ourselves from. Moreover, they are friends on the basis not of their behaviour, or their attractiveness to us, but of their shared createdness. Welcoming others involves a choice basically to trust them, and it implies vulnerability: making ourselves open to others in conversation, sharing our time or resources. Being welcoming is not, however, indiscriminate: it implies responsibility. Closing the door on someone else may be necessary and right when it is done to protect the vulnerable and to help the other to take responsibility for their actions.

Stewarding

We understand that the world we have been given is finite and so are its resources. We also understand that those resources, of energy, food, space and raw materials, are being consumed recklessly, unfairly and unsustainably. We also understand that when we consume resources unsustainably we are stealing, not only from people living elsewhere on this planet but also from our children and our children's children. The obligation on us all is to 'tread lightly' on our environment—whether emotional, social, biological or physical—and to be deeply aware of the footprint we are leaving on the surface of our world.

Value 1: Receiving	Value 2: Welcoming	Value 3: Stewarding
...a daily rhythm of receiving at the start of the day before giving or taking, through simple, personal acts of prayer, contemplation, meditation or praise	...cultivating the patience and stillness to listen attentively to those we meet so that each person feels heard and not ignored, used or passed over	...choosing to engage in creative activity—social enterprise, creative or intellectual innovation or experimentation, and so on—so that our overall impact is positive, not negative
...a practice of pausing before eating a meal in thanksgiving for the gift to be received	...resisting the temptation to condemn others who hold different beliefs, and choosing instead to listen and understand their perspective and concerns in order to find ways to live as friends	...adding to the social capital of our neighbourhood by visiting the vulnerable
...a weekly discipline of setting aside time, at the start of the new week, to look ahead and receive its tasks, pleasures and encounters as opportunities for growth	...communicating our beliefs, or those of our community, clearly and authentically so that others can see how they can relate to us, understand us and accept us	...strengthening bonds in our family by being a peacemaker
...a practice of cultivating an awareness of each season of nature, or 'season' of life, and adjusting what we eat, do and how we work accordingly	...developing a commitment to help others to understand the impact of their actions and beliefs both on those around them and themselves, so that they can better take responsibility	...deepening the relationships we have committed ourselves to so they with integrity and generosity
...an annual discipline of beginning each new year with a day (or more) of retreat	...choosing to view encounters with strangers as meetings with potential friends—a gift rather than a burden	...working to protect social structures and institutions that increase social capital and trust and opposing that which subverts them
...an attitude of thankfulness throughout the day for the things in life we take for granted (rain, fruit juice for breakfast, a warm bed, a job, income, family and so on)	...choosing to be especially attentive, in the use of our time, skill and money, to the vulnerable, the dispossessed, the homeless and the lost	...cultivating our own skills as gifts entrusted to us for the good of others, so that we can make the best contribution we can to the world

Value 1: Receiving	Value 2: Welcoming	Value 3: Stewarding
...a freedom to enjoy without guilt the delights, riches and goods of the world that come to us	...choosing to welcome visitors generously, whether they are expected or not, being willing to share with them as far as possible our home, our time and our food so that we may bless them as we have been blessed	...choosing to limit our consumption of the world's resources—energy, food, water, raw materials and so on—according to what we need, by being careful, efficient and restrained
...a conscious check on our impatience, frustration and even rage when circumstances appear to conspire against us	...choosing to offer back a proportion of our time and/or money as a gift, to be given away freely with no thought of a return, as an act of dependence, trust and generosity and a sign that we are not mastered by greed	...considering the impact on the environment of our means of transport
...a decision to try to seek the learning and growth that may lie within the difficulties and afflictions that from time to time we have to endure	...developing a practice of confessing to those we may have hurt and asking for and receiving their forgiveness	...choosing to reduce the impact of our consumption on the planet by reducing waste (including packaging) and, as far as possible, repairing rather than replacing (including white goods, electronics, cars and so on)
...a pattern of periodic planned fasting (from such things as television, food, alcohol etc) as a way to master our desires	...seeking to surrender our anger over what has been wrongly done to us, rather than allowing it to fester and turn into bitterness, and in this way to find the resources to forgive those who hurt us	...choosing to consider the origins of all we consume, the conditions of those who produced it and the impact of the processes and materials used in its production (which may involve switching to a renewable-power supplier, for example, or buying local produce)

Bibliography

R F Baumeister, L Smart and J M Boden. *'Relation of Threatened Egotism to Violence and Aggression: the Dark Side of High Self-Esteem'*, Psychological Review 103

Peter G Bourne. *Jimmy Carter: A Comprehensive Biography From Plains to Post-Presidency*. New York, Scribner, 1997

John Bowlby. *Attachment and Loss*. New York: Basic Books, 3 vols, 1969–80

Clayton Carson, ed. *The Autobiography of Martin Luther King*. Abacus, 1999

Richard J Carwardine. *Lincoln*. Pearson Educational/Longman, 2003

Charles Darwin. *On the Origin of Species: By Means of Natural Selection or The Preservation of Favoured Races in the Struggle for Life*. London: J Murray, 1859

Emile Durkheim. *Suicide: A Study in Sociology*. Translated by J A Spaulding and G Simpson. London: Routledge & Kegan Paul, 1952

T S Eliot. 'Choruses from The Rock', in *Collected Poems 1909–1962*. Faber and Faber, 1963

Robert Fulghum. *All I Really Need to Know I Learned in Kindergarten: Uncommon Thoughts on Common Things*. New York: Ballantine Books, 2003

Robert M Galford and Anne Seibold Drapeau. *The Trusted Leader*. The Free Press, 2002

David Harvey. *The Condition of Postmodernity: An Enquiry into the Origins of Cultural Change*. Cambridge, MA: Blackwell, 1990

Irenaeus. *Irenaeus Against Heresies: Book 4*. Whitefish, Mont: Kessinger Publishing, 2007

Oliver James. *Britain on the Couch: Why We're Unhappier Compared with 1950 Despite Being Richer: a Treatment for the Low-Serotonin Society*. London: Century, 1997

Roy Jenkins. *Churchill: A Biography*. Farrar, Straus and Giroux, 2001

Manfred Kets de Vries. *The Leadership Mystique: A User's Manual for the Human Enterprise*. Financial Times Prentice Hall, 2001

James Lawrence. *Growing Leaders: Reflections on Leadership, Life and Jesus*. Bible Reading Fellowship, 2004

Joseph LeDoux. *The Emotional Brain*. London: Phoenix, 1999

Nelson Mandela. *Long Walk to Freedom: The Autobiography of Nelson Mandela*. Little Brown & Co, 1994

J Richard Middleton and Brian J Walsh. *Truth Is Stranger than It Used To Be: Biblical Faith in a Postmodern Age*. London: SPCK, 1995

Jae Yun Moon and Lee Sproull. '*Essence of Distributed Work: The Case of the Linux Kernel*'. First Monday 5, No. 11 (November 2000)

Henri J M Nouwen. *The Wounded Healer: Ministry in Contemporary Society*. Doubleday, 1972

John Perkins. *Confessions of an Economic Hit Man*. San Francisco: Berrett-Koehler Publishers, 2004

Richard Reeves. *President Reagan: The Triumph of Imagination*. New York, Simon & Schuster, 2005

Robert A Rosenbaum and Doublas Brinkley. *The Penguin Encyclopedia of American History*. New York: Penguin Reference, 2003

Anthony Sampson. *Mandela: The Authorized Biography*. Random House, 2000

Larry C Spears, ed. *Reflections on Leadership: How Robert K. Greenleaf's Theory of Servant-Leadership Influenced Today's Top Management Thinkers*. John Wiley & Sons, 1995

Robert A Strong. *Working in the World: Jimmy Carter and the Making of American Foreign Policy*. Baton Rouge, Louisiana State University, 2000

— "*Recapturing leadership: The Carter Administration and the Crisis of Confidence*", Presidential Studies Quarterly 16, Fall 1986

Margot Sunderland and Nicky Armstrong. *Helping Children who Bottle Up their Feelings & A Nifflenoo Called Nevermind*. Speechmarks, 2004

Dylan Thomas. '*Do Not Go Gentle*' in Collected Poems 1934–1953, edited by Walford Davies and Ralph Maud. Phoenix, 2000. Reprinted by permission of New Directions Publishing Corp., NY, and David Higham Associates, London

Jim Wallis. *Faith Works: Lessons on Spirituality and Social Action*. SPCK, 2002

Philip Yancey. *The Jesus I Never Knew*. Zondervan, 2002

The Undefended Leader trilogy
by Simon P Walker

LEADING OUT OF WHO YOU ARE

Discovering the Secret of Undefended
Leadership

ISBN: 978 1903689 43 1

LEADING WITH NOTHING TO LOSE

Training in the Exercise of Power

ISBN: 978 1 903689 44 8

LEADING WITH EVERYTHING TO GIVE

Lessons from the Success and Failure of Western
Capitalism

ISBN: 978 1903689 45 5

PiQUANT
editions

www.piquanteditions.com

The Leadership Community

Simon Walker's The Undefended Leader trilogy developed out of his work with a number of leaders in business, charity, politics or the church who make up an on-line community, The Leadership Community. The Community is an ongoing association which is supported by a website (www.theleadershipcommunity. org). It provides many resources for those who want to offer undefended leadership, including training courses, conferences, web tools and on-line discussion forums. You can become a free guest member of the community through a simple online registration process.

The Leadership Community is committed to practice: we are members because we are trying to live out a certain kind of life. The only condition of membership is that you choose to join us.

www.theleadershipcommunity.org

Lightning Source UK Ltd.
Milton Keynes UK
UKOW06f0158060315

247337UK00001B/16/P